China Insights

This book series collects and presents cutting-edge studies on various issues that have emerged during the process of China's social and economic transformation, and promotes a comprehensive understanding of the economic, political, cultural and religious aspects of contemporary China. It brings together academic endeavors by contemporary Chinese researchers in various social science and related fields that record, interpret and analyze social phenomena that are unique to Chinese society, its reforms and rapid transition. This series offers a key English-language resource for researchers and students in China studies and related subjects, as well as for general interest readers looking to better grasp today's China. The book series is a cooperation project between Springer and China Social Science Press of China.

More information about this series at http://www.springer.com/series/13591

Shiyuan Hao

China's Solution to Its Ethno-national Issues

CHINA SOCIAL SCIENCES PRESS

 Springer

Shiyuan Hao
Chinese Academy of Social Sciences
Beijing, China

Translated by
Jianping Zhang
Faculty of Foreign Studies
Jiangxi University of Science & Technology
Ganzhou, China

Mingxing Ke
Faculty of Foreign Studies
Jiangxi University of Science & Technology
Ganzhou, China

Sponsored by Chinese Fund for the Humanities and Social Sciences (本书获中华社会科学基金资助).

ISSN 2363-7579   ISSN 2363-7587   (electronic)
China Insights
ISBN 978-981-32-9518-6   ISBN 978-981-32-9519-3   (eBook)
https://doi.org/10.1007/978-981-32-9519-3

Jointly published with China Social Sciences Press
The print edition is not for sale in the Mainland of China. Customers from the Mainland of China please order the print book from: China Social Sciences Press.

This Springer imprint is published by the registered company Springer Nature Singapore Pte Ltd.
The registered company address is: 152 Beach Road, #21-01/04 Gateway East, Singapore 189721, Singapore

Series Foreword

Since the Opium War, modern China has come under attack and been bullied for its backwardness; this cultural circumstance has given many Chinese people a psychological inferiority complex, as China has lagged behind other countries technologically, institutionally, and culturally. Efforts to change the situation in which Western countries were strong but China was weak and to revitalize China needed to start with cultural criticism and culture renovation. Therefore, the Chinese people turned their eyes to the outside world and learned from Japan, Europe, the USA, and even Soviet Russia. We have always been overwhelmed by stress and anxiety and have had a burning desire to reverse the state of being bullied as a result of underdevelopment, poverty, and weakness and to catch up with and surpass the Western powers. In pursuing the more than one-hundred-year-old dream of building a powerful country and reviving China, we have focused on understanding and learning from others, but seldom, if ever, have others learned from and understood us. This has not greatly changed in the course of modernization since China's reform and opening-up in 1978. The translation and introduction of many Western works in the 1980 and 1990s is a very good example. This is the history of the Chinese people's understanding of the relationship between China and the rest of the world since the beginning of modern times.

At the same time, in pursuing the dream of turning China into a powerful country and rejuvenating it through material (technological) criticism, institutional criticism, and cultural criticism, the Chinese people have struggled to find a path that would make the country prosperous and the people strong while preventing the country from being ruined and the race from being destroyed. This path first represents a thought, a banner, and a soul. The key issue has been what kind of thought, banner, and soul can save the country, making it prosperous and the people strong. For more than one hundred years, the Chinese people have constantly carried out experiments and attempts amidst humiliation, failure, and anxiety. They have experienced failure in adopting advanced Western technology and thought on the basis of safeguarding China's feudal system and practicing a constitutional monarchy after the collapse of the Western capitalist political path and a great setback in worldwide socialism in the early 1990s. The Chinese people ultimately embarked on a path toward a successful revolution with national independence and liberation; in particular, they have adopted a path leading to the socialist modernization of China—a road toward socialism with Chinese characteristics—by combining the theoretical logic of scientific socialism with the historical logic of China's social development. After more than 30 years of reform and opening-up, China's socialist market economy has rapidly developed; tremendous achievements have been made in economic, political, cultural, and social constructions; comprehensive national strength, cultural soft power, and international influence have substantially improved; and a great success has been achieved in socialism with Chinese characteristics. Although the latter project has not yet become full-fledged, its systems and institutions have basically taken shape. After more than one hundred years of pursuing dreams, China is rising among the nations of the world with a greater degree of confidence in the path it has chosen, the theory it has adopted, and the institutions it has created.

Meanwhile, we should be aware that given the long-standing cognition and cultural psychology of learning from Western countries; we seldom take the initiative in showcasing ourselves—historical China and current China in reality—to the world, though China has emerged as a great world power. Due to a deeply rooted view that "Western countries are strong and China is weak," developed through Western-Chinese cultural exchanges, Western people and nations seldom have a sense of Chinese history or the current developments in China, let alone an understanding of China's developmental path and such in-depth issues as the scientificity and effectiveness of China's theory and institutions or their unique value for and contributions to human civilization. As self-recognition is not displayed, the "China Collapse Theory," "China Threat Theory," "China State Capitalism," and other so-called theories coined by certain people with ulterior motives and differing political views have been widely spread.

During our development, based on "crossing the river by feeling the stones," we have paid attention to learning from Western countries, understanding the world and learning to know ourselves through Western experience and discourse but have neglected self-recognition and efforts to let others know us. When we strive to become part of the world in a more tolerant and friendly way, we are not objectively, truly understood. Therefore, we should describe the path to the success of socialism with Chinese characteristics, tell Chinese stories, disseminate Chinese experiences, use international expressions to show a real China to the world, and help people around the world realize that the Western manner of modernization is not the endpoint of human historical evolution and that socialism with Chinese characteristics is also a valuable treasure of human thought. This is undoubtedly a very important task for an academic cultural researcher with a sense of justice and responsibility.

In this connection, the Chinese Academy of Social Sciences organized its top-notch experts and scholars and several external experts to write the China Insights series. This series not only provides an overview of China's path, theories, and institutions but also objectively describes China's current development in the areas of political institutions, human rights, the rule of law, the economic system, finance, social governance, social security, population policies, values, religious faith, ethnic policies, rural issues, urbanization, industrialization, ecology, ancient civilization, literature, art, etc., thus depicting China in a way that helps readers visualize these topics.

We hope that this series will help domestic readers more correctly understand the course of the more than 100 years of China's modernization and more rationally look at current difficulties, enhance the urgency for and national confidence in comprehensively intensifying reform, build a consensus on reform and development, and gather strength in this regard, as well as deepen foreign readers' understanding of China, thus fostering a better international environment for China's development.

January 2014   Zhao Jianying

Preface

The Ethno-national Policies of the CPC During Its Time Based in Yan'an: 1935–1948

A large number of countries in this world, including China, are characterized by their diverse ethnic or racial composition. *The Constitution of the People's Republic of China* declares that the country is "a unitary multi-national state created jointly by the people of all its nationalities." China is a unified multi-ethnic country with a long history, and this is the most important starting point for understanding China. It took thousands of years for China to form a unified multi-ethnic country, toward which all ethnicities of China have made great contributions, and the sustained development of Chinese civilization over millennia is the result of the ethnic pursuit of national unification. As early as 221 BC, the Qin Dynasty (221–206 BC), the first feudal empire in the history of China, brought about the unification of the country for the first time. The subsequent Han Dynasty (206 BC–220 AD) further consolidated the country's unification. Later dynasties, whether they were established by Han people, such as the Sui (581–618), Tang (618–907), Song (960–1279), and Ming (1368–1644), or by ethnic minority groups, such as the Yuan (1271–1368) and Qing (1644–1911), all considered themselves as "orthodox reigns" of China and regarded the establishment of a united multi-ethnic state their highest political goal.

As an indispensable precondition to understanding China, in particular, the answer to its ethno-national issues, such historical experience, is extremely rare in the world. On the one hand, unity represents a stable and solid-state system; on the other hand, multi-ethnicity implies the existence of a long-standing and complicated ethnic relationship. The state governance capacity to effectively handle ethnic affairs is greatly needed to achieve development and prosperity in a unified country with a diverse ethnic makeup. However, the principles, policies, and guidelines on addressing the ethno-national issues of the country were not chartered in the lofty and stately palaces; rather, they should be traced to the Chinese Communists' time based in Yan'an, a remote and mountainous town in northern Shaanxi.

I

In March 1947, people in North China still felt a chill in the early spring air. After experiencing a long and extremely cold winter, the Loess Plateau was covered by ice and snow. In spite of the freezing weather, farmers in northern Shaanxi were busy preparing for the spring cultivation. The cloud of war that had a bearing on China's future and destiny was approaching Yan'an, reputed to be the wartime stronghold of the Chinese Communists from the mid-1930s to 1949.[1] In the cave dwellings of the Loess Plateau, the leadership of the Chinese Communists formulated the basic policies to address the ethno-national issues of China.

For a relatively long period of time since the founding of the Chinese Communist Party (CPC) in 1921, China had formed a political party pattern represented by the ruling Chinese Nationalist Party (Kuomingtang, or KMT) and the opposition CPC. In May 1928, the CPC created its own armed forces, the Red Army. After being forced out of the Jinggang Mountains by the Kuomintang Army, the Communists fled to Ruijin, taking advantage of its relative isolation in the rugged mountains along Jiangxi's border with Fujian. In 1931, this fledging political force inaugurated the Chinese Soviet Republic (CSR). Its constitution declared: "all the workers, peasants, officers and soldiers of the Red Army, and other working classes within the jurisdiction of the CSR, regardless of their ethnicities and religious beliefs, are equal citizens."[2]

The CSR Constitution put forward the CPC's political initiative of resolving domestic ethno-national issues: "We recognize the self-determination rights of all the ethnic minorities, including the Mongols, Huis, Tibetans, Miaos, Lis and Koreans. They are free to decide whether to join or secede from the CSR or establish their own autonomous governments. The Chinese Soviet administration shall make every effort to assist the ethnic minorities for their freedom and democracy by eradicating the cruel oppression of imperialism, the Kuomintang government, the warlords, religious upper classes and chieftains." Apparently, the CPC's propositions of acknowledging the ethnic minorities' rights of self-determination and organizing a federal government were derived from the Soviet Union. Under the historical conditions at that time, it was quite natural for the CSR Constitution to draw on the Soviet Union Constitution for the Chinese Communists openly declared Marxism–Leninism as its guide for action. In their rudimentary stage, the CPC's guidelines to solving domestic ethno-national issues, due to lack of understanding of the historical and actual conditions of the ethnic minorities, were in large part influenced by the Soviet Union and the Communist International. However, it did not exclude the CPC's initiative to work out answers to the ethno-national issues of China based on the national conditions of the country.

It was en route to the epic Long March that the CPC directly understood the social situations of the Chinese ethnic minorities. Defeated in the Fifth Anti-encirclement Campaign against the KMT's National Revolution Army in

---

[1]Hsu (2008).

[2]*Collected Documents of Ethnic Affairs Administration* (1991).

October 1934, the Chinese Communists and the Red Army were compelled to retreat from their base in south Jiangxi. The Red Army, under the eventual command of Mao Zedong and Zhou Enlai, escaped in a circling retreat to the west and north, which reportedly traversed over 9000 km over 370 days. In spite of high casualties, the Long March gave the CPC the isolation it needed, allowing the Red Army to recuperate in northern Shaanxi. It was also vital in helping the Chinese Communists to gain a positive reputation among the Chinese peasantry due to the determination and dedication of the surviving participants. Passing through some of the most difficult terrains of Western China by traveling west, then north to Yan'an, the Long March provided rare opportunities for the CPC's contact with ethnic minorities, which greatly deepened the Chinese Communists' perception and cognition about the multi-ethnic national condition of China.

The policies and actual deeds of the Red Army, for instance, treating ethnic minorities on an equal footing, respecting their religious belief, folkways and customs, won the trust of minority ethnic groups. In addition, the Long March widely publicized the CPC's basic concepts in handling domestic ethnic issues, including ethnic equality and unity, opposing ethnic discrimination and oppression, which laid a solid foundation for the CPC's ethno-national policies.

II

In October 1935, some 30,000 ragged and exhausted Red Army officers and soldiers reached northern Shaanxi and joined with the local Communist forces there. The year in which the Red Army arrived in Yan'an was a critical moment for China and the Chinese nation: In the civil society, the lyrics of *The March of the Volunteers*, "The peoples of China are at their most critical time, everybody must roar defiance" became wildly popular among the Chinese public; in the Soviet Union, the CPC's delegation to the Communist International, in the name of the Chinese Soviet Republic and the CPC Central Committee, made public the *Message to all Compatriots on Resistance against Japanese and National Salvation*, which called upon the Chinese Nationalist Party to end the Civil War and to unite the people in resisting the Japanese invasion.

Pressed by a growing population, Japan initiated the seizure of Manchuria (Northeast China) in September 1931 and established the abdicated emperor of the Qing Empire, Puyi, as head of the "Manchukuo," a puppet state under the control of Japan. The Japanese began to push from south of the Great Wall into Northern China and its coastal provinces. After occupying Manchuria, the Imperial Japanese Army gradually began its southward advance. In 1935, Beiping (today's Beijing) and Tianjin were both captured by Japan. As a consequence, the North China Plain was helpless against the Japanese forces. The Chinese nation was faced with the danger of life or death. Chinese fury against Japan was predictable, but anger was also directed against the KMT Government headed by Chiang Kai-shek, which at the time was more preoccupied with anti-Communist extermination campaigns than with resisting the Japanese aggression. At a conference held in Yan'an in December 1935, Mao Zedong delivered a speech entitled *on tactics against Japanese imperialism.*

The appeal of Mao Zedong struck a responsive chord among people throughout China. Yan'an, the headquarters of the CPC, became the political center from which to mobilize the Chinese people for the common fight against the Japanese invasion.

After the humiliating defeat in the First Opium War (1840), the Qing Empire was coerced into signing *the Treaty of Nanking*, which became the first step toward opening the lucrative coastal areas of China to global commerce and opium trade. With the advent of modern times, Chinese society became embroiled in intense upheavals. The imperialists launched one aggression after another against the Chinese borderlands, including Yunnan, Tibet, Xinjiang, Mongolia, and Manchuria. Taking advantage of their superior military capabilities, they imposed a series of unequal treaties on the weak and incompetent Qing Dynasty. China was plunged into the darkness of domestic turmoil and foreign aggression; its people, ravaged by war, saw their homeland torn apart and lived in poverty and despair.

As a result, the modern era of China between 1840 and 1949 was a time of fierce struggle as the Chinese people resisted feudal rule and foreign aggression. With tenacity and heroism, countless dedicated patriots fought, pressed ahead against the odds, and tried every possible means to seek the nation's salvation. These heroic efforts culminated in the Revolution of 1911. It is commonly known as the Xinhai Revolution for the year of 1911 was the Xinhai stem-branch in the sexagenary cycle of the Chinese calendar. With the abdication of the last emperor of the Qing Dynasty, the radical revolutionaries led by Dr. Sun Yat-sen toppled the Qing Dynasty and established the Republic of China (ROC), marking the end of 2000 years of imperial rule and the beginning of China's early republican era.

The newly founded ROC government was facing enormous challenge in its borderland defense. In the wake of the Xinhai Revolution, Jebtsundamba Khutughtu, the religious leader of the Gelug School of Tibetan Buddhism in Mongolia, proclaimed the independence of Outer Mongolia and founded the "Great Mongolian Government." Three years later, the British colonists attempted to instigate the "independence of Tibet" in the Simla Accord (1914). After seizing Northeast China following the Mukden Incident, a staged event engineered by Japanese military personnel as a pretext for the Japanese invasion of northeastern China in 1931, the pro-Japanese puppet government "Manchukuo" was installed in Manchuria. The following year, the Uygur separatists founded the "East Turkestan Islamic State" in Xinjiang. In 1935, Japan started its conspiracy of founding "Mongolian State" in Inner Mongolia by collaborating with Demchugdongrub, a Mongol Prince of the First Rank, who was one of the most influential figures in the local politics. It heralded the full implementation of a brand new strategy first put forward by the Japanese Prime Minister Tanaka Giichi in the controversial *Tanaka Memorial*, "the Japanese Empire needs to take over Manchuria and Mongolia at first for the purpose of dominating China." Moreover, the Black Dragon Society, a paramilitary and ultranationalist right-wing group in Japan, was busy for the preparations of establishing "Huihuiguo" (the State for the Hui people) in Northwest China's Ningxia region.[3]

---

[3]*The CPC's Collected Documents on the Ethno-national Issue.* p. 165.

After arriving at Yan'an in 1935, the CPC, fully perceiving the Japanese imperialists' conspiracy to split China, issued *A Message to the Inner Mongols*. It proclaimed that the answer to the ethno-national issues of Inner Mongols should be the top priority in the people's revolution against imperialism, feudal oppression, and the bureaucratic bourgeoisie.[4] In addition, the Chinese Communists strongly advocated the cessation of all civil wars and the common resistance against Japan and called for the establishment of an anti-Japanese National United front.

As the Japanese imperialists launched a full-scale war of aggression against China, Europe was on the eve of the Second World War. Though the rise of Nazi Germany with its audacious ambition of dominating the world became an evident reality, Britain and France were complacent with the policy of appeasement framed by *the Treaty of Versailles*. In 1936, Germany and Italy established the "Berlin-Rome Axis," which grew out of their diplomatic efforts to secure their own expansionist interests. Oblivious to what was happening in Asia, the Europeans failed to anticipate that Japan would immediately join the Fascist Axis after the outbreak of the Second World War in Europe. It was not until late 1936 that the world finally diverted its attention to China. On December 12, 1936, Kai-shek Chiang, chairman of the KMT-controlled Nationalist Government of China, was arrested by Xueliang Zhang, a former warlord of Manchuria and commander of the Northeastern Army, in order to force Chiang to enter into a cease-fire with the CPC and form a united front against Japan. Historically reputed as the Xi'an Incident, it led to a truce between the KMT and the CPC. At the same time, the CPC won considerable support from the Chinese people for being an open advocate of the anti-Japanese united front.

III

During that time, Edgar Snow, an American journalist, was in Yan'an, sorting out his extensive first-hand interviews with Mao Zedong and other CPC top leaders. In October 1937, *Red Star over China*, an account of the Chinese Communist Movement from its foundation until the late 1930s, was published in London. Presenting vivid descriptions of the Long March, as well as biographical accounts of leaders on both sides of the armed conflict of China, the book became an instant bestseller upon its publishing. Snow's status as an international journalist not previously identified with the communist movement gave his reports the stamp of authenticity. The glowing pictures of life in the communist areas contrasted with the gloom and corruption of the Kuomintang government. The book has an unparalleled importance in "establishing a positive image of the emerging Chinese Communist movement," which had long been blockaded and demonized by the mainstream Western media.[5]

Following Edgar Snow's footsteps, a large number of overseas journalists, doctors, academics, and experts, including Agnes Smedley, Norman Bethune, Hans

---

[4]Ibid., p. 322.

[5]Mackerras (2013).

Shippe, Kwakanath S. Kotnis, James Bertram, Owen Lattimore, Mical Lindsay, Alley Rewi, and George Hatem, arrived at Yan'an to help the Chinese people in their war of resistance against Japan. They made significant contributions to the great cause of Chinese people's liberation through their altruistic and humanitarian assistance to China. Yan'an, once an obscure town nestled in Northwest China, was thrust into the global limelight.

After the Long March, Mao Zedong systematically summarized the experiences and lessons of the Chinese people's liberation cause against the backdrop of the Second Sino-Japanese War, which had a bearing on the survival of the Chinese nation. Illuminated by the kerosene lamp in his Yan'an cave dwelling, MaoZedong explored the objective law of the Chinese Revolution, laying a sound foundation for the formation of Marxism–Leninism with Chinese characteristics. In *Red Star over China*, Edgar Snow commented that "Mao Zedong succinctly summarizes and vividly expresses the demands of the Chinese working classes, in particular, the impoverished, oppressed and illiterate Chinese peasants, who account for the majority of the population of China." Snow was deeply convinced that Mao Zedong might become a great figure if the appeals of the peasantry were to become "the motive force to revive China" under the CPC's leadership.[6] History has testified the vision of the American journalist.

In the CPC's infancy, its political programs of solving China's ethno-national issues had been in large part influenced by the Soviet Union. However, *the Resolution on the Issues of Chinese Ethnic Minorities* by the Chinese Soviet Republic, which was co-established by Mao Zedong and other CPC leaders in November 1931, declared that: "the ethnic minorities in Mongolia, Tibet, Xinjiang, Yunnan and Guizhou are entitled to establish autonomous governments." It showed that regional autonomy for ethnic minorities was also considered as an alternative approach to realize national self-determination.[7] While talking with Edgar Snow in Yan'an, Mao Zedong specifically pointed out the prospect for Inner Mongolia: "We will assist the Mongols to establish an autonomous government after driving the Japanese aggressors out of China."[8] More than a policy statement, it was put into practice in the Shaan-Gan-Ning Border Region, which was created by the CPC in agreement with the ruling KMT as a part of the national united front policy during the Second Sino-Japanese War.

With a population of 1.5 million and a size of 130,000 km^2, the Border Region covers northern Shaanxi, eastern Gansu and parts of Ningxia. During his stay in Yan'an, Edgar Snow visited Yuwang Township, a concentrated community of the ethnic Hui people. At that time, the locals were busy themselves with inaugurating an autonomous government. While conversing with them, Snow was surprised to find that they had deep trust in the CPC's ethnic and religious policies.

---

[6]Snow (1984).

[7]The United Front Department of the CPC Central Committee. *Collected Documents of Ethnic Affairs Administration*. p. 170.

[8]Snow E. *Red Star over China*. p. 85.

He commented that it was "simply unbelievable" for the Chinese Communists to eliminate the deep-rooted historical ethnic grievances within such a short period of time. At first, he was skeptical about the credibility of the CPC's commitment to the Hui People's autonomy. Coincidentally, he witnessed the inauguration conference of Yuhai Hui Autonomous Government, which effectively dispelled his doubts.[9] The Lebanese-American doctor Shafick George Hatem, who was with Edgar Snow in Yan'an, was asked to translate the conference posters into Arabic. It played a symbolic positive effect on the local Hui people, who were predominantly adherents of the Muslim faith.[10] In December 1936, Yuhai Hui Autonomous Government was officially inaugurated in a mosque in Tongxin County in Northwest China's Ningxia province. In spite of its existence of only six months, the autonomous regime, which combined Worker–Peasant Revolution with ethnic liberation movement, is accepted as a rudimental practice of regional autonomy for ethnic minorities.[11]

IV

During its time headquartered in Yan'an, the CPC's ethnic minority affairs were concentrated in the northwest provinces and Inner Mongolia due to the strategic geopolitical importance of these regions against the background of China's armed conflict with Japan. In October 1937, Demchugdongrub, a Mongolian prince descended from the Borjigin imperial clan, proclaimed the independence of Inner Mongolia and founded the "Mongol United Autonomous Government," with Kweisui (today's Hohhot) as the capital. At the same time, the Japanese Army invaded Baotou, the largest industrial city of Inner Mongolia, attempting to occupy the vast northwest China. Promising to help the Hui warlords with their plan of establishing an independent state for the Hui People, Japan intended to create an internal discord in China's national united front by taking advantage of the ethnic minorities' grievances against the Han people. Therefore, the ethnic policy of the CPC became an important part of consolidating and expanding the anti-Japanese national united front.

As mentioned earlier, the Chinese Communists conveyed their respect for the Hui People's regional autonomy and religious belief when Yuhai Hui Autonomous Government was established in 1936. Likewise, the CPC leadership demonstrated their reverence for the Mongols' ancestral worship by paying homage to the Mausoleum of Genghis Khan en route to its southward relocation during the Second Sino-Japanese War. With ties to traditional Mongolian shamanism, the worship of Genghis Khan is a religion popular among the Mongols. With the intensification of Japan's incursion into North China, the Japanese Army attempted to use the cult of Genghis Khan to fan Mongolian nationalism. At the request of the

---

[9] Snow E. *Red Star over China*. pp. 301–302.

[10] Yang and Hui (1996).

[11] *The Collected Documents of the Ethnic Affairs of China*, p. 367.

Mongol nobility, the Mongolian and Tibetan Affairs Commission of the ruling Nationalist Government of China submitted a report to the Supreme State Defense Council, suggesting that the mobile tomb and its relics be relocated elsewhere. Actively responding to this patriotic event, the Shaan-Gan-Ning Border Region government erected a mourning hall in Yan'an. The Chinese Communists held a large public sacrifice to Genghis Khan with a crowd of about 20,000 spectators. The CPC Central Committee and Mao Zedong presented memorial wreathes.[12] In addition to being a much-told story of KMT-CPC cooperation, this grand ceremony had an important impact on advancing the autonomous movement of Inner Mongolia.

The CPC's policies toward the ethnic minorities are aligned with the history and national conditions of China. After the 1911 Revolution, the intellectual elites of China, including Sun Yat-sen, were concerned with what kind of modern China to build. A range of nation-state construction programs came into being, for example, "a republic of five ethnicities" (a union of five races), the US-style "one of many," and the Soviet-style "federal republic." All these were related to the history and territory of China as a unified multi-ethnic state, as well as the diversity and complexity of national components in blood, language, culture, customs, religion, and other aspects, in particular, the equal status and rights of ethnic minorities in modern China. During its time based in Yan'an, the CPC leadership provided theoretical solutions to these problems.

V

The Chinese Revolution of 1911 terminated the timeline of China's feudal dynasties. As a consequence, establishing a nation-state in the country became a natural choice. Derived from the development process of Western capitalism, the nation-state has the characteristics of sovereign independence, territorial integrity, and conversion from 'subjects' loyal to the emperor to citizens loyal to the country. According to Marxism, the substitutions of capitalism for feudalism, nation-state for dynastic empire, citizens for subjects, are great progress in social development. However, the Western capitalists, upon the founding of their nation-states, embarked on a path of global expansion and colonial empire building with their superior military forces. After the fall of the Manchu Dynasty, the primary concern of the republican government was to abolish the unequal treaties imposed on China by the foreign powers. Therefore, the establishment of a modern nation-state in China needed to, in the first place, liberate the Chinese people from the yoke of imperialism and realize the self-determination of the Chinese nation. The fulfillment of this historical task became the inescapable duty of the Chinese Communists.

The road explored by Sun Yat-sen, the federal system of the "republic of five ethnicities," included elements that emulated the Soviet Union, and was not aligned with the history and national conditions of China. The Chinese Communist Party seized the situation and began to explore the path of regional ethnic autonomy

---

[12]Jin and Sai (2011).

within a unified country. After making the Long March exodus, the Red Army controlled by the CPC took over Yan'an. It became the seat of the Communist Government of what became known as the Shaanxi-Gansu-Ningxia Border Region, whose political principle, economic institution, educational system, and social policy incarnated the embryonic form of state governance. Yan'an Institute of Nationalities founded in 1941 became an important base for training ethnic minority officials and promoting the CPC's ethno-national policies. Some Mongol members of the CPC, including Ulanhu, made great contributions to the autonomous movement of Inner Mongolia. In July 1945, Ulanhu was appointed by the CPC Central Committee as Chairman of the newly established Suiyuan-Mongolia Provincial Government.

On August 15, 1945, the Japanese Emperor Hirohito officially capitulated to the Allies, symbolizing the end of the Second Sino-Japanese War. However, the brief period of celebration was soon shadowed by the upcoming civil war between the KMT and the CPC. At that time, the CPC advocated that "a democratic coalition government be established for the target of building China into an independent, democratic, united and prosperous country." It voiced the Chinese people's long-awaited wishes of peace and democracy.[13] On August 27, 1945, the CPC delegation headed by Mao Zedong flew to Chongqing, which served as Kai-shek Chiang's provisional capital during the Second Sino-Japanese War, to begin the first postwar negotiations. Though both sides stressed the importance of a peaceful reconstruction, the conference did not produce any concrete result.

While visiting Westminster College in the USA in March 1946, the British Prime Minister Winston Churchill delivered his "Sinews of Peace" address, which was commonly known as the "Iron Curtain Speech" for Churchill used the term "iron curtain" in the context of Soviet-dominated Eastern Europe. It declared the commencement of the "Cold War," a state of geopolitical tension after Second World War. In June of that year, only one year after the end of China's enduring hostilities with Japan, the forces of the Nationalist Government launched a full-scale civil war against the forces of the CPC. In March 1947, Yan'an, the headquarters of the Chinese Communists and the People's Liberation Army, was captured by the KMT forces. However, the Communist leadership learned of the attack in advance and pulled out. Almost at the same time, Inner Mongolia People's Congress was convened in Ulanhot in the eastern part of Inner Mongolia. The founding of Inner Mongolia Autonomous Government represents the basic political system design for the CPC's answer to the ethno-national issues of China.

In China's traditional political wisdom, "he who wins the support of the people will flourish, he who loses the backing of the public will perish" is an incontrovertible truth repeatedly verified by facts. In other words, any power politics or ruling force can never triumph over the general trend of development and the common aspiration of the people. When the CPC's Red Army arrived in northern Shaanxi in 1935, they numbered only in around 30,000. However, the balance of power shifted in favor of the Chinese Communists with their main force growing to

---

[13]*The Selected Works of Mao Zedong. Volume III* (1991).

1.2 million troops by the end of the Second Sino-Japanese War. Their liberated zones covered one-quarter of the country's territory and one-third of its population. On October 1, 1949, Mao Zedong proclaimed the founding of the People's Republic of China (PRC) with its capital at Beiping, which was renamed Beijing. Kai-shek Chiang and approximately one million KMT troops retreated from mainland China to the island of Taiwan in December after the loss of Sichuan. In the final analysis, the Chinese Communists' victory in their battle over the KMT forces shall be ascribed to the popular support of the people. After waging protracted and arduous struggles, armed and otherwise, along a zigzag course, the Chinese people of all nationalities led by the Communist Party of China with Mao Zedong as its leader ultimately, in 1949, overthrew the rule of imperialism, feudalism, and bureaucrat-capitalism, won a great victory in the New-Democratic Revolution and founded the People's Republic of China. Since then, the Chinese people have taken control of state power and become masters of the country. After the founding of the People's Republic, China gradually achieved its transition from a New-Democratic to a socialist society.

The establishment of the PRC realized the self-determination of the Chinese nation. The Chinese people of all ethnic groups embarked on a new journey of great rejuvenation. Since 1949, China's ethno-national policies, which are legally guaranteed by *the Law on Regional Ethnic Autonomy*, have formed a holistic system, covering areas of politics, economy, culture, and society. In the national conference on ethnic minority affairs held in 2014, the Chinese President Xi Jinping succinctly summarized the set of laws, systems, and policies as "the Chinese characteristic solution to its ethno-national issues." Upon its founding, the People's Republic of China largely copied the Soviet Union's socialist system. Since reform and opening-up, China has embarked on a socialist path with Chinese characteristics and become the world's second-largest economy. This shows political independence is key to how far China can go. Most major phenomena facing China cannot be explained by Western theories. China must find solutions with its own wisdom. Whether our practices are good should be assessed by whether they respond to and promote China's mission and the actual results.

China's opening up is intended to draw lessons from others' experience and absorb the achievements of other parts of civilized human society, but it would be impossible for China to introduce systems and development models of other countries completely. The success of China's reform mainly rests with a developmental path based upon its own reality, which conducts exploration in accordance with its own conditions. This is the most important strategy since China's reform and opening up and is a development idea that China should continue to follow in the future. Xi Jinping pointed out: "Which path should we follow? This is the paramount question for the future of the CPC and the success of its cause. Socialism with Chinese characteristics is the integration of the theory of scientific socialism and social development theories of Chinese history. Socialism has taken root in China. It reflects the wishes of the people and meets the development needs of the country and the times. It is a sure route to success in building a moderately prosperous society in all respects, in the acceleration of socialist modernization, and in the great renewal of the Chinese nation."[14]

As an organic part of socialism with Chinese characteristics, or Marxism–Leninism adapted to Chinese conditions, it is the CPC's conscious choice on the basis of China's historical and national conditions. Xi added: "What doctrine a country may choose is based on whether it can resolve the historical problems that confront that country. Both history and reality have shown us that only socialism can save China and only socialism with Chinese characteristics can bring development to China. This conclusion is the result of historical exploration, and the choice of the people."[15] Thus, the knowledge of the historical basis, advanced concepts, and practical results for China's answer to its ethno-national issues is an indispensable perspective for a full and objective understanding of China.

Beijing, China   Shiyuan Hao

References

Hsu, I. C. Y. (2008). *The rise of Modern China: 1600–2000* (p. 480). Beijing: World Book Inc.

Collected Documents of Ethnic Affairs Administration (p. 166). Beijing: Press of the CPC Party School (1991).

The CPC's Collected Documents on the Ethno-national Issue (p. 165).

Mackerras, C. P. (2013). *The western image of China since 1949* (p. 36) (Y. Zhang & D. Wu, Trans.). Hong Kong: Open Page Publishing Co. Ltd.

Snow, E. (1984). *Red Star over China* (p. 63). Beijing: Xinhua Press.

Yang, W., & Hui, Y. (1996). *Autonomous government: The first county-level organ of self-government* (5). Ningxia Pictorial.

Jin H. & Sai H. (2011). *The comprehensive history of inner Mongolia. Vol. II* (p. 704). Beijing: People's Press.

The selected works of Mao Zedong. Vol. III (p. 1029). Beijing: People's Press (1991).

The governance of China (p. 35). Beijing: Foreign Languages Press (2014).

---

[14]*The Governance of China* (2014).

[15]Ibid., p. 155.

Contents

Chapter 1
The Historical Gene of China: A Unified Multi-ethnic State

The thinker Gong Zizhen in Qing dynasty said, "If you wish to know the Great Way, you must first know history; conversely, to annihilate a country, you must first remove its history." Our perspective of history shapes the way in which we view the present, and therefore, it dictates what answers we offer for existing problems. As we study the history of a country, we will learn about the challenges and achievements of its people in different historical periods. China has been a unified multi-ethnic state since ancient times, which can be defined as the historical gene of the Chinese nation. Therefore, understanding the formation of China into a multi-ethnic state is a prerequisite to the solution to its ethno-national issues.

1.1 The Early Chinese Civilization Jointly Created by the "Five Ethnicities"

China is a unified multi-ethnic country with a long history, and this is the most important starting point for understanding China. As a modern nation-state, China has the task of building and realizing the great rejuvenation of the Chinese nation. It took thousands of years for China to form a unified multi-ethnic country, in which all ethnicities of China have made great contributions; and the sustained development of Chinese civilization over millennia is the result of the ethnic pursuit of national unification. It endured for hundreds of years, surviving the rise and fall of many ruling houses and the constant threat of invasion. However, the systematic interpretation of Chinese civilization remains an enigma for the outside world. At the same time, the feature of multi-ethnicity is encoded in the unity of China, which is undoubtedly a historical driving force for the continuity of Chinese civilization.

In the long process of historical development, China has formed a unified multi-ethnic state structure, boasting extensive ancient human history and cultural diversity. In China, there are hundreds of sites containing ancient human remains and fossils, and thousands of Paleolithic and Neolithic sites. Voluminous historical literatures

© China Social Sciences Press 2020
S. Hao, *China's Solution to Its Ethno-national Issues*, China Insights,
https://doi.org/10.1007/978-981-32-9519-3_1

record a large number of culturally diverse groups and their interactions. The connection between the various Chinese cultural systems of the Neolithic Age with the early human groups can be briefly summarized in the following outline. The *huaxia* people were descended from the Neolithic *yangshao* culture, which existed from around 5000–3000 BC along the Yellow River, and the *longshan* culture, a late Neolithic culture from the middle and lower Yellow River valley areas of Northern China, dating from about 3000–1900 BC; the *dongyi* people were descended from the cultures of *dawenkou* and *longshan*; the *nanman* from the various Neolithic cultures to the south of Yangtze River, including those of *hemudu*, *majiabang*, *liangzhu*, *daxi*, and *qujialing*; the *beidi* people rose out of the Neolithic cultures to the north of the Yangtze River, including the cultures of *xinle*, *fuhe*, and *hongshan*; the *xirong* people originated from the *majiayao* culture of Northern China. In the *Book of Rites*, which brings together Confucian thoughts before the Qin dynasty, the five early human groups, including *huaxia* (the Han people based in the North China Plain), *dongyi*, *nanman*, *xirong*, and *beidi* (eastern, southern, western, and northern barbarians, respectively), are collectively termed as "five ethnicities," which set a precedent for Chinese classical ethnography.

In its original sense, *huaxia*, the ancestors of what later became the Han people, refers to a confederation of tribes living along the Yellow River. They were seen as a civilized society that was distinct and stood in contrast to what was perceived as the four barbaric peoples around them. The *huaxia* people classed their neighbors by compass direction as *Siyi* (literally "four barbarians"), including the *beidi*, *nanman*, *dongyi*, and *xirong*. According to *The Book of Rites*, people's qualifications and accomplishments vary with the climate and natural geographical environment. Such differences are reflected in temperament, attitudes, and behavior, and also in food, utensils, tools, clothing, housing, and so on. The "five ethnicities" had different languages and ideas, and needed translators for communication with each other. It produced a very classical description of the many diverse human groups and their mutual interactions on the vast land of China.

The "Hua-Yi distinction," also known as the "Sino-barbarian dichotomy," is an ancient Chinese concept that differentiates a culturally defined "*huaxia*" (Han people) from cultural or ethnic outsiders ("*yi*" or "barbarians"). Although "*yi*" is often translated as "barbarian," other renderings of this term include "foreigners," "wild tribes," or "uncivilized tribes." The "Sino-barbarian dichotomy" was basically cultural, but it could take ethnic or racist overtones, in particular in times of war. In the former cases, it asserted the cultural superiority of the Han people but implied that the "four barbarians" could evolve into "huaxia" by adopting their values and customs. When this "cultural universalism" took a more racial guise, it could have harmful effects on those groups not considered "huaxia."

The perceived contrast between "*huaxia*" and "*yi*" was accentuated during the Eastern Zhou period (770–256 BC), when adherence to Zhou rituals became increasingly recognized as a "barometer of civilization," a meter for sophistication and cultural refinement. It is widely agreed by historians that the "Hua-Yi distinction" emerged during that period. The conclusion of the Warring States Period (475–221 BC) brought about the first unified Chinese state established by the Qin dynasty (221–207 BC). Qin Shi Huang, who was both the founder of the Qin dynasty and the first emperor of a unified China, initiated the imperial system and forcibly standardized the traditional Chinese script, leading to the first of the distinctions between the refined "hua" and the increasingly marginalized "yi." The Han dynasty (202 BC–220 AD) further contributed to the Hua-Yi division with its creation of a persistent Han cultural identity. Spanning over four centuries, the Han period is considered a golden age in Chinese history. To this day, China's majority ethnic group refers to themselves as the "Han people" and the Chinese script is referred to as "Han characters."

Throughout history, Chinese frontiers had been periodically attacked by nomadic tribes from the north and west. These peoples were considered "barbarians" by the Han, who believed themselves to be more refined and who had begun to build cities and live urban lives based on agriculture. It was in consideration of how best to deal with this threat that Confucius was prompted to formulate principles for relationships with the barbarians, briefly recorded in *Analects*.[1] Confucius regarded people who did not respect "Li" (literally "ritual propriety") as "barbarians," for he believed the workings of a state should be founded on ethical conduct rather than the relatively cruel social codes imposed by conquering princes.

Early Chinese rulers were thought to be "sons of heaven" and were given the "Mandate of Heaven," the approval of the gods to rule as long as they ruled well. China's first ruling dynasty, the Xia, was established around 2000 BC. According to tradition, the late Xia rulers were so cruel that they lost the "Mandate of Heaven" to the Shang dynasty (1600–1046 BC). The Shang rulers controlled a fairly small state near the Yellow River but influenced a much larger area. They were often at war with neighboring peoples and with sheep-herding nomads. One of these neighboring peoples, the Zhou from the Wei River region to the west, overthrew the Shang dynasty in around 1100 BC. The Zhou reigned for nearly 900 years, longer than any other dynasty in Chinese history. Although the last Zhou rulers had little power, their fall in 256 BC was a turning point in the country's history. The dynasties that followed the Zhou established, extended, and maintained the Chinese Empire.

The "five ethnicities" in ancient China correspond to the geographical location of different cultural groups. The Huaxia, living and farming in the Central Plains, led in terms of economic and cultural development; and the "four barbarian tribes on the borders" (dongyi, xirong, nanman, and beidi) engaged in nomadic activities, fishing, hunting, and mountain agriculture. The diverse groups in the periphery maintained an economic cultural exchange with the Central Plains, but they used various ways to merge into the Central Plains region. The "center-periphery" interactive economic and cultural activities caused the Central Plains region's agricultural civilization to develop, the population to increase, and the national governance model to mature.

---

[1]*Analects* is a collection of sayings and ideas, which is believed to have been compiled and written by Confucius' disciples.

1.2   The Dynasties of Qin and Han: Centralized and Unified Empires

In 221 BC, Qin Shi Huang (literally "the first emperor of the Qin dynasty") founded the Qin dynasty, the first centralized dynasty of China, upon conquering the other six states. The establishment of the Qin dynasty, as a landmark of progress in Chinese history, laid a solid historical foundation for the formation and development of a unified multi-ethnic state. The Qin dynasty implemented a series of social integration systems and policies, such as "book with the same script," "vehicle on the same track," uniform weights and measures, and developed unified national laws. The unification of the written language had a particularly profound impact on Chinese society. These measures initiated the historical trend of China's unification, and its geographical stability and socio-cultural identity accelerated the consolidation process of Chinese ethnicities in the Central Plains. This group of ethnicities later developed into the most populous Han.

With no interest in territorial expansion, the Qin dynasty was content with its internal unity. The Roman Empire founded a century later in Europe, on the contrary, was committed to military conquest and expansion. Rome established hundreds of provinces in its overseas dominions. The French historian Fustel de Coulanges commented: "it never occurred to the rulers of the Roman Empire to create new governance systems for the overseas dominions after the former city-state institutions were forcibly abolished. They proposed no new regulations to govern their subjects, let alone a unified law applicable to the whole empire."[2] The imperial ruling systems initiated by the Chinese Qin dynasty were inherited and developed by the Han dynasty (202 BC–220 AD). In addition, these institutions turned out to be stable national systems for all the succeeding Chinese feudal dynasties. After its collapse, the Roman Empire left a great deal of architecture, such as amphitheaters, water diversion canals, triumphal arches, and domes. The once-powerful empire had no direct heir. As a matter of fact, the successive regimes after the division of the Roman Empire, from the Eastern and Western Roman Empires, to the Holy Roman Empire, were mere "Romanization" labels which the European powers chased after. The subjects of the Roman Empire had never been integrated into a unified "Roman nation."

The Qin dynasty's unification of China and its rule over Chinese society had far-reaching significance for the formation of Chinese culture. The identification, inheritance, and maintenance of the political culture centered on the teachings of Confucius have been established as the yardstick to assess the legitimacy of the succeeding feudal dynasties. During this process, the "four barbarians," or the various minority ethnic groups of China, also experienced an integration process from clan, to tribe, to national community. Influenced by the relatively advanced agricultural civilization in the North China Plain, the nomadic tribes were increasingly assimilated into the Han people and the agricultural society. This assimilation process was

---

[2]Fustel de Coulanges (2006): 350.

never interrupted throughout the Chinese feudal dynasties. As a consequence, the traditional culture of China produced a tolerance for diversity under the conditions of unified ethical codes, institutions, decrees, and laws.

After conquering the six other states, the Qin dynasty initiated the "grand unification" process of China. Almost at the same time, Modu Chanyu, the supreme leader of the Xiongnu people,[3] created the Xiongnu Empire in 209 BC. The Xiongnu people's relations with adjacent Han Chinese dynasties were complex, with repeated periods of conflict and intrigue, alternating with exchanges of tribute, trade, and marriage treaties. The interaction between the northern nomads and the agricultural peoples in the Yellow River Valley became the most important factor affecting the rise and fall of the Chinese feudal dynasties. The agricultural society had great demands for draft animals, such as cattle, horses, or camels, and livestock products, including leather, wool, and meat. Meanwhile, the nomads were eager to get iron tools, textiles, grains, and handicraft products. The two civilizations formed a complementary relationship in terms of their economic and social development, although armed conflict, the inevitable feature of that historical era, did occur.

To protect the empire against the raids and invasions of the northern nomads, the first emperor of the Qin dynasty had the Great Wall built along an east–west line across the northern borders. Since then, the Great Wall has been sporadically rebuilt, maintained, and enhanced. The defensive characteristics of the Great Wall were enhanced by the construction of watch towers, troop barracks, garrison stations, signaling capabilities through the means of smoke or fire, and the fact that the path of the Great Wall also served as a transportation corridor. Some overseas Sinologists have argued that "the regions beyond the Great Wall of China cannot be identified as Chinese territories." As a matter of fact, these people erroneously associated the historical territory of ancient China with the border concept of the modern state, which is a misconception about China's national condition as a unified multi-ethnic state. In almost the same period when the Chinese Great Wall was erected, Europe witnessed the construction of Hadrian's Wall and the Upper Germania-Raetia Wall for defense against the invasions of nomadic tribes. However, European historians will never equate these ancient military fortifications with the territorial boundaries of modern Italy, Britain, or Germany. With the disruption of the Roman Empire, these defense facilities built for the use of military expansion were abandoned in the foreign lands. Nonetheless, the Great Wall of China remained inside the Chinese territory with the northern nomads' conquest of the North China Plain.

The formation of the Chinese state was a process in which the Han agricultural society in the North China Plain ("Zhongyuan") functioned as the center and the peripheral "Siyi" (literally "four barbarians") were increasingly integrated. The Western world's perception of Chinese culture was built on its bilateral trade and cultural exchanges with China. The Silk Road, which was started during the Eastern Han dynasty (25–220 AD), was central to the economic and cultural links between the East and the West. Trade on the Silk Road played a significant role in the development

---

[3]The Xiongnu people a confederation of nomadic tribes who inhabited the east Asian steppe from the third century BC to the late first century AD.

of civilization in China, as well as the Indian subcontinent, Persia, Europe, the Horn of Africa, and Arabia, opening political and economic engagements between these regions. Though silk was certainly the major product exported from China, religions, syncretic philosophies, and various technologies also spread along the Silk Route. In addition to economic trade, the Silk Road served as a means of carrying out cultural trade among the civilizations along its network. In *The Geography*, a compilation of geographical coordinates of the part of the world known to the Roman Empire compiled by Claudius Ptolemy, China was addressed as "Sinae" or "Serice," meaning "land where silk comes from." Toward the end of the Qin dynasty, a military leader named Bang Liu declared himself emperor and established the Han dynasty in 202 BC. Bang Liu and his successors drew on the Qin patterns of governance but avoided the extremes of that rigid rule. At that time, the Xiongnu people were recognized as the most prominent of the nomads bordering the Han Empire. After a series of battles, the Han Empire controlled the strategic region from the Ordos and Gansu corridor to Lop Nor. As a result, the Xiongnu Empire became unstable and was no longer a threat to the Han Chinese. After the Xiongnu Civil War, the Southern Xiongnu entered into tributary ties with the Han Empire, while the northern contingent migrated westwards.

After the collapse of the Han dynasty, feudal China experienced several centuries' chaos and warfare. By the early second century AD, the later Han rulers were facing economic ruin. There were rivalries among powerful families at court and between generals in the provinces, as well as widespread peasant rebellions. In 220, the Han Empire split into three kingdoms, the tripartite division of China between the states of Wei, Shu, and Wu. Nomads crossed the frontier and swept into North China. Constant warfare caused great hardship for the peasants throughout the country. This time of trouble came to be called the Age of Disunity, which continued for more than 300 years. Upon crossing the Great Wall and settling in the North China Plain, the nomadic peoples joined in the fighting for the central power. As the heir of the northern nomadic empire, the Xianbei people dominated North China and founded the Northern Wei dynasty. In addition, the sinicized barbarians established some other regimes in North China between 439 and 589. These states founded by the ethnic minorities were collectively named the Northern Dynasties. Over the same period, a large number of Han gentry, merchants, craftsmen, and farmers migrated to the regions south of the Yangtze River, which witnessed the successive existence of a series of dynasties: Liu Song (420–479), Southern Qi (479–502), Liang (502–557), and Chen (557–589). Because these regimes had their capital at Southern China's Nanjing city, they are grouped as the Southern dynasties. The rulers of these short-lived dynasties were generals who seized and then held power for several decades but were unable to securely pass the ruling power onto their heirs.

After approximately four centuries' separation and division, unification was achieved in the Sui and Tang dynasties. Near the end of the Age of Disunity, a warlord in Northern China conquered the south and declared himself as the first emperor of the Sui dynasty. At that time, the territories of the Western Roman Empire were carved up by the Germanic tribes. Voltaire vividly described the decadence of the empire: "Latin was replaced by 20 languages of the barbarians. The magnificent arenas and amphitheaters in the various provinces of the Roman Empire gave way to thatched huts."[4] Meanwhile, the majority of the Iberian Peninsula was occupied by the Moors, and the Byzantine Empire lost its governance over North Africa due to the rise of the Islamic Khalifa Empire.

1.3   The Tang Dynasty: Discontinuing the Tradition of Building the Great Wall

The Tang dynasty (618–907) was preceded by the Sui and followed by the "Five Dynasties and Ten Kingdoms period." It is generally regarded as a high point in Chinese civilization and a golden age of cosmopolitan culture. Its territory, acquired through military campaigns by its early rulers, rivaled that of the Han dynasty. The Tang dynasty inherited the system of "grand unification" initiated by the Qin and Han dynasties, but gave up the tradition of building the Great Wall. Actually, the Great Wall, established as the dividing line between farming civilization and the nomadic, was established as merely the extension of the Chinese agricultural society. Just as the famous Sinologist Owen Lattimore said: "the economic differences inside and outside the Great Wall did not form a political isolation. Although the Chinese emperors made great efforts to build the Great Wall, there had never been a clear-cut demarcation for the borderland."[5] Thus, the Great Wall is a "resource boundary" between farming society and the northern nomads. Though the dynasty based in the North China Plain was regarded as the orthodox central power following the unification of China during the Qin and Han dynasties, the identity of the ruler who ascended the throne was no longer limited to the Han people; rather, the "four barbarians" (the marginalized ethnic minorities) had also access to the supreme power.[6] The Tang dynasty, a golden age of cosmopolitan culture, was "a new regime that accepts and mixes diverse traditions." Since the Han and Tang dynasties are considered to be the high points of Chinese civilization, the Chinese would refer to themselves as either Han or Tang. Therefore, people in the Tang dynasty were commonly referred to as "Tangren" or "Tang Chinese," which is, in essence, another word for Han people. Today, the "China Town," an ethnic enclave of Chinese outside China, is traditionally expressed as "Tang People's street."

The Tang emperors encouraged trade and engagement with other Asian countries. There was great demand in both Europe and Asia for Chinese silk and porcelain. Foreign religions, including Buddhism, Islam, and Christianity, were brought into China. The Tang dynasty, a climax of economic and cultural exchanges between the East and the West, created a prosperous and open era. The Silk Road connected China directly to the West for land-based trade. Regrettably, the business caravans, missionaries, and travelers to the Tang Empire at that time did not leave many written

---

[4] Voltaire (1995): 308.

[5] Lattimore (2005): 45.

[6] Wang (2008): 223.

records about their travel experiences. Except for the exquisite silk and porcelain, China was still a mystery in the Western world.

The Greek-Canadian historian Leften Stavros Stavrianos pointed out: "the tension between nomads and agricultural society is the central mechanism of human history for thousands of years."[7] It is no exception in the history of China. In addition, class oppression and the incurred ethnic conflict must be taken into account while analyzing the dynastic pattern of China. The dynastic cycle of China followed a pattern generally like this: a new dynasty begins with a period of peace, prosperity, and loyalty to the ruler. Population increases. The government spends money on public works: walls, canals, and roads. As the dynasty continues, a less able ruler comes to power. Court officials and bureaucrats become corrupt and used to luxury, which causes them to spend more of the government's money. More money also may have to be spent on defending newly won lands or holding off invaders. The peasants are taxed more heavily, but the government still does not have enough money to keep things in repair. Peasant's rebellion breaks out. During the uprisings, dams and walls are weakened by neglect, allowing floods or invasions. Crops are destroyed, and famine may result. These weaken the government still more, and nobles begin to seize power from the ruling dynasty. The population decreases, and tax revenues are smaller. Finally, the old dynasty falls. The new dynasty starts by establishing a period of peace and prosperity, and the cycle begins again. Accordingly, China embarked on a new cycle of disintegration and unification at the end of the prosperous Tang dynasty. In this process, the nomadic people's raids and their challenges against the imperial power were particularly intense. In fact, the imperial Tang government was steadily weakened by enemy attacks on its borders from the eighth century onward. At the same time, the military leaders in the provinces rebelled and drove the last Tang Emperor from the throne in 907.

Around the time of the collapse of the Tang Empire, the Khitan, a nomadic people originally from Mongolia, founded the Liao Empire. Over the same period, the Jurchen, a Tungusic people who inhabited the region of Manchuria, established the Jin dynasty and later gained control of most of Northern China. The Liao Empire was destroyed by the Jin in 1125 with the capture of the Liao Emperor. However, the remnant Khitan, led by Yelü Dashi, inaugurated the Qara Khitai (Western Liao dynasty), which ruled over parts of Central Asia for almost a century before being conquered by the Mongols. At that time, the Tangut people, who lived in Northwest China, founded the Western Xia Empire, which existed from 1038 to 1227. The disunity process, which continued for two centuries, ended with the founding of the Mongolian nomadic empire by Genghis Khan in the northern grasslands in 1206. After Genghis Khan's death in 1227, his grandson Kublai Khan completed the conquest of the Southern Song dynasty. For the first time in China's long and brilliant history, foreign "barbarians" ruled the entire country. By 1279, the Mongol conquest of the Song dynasty was completed and Kublai became the first non-native emperor to conquer all of China. The famous British historian Arnold Joseph Toynbee commented: "Generally speaking, the empires established by the nomadic conquerors cannot sur-

---

[7]Stavrianos (1992): 102.

vive long. They are bound to decline even before their growth."[8] It is, admittedly, a universal fact. Although known for the brutality of his campaigns, Genghis Khan is credited with bringing the Silk Road under one cohesive political environment. This brought communication and trade from Northeast Asia into Muslim Southwest Asia and Christian Europe, thus expanding the horizons of all three cultural areas.

1.4   The Yuan Dynasty: Forming the Territorial Base of China

Isolated by the vast oceans, people from different continents had a very limited understanding of each other in the thirteenth century. As a network of trade routes that had been for centuries central to cultural interaction through regions of the Asian continent connecting the East and the West, the Silk Road was far from a secure and smooth thoroughfare. The harsh environment of the Gobi desert, complicated by the tedious protracted journey, posed numerous challenges in addition to the tempting business opportunities and profits. As a consequence, this trade route witnessed frequent harassments and lootings from the nomadic powers in the Inner Asia grasslands. At the same time, this highway of culture and commerce had been dominated for several centuries by the Islamic empire which emerged in the Middle East and later expanded to West Asia and Central Asia. Stavrianos pointed out: "It wasn't until the thirteenth century when the Mongols conquered the entire Eurasian continent stretching from the Pacific to the Baltic and the Black Sea that the Silk Route was reopened, which made it possible for Marco Polo's voyage to China."[9] In addition to being the heir and terminator of the Inner Asian nomadic society, the vast territory of the Mongol Yuan dynasty was unprecedented in Chinese history.

Before the establishment of the Yuan dynasty, the northern nomads, including the peoples of Hun, Xianbei, Rouran, Uighur, Turks, Khitan, and Jurchen, successively crossed the Great Wall and inaugurated a variety of short-lived dynasties. However, most of these regimes were assimilated into the mainstream Han Chinese culture. For example, the Northern Wei dynasty created by the Xianbei people underwent a gradual sinicization process by adopting the attires, family names, languages, administrative systems, and penal codes of the Han society. The Liao and Jin dynasties, which were, respectively, established by the peoples of Khitan and Jurchen, also introduced the Han Chinese governance methods. Moreover, they created their own scripts by drawing on the form and strokes of Chinese characters.

Although these dynasties failed to achieve the goal of unifying China, they were included in *Books of the Twenty-Four Histories*, the ancient Chinese official dynasty chronologies. Likewise, some other influential regimes founded by the minority eth-

---

[8] Toynbee (1966): 216.
[9] Stavrianos (1988): 137.

nic groups, such as the Tibetan Empire,[10] and the Western Xia Empire,[11] established close political, economic, and cultural ties with the Chinese central dynasties based in the North China Plain. The Tangut script, a logographic writing system used for writing the extinct Tangut language of the Western Xia dynasty, was designed by emulating the shape and strokes of Chinese characters. Some aboriginal peoples in Southwest China, including the Zhuang, Yao, Miao, Bai, and Shui, also created their own square scripts by imitating Chinese characters. Likewise, the Mongols created their own script by using the Uighur alphabet during the reign of Genghis Khan. After the founding of the Yuan dynasty, Kublai Khan, the Mongol Emperor and grandson of Genghis Khan, ordered the creation of the Phag-spa Script, an alphabet designed by Drogön Chögyal Phagpa, the Tibetan monk and state preceptor, as a unified script within the Yuan Empire. Therefore, we can clearly observe an ever-increasing political, economic, cultural, and social engagement among the "five ethnicities" and their descendants.

Considered the rightful heir to Chinese central power, the Yuan dynasty achieved an extensive national unification for the first time in the history of China. The Yuan Emperor set up in Tibet the Chief Military Command under the Pacification Commissioner's Office to directly manage the political and military affairs of the region. The Yuan court set up courier stations on the road leading from Lhasa to the capital city of Dadu and sent officials to Tibet three times to conduct census. Thanks to the invincible Mongol cavalry, the Mongols succeeded in the series of military operations in the Eurasian Continent and their final conquest of the Southern Song dynasty paved the way for the unification of China. In 1271, Kublai renamed the new Mongol regime as the Yuan dynasty and sought to sinicize his image to that of Emperor of China to win control of the Han people. Kublai moved his headquarters to Dadu, the seed for what later became the modern city of Beijing. Kublai also ordered the digging of the Grand Canal, which linked Hangzhou and Beijing with a direct north–south waterway for the first time. In addition to the expanded marine transport capacity, the Yuan dynasty established a state-run courier system which connected the vast empire. The development of transportation facilities created favorable conditions for the Westerners' visits in the Chinese interior. In the thirteenth century, a large number of Western missionaries, merchants, and craftsmen traveled to China. Among them, Marco Polo was the most famous.

Born into a merchant family in Venice, the 17-year-old Marco Polo, together with his father and uncle, set off for Asia in 1271 on the series of adventures that brought him at first to Xinjiang, then to Dadu. He even had the privilege of having an audience with Kublai Khan. Later, Marco Polo traveled extensively in China. These adventures were later documented in *The Travels of Marco Polo*, which vividly described to Europeans the wealth and vastness of China, as well as the metropolitan Dadu and other cities. Regarding the Yuan dynasty's governance in Tibet, Marco

---

[10]The Tibetan Empire was called Tubo (or Tufan) in Chinese historical texts and existed from the seventh to ninth centuries.

[11]The Western Xia Empire was a regime existent from 1038 to 1227 in what are now the northwestern Chinese provinces.

Polo recounted: "under the rule of the Yuan Emperor, the Tibetans have their own language. In addition, they are devout adherents of Buddhism."[12] It should be pointed out that Western academia is still divided in the authenticity and veracity of Marco Polo's narrative of his travels. Many scholars even questioned if he had visited the places he mentioned in his travel notes.[13] In spite of that, it is an established fact that Marco Polo's accounts of China are more accurate and detailed than those of his contemporaries. Since its publication, the book has been translated into 120 languages and widely circulated throughout the world, which is adequate to verify its irreplaceable historical status in the cultural exchanges between the East and the West.

Almost over the same period as Marco Polo's journeys in China, Rabban Bar Sauma, an ethnic Uyghur born in Dadu, embarked on a journey to Europe as the emissary of the Yuan Emperor. He met with many of the European monarchs in an attempt to arrange a Franco-Mongol alliance. Though the mission bores no fruit, the Uyghur documented his lifetime of travel in his later years. His written account of the overseas journey, painted by a keenly intelligent, broadminded, and statesmanlike observer, is of unique interest to modern historians as it gives a picture of medieval Europe at the close of the Crusades period.[14] At that time, most of the diplomatic envoys sent by Western countries to the Yuan dynasty were Christian priests; this could, to a large extent, be attributed to the Mongol rulers' inclusiveness of different religions. Such liberal religious policy accelerated the compatible development of indigenous beliefs and foreign religions. Also for this reason, a large number of immigrants from Europe and Central and West Asia found their homes in China.

During Kublai's reign, a form of caste or social stratification was introduced. The population was divided into the following classes: Mongols, Semu, "Hanren" (all subjects of the former Jin dynasty), and Southerners (all subjects of the former Southern Song dynasty, including Hans and minority native ethnic groups in Southern China). The Mongols and Semuren were given certain advantages in the dynasty. Among the Semu were Uyghurs, Tibetans, Muslim Central Asian Persian and Turkic peoples, West Asian Jewish, and other minority groups from even further Europe. With the help of the Semuren, Kublai Khan mapped his vast empire, reaching from the Pacific Ocean to the Black Sea, from Siberia to what is now Afghanistan.[15] The Yuan Emperors' reverence and support for Tibetan Buddhism exerted a significant impact on the formation and development of theocracy in Tibet. Moreover, it provided favorable conditions for the spread of Tibetan Buddhism in the Chinese interior. The White Stupa Temple in Beijing was a famous monastery erected under the patronage of Kublai Khan.

It is no exaggeration to say that the global horizon of the Yuan dynasty was unprecedented in Chinese history. Jack Weatherford, an American professor of anthropology, commented that ancient Chinese intellectuals had always been hold-

---

[12]Polo (2000): 278.

[13]Wood (1997): 6.

[14]Zhang (1977): 213.

[15]Liu (2011): 217–218.

ing fast to an ideal that was hard to make true, "to establish a unified country, under which all the people are governed by the central authority." "Such a concept of "China" had become a perennially popular subject among the Chinese elites,"[16] added Weatherford. The Yuan dynasty turned the political ideal into a reality, achieving an unprecedented national unity. Moreover, the vastness of the Yuan dynasty formed the territorial base of succeeding Chinese dynasties.[17]

Among the scholars on the history of the Mongol Empire and the Yuan dynasty, some argued that the Yuan dynasty could not be categorized as one of the Chinese dynasties. For example, the Japanese historian Sugiyama Masaaki believed that "the Yuan dynasty established by Kublai Khan was never a true Chinese feudal dynasty and it is, in its essence, merely the reformation of the "Mongol world empire" by partially introducing the political systems of the Chinese central dynasty."[18] As mentioned earlier, Kublai Khan classified his subjects into four castes to strengthen the dominant status of the Mongols. At the same time, he inherited the norms of the Chinese central dynasties in terms of state governance system and mode from the beginning of his reign.

Actually, the scrambling for the right of inheritance had already split the Mongol Empire during the reign of Ögedei Khan, the third son of Genghis Khan. As a result, the descendents of Genghis Khan, as the orthodox heir of the Great Khan, gradually abandoned the basis of Khural as the Mongol Empire's Khan succession while adapting to the imperial power of the Chinese dynasty. As a matter of fact, the emperor of the Yuan dynasty held merely nominal suzerainty over the three western Mongol khanates. These were essentially autonomous and ruled separately due to the division of the Mongol Empire after the Toluid Civil War in the 1260s. By the time of Kublai's death in 1294, the Mongol Empire had fractured into four separate khanates, including the Golden Horde khanate in the northwest, the Chagatai Khanate in Central Asia, the Ilkhanate in the southwest, and the Yuan dynasty in the east based near modern-day Beijing, each pursuing its own separate interests and objectives. In 1304, the three western khanates briefly accepted the nominal suzerainty of the Yuan dynasty, but in 1368 the Ming dynasty took over the Mongol capital. The rulers of the Yuan retreated to the Mongolian homeland and continued to rule there as the Northern Yuan dynasty, while the Golden Horde and the Chagatai Khanate lasted in one form or another for some additional centuries. Therefore, the Yuan dynasty created by Kublai Khan can be regarded as a deconstruction, rather than a reformation, of the "Mongol world empire" during his transformation from the Great Mongol Khan to the emperor of the Chinese central dynasty. The establishment of the Yuan dynasty ended 300 years of dynastic separation in the course of Chinese history. In addition, Tibet was brought under its direct rule. With the disintegration of the three western Mongol khanates, the looted territories of the "Mongol world empire" were restored to their original masters. However, the territories under the rule of the Yuan dynasty laid the domain foundation for the succeeding Chinese dynasties.

---

[16]Weatherford (2006): 207–208.

[17]Xiao (2007): 148, 164.

[18]Masaaki (2013): 134.

In each historical dynastic change of China, the new rulers were destined to confront the challenges of governance legitimacy, in particular, resistance or non-cooperation from the intellectuals. For example, Tianxiang Wen, a scholar-general in the last years of the Southern Song dynasty (1127–1279), refused to yield to the Mongol Yuan dynasty despite being captured and tortured. It can be partially ascribed to the Han intellectuals' disdain for the ethnic outsiders, or "northern barbarians." Following the collapse of the Yuan dynasty, some famous ethnic Han scholar-bureaucrats, declined to swear allegiance to the newly established Ming dynasty, which was ruled by the Han people. It can be, to a large extent, ascribed to the "dynastic identity" in the course of Chinese history.[19] Such political culture brings about the tradition that the succeeding dynasty compiles the dynastic history of the former one. For example, the Yuan rulers edited the historical records of the Song, Liao, and Jin dynasties. After establishing the Ming dynasty with the banner of "ousting the Mongols and restoring Chinese central power to the Han people," Yuanzhang Zhu, the founder and first emperor of the Ming dynasty, ordered the compilation of the official history of the preceding Yuan dynasty.

1.5   The Ming Dynasty in the Wake of He Zheng's Overseas Expeditions

After the wide circulation of *The Travels of Marco Polo* in Europe, the Westerners' understanding of Asia changed from the nightmare of Genghis Khan's cavalry conquests to the earnest longing for prosperity and wealth. In the history of human society, the fifteenth century is considered an outset from regional to global. With seafaring developments, people explored beyond their isolated continents and found new global perspectives. The global conquest of the Mongol Empire in the thirteenth century opened up a smoother exchange and engagement in Eurasia; 200 years later, the overseas voyages of He Zheng heralded China's navigation toward the maritime era.

Relying on its developed shipbuilding industry and sophisticated seafaring technology, the Ming dynasty realized the Chinese people's wish to understand the diversity of the world through sea routes. In the years from 1405 to 1433, He Zheng (1371–1433), a mariner, explorer, diplomat, fleet admiral, and court eunuch during the early Ming dynasty, led a large official fleet for seven expeditions, setting foot in Southeast Asia, Southern Asia, Western Asia, and as far as the East African coast, visiting more than 30 countries and regions, bringing about an unprecedented intercontinental exchange of human society through the sea routes of the time. It was undoubtedly a magnificent feat, and a progenitor of human society's intercontinental exchange. Then, a perplexing question arose: why was Christopher Columbus, instead of He Zheng, credited with discovering "New World"? It has been, and still remains, an enigma among scholars of world history. In 2002, Gavin Menzies, a

---

[19]Yao (2007): 259, 273.

retired British submarine lieutenant-commander, alleged that the fleet of He Zheng had visited the Americas prior to the European explorer and that the Chinese had circumnavigated the globe a century before the expedition of Ferdinand Magellan.[20] Of course, even if this assumption was true, it could not change the fact that the massive expeditionary voyages of He Zheng failed to have a direct and significant impact on world history. It might be that the Chinese had discovered the "New World," but they had no intention of occupying it.

These voyages were not designed to have a direct impact on the history of the world. China's exchanges with the world at this time were indications of the vast generosity of the emperor, with global diplomatic exchanges paramount; it did not affect China's closed "heavenly kingdom" cultural system, and China was satisfied with the traditional values of the imperial system and favoring agriculture while discouraging commerce. David S. Landers, a professor of economics and of history at Harvard University, made an incisive comment: "their voyages were to show off heavenly kindness, not broaden views and learn; to show their existence, not stay; and to receive respect and tribute, but not purchase."[21] The Chinese emperor's disdain for trade, and his firm belief that Chinese civilization had no need of products or technology from the outside world meant that trade, when it was permitted, was also construed as a tributary. Under this construction, the goods received by China constituted a tributary offering, while those that the visitors received were intended as gifts that the emperor in his kindness had bestowed upon his distant tributaries. The gifts shipped back by He Zheng's fleet were only some exotic animals, such as giraffe, zebra, and ostrich, which to a large extent consolidated the Chinese emperor's resolve to refrain from exchange with the "foreign barbarians." After He Zheng's overseas voyages, state-sponsored Ming naval efforts declined dramatically and China turned away from the seas with the implementation of the "Sea Ban," a series of policies restricting private maritime trading and coastal settlement during most of the Ming dynasty. Accompanied by the loss of the world-leading shipbuilding capacity and seafaring technology, China was isolated from European technological advancements. Stavrianos commented: "the "Sea Ban" of China was absolutely incomprehensible for the European countries, in which business firms were competing feverishly for the lion's share in their overseas ventures."[22]

More than 50 years after He Zheng's expeditionary voyages, Christopher Columbus set sail across the Atlantic Ocean under the auspices of the Catholic monarchs of Spain.[23] During his first voyage in 1492, he reached the American continent, landing on an island in the Bahamian archipelago. These voyages and his efforts to establish permanent settlements on the island of Hispaniola initiated the European colonization of the "New World." Columbus never admitted that he had reached a continent previously unknown to Europeans, rather than the East Indies for which he had set course. Columbus' exploration and discovery of the "New World" set off European

---

[20]Menzies (2005): 42.

[21]Landers (2001): 120.

[22]Stavrianos (1988): 120.

[23]de Carla (2003): 297.

interest in voyage and adventure. "Western society has reached the takeoff point. It is to take off, but once it takes off, it will clear the sea, and start an irresistible global expansion."[24] This expansion was destined to be a disaster to ancient civilizations and traditional societies; and China was no exception.

After the collapse of the Yuan dynasty, the Mongol remnants retreated to the Mongolian Plateau, where the name Great Yuan was carried on. It still posed a huge challenge to the newly established Ming dynasty, which failed to gain a clear upper hand over the Mongolian tribes after successive battles. The long-drawn conflict was taking a toll on the Ming Empire. Therefore, the Ming court abandoned the strategy of annual land expeditions; instead, it embarked on a massive and expensive expansion of the Great Wall along the northern border. Unlike the earlier fortifications, the Ming construction was stronger and more elaborate due to the use of bricks and stone instead of rammed earth. With a length of 8850 km, the Ming wall extends from the Yalu River in the east to the Qilian Mountains in the west. Sections near the Ming capital of Beijing were especially strong. Though the Chinese Great Wall to a large extent acted as a deterrent to the southward raids of the Mongol cavalry, the Northern Yuan dynasty based in the Mongolian Plateau still extended its sphere of influence to the Western Region (today's Xinjiang) and Qinghai. The frequent harassments by the nomadic neighbor were like fish bones sticking in the throat of the imperial Ming dynasty. In this regard, the Ming throne adopted diplomatic carrots, rather than sticks, to appease the Mongol rulers. The sectarian conflict of Tibetan Buddhism in the Tibetan Plateau provided a rare opportunity for the Ming court to mitigate the threat from the Mongols.

The Ming court inherited the Yuan dynasty's governance policy in Tibet by supporting the dissemination of Tibetan Buddhism. To oversee the Lhasa authorities, the Ming government conferred new princely titles on leaders of Tibetan Buddhism sects after the local leaders pledged allegiances to the Ming Emperor. During this period, the Gelug school of Tibetan Buddhism founded by Je Tsongkhapa (1357–1419) was widely popularized in Tibet and Mongolia. In an agreement concluded between the Ming Empire and the spiritual leader of Tibetan Buddhism, the latter agreed to persuade the Mongol forces to retreat to the Mongolian Plateau.[25] Allying themselves with the Mongols as a powerful patron, the Gelug emerged as the pre-eminent Buddhist sect in Tibet at the end of the sixteenth century. In 1578, its chief Sonam Gyatso formed an alliance with Altan Khan, the most powerful Mongol leader at that time. Altan Khan perceived that through the Buddhist faith he could gain governance legitimacy. As a response, Sonam Gyatsho proclaimed Altan Khan to be the reincarnation of Kublai Khan, and in return, Altan Khan gave the title "Dalai Lama" to Sonam Gyatso. Therefore, the Gelug tradition became the most influential religious belief among the Mongols in the ensuing centuries. With the shared faith of Tibetan Buddhism, Mongolia established ever-increasing close ties with Tibet.

After becoming a Tibetan Buddhism convert, Altan Khan returned to Mongolia and built the first Buddhist monastery in Kuku-Khoto (today's Hohhot of Inner Mon-

---

[24]Ibid., p. 474.

[25]Ya (1984): 12.

golia). After that, Tibetan Buddhism began its wide propagation among the Mongols. After the collapse of the Yuan dynasty, the Mongols gradually fragmented into three subgroups, including south Mongolia, north Mongolia, and west Mongolia. After Sonam Gyatso's death in 1588, Altan Khan's great-grandson was anointed as the 4th Dalai Lama. It further strengthened the Tibetan-Mongol alliance. While exerting extensive influence on the Mongolian region, the spread of Tibetan Buddhism provided space for the Mongols' interference with the political and religious affairs of Tibet.

As Mongol raids continued periodically over the years, the Ming Empire devoted considerable resources to expanding and reinforcing the Great Wall along its northern border. Though the Mongol cavalry no longer gained a clear upper hand over the Ming frontier guards, the Ming rulers were facing increasing challenges in coastal defense. At that time, the southeast coastal areas of China had long been subjected to frequent raids by Japanese pirates. In 1517, the armed merchant ships of Portugal arrived in Guangzhou and heralded the enduring conflicts between China and the Western world. In 1521, the Ming Imperial Navy defeated a Portuguese fleet in the Battle of Tunmen. In spite of the victory on the battlefield, the Ming Empire ultimately agreed to allow the Portuguese to settle at Macao with gradual improvement of Sino-Portuguese relations and Portuguese aid given to the Ming forces against the Japanese pirates along China's shores. Thus, Macao became a gateway for European missionaries to enter China. In 1582, the Italian Jesuit priest Matteo Ricci (1552–1610) arrived at Macao where he began his gospel preaching in China. He became the first European to enter the Forbidden City, the imperial palace of the Ming dynasty, in 1601 when invited by the Wanli Emperor, who sought his selected services in matters such as court astronomy and calendrical science. Ricci laid the foundation for the spread of Western Catholicism in China by using existing Chinese concepts to explain Christianity. For example, he did not explain the Catholic faith as entirely foreign or new; instead, he argued that the Chinese culture and people had always believed in God and that Christianity was simply the completion of their faith. In addition, the Italian missionary made commendable contributions to the cultural exchanges between China and the West in the aspects of astronomy, geography, mathematics, and map-making. In 1610, Ricci died in Beijing, aged 57. By the code of the Ming dynasty, foreigners who died in China had to be buried in Macau. In light of Ricci's contributions to China, the Ming Emperor granted a burial plot in the Chinese capital for Ricci's remains and designated a Buddhist temple for the purpose. Ricci's successor, Johann Adam Schall von Bell (1591–1666), a German Jesuit and astronomer who is known in China as Ruowang Tang, participated in modifying the Chinese calendar and compiling what is known as the Chongzhen Calendar. The German was also credited with manufacturing artillery and introducing Western metallurgical technology to China.

In the late Ming, the Europeans started their global voyages in the Americas, East Asia, and Southeast Asia, overseas trade becoming the "engine of national growth" for the European powers.[26] While elaborating his theory of modern world-system

---

[26]Fairbank (2000): 6.

approach, the American sociologist Immanuel Wallerstein tried to find a compelling answer to the puzzling question, "why did the Chinese Ming Empire refrain from overseas expansion?" He argued that China was keen on "internal expansion" for the purpose of promoting rice growing; however, the emerging bourgeoisie and "new world economic system" in Europe, which was composed of "small empires, nation-states and city-states," was in urgent need of geographical expansion.[27] Admittedly, the multi-factor reasoning of Wallerstein was to some extent justifiable. Nevertheless, the so-called internal expansion ignored the ever-increasing engagements between the Han people ("huaxia") and the ethnic minorities ("yi" or "barbarians") throughout the Chinese history. Besides, world history was experiencing a series of fundamental changes. Though China refrained from overseas colonization in spite of its earliest command of global navigation capacity, the country was facing a national crisis of being colonized by foreign powers.[28] After gaining independence from Spain, the Netherlands founded in 1602 the "Dutch East India Company," which competed with Spain and Portugal for dominance in East Asia. In the context of the Age of Discovery in which extensive overseas exploration emerged as a powerful factor in European culture, Dutch colonists established their presence in Taiwan to trade with the Chinese Ming Empire in 1624. Two years later, Spanish invaders landed on Taiwan and continued westwards along the coast until they arrived at Keelung harbor. After seventeen years, the last fortress of the Spanish was besieged by Dutch forces and eventually fell, giving the Dutch control over most of the island.

In addition to the Western colonists' repeated raids along China's coastline, the internal forces that challenged the reign of the Ming dynasty also gathered momentum. The Jurchen people, whose ancestors had established the Jin dynasty and gained control over most of North China five centuries ago, once again rose in Manchuria (Northeast China). The Jurchen chieftain Nurhaci united the various tribes and consolidated the Eight Banners system. A banner under the Qing regime was an integrated military and civilian organization or unit formed on the principles that "all are fighting men on an expedition and civilians back in the home region" and "till the land or go hunting when there is no war but join up when fighting breaks out." In this way, the whole of the Manchu nation, irrespective of social strata, was divided into what are known as the Eight Banners. After that, Nurhaci launched attacks on the Ming Empire. His conquest of Liaoning laid the groundwork for the domination of the rest of China by his descendants. He is also generally credited with ordering the creation of a new writing system for the Manchu people based on the Mongolian vertical script. In 1636, Nurhaci's son Hong Taiji changed the appellation of his people from Jurchen to Manchu. One year later, he ascended the throne, which symbolized the inception of the Qing dynasty.

Almost over the same period of time, the political and religious power struggle in Tibet intensified. Due to the internal strife between the two lineages of Tibetan Buddhism, Gelug Sect and Kagyu Sect, the fifth Dalai Lama turned to Gushri Khan, a Khoshut prince and leader of the Khoshut Khanate who supplanted the Tumed

[27] Wallerstein (2013): 39.

[28] Fairbank J. K., *The Great Chinese Revolution: 1800–1985*, p. 12.

descendants of Altan Khan as the main benefactor of the Dalai Lama and the Gelug Sect. In 1637, Güshi Khan defeated a rival Mongol prince Choghtu Khong Tayiji, the political patron of the Kagyu Sect, and established his khanate in Tibet over the next few years. His military assistance to the Gelug Sect enabled the 5th Dalai Lama to establish political control over Tibet. While supporting the theocratic authority of the Dalai Lama, Güshi Khan accorded the title of the Panchen Lama to Losang Chökyi Gyaltsen, the teacher and close ally of the 5th Dalai Lama. The title of Panchen Lama has continued to be given to the successors of Losang Chökyi Gyaltsen and, posthumously, to his predecessors starting with Khedrup Gelek Pelzang, the 1st Panchen Lama. Thus, the Panchen lineage of the Gelug School was established. Traditionally, the Panchen Lama was the head of Tashilhunpo Monastery and held religious and secular power over the Tsang region centered in Shigatse, independent of the Ganden Podrang authority led by the Dalai Lama.

1.6   The Consolidation and Splendor of "High Qing": 1662–1795

When the fully fledged Manchu forces marched to the foot of the Great Wall in 1643, the peasant rebels led by Zicheng Li, a former minor official of the Ming dynasty, conquered Beijing. The Chongzhen Emperor committed suicide in the Forbidden City when the city fell, marking the end of the Ming dynasty. The Ming general Sangui Wu, who controlled the largest armed force under the Ming in Northern China, made an alliance with the Manchus and opened the Shanhai Pass, one of the major passes along the Great Wall of China, to the Manchu banner armies. Thereafter, the Manchu Army defeated Zicheng Li's rebel forces and seized the capital. The Qing dynasty, lasting for over 270 years, inherited China's 2000 years of political rule and cultural tradition, but further integrated the country's unified state and multi-ethnic national structure. It also formed the territorial base for the modern Chinese state.

The reigns of Kangxi and Qianlong emperors witnessed long-term stability and relative wealth after years of war and chaos. In the meantime, state unity, territorial consolidation, and borderland governance were unprecedentedly strengthened. Therefore, this period was acclaimed by the historians as the "Prosperous Era of Kangxi and Qianlong" or "high Qing era." Military expeditions were dispatched to the far corners of the empire to quell revolts and expand frontiers, making the dynasty the second largest in Chinese history, second only to the Yuan Empire created by the Mongols. The Kangxi Emperor (1654–1722) suppressed the Revolt of the Three Feudatories, conquered the Kingdom of Tungning in Taiwan and forced the Mongol rebels in the north and northwest to submit to Qing rule, and blocked Tsarist Russia on the Amur River. During the reign of the Qianlong Emperor, the Dzungar Khanate was incorporated into the Qing Empire's rule and renamed as Xinjiang. To the west, Ili was conquered and garrisoned. The incorporation of Xinjiang into the Qing Empire resulted from the final defeat and destruction of the Dzungars, a coalition of western

Mongol tribes. Throughout this period, there were continued Mongol interventions in Tibet and a reciprocal spread of Tibetan Buddhism in Mongolia. After the Lhasa riot of 1750, the Qianlong Emperor sent armies to Tibet and firmly established the Dalai Lama as the religious and secular leader of Tibet, with the Amban (the Qing imperial resident in Lhasa) and garrison to preserve Qing presence.

To win the good will and acceptance of the Han society, the early Qing Emperors identified themselves with the traditional order of the Han people, kept the Ming governance and social institutions, embraced Confucianism as a state philosophy, and absorbed the Han scholars into their bureaucracy to work alongside the Manchus. They equated the lands of the Qing Empire, including present-day Manchuria, Xinjiang, Mongolia, Tibet, and other areas as "China" in both the Chinese and Manchu languages, thus defining China as a multi-ethnic state, rejecting the idea that China only meant Han areas and proclaiming that both Han and non-Han peoples were part of China. In spite of its ostensible national prosperity and vast territory, the Qing Empire was threatened with the expansion of foreign powers. If the Gurkha's invasion of Tibet was just a footnote in history, then the Russian Empire as a rising power posed an enduring threat to the northern border of China. With a firm control over the whole of the country, the Qing rulers were in a position to deal with what they saw as Russian encroachment in Manchuria, the ancient homeland of the Manchu nobility. In 1689, the Qing government and Russia concluded *the Treaty of Nerchinsk*. As China's first international treaty with modern significance, the agreement defined the border between China's northeastern region and Russia.

During this period, the Chinese traditional border governance policies such as "rule by customs" became more systematic, and ethnic minorities in border areas further strengthened the national identity. The Qing dynasty, regarded as an ethnic minority that had entered the Central Plains to establish a unified dynasty, supported the coexistence and stable development of different ethnicities, religions, cultures, and languages in a unified national pattern. The Manchu ruler's governance capacity in the border areas was significantly strengthened with the enhanced composite national strength. In the early Qing dynasty, the central government acknowledged the secular dominant status of the Gushi Khan, a Khoshut prince and leader of the Khoshut Khanate, in Tibet. Through the official canonizations of the Dalai Lama and Panchen Lama, the Qing rulers succeeded in incorporating the political and religious power of Tibet into the structure of the central government. In 1793, the Qianlong Emperor issued *the 29-Article Imperial Decree for a Better Governance of Tibet*, tightening the Qing throne's control over the region. The ambans (the Qing imperial residents) were elevated above the Kashag (the governing council of Tibet) in responsibility for Tibetan political affairs. The imperial decree also outlined a new approach, which was termed the "Golden Urn," to select the incarnations of the Dalai Lama and Panchen Lama. Children believed to be the reincarnations of the Dalai Lama or the Panchen Lama were identified by a lottery method, in which names of competing candidates were written on folded slips of paper placed in a golden urn (hence the name). The theocratic system supervised and coordinated by the Qing Amban effectively consolidated the Qing Empire's governance of Tibet. In addition to encouraging intermarriage between the Manchu and Mongol nobilities, the Qing court introduced the Eight Banner system, referring to the administrative/military divisions under the Qing dynasty into which all households were placed, to Mongolia. The Qianlong Emperor created in Xinjiang the General of Ili, a position to pacify Dzungaria (now part of Xinjiang) and suppress uprisings by the Khoja rebels. The General of Ili governed the entirety of Xinjiang during Qing rule until it was turned into a province. At the same time, the offices of military attache and imperial resident were established under the General of Ili to manage military affairs north and south of the Tianshan Mountains.

From the late seventeenth century, Tsarist Russia had intensified its encroachments on Heilongjiang Province in Northeast China. At the same time, Prince Gaerdan of the Mongolian tribe Zhungaer that lived near the northwest borders of China was actively trying to split off from the Qing regime with the support of Tsarist Russia. For the purpose of defending China's unity against further Russian invasion, the Kangxi Emperor took a series of countermeasures to strengthen his control over the northern borderland and improve his relationship with the many Mongolian tribes in the region. One decision he made was to make personal inspection tours to the northern borderland. He also set up there the Imperial Hunting Grounds, in which he would meet with the princes of various nationalities in the northwest borderland for such activities as horse-racing, archery, and other martial sports during his inspection tour. In this way, he not only succeeded in improving his ties with the minority nations but also the military preparedness of the country.

The inspection and hunting tours would take some three or four months during which the emperor necessarily would have to take care of state affairs, granting audiences to ministers and other officials and reading and writing comments on memorials. This made it necessary to have temporary abodes on the journey and supplies of all kinds. Thus, began in 1703 the construction of the Imperia Summer Villa in Chengde, on the outskirts of the capital city. Commonly known as Chengde Mountain Resort, a large complex of imperial palaces and gardens, it was not fully completed until almost 90 years later, although in five years' time a resort was beginning to take shape. The Imperia Summer Villa, thanks to its vast and rich collection of Chinese landscapes and architecture, became a culmination of all the variety of gardens, pagodas, temples, and palaces from various regions of the empire. Temples of different architectural styles and imperial gardens blend harmoniously into a landscape of lakes, pastureland, and forests. The resort's plain area also possesses characteristics of the scenery of the Mongolian grasslands. The royal monastery complex in the resort, in particular, the palaces modeled after the Potala Palace in Lhasa and Tashi Lhunpo Monastery in Shigatse, highlighted the symbolic significance of Mongolia, Tibet, and Xinjiang in the Qing dynasty's borderland governance. In the Qing dynasty, Kangxi, Qianlong and a succession of other emperors after them used to spend several months a year here, administering state affairs and receiving princes of the minority nations or foreign envoys. Hence, this resort was more than just a summer retreat but a second palace away from the capital.

The resort became an ideal venue for the Qing Emperor's reception of high officials and ethnic minority aristocracy. It was in the main hall of the architectural complex that Emperor Qianlong received Ubashi Khan, a Torghut prince, who led his tribesmen on their massive migration back to China from Russia.[29] After overcoming untold difficulties and suffering heavy losses at the hands of the Tsarist forces who pursued and tried to block their way, they finally arrived back in China in 1761. To show his admiration for the heroic feats of Ubashi Khan, the Qianlong Emperor gave an audience with the Mongol chieftain in the mountain resort and gave a banquet in his honor. Also during the reign of the Qianlong Emperor, the aborigines of Taiwan paid homage to the emperor's birthday in the venue.[30]

The Qing court's effective governance in Mongolia eliminated the northern nomads' long-standing threat to Chinese central power, which meant the Great Wall had completed its historical mission of fending off the northern nomads. During the reign of the Kangxi Emperor, some senior officials jointly presented a memorial to the throne, suggesting the Great Wall be repaired for the consolidation of frontier defense. Nevertheless, Kangxi disapproved of the proposal, refuting: "the national strength and people's endorsement are fundamental to resisting foreign aggression. It is, therefore, absolutely unnecessary to divert enormous manpower and material resources to the building and maintenance of the Great Wall."[31] After this, China's established practice of building the Great Wall along the northern border to protect the country against enemy states was discarded.

After the introduction of Tibetan Buddhism in the sixteenth century, two Gelug lineages of Tibetan Buddhism, including Jebtsundamba and Changkya Khutukhtus, were instituted in Outer Mongolia and Inner Mongolia, respectively. Following the practices for the Dalai Lama and the Panchen Lama in Tibet, the Qing government granted a goldenseal and nobility title to the Jebtsundamba Khutuktu, the spiritual head of the Gelug lineage in Outer Mongolia. To prevent a power struggle arising from the Mongol nobility's divided opinions on the reincarnation selection of Jebtsundamba Khutuktu, the Qianlong Emperor decreed that all future reincarnation candidates were to be located in the Tibetan area after the death of the 2nd Jebtsundamba Khutuktu. The decree added that the lot-drawing ritual should be applied in the reincarnation selection, in which names and birth dates of competing candidates were written on folded slips of paper placed in a golden urn and then drawn. In addition, the lot-drawing ritual had to be jointly supervised by the Dalai Lama, the Panchen Lama, and the Qing Imperial Resident in Tibet.[32] Similarly, the power of Changkya Khutukhtu, the title held by the spiritual head of the Gelug lineage of Tibetan Buddhism in Inner Mongolia during the Qing dynasty, was restricted to religious affairs. Thus, Tibetan Buddhism was effectively applied by the Qing government to weaken the power of the religious leaders of Outer and Inner Mongolia.

---

[29]The Torghut was a Mongol clan who were compelled to migrate westward toward the end of the Ming dynasty (1368–1644) after repeated attacks by the Zhungaer tribe. They then settled in the lower reaches of the Volga in Russia. There for a long time they were subjected to oppression and plundered by the government of Tsarist Russia and unable to stand this any longer, they finally decided to migrate back to China.

[30]Hao (2008).

[31]*Imperial Collection of Four, Volume VII.*

[32]Delager (1998): 165.

In the early seventeenth century during the Manchu conquest of China proper, the Manchu male hairstyle, or queue, in which the hair on the front of the head was shaved off above the temples and the remainder of the hair was tied into a long braid, was forcefully introduced to the Han society for it signified the Han people's submission to Qing rule and also aided the identification of those Han who refused to accept Manchu domination. Though the Qing Emperors violently imposed the queue order on the Han society, they were more broadminded and liberal than the ruling elites of the Mongol Yuan dynasty in terms of drawing on the culture of the Han people. In addition to consciously advocating the political culture and etiquette of the North China Plain, the Qing court greatly encouraged the Manchu people to learn the Chinese language. The early Qing Emperors identified themselves with the traditional order of the Han people, kept the Ming governance and social institutions, embraced Confucianism as a state philosophy, and absorbed the Han scholars into its bureaucracy to work alongside the Manchus. Many European missionaries, such as Johann Adam Schall von Bell from Germany, Ferdinand Verbiest from Belgium, and Giuseppe Castiglione from Italy, were highly esteemed and appointed to be trusted counselors by the Qing rulers. The Kangxi Emperor frequently requested the teaching of Ferdinand Verbiest, who is known in Chinese as Huairen Nan, in geometry, philosophy, and music. As an accomplished mathematician and astronomer, the Belgian priest corrected the Chinese calendar and was later asked to rebuild the Beijing Observatory. Due to his great contributions to Chinese society, he was the only Westerner in Chinese history to ever receive the honor of an imperial posthumous title after he died in Beijing in 1688. The Jesuit painter Giuseppe Castiglione, who served at the imperial courts of the emperors of Kangxi, Yongzheng, and Qianlong, painted in a style that is a fusion of European and Chinese traditions. In addition to his brilliant expertise as a painter, he was also in charge of designing the Western-style palaces in the imperial gardens of the Summer Palace. While spreading Western science and technology among the Chinese society, these European pastors also gained spaces for their missionary work.

By virtue of the scaling down of hostilities as peace returned to China after the Manchu conquest, and also as a result of the ensuing rapid increase of population, land cultivation, and therefore tax revenues based on agriculture, the Qing dynasty during the reigns of the Kangxi and Qianlong became the largest economy in the world. It has become an established fact in China and beyond. In 1750, the industrial output of China accounted for 32.8% of the world, while the respective proportion of the whole of Europe was only 23.2%.[33] With a population of 300 million, China became the center of absorbing the silver capital of the world. Its foreign trade has maintained the largest surplus based on its "dominant position in the world economy in textile, porcelain and tea exports."[34] This was also one of the reasons why the Qianlong Emperor refused the Macartney Embassy's request for a bilateral trade agreement with the Qing Empire.

---

[33] Kennedy (1992): 176.

[34] Frank, A. G. *Reoirent: the Global Economy in the Asian Age*, p. 232.

1.7 The Late Qing: The Turn of the Dynastic Fortune

In 1793, Lord George Macartney led a British special envoy and large fleet to China, with the purpose of opening Chinese markets and establishing trade relations. However, there were cultural etiquette disputes between the British and the Chinese, and the Chinese feeling of superiority caused the Emperor Qianlong to state that "our Celestial Empire possesses all things in prolific abundance and lacks no product within its borders. Therefore, there is no need to import the manufactures of outside barbarians in exchange for our own produce."[35] Even before Macartney's departure from London, he had anticipated that there might be some disagreement with the Chinese side on the details of the ceremonies and rituals to be performed at the meeting. The ritual of the kowtow, which requires an individual to kneel with both knees on the ground and bow so as to touch the forehead to the ground, presented a particular dilemma. For Macartney, one sticking point was the relative status of the two sovereigns, King George III of Britain and the Qianlong Emperor of China. Macartney believed that Britain at that time was the most powerful nation in the world. However, the Chinese emperor, who believed himself the "Heavenly Son" of the "Celestial Empire," merely treated the British embassy as a tribute mission. The Qianlong Emperor's compromise on the issue was that Macartney could perform a single prostration in lieu of the nine typically called for. Finally, it was agreed that Macartney would genuflect before the Qing Emperor as he would before his own sovereign, touching one knee to the ground. There are different interpretations of these historical, anthropological, and political etiquette disputes, but it was regarded as a significant collision of East–West political culture and values. The exchange ended in failure due to the cultural differences and tradition–modernity conflicts, imperialist expansionist ambitions, and heavenly kingdom self-protection; it showed the different political philosophies of the British "sovereign equality" and the Qing dynasty "order containment" empire-building.

Although ultimately unsuccessful in its primary objectives, the circumstances surrounding the mission provided ample opportunity for both British and Chinese parties not to feel totally disgruntled about the compromises and concessions they had made. The failure of the primary objectives was, to a large extent, not due to Macartney's refusal to kowtow in the presence of the Qianlong Emperor, as is sometimes believed. It was also not a result of the Chinese reliance on tradition in dictating foreign policy, but rather a result of competing world views which were uncomprehending and to some degree incompatible. While to a modern sensibility the failure of the Macartney Mission marked a missed opportunity by both sides to explore and understand each other's cultures, customs, diplomatic styles, and ambitions, it also prefigured increasing British pressure on China to accommodate its expanding trading and imperial networks. The mutual lack of knowledge and understanding on both sides would continue to plague the Qing dynasty as it encountered increasing foreign pressures and internal unrest during the nineteenth century.

---

[35] Xiao and Yang (1986): 254.

During the Qing dynasty, China kept its leading position in the world in many aspects, but the world experienced substantial changes. Driven by the commercial revolution of colonial trade, the Western world was constantly accumulating potential for industrial revolution. In the West's global expansion, the East and China were the "mainland myth" because at that time the center of the world economy was in Asia, with "China, Japan and India as its leaders, followed by Southeast Asia and West Asia."[36] The "global impulse" of the European countries to open up overseas markets was backed by industrial revolution and technological advancement. In addition, their economic strength also witnessed an ever-enhancing tendency. The global share of Europe's industrial output rose from 28.1% in 1800 to 34.2% in 1830, while the percentage of the Chinese economy dropped from 33.3 to 29.8%.[37] Therefore, the Europeans were no longer contented with the Qing Empire's Canton System, or "single port trading policy"[38]; rather, they coveted the huge market prospect and abundant resources in the vast Chinese interior. The traditional Chinese political system, the economic order, and social and cultural life were bound to encounter pressure from the globally expanding Western world. This lack of agreement led to rise of the opium smuggling trade, triggering the Opium War in 1840.

In an article covered in the *New York Daily Tribune* in 1858, Karl Marx vividly exposed the cause of the Opium War and its aftermaths. "The Chinese emperor, in order to put an end to the opium consumption of his subjects, decreed that opium import should be banned. However, the opium trade had already become an indivisible part of the financial system of the British East India Company." Marx defined the armed conflict between the Qing Empire's resistance, which "stood on the moral high ground," and the British colonists' profit-seeking privilege as "a bizarre elegy which was beyond the imagination of any great poet."[39] John K. Fairbank commented: "Opium trade, as an enduring organized international crime, gave a blood transfusion to British aggression against China. Moreover, it became the most effective commodity for the British Empire to offset China's long-term foreign trade surplus."[40] With the large outflow of silver, the government finance and currency circulation of the Qing Empire was "in serious chaos due to opium imports with a total value of £7 million."[41] After the Opium War, the Qing Empire, which for a long time proclaimed itself as the "Celestial Empire" endowed with the "Mandate of Heaven," was forced to open its door to the imperialist powers. China's 2000-year-old feudal society and its colonial and semi-colonial characteristics crossed the threshold into modern times. Ancient and traditional China was incorporated into

---

[36]Frank, A. G. *Reoirent: the Global Economy in the Asian Age*, p. 232.

[37]Kennedy (1992): 176.

[38]The Canton System arose in 1757 as a response to a perceived political and commercial threat from abroad on the part of successive Chinese emperors and served as a means for the Qing court to control China's trade with the West by focusing all trade on the southern port of Canton (now Guangzhou).

[39]Marx (2009): 632.

[40]Fairbank and Liu (1985): 233.

[41]Marx (2009): 641.

the Western-dominated world system in the contest of antiquated weaponry against guns and bullets.

For the Chinese people at that time, from the supreme emperor down to the peasants tied to the land, the stunning defeat of China in the Opium War was a huge psychological shock: from pride in their "heavenly kingdom" to surrendering sovereign rights under humiliating terms; and from the superiority in broad culture to inferiority in skills. The northern nomads no longer posed a threat to the Chinese central dynasty, as had been the case for centuries; rather, the Chinese were confronted with the sophisticated weaponry of the imperialist powers. Gunpowder, which was discovered in the ninth century by Chinese alchemists searching for an elixir of immortality, found its application in military use, such as primary rockets and guns, by the Qing banner army during the Anglo-Chinese Opium War. However, these primary firearms were no match for the Britons' sophisticated bullets and artillery with their advantages in metallurgy, machinery, and technology.

The industrial revolution achievements of the Western powers inflicted one calamity after another on the ancient Chinese society. In 1842, British troops occupied Hong Kong. Eighteen years later, the Anglo-French expeditionary forces invaded Beijing. They looted the Summer Palace, a complex of palaces, and gardens known for its extensive collection of gardens and architecture and other works of art, setting the entire place ablaze. After the defeat of the Qing Navy in the Sino-Japanese war in 1894, Taiwan became a colony of Japan. In 1900, the forces of the Eight-Nation Alliance, including Japan, Russia, the British Empire, France, the USA, Germany, Italy, and the Austro-Hungarian Empire, raided Beijing and looted the Chinese capital and ransacked the Forbidden City, with many Chinese treasures finding their way to Europe. These tragedies exacerbated the domestic class contradictions, ethnic conflicts, and national decline; China was gradually reduced to a semi-feudal and semi-colonial state with the impending menace of being carved up by the foreign powers.

1.8 The Genetic Code for the "Grand Unity" of China

Each war launched by the imperialist powers against China was accompanied by the conclusion of unequal treaties. "The treaty relation created by military force can only be sustained by gunboat diplomacy."[42] Starting with *the Treaty of Nanking*, which ended the First Opium War, the imperialist powers coerced the Qing government into signing more than 30 unequal treaties on the grounds that the foreign powers had no obligations in return. These treaties inflicted sovereignty loss, territorial division, and huge indemnities on China. Over a course of six decades between 1840 and 1900, the Chinese were to pay 1.3 billion taels of fine silver as war indemnities to the imperialists.[43] In other words, each of the 400 million Chinese nationals had to

---

[42]Fairbank J. K. & Liu G. J., *The Cambridge History of China: Late Qing 1800–1911*, p. 225.

[43]Map of the Century of National Humiliation (1997).

bear a "debt" of 3 taels of silver. Such shameless plundering is second to none in the history of the world.

To pay indemnities to the foreign invaders can be defined as bizarre bandit logic. Marx pointed out: "the indemnity paid to the British colonists, who are used to crowing about their high moral standards, is for the practical purpose of 'making up their trade deficit'."[44] The Qing dynasty was on the verge of subjugation due to the imperialist invasions and domestic unrest at the turn of the twentieth century. The Chinese people were at their most critical juncture when the fate of the Chinese nation was hanging in the balance. "The once largest and most progressive dynasty was reduced to being one of the poorest countries on earth in just a few hundred years," lamented Konrad Seitz, a German academic and diplomat.[45] At the same time, the imperialist powers were transformed into modern developed countries powered by cheap labor, large overseas markets, and wealth looted from colonial aggression.

From the Qin dynasty (221–206 BC) to the Qing dynasty (1644–1912), the history of China has gone through two millennia in a political structure as a unified multi-ethnic state. In the eyes of Western historians, the failed attempts to rebuild a unified empire in the history of Europe were to a large extent ascribed to the internal weak points unique to the region and the turmoil caused by the ceaseless invasion of nomads. The situation was quite different in imperial China. Stavrianos commented: "the Han dynasty (202 BC–220 AD) collapsed due to land acquisitions, invasions, and feuding between consort clans and eunuchs. After a period of chaos and division in the North China Plain, the Sui dynasty again unified the country. The Chinese civilization has long been in a prosperous period, with almost no interruption."[46] This is indeed a unique national history. In fact, the warfare and destruction inflicted by the northern nomads on the North China Plain were by no means less than the historical experiences of Europe. After dominating the central authority with military force, both the Yuan dynasty and the Qing dynasty had to succumb to the relatively advanced Han civilization. Due to this kind of Chinese political identity, the Qianlong Emperor of the Qing dynasty rejected the earlier preconception that only the Han people could be masters of Chinese central power. Voltaire concludes that it is the deep-rooted mentality of "grand unity" that binds the vast country into an extended family.[47]

History has already testified that the successive Chinese central authorities, including those established by the ethnic minorities, would inherit, identify, and maintain this unified dynastic system since the unification of the North China Plain by the Qin dynasty. It is, therefore, the cypher code for the historical gene of China. The four grand unifications in the history of China, including the dynasties of Qin and Han (221 BC–220 AD), the dynasties of Sui and Tang (581–907), the Yuan dynasty (1271–1368), and the Qing dynasty (1644–1911), and the numerous short-lived regimes in between, are parts of the historical formation and development process

---

[44]Marx (2009): 641.

[45]Seitz (2007): 63.

[46]Stavrianos L. S., *Lifelines from Our Past: A New World History*, p. 109.

[47]Voltaire. *On the Spirit and Customs of Various Nationalities*, pp. 212–216.

of the unified multi-ethnic state. The notable economic historian Roy Bin Wong concluded: "As a matter of fact, the Yuan dynasty and the Qing dynasty founded by the Mongols and Manchus respectively, and the repeated raids of the northern nomads against the Chinese central dynasties, actually led to the reconstruction and reunification of the Chinese empire, rather than the division of the country."[48] The supreme principle of the "grand unity", the strategy of "governing a region in accordance with its specific customs," and the goal of "harmony without uniformity" have been running through the history of China. All these constitute the inner logic of the time-honored Chinese civilization. History indicates that with the mutual interaction in China between the Huaxia (Han people) center and the Siyi (the ethnic minorities) periphery, unification was always the trend in Chinese history, and all ethnicities were builders of the unified multi-ethnic state. Such historical conditions are said to be rare in the world.

The "five ethnicities" (huaxia, dongyi, nanman, xirong and beidi), the many diverse ancient human groups living on the vast land of China, and their descendants had jointly established a unified multi-ethnic country. Then, could such kind of fine tradition be carried on after China terminated the dynastic history in 1911? Obviously, it is not a question to be naturally addressed by following the fixed historical course, for the semi-colonial and semi-feudal Chinese society after the Opium War was dominated by imperialist powers. After the completion of their encroachment and colonization of the countries near to China, the imperialist powers accelerated the pace of infiltration and aggression toward the Chinese borderland. By then, the British colonists had successfully destroyed the whole structure of Indian society through the invincible strategy of "divide and rule" after transforming India into the largest colony in Asia.[49] After that, the Tibetan region of China became their next prey. Taking advantage of the domestic chaos and ethnic conflict in China, the British colonists invaded Tibet. However, just as Marx predicted at that time: "currently, the Britons have inadequate capacity to colonize China and they may not be able to do so in the future, for the history of China is different from that of India."[50] The imperialist powers' aggression toward China cannot change the historical gene of the country as a unified multi-ethnic state.

References

de Carla, J. (2003). *The history of Spain*. Beijing: The Commercial Press.
de Coulanges, Fustel. (2006). *The ancient city: A study on the religion, laws and institutions of Greece and Rome*. Guiling: Guangxi Normal University Press.
Delager, (1998). *The history of Tibetan Buddhism in Inner Mongolia*. Hohhot: Inner Mongolia People's Press.
Fairbank, J. K. (2000). *The great Chinese revolution, 1800–1985*. Beijing: World Affairs Press.

---

[48] Wang (1998): 89.

[49] Marx, K., *The Collected Works of Marx and Engels*. Volume II, p. 679.

[50] Ibid., p. 676.

Fairbank, J. K., & Liu, G. J. (1985). *The Cambridge history of China: Late Qing 1800–1911*. Beijing: China Social Sciences Press.

Hao, S. (2008). The Taiwan Aborigines' homage to the Qing emperor. *Journal of Chinese Social Sciences, 2,* 15–19.

Kennedy, P. (1992). *The rise and fall of great powers*. Beijing: World Affairs Press.

Landers, D. S. (2001). *The wealth and poverty of nations: Why some are so rich and some so poor?*. Beijing: Xinhua Press.

Lattimore, O. (2005). *Inner Asian Frontiers of China* (X. Tang, Trans.). Nanjing: Jiangsu People's Press.

Liu, Y. (2011). *Sea and land: A study of east-west communication in medieval times*. Beijing: Peking University Press.

Map of the Century of National Humiliation. (1997). Beijing: People's Press.

Marx, K. (2009). *The collected works of Marx and Engels*. Beijing: People's Press.

Masaaki, M. (2013). *The challenges of Kublai Khan*. Beijing: Social Sciences Academic Press.

Menzies, G. (2005). *1421: The Year China discovered the world*. Beijing: Jinghua Press.

Polo, M. (2000). *The travels of Marco Polo*. Shanghai: Shanghai Bookstore Publishing House.

Seitz, K. (2007). *China: The revival of a world power*. Beijing: International Cultural Publishing Company.

Stavrianos, L. (1988). *A global history: The world before 1500*. Shanghai: Press of Shanghai Social Sciences Academy.

Stavrianos, L. (1992). *Lifelines from our past: A new world history*. Beijing: China Social Sciences Press.

Toynbee, A. (1966). *Historical research* (W. Cao, Trans.). Shanghai: Shanghai People's Press.

Voltaire, (1995). *On folkways and customs* (Vol. I). Beijing: The Commercial Press.

Wallerstein, I. (2013). *The modern world-system*. Beijing: Social Sciences Academic Press.

Wang, G. (1998). *China transformed: Historical change and the limits of European experience*. Nanjing: Jiangsu People's Press.

Wang, M. (2008). *Choice of nomads: The nomadic tribes in Northern Asia vs. the Han Empire*. Guilin: Guangxi Normal University Press.

Weatherford, J. (2006). *Genghis Khan and the making of the modern world* (H. Wen & J. Yao, Trans.). Chongqing: Chongqing Press.

Wood, F. (1997). *Has Marco Polo been to China?*. Beijing: Xinhua Press.

Xiao, Q. (2007). *The history of Mongol-dominated Yuan empire* (Vol. I). Beijing: Zhonghua Book Company.

Xiao, Z., & Yang, W. (1986). *A chronicle of Sino-Western relations before the opium war*. Hubei People's Press.

Ya, H. (1984). *The biography of the 13th Dalai Lama*. Beijing: The People's Press.

Yao, D. (2007). *Ten papers on the history of the Northern Nomads of China*. Guiling: Press of Guangxi Normal University Press.

Zhang, X. L. (1977). *Historical documents on east-west communication* (Vol. 1). Beijing: Zhonghua Book Company.

Chapter 2
A Century of National Humiliation: Threats of Border Areas Fragmentation by the Imperialist Powers

Ancient Chinese states were typified by variously sized city-states that existed prior to the country's unification by Qin Shi Huang, the first emperor of the Qin dynasty, in 221 BC. In many cases, these were vassal states characterized by the tribute paid to the ruling central dynasty. According to the Sinocentric viewpoint and the "Mandate of Heaven," China was the center of the world and the incumbent emperor its only ruler; all other would-be potentates were merely vassals of the "Celestial Empire." As a result, from the earliest times, the Chinese viewed the world as a series of concentric spheres of influence emanating outward from their capital. Within the closest circle lay the vassal states who pledged allegiance to the central ruling dynasty. However, the sovereignty and territorial integrity of China had been trampled by the imperialist powers during the century of national humiliation between the First Opium War (1840) and the founding of the People's Republic of China (1949). All efforts to maintain the dignity and sovereignty of the Chinese central authority were met with the imperialist powers' sophisticated weaponry and gunboat diplomacy. With the conclusion of unequal treaties, the southeast coastal areas of China were successively forced open. At the same time, the land borders of the country were invaded and carved up by the foreign powers.

2.1 The Decline of the Qing Dynasty and Ensuing Border Crisis

In the early seventeenth century, the Italian missionary Matteo Ricci was appointed as an imperial adviser of the Wanli Emperor of the Ming dynasty. Ricci presented gifts, including a world atlas, chime clock, and octaves, to the Ming Emperor. The official historians of China recorded these gifts as tributes paid to the "Celestial Empire." Prior to this, the tributes paid to the Chinese central authority by the tributary states in Asia were nothing more than native products or exotic animals of the agricultural society. Therefore, these technologically advanced products presented by the

© China Social Sciences Press 2020
S. Hao, *China's Solution to Its Ethno-national Issues*, China Insights,
https://doi.org/10.1007/978-981-32-9519-3_2

European missionary definitely appealed to the Chinese Emperor. The ruling elites of the Chinese central authority began to show interest in the modern scientific knowledge and industrial skills of Western countries. However, most of these innovative products were merely utilized to please the royal family. This fleeting sense of novelty inflicted no fundamental impact on the self-sufficient agricultural society of China.

That said the dynastic rulers of China did not lack geographical knowledge, including the concepts of the "world" or "universe." Even as early as the late fourteenth century, the cartographers of the Ming dynasty had already scaled the world atlas, which was acclaimed as the earliest map to correctly depict the shape of Eurasia and Africa. The map was used as the most important orientation instrument by He Zheng's overseas expedition fleet.[1] Nevertheless, the Ming Empire's "sea ban," the series of isolationist policies restricting private maritime trading and coastal settlement, shelved the relatively sophisticated geological knowledge to royal collections. Proclaiming himself as the legitimate holder of the "Mandate of Heaven," the Ming Emperor arrogantly categorized the technology-intensive produce presented by the Western clergy as "tributes," rather than gifts. In the mind of the emperor, these Christian pastors were merely "foreign barbarians from the far corners of the globe."

Thanks to their expertise with the astronomical calendar, the Jesuit clerics were highly revered by the Ming rulers, for astronomy was closely related to the Chinese tradition of "Mandate of Heaven," a principle used to justify the power of the emperor, as well as explaining suitability for the office. According to this belief, Heaven bestowed its mandate to a just ruler, the "Son of Heaven." After winning the emperor's trust, these Jesuit pastors introduced a large number of western writings to China. Among them, Giulio Aleni (1582–1649), an Italian Jesuit missionary and scholar who was proficient in the Chinese language, made an important contribution to the royal court's understanding of the world by compiling the *Zhifang Waiji* (Chronicle of Foreign Lands), the first detailed atlas of global geography available in Chinese. The eight scrolls of the book divide the world into five continents, each with separate maps and descriptions. These western priests initiated the first wave of "Western learning's dissemination to the East", the introduction of western knowledge systems, and world outlook into China during the Ming and Qing dynasties. This "eastward transmission of western sciences" had a tremendous impact on modern Chinese history. These works introduced new ideas to the Chinese people, for example, the theory of evolution and the "survival of the fittest." At the same time, the Law of the Jungle, namely "the superiority of brute force or self-interest in the struggle for survival," jeopardized the land borders of China. From the British invasion of Tibet in the late nineteenth century to the Japanese invasion of northeast China in the twentieth century, imperialist forces have conducted activities to split China. China's north-east, north, north-west, and south-west border areas have faced the threat of fragmentation by imperialists.

The Silk Road formed in the Han dynasty declined with the collapse of the Mongol Yuan dynasty. The infant Ming dynasty was confronted with a changing domestic and

---

[1]Liu Y. *Sea and Land: a study of East-West Communication in Medieval Times*. Beijing: Press of Peking University, pp. 219–220.

international environment. Internally, the Ming rulers failed to break a stalemate over its confrontation with the Mongol nomads; externally, the Ottoman Empire, which had already conquered West Asia and North Africa, was expanding into Europe.[2] Moreover, the Europeans had already opened sea routes to Asia in the fifteenth century. When the Western imperialists forced open the door of China from the sea, Tsarist Russia, which was lacking in maritime competitiveness, committed aggressions against Chinese borderlands, attempting to change frontiers by force.

In the late sixteenth century, the Cossack cavalry of the Russian Empire crossed the Ural Mountains and entered vast Siberia. The region was recorded in the *Shan-hai Ching (the Classic of Mountains and Seas)*, a Chinese classic text which was a compilation of mythic geography and myth. The geographical orientation, group appellation, production methods, and living customs of Siberia had frequently appeared in Chinese classical documents since the dynasties of Qin (221BC–207BC) and Han (202BC–220AD). These regions were either incorporated into the rising nomadic empires or governed by the frontier administrations of the Chinese central authority. The Lake Baikal region and the river basins of northeast China had long been the traditional habitats of the ancient tribes of Mongols and Tungusic peoples. The expansion of the Russian Empire and the brutal massacre by the Cossacks were met with strong resistance from the Mongol and Daur tribes. Thereafter, the frequent Sino-Russia border conflicts led to the conclusion of the *Treaty of Nerchinsk* in 1689. According to the treaty, the Russians gave up the area north of the Amur River as far as the Stanovoy Mountains and kept the area between the Argun River and Lake Baikal.

Symbolizing China's beginning of delineating state borders with boundary stones, *the Treaty of Nerchinsk* had a significant impact on the Manchu rulers. The Kangxi Emperor of the Qing dynasty came to realize that the existing Chinese maps were far from accurate. In 1708, he sponsored a nationwide geodesy and mapping program based on the astronomical observation and triangulation measurements of the Christian missionaries. *The Atlas of China (huangyuquanlantu* in Chinese) took over 10 years to complete.[3] During the reign of the Kangxi Emperor, two Tibetan monks were entrusted to survey and map the vast Tibet. In 1717, the first-ever atlas of Tibet was scaled.[4] After suppressing the rebellion of the Dzungar Khanate, a coalition of Western Mongol tribes, in 1755, the Qianlong Emperor incorporated the land of the Dzungars into the Qing Empire. Soon after that, Xinjiang was also surveyed and mapped.[5] The scaling of the map of China marked fundamental progress of the Chinese nationals' sovereignty concept.

Heralded as the Qing government's earliest effort to safeguard the territory and sovereignty manifested by *the Atlas of China*, the conclusion of *the Treaty of Nerchinsk* failed to discourage the Russian Empire's determination to annex the

---

[2]Stavrianos (1992): 52.

[3]Sun (2003).

[4]Shen and Liu (2014): 6.

[5]Sun Z. *Map Scaling and Territory Formation during the Reigns of Kangxi, Yongzheng and Qianlong*, pp. 59 62.

strategic Mongolia region. For the purpose of seeking more territory and commerce interests, Russia succeeded in persuading the Qing government to shelve the issue of the Sino-Russia border along Outer Mongolia in the lengthy negotiations in the wake of signing the treaty. After that, Russia continued to penetrate Outer Mongolia under the pretext of opening up new trade routes. In 1727, China and Russia signed the *Treaty of Kyakhta*; large tracts of land to the south and west of Lake Baikal and Mongolia Buryatia were incorporated into the Russian Empire. The Russians quickly built the post of Kyakhta at the border. The region where Kyakhta stands is a natural location for the Russo-Chinese trade. The Siberian River Routes connect the fur-bearing lands of Siberia to Lake Baikal.

As a response, the Qing government built the fort of Maimaicheng, a Chinese toponym meaning literally "trade town" or "trading post," on the border with Russia opposite to the town of Kyakhta. Officials on both sides dealt with diplomatic exchanges between the two empires, trade disputes, and the usual police matters to be expected on a long border inhabited by nomads. The Kyakhta trade route followed the usual route to Irkutsk, by flatboat across Lake Baikal, and south by poling up the Selenge River past Selinginsk. Much barter was done at Kyakhta during the winter, and Chinese goods were shipped west when the rivers melted. To the south, the route went south to Urga, southeast to Kalgan on the Great Wall and then Beijing. Trade was mostly Siberian furs for Chinese cotton, silk, tobacco, and tea. Most of the tea trade along the trade route was managed by merchants from Northern China's Shanxi province. The merchants dealt in other goods and interacted with the numerous lamaseries which were also political and economic centers. Historically, the Kyakhta trade route was analogous to the Tea Horse Road, a network of caravan paths winding through the mountains of Sichuan, Yunnan, and Guizhou in southwest China.

The Russia Empire benefited a lot from this trade route. After the outbreak of the First Opium War in 1840, Russia was eager to compete with the Western powers to carve up China. During the Second Opium War, Russia incorporated large swathes of Chinese territory. In addition, Russia was granted the privileges of free trade and customs duty exemption in Outer Mongolia. After the First Sino-Japanese War, the Qing Empire was coaxed into signing *the Sino-Russian Secret Treaty*, which gave Russia to the exclusive right to build railroads and extract minerals in Mongolia and Manchuria. Almost over the same period, the Western powers' colonial conquest of Southeast Asia and South Asia blocked the traditional tributary ties between these areas and the Qing Empire. As a consequence, the southwest border regions of China were subject to the aggression of Britain and France. The imperialist powers' illegal field surveying or explorations in the border areas of China were bound to meet with the resistance of the local ethnic minorities. For example, the Tibetans deported the western missionaries in 1643.[6] Thereafter, the foreign powers engineered a series of "incidents," which became pretexts to coerce the Qing government into signing unequal treaties.

---

[6]Taylor (1995): 35.

In the era of the Europeans' colonization of the Americas and Asia, the Christian missionaries were pioneers in Tibet. To convert the Tibetans, the Jesuit priests had to compete with the deep-rooted influence of the Buddhist Vajrayana doctrine and Tibetan institutions. Rather than a rudimentary religious belief, Tibetan Buddhism derives from the latest stages of Indian Buddhism and preserves "the Tantric status quo of eighth-century India." After repeated failed attempts to convert Tibetans, the western missionaries could only excuse themselves by denouncing the absurdity of the teachings of Tibetan Buddhism. For example, Ippolito Desideri (1684–1733), an Italian Jesuit missionary and the first European to have successfully studied and understood the Tibetan language and culture, declared: "the 'source of error' of Tibetans lies in their ridiculous argument of 'denying the existence of God'; in addition, Tibetan Buddhism, a most vicious enemy, adorns this absurd argument with subtle artistic techniques."[7] Therefore, the European missionaries had to retreat ignominiously from Tibet in the mid-eighteenth century, only comforting themselves with the oldest strategy of the Christian church: not everything in the world can be conquered.[8]

However, the missionaries' vivid narratives on Tibet aroused the Westerners' everlasting interest in the remote and mysterious "roof of the world." After occupying India, the British colonists coveted to chart the unknown territory beyond the northern borders of Bengal, with a view to opening up trade with Tibet and possibly establishing a backdoor trade relationship with the Chinese Qing dynasty, which tightly controlled foreign trade under the Canton System, or "single port commerce system." Taking advantage of the infighting between the two sects of Tibetan Buddhism, the Panchen Lama, and the Dalai Lama, the envoy of the East India Company won access to Tibet and met the Panchen Lama in November 1774. However, the British colonists' ultimate goal of establishing a trade route to Tibet was not secured. [9] In spite of the aborted efforts to establish direct trade ties with Tibet, the mission of the East India Company to Lhasa provided the first-hand accounts on the local customs and produce of the Tibetan Plateau, which further stimulated the Western powers' desire to open up colonial trade.

Although the Britons believed that "Tibet has the worst natural conditions in the world," they had long coveted the region's potential commerce and trade interests. As a result, they concluded that the "culturally incompetent and inferior Tibetans" deserved to be conquered by force.[10] Under the secret assistance of the East India Company, Nepalese Gurkha troops invaded Tibet successively in 1788 and 1791. At the request of the Dalai Lama, the Qianlong Emperor of the Qing Empire sent a strong troop of 70,000 soldiers to defend Tibet in 1792. Thus, the Nepal–Tibet conflict turned into a war between Nepal and the Qing Empire. The Nepalese troops attempted to defend against the Qing attack, but were faced with overwhelming odds. Both sides had suffered heavy casualties and the Chinese Army pushed the Gurkhas back to

---

[7]Ippolito Desider (2004): 238.

[8]Taylor (1995): 56.

[9]Liang (2012).

[10]Turner (2004): 156.

the inner hills close to the Nepali capital. During the armed conflict, the so-called Phe-rang forces (literally "foreigners" in Tibetan) secretly assisted the Gurkhas. It was not until the eruption of the First Opium War in 1840 that the Qing government came to realize that "the Phe-rang forces" were actually the British colonists."[11]

2.2 The Self-Strengthening Movement: To Learn the Superior Techniques of the Barbarians in Order to Repel Them

The acquired geographical knowledge of the Chinese Emperors, be it the world atlas charted by Matteo Ricci, or the *Huangyu Quanlantu*, the map of China scaled during the reign of the Kangxi Emperor of the Qing dynasty, was mothballed, failing to be integrated into the knowledge system of Chinese society. The American sinologist Immanuel C. Y. Hsu concluded: "Western learning's dissemination to the East during the late Ming and early Qing dynasties enlightened only a small number of progressive Chinese intellectuals."[12] It was not until the imperialist powers' sophisticated weaponry forced open the door of China that the Chinese elites began to reconsider the position of China in the world.[13] After its disgraceful defeat in the First Opium War, the Qing Empire, which had long taken pride in its status as "the Celestial Empire," painfully felt the degradation of technological inferiority in comparison with the Western powers. The Chinese were forced to "open their eyes and see the world," and a group of pioneers emerged to save the nation from extinction. They began translating and introducing western literature and broadened the global horizon of the Chinese people. Known as "the first Chinese looking at the world," Zexu Lin (1785–1850), a skilled bureaucrat known for his opposition to opium, presided over the editing of the *Si Zhou Zhi (the Geography of the Four Continents)* and took the lead in developing a Chinese world vision. Over the same period, Yuan Wei (1794–1857) edited *Hai Guo Tu Zhi (the Illustrated Treatise on the Maritime Kingdoms)*, the first significant Chinese work on the West and one of China's initial responses to the Anglo-Chinese Opium War. As well as mapping various countries, Wei's objective was to provide as complete a picture as possible of the advantages the Western powers possessed in shipbuilding techniques and weaponry production so that these "might be turned to use for subduing them." Wei believed that the Chinese people should "learn the superior technique of the barbarians in order to repel them." In the longer term, Wei and his contemporaries helped change the Chinese view of the outside world not only through the dissemination of new material but also by starting to change the view that China was the "center of the world."

With the advent of modern times, Chinese society became embroiled in intense upheavals; this was a time of fierce struggle as the Chinese people resisted feudal

---

[11]Liang J. *The British Empire and Tibet: 1774–1904*, p. 179.

[12]Hsu, I. C. Y. *the Rise of Modern China: 1600–2000*, p. 84.

[13]Zou (2000).

rule and foreign aggression. Following the series of military defeats and concessions to foreign powers in the late Qing dynasty, the ruling elites of the Qing Empire came to understand that it was necessary to adopt Western military technology and armaments. They believed that this could be achieved by establishing shipyards and arsenals and by hiring foreign advisers to train Chinese artisans to manufacture such wares in China. These reforms were collectively termed the Self-Strengthening Movement by the historians. In 1861, the Qing government created the *Zongliyamen* (literally the "office in charge of affairs of all nations"), which was actually a government body in charge of foreign policy during the late Qing dynasty. A number of reforms were implemented, such as the restoration of regional armies, territory, paying indemnities, and arsenals, an increase in industrial and commercial productivity, and the institution of a period of peace that allowed China time to modernize and develop. In April 1861, the Qing government established the Imperial Maritime Customs Service to collect tariffs equitably and generate new revenues from the import dues on foreign goods. These efforts, in particular, the translation and promulgation of *the Elements of International Law*, showed the Qing Empire's eagerness to integrate proactively into the international order laid down by Western powers. In addition, the Qing government was committed to the introduction of western technology and personnel training. In 1862, *Tongwen Guan*, a government school for the teaching of Western languages, was founded in Beijing. Its establishment signified the Qing Empire, after years of reluctance, at last tried to learn about the West of their own accord. In addition, the Qing government organized what came to be known as the Chinese Educational Mission, which included 120 students, some under the age of ten, to study in New England in 1872. However, the Qing government's intention of dynastic revival could only be a fantasy against the backdrop of the imperialist powers' profit-seeking nature.

Admittedly, the Self-Strengthening Movement led to the significant improvement of military industries, which directly enhanced the Imperial Qing Army's armament. To assist the suppression of the Taiping Rebellion,[14] the Qing Empire's state-run arsenals and the imperialist powers provided a large number of modern weapons to the Hunan Army, a standing army organized by Guofan Zeng, a statesman, military general, and Confucian scholar of the late Qing dynasty, from existing regional and village militia forces to contain the rebels.[15] In addition to providing military equipment to the Hunan Army, the imperialists armed the Anhui Army founded by Hongzhang Li, who quelled several major rebellions and pioneered China's industrial and military modernization. According to the study of John King Fairbank, "the Anhui Army had around 15,000 rifles towards the end of the Taiping Rebellion in 1864."[16] Equipped merely with "cold weapons" without fire or explosives, the Taiping rebels were in a disadvantageous position while combating with the imperial Qing forces, the Hunan Army, and the Anhui Army. The foreign powers' support

---

[14] A massive insurgency fought between the Manchu Qing dynasty and the Christian millenarian movement of "the Heavenly Kingdom of Peace" that lasted from 1850 to 1864.

[15] Fairbank J. K. *The Great Chinese Revolution: 1800–1985*, p. 131.

[16] Fairbank J. K. & Liu G. *The Cambridge History of China: Late Qing*, p. 340.

given to the Qing government was aimed at sustaining the Manchu-dominated Qing Empire, for only in this way could their colonial interests in China be "legalized" and bolstered.

Although the Taiping had been suppressed by 1864, several other rebellions of a smaller order still raged over different parts of the country. The Nien Rebellion, which broke out in 1853 and lasted until 1868, focused its activities in the southern part of North China. The Moslem Rebellion in Yunnan lasted from 1855 to 1873 and the Tungan Rebellion in the northwest from 1862 to 1878. These long-lasting rebellions were extremely debilitating in their effects, but they established no rival governments to contest the court in Beijing. The primary cause of their failures was that the social stratification of China did not create the necessary conditions for a bourgeois revolution. In all fairness, the military modernization endeavors of the Self-Strengthening Movement did enhance the Qing Empire's state machinery to suppress the domestic riots. In the face of the imperialist powers' aggression, the Qing Imperial Army reclaimed Xinjiang from Muhammad Yaqub Bek, a Tajik adventurer who had been master of the Tarim Basin from 1865 to 1877. This victory of maintaining the territorial integrity of China was, to a large extent, connected with the "increasing armament of imported or self-made firearms" of the Qing troops.[17]

With the intention of revitalizing government and improving economic and cultural conditions in China, the Self-Strengthening Movement directly led to the "Tongzhi Restoration." Named after the reigning Tongzhi Emperor, it was an attempt to arrest the dynastic decline of the Great Qing by restoring the traditional order. With the old mentality, "Chinese learning for fundamentals and Western learning for practical application" as the guiding principle, the self-strengtheners failed to bring about a genuine program of modernization in China. Of course, the rulers of the Qing dynasty already realized that their excessive reliance on the foreign powers would inevitably subject China to the imperialists' political interference and economic colonization. However, they were also crystal clear that only by choosing to cooperate with the imperialists could the Qing government get the foreign powers' crucial military and economic assistance to suppress the domestic rebellions, which would, in turn, prolong the existence of the Qing dynasty.[18] Therefore, the Self-Strengthening Movement and the "Tongzhi Restoration" failed to arrest the dynastic decline of the "Celestial Empire." Ancient and traditional China was incorporated into the Western-dominated world system in the contest of antiquated weaponry against guns and bullets. In the years when China suffered aggression from imperialist powers, the Qing government was coerced into ceding territory, paying indemnities, and committing other humiliating acts. In 1888, British troops invaded Tibet, which led to the conclusion of the *Convention Between Great Britain and China Concerning Sikkim and Tibet*. The signing of the treaty opened the door for the British colonists' invasion of Tibet. Japan's incursion into Taiwan in 1874 exposed the vulnerability of the existing pre-modern Chinese Navy. The Qing court came to realize that the building of a powerful navy was a priority to protect its national sovereignty. A proposal was made

---

[17]Fairbank J. K. & Liu G. *The Cambridge History of China: Late Qing*, pp. 280–283.
[18]Wright (2002): 269.

to establish modern coastal fleets. With a remit to defend the section of coastline closest to the capital, the Beiyang Fleet (literally "Northern Ocean Fleet") sponsored by Hongzhang Li garnered much greater resources than the other three fleets of the Imperial Qing Navy. In 1894, the Japanese Navy initiated the First Sino-Japanese War. At the Battle of Yalu River, the Beiyang Fleet suffered heavy losses due to the surprise attack of the Japanese forces and the inferiority of its equipment and was eventually annihilated in the Battle of Weihaiwei.[19]

2.3   The First Sino-Japanese War and Japan's Subsequent Annexation of Taiwan

Intimidated by Western powers' war threats, Japan was coerced into opening its doors in the mid-nineteenth century. In spite of great efforts to introduce western technology at this stage, Japanese society continued to revere Chinese culture.[20] After the Opium War, Chinese publications on Western learning were highly valued in Japan. For example, *the Illustrated Treatise on the Maritime Kingdoms* compiled by Yuan Wei was widely read by the Japanese elites in the late Tokugawa Shogunate.[21] In addition, a large number of Chinese texts on world geography and international law, even the Chinese periodicals run by the Western missionaries, were introduced to the island country.

In spite of Japan's isolationist foreign policy in the Tokugawa period (1603–1868), Takasugi Shinsaku, a samurai who contributed significantly to the Meiji Restoration, was ordered to lead a diplomatic mission to Shanghai in 1862. Shocked by the effects of European imperialism on the Qing Empire, Takasugi was convinced that Japan must strengthen itself to avoid being colonized by the Western powers, or else suffer a similar fate. This coincided with the growing social movement of "expelling the barbarians and revering the Emperor," which attracted certain radical sections of Japan's warrior class and court nobility.[22]

In 1867, the Tokugawa Shogunate came to an end, which initiated the Meiji Restoration, an event that restored practical imperial rule to Japan the following year. Spanning both the late Edo period and the beginning of the Meiji period, the restoration led to enormous changes in Japan's political and social structure. It was responsible for the emergence of Japan as a modernized nation in the early twentieth century and its rapid rise to a status of great power in the international system.[23] The years following the Meiji Restoration and the fall of the Shogunate had seen Japan transform itself from a feudal society into a modern industrial state. The Japanese government sent delegations and students around the world to learn

---

[19]Fairbank J. K. *The Great Chinese Revolution: 1800–1985*, p. 145.

[20]Wang (2000): 21.

[21]Yoda (2004): 58.

[22]Feng (2001): 209.

[23]Stavrianos, L., *A Global History: the World after 1500*, p. 482.

and assimilate Western arts and sciences, with the intention of making Japan an equal to the Western powers. The success of the Japanese expedition to Taiwan in 1874, which marked the first overseas deployment of the Imperial Japanese Army, revealed the fragility of the Qing dynasty's hold on the island and encouraged further Japanese adventurism. Though Japan's embroilment with China was eventually resolved by a British arbitration under which the Qing government agreed to compensate Japan for property damage, this diplomatic dispute highlighted the intention of Japan's external expansion. After fighting two opium wars, the Qing dynasty was unable to resist the encroachment of Western powers. As a consequence, Japan saw the opportunity to take China's place in the strategically vital Korean peninsula. In 1876, Japan employed gunboat diplomacy, implying or constituting a direct threat of warfare, to press Korea to sign *the Japan–Korea Treaty*, which ended Korea's status as a tributary state of the Qing dynasty.

In 1894, the Donghak Peasant Revolution, an armed rebellion led by aggravated peasants and followers of the Donghak religion, broke out in Korea. At the Korean government's request, the Qing Emperor sent troops to Korea to help suppress the riot. Under the pretext of "protecting Japanese nationals and embassy," the Japanese government dispatched troops to Korea. As a result, the forces of China and Japan underwent an intense confrontation in Korea. On Aug 1, the First Sino-Japanese War was formally declared. Despite fighting bravely against the Japanese forces, the Chinese Navy lost the Battle of the Yellow Sea. The Beiyang Fleet, the only trump card of the Qing dynasty, was ambushed and wiped out by the Japanese Navy. In January 1895, the two Japanese forces joined and occupied the Chinese northeastern frontier. *The Treaty of Shimonoseki* ended the war as a clear victory for Japan. In this treaty, China recognized the independence of Korea and renounced any claims to that country. It also ceded the Liaodong Peninsula, Taiwan, and Penghu to Japan. In addition, China was to pay Japan a war indemnity of 230 million taels of silver. The First Sino-Japanese War demonstrated the failure of the Qing Empire's attempts to modernize its military and fend off threats to its sovereignty, especially when compared with Japan's successful Meiji Restoration. For the first time, regional dominance in East Asia shifted from China to Japan. The prestige of the Qing Empire, along with the classical tradition in China, suffered a serious setback.

The island of Taiwan was inhabited by Taiwanese aborigines before the seventeenth century when Dutch and Spanish colonists opened the island to mass Han immigration. After a brief rule by the Kingdom of Tungning, a regime founded by a Chinese Ming loyalist Chenggong Zheng,[24] the island was placed under the jurisdiction of Fujian province. The Kangxi Emperor annexed Taiwan to remove any threat to his dynasty from remaining resistance forces on the island. In 1885, the Qing upgraded the island's administration status from prefecture to province. In accordance with *the Treaty of Shimonoseki*, Taiwan, along with Penghu and the Liaodong Peninsula, were ceded in full sovereignty to Japan.[25] The short-lived resis-

---

[24]Chenggong Zheng, who was known in the West by his Hokkien honorific Koxinga, as part of the loyalist movement to restore the Ming dynasty after it was overthrown by the Manchu people.
[25]Hao and Chen (2012): 2.

tance movement of the pro-Qing Taiwanese ended to no avail when it was suppressed by the Japanese troops. The fall of Tainan wrapped up the organized resistance to Japanese occupation and inaugurated five decades of Japanese rule (1895–1945). The Japanese began an island-wide assimilation project to bind Taiwan more firmly to the Japanese Empire and the Taiwanese were taught to identify themselves as Japanese under the Kominka Movement, literally "to make people become subjects of the Japanese Emperor." Accordingly, Taiwanese culture and religion were outlawed, and the citizens were encouraged to adopt Japanese surnames.

2.4   The Boxer Protocol and the Anglo-Tibetan Treaty of Lhasa

Marking the complete failure of the Qing government's Self-Strengthening Movement, China's terrible defeat in the First Sino-Japanese War heralded the impending demise of the Qing dynasty and ushered in a period of exacerbated foreign aggression and domestic political movements. The imperialist powers carved China into leased territories and spheres of influence. China was plunged into the darkness of domestic turmoil and foreign invasion; its people, ravaged by war, saw their homeland torn apart and lived in poverty and despair. Sheng Hu, a renowned Chinese historian, pointed out: "The need for a more extensive institutional reform was recognized by scholars, officials, and even the Qing Emperor, although they differed on the question of its nature, scope, and leadership."[26] The representative figures for such a radical reform were Han intellectuals, including Youwei Kang, Fu Yan, Qichao Liang, and Sitong Tan. After formulating the political program of constitutional monarchy, they recommended that the Qing Emperor pursues three courses of action: proclaim a national policy on reform after the fashion of Russia's Peter the Great and Japan's Meiji Emperor; gather all the talents of the country to prepare for an institutional reorganization; allow provincial authorities to initiate institutional reform within their own jurisdictions. The reformers declared that China needed more than "self-strengthening" and that innovation must be accompanied by institutional and ideological change.

On June 11, 1898, the young Guangxu Emperor of the Qing dynasty ascended the Tiananmen of the Forbidden City and issued an imperial edict, ordering a series of reforms aimed at making sweeping social and institutional changes. In the following three months, some forty to fifty reform decrees were promulgated in rapid succession in the areas of education, government administration, industry, and diplomacy. Although the Qing Emperor and the reform-minded supporters vigorously pushed the reform program, it was boycotted by most of the high officials in the central and provincial administrations. The abolition of the eight-legged essay met with strong opposition from the Ministry of Rites, which was in charge of the civil service examinations. Most of the provincial authorities ignored or delayed the orders for reform.

---

[26]Hu (1981): 346.

These officials dared to challenge or disregard the emperor's orders in full knowledge of the fact that the real power of state was not in his hands but in those of the Empress Dowager Cixi, who effectively controlled the Chinese government in the late Qing dynasty for 47 years from 1861 until her death in 1908.

Opposition to the reform was intense among the conservative ruling elites, who, condemning the announced reform as too radical, proposed instead a more moderate course of change. With the tacit support of the political opportunist Shikai Yuan, a statesman and warlord famous for his influence during the late Qing dynasty, and the backing of conservatives, Empress Dowager Cixi engineered a coup on September 21, 1898, forcing the Guangxu Emperor into seclusion. Cixi then took over the government as regent. Historically known as the Hundred Days' Reform, it ended with the rescinding of the new edicts and the execution of six of the reform's chief advocates.[27]

The coup reversed the entire power structure of the Qing dynasty, restoring reactionary Manchu ruling elites to office at the expense of both radical and moderate reformers. After the Hundred Days' Reform, the Guangxu Emperor was put under house arrest within the Summer Palace. A crisis over the issue of the emperor's abdication emerged, which was actually supported and masterminded by Empress Dowager Cixi. However, the foreign powers voiced their public disapproval of dethroning the Guangxu Emperor since the conservative political orientation of Cixi undermined the efforts of imperialist powers to integrate China into the Western regulation. Bowing to increasing pressure from the Western powers, Cixi did not forcibly remove the Guangxu Emperor from the throne. Nonetheless, it became one of the motivations for her patronage of the anti-foreign Boxer Rebellion.

Strong anti-foreign sentiment permeated not only the court under the Empress Dowager, but the Chinese scholars, officials, gentry, and the people at large. Half a century of foreign humiliation, in war as well as in peace, had deeply wounded their national pride and self-esteem. The presence of haughty foreign ministers, consuls, aggressive missionaries, and self-seeking traders constantly reminded them of China's misfortune. This gnawing sense of injustice generated a burning desire for revenge until it burst out in a vast anti-foreign movement, the Boxer Rebellion, a violent anti-foreign, anti-colonial, and anti-Christian uprising that took place in China between 1899 and 1901, toward the end of the Qing dynasty. The uprising took place against a background of severe drought and disruption caused by the growth of foreign spheres of influence. After several months of growing violence against both the foreign and Christian presence in Shandong and the North China Plain in June 1900, the Boxer fighters, convinced they were invulnerable to foreign weapons, converged in the capital city with the slogan, "support the Qing government and exterminate the foreigners." Foreigners and Chinese Christians were compelled to seek refuge in the Beijing Legation Quarter.

Perhaps fearing further foreign intervention, Cixi threw her support to these anti-foreign bands by making an official announcement of her support for the movement and a formal declaration of war on the Western powers. In the summer of 1900, when

---

[27] Hsu, I. C. Y. *The Rise of Modern China: 1600–2000*, p. 299.

the international legations in Beijing came under attack by Boxer rebels supported by the Qing government, the coalition dispatched their armed forces, in the name of "humanitarian intervention," to defend their respective nations' citizens, as well as a number of Chinese Christians who had taken shelter in the legations. On the morrow of the Allied advance into Beijing, the Empress Dowager, the Guangxu Emperor, and a small entourage fled in disguise. Clad in coarse commoner's clothes to avoid identification, they escaped westward under pitiful conditions. After a long and hard journey, the court was re-established in Xi'an of Shaanxi province. After conquering Beijing, the Eight Power Allied Forces plundered the Chinese capital. The aggressors dividedly occupied Beijing for as long as a year, during which they wantonly looted priceless valuables, burned palaces and houses, destroyed properties, raped women, and slaughtered civilians.[28] At the end of the nineteenth century, the Qing dynasty's last attempt to stand up to the imperial powers ended again in a fiasco.

After the fall of Beijing, the Eight-Nation Alliance negotiated a treaty with the Qing government, sending messengers to the Empress Dowager in Xi'an. The imperialist powers needed a government strong enough to suppress further anti-foreign movements, but too weak to act on its own; they supported the continuation of the Qing dynasty, rather than allowing it to be overthrown. On September 7, 1901, the Qing court signed *the Boxer Protocol* with the Eight-Nation Alliance. The major clauses included: The execution of ten high-ranking officials linked to the Boxer Rebellion and other officials who were found guilty of the slaughter of foreigners in China; China to be fined war reparations of 450,000,000 taels of fine silver for the losses that it caused; legation quarters occupied by the foreign powers to be considered a special area reserved for their use under exclusive control, in which Chinese shall not have the right to reside, and which may be defensible. China to recognize the right of each power to maintain permanent guard in said quarters for the defense of its legation; the Boxer rebels and the Qing government officials to be punished for crimes or attempted crimes against the foreign governments or their nationals. Thus, the Qing government was completely reduced to being the puppet of the imperialist powers. The conclusion of *the Boxer Protocol*, "on the one hand, nominally maintained the sovereign independence of China; on the other hand, it led to the collapse of the world's oldest political entity."[29] China became a semi-colony, losing the power and ability to defend its sovereignty and territorial integrity.

The enormous colonial interests the Japanese government grabbed from the destitute Qing Empire in the wake of the First Sino-Japanese War whetted the imperialist powers' appetite for carving up China. In addition to its economic control over Outer Mongolia, Russia blatantly sent troops to Urga (today's Ulaanbaatar) under the pretext of protecting Russian nationals. For its eastward expansion and more stakes in Mongolia, it made every effort to foster pro-Russian forces among the Mongol elites, which created favorable conditions for Outer Mongolia's future independence. After the conclusion of *the Boxer Protocol*, the competition between Britain and Russia for spheres of influence in Xinjiang and Tibet intensified. To coerce the Qing

---

[28] Hu (1981): 346.

[29] Hobsbawm (1999a): 364.

government into further opening the door of Tibet, the British colonists threatened to establish direct political and economic ties with Tibet by resorting to the use of force. Of course, no matter how feeble and incompetent the Qing government was at that time, it would not readily yield to the imperialist powers on issues concerning state sovereignty and territorial integrity. Sandwiched between Russia's carrot and Britain's stick, the Tibetan local government found itself in a most awkward predicament. The subsequent story could only be narrated in accordance with the "political trap" pre-designed by the aggressors.

With the purpose of countering Russia's perceived ambitions in the East, the British Indian government dispatched an expeditionary force to Tibet in 1903. Headed by Francis Younghusband, the British troops fought their way to Gyantse. Thousands of Tibetans armed with antiquated hoes, swords, and flintlocks were mown down by modern rifles and machine guns while attempting to block the British advance. The aggressors, relying on their sophisticated weaponry, broke through the Tibetan forces' several lines of defense. Even the British invaders were terribly shocked by the tenacious resistance of the Tibetans. Edmund Candler, who gained a post as the Daily Mail correspondent accompanying the expeditionary force into Tibet, later recalled the combat in his memoirs: "the Tibetan soldiers, who were armed merely with hoes, swords or whatever you call those thing, made their tragic and heroic last stand against the 3,000 strong well-equipped British troops, who were experienced veterans of mountainous border warfare. In spite of the great disparity in military strength, the Tibetan soldiers, who actually lacked discipline and training, had the guts to sacrifice their blood and flesh for the protection of their home village."[30] While the British troops were moving in on Lhasa, the 13th Dalai Lama fled to Outer Mongolia. At the suggestion of the Imperial Resident in Tibet, the Qing Emperor deposed the Dalai Lama. This, however, raised a storm of protest from the Tibetans.

On September 7, 1904, the representatives of the British expeditionary force and Tibetan government, without the knowledge and approval of the Qing Throne, concluded *the Treaty of Lhasa,* officially *the Convention Between Great Britain and Tibet.* The main points of the treaty allowed the Britons to trade in Yadong, Gyantse, and Gartok while Tibet was to pay a large indemnity, with the Chumbi Valley, a river valley at the intersection of Sikkim, Bhutan, and Tibet, ceded to Britain until payment was received. Further provisions recognized the Sikkim–Tibet border and prevented Tibet having relations with any other foreign power. It thereby effectively converted Tibet into a British protectorate. The treaty placed Tibet directly under British military and political control. The inking of the treaty aroused strong indignation in the Chinese people. The Qing government publicly repudiated the treaty and refused to sign it, maintaining that it violated the British government's commitment of "non-occupation to Tibet and non-invasion of Chinese sovereignty."[31]

In September 1904, the British expeditionary force pulled out of Lhasa without actually achieving any tangible results. During their eight-month expedition to the high-altitude Tibetan Plateau, the Britons looted Buddhist monasteries, plundering

---

[30]Candler (1989a): 112.

[31]Ya H. *The Biography of the 13th Dalai Lama*, p. 181.

numerous cultural relics and religious classics. These invaders, holding the same view as the Western missionaries who entered Tibet in the early eighteenth century, strongly disapproved of "the absurd doctrines of Tibetan Buddhism" . The war correspondent Edmund Candler later recalled: "in the monasteries of Tibetans, there are always gold-plated Buddha statues, garish paintings, colorful murals with terrible devil masks and deceptive gadgets of the Dalai Lama."[32] However, these bandits spared no efforts to the looting of these "deceptive gadgets." According to the self-statement of David McDonald, the British officer who was tasked with transporting these relics out of Tibet, "we hired 400 mules to carry these items, including rare and precious Tibetan Buddhism scriptures, statues, armors, weapons, Thangkas and porcelain."[33] The British colonists' indiscriminate plundering and looting inflicted heavy losses on the traditional culture of Tibet.

In 1905, the Qing court appointed Shaoyi Tang, a widely respected Chinese politician, to be the envoy of China to negotiate with the Britons about the matter of revising *the Treaty of Lhasa*. Fruitless negotiations dragged on for a year. The British representative disagreed with the suggestion that the Qing government, on behalf of the Lhasa authorities, pay the war indemnity, for it would actually acknowledge Chinese sovereignty over Tibet. Stipulating that "any foreign country, other than Great Britain, is not allowed to send diplomatic missions or representatives to Tibet," *the Treaty of Lhasa* highlighted the British colonists' exclusive interests in Tibet. It aroused strong opposition from other imperialist powers. Therefore, the Britons were compelled to make a concession.

In April 1906, the representatives of the British government and the Qing throne concluded *the Convention between Great Britain and China Respecting Tibet*, which re-affirmed the Chinese possession of Tibet after the British expedition to the region. The British, for a fee from the Qing government, agreed "not to annex Tibet or to interfere in its administration," while China agreed "not to permit any other foreign country to interfere with the territory or internal administration of Tibet." Through these privileges, the Britons gradually dominated Tibet politically and economically. Tibet was effectively converted into a British protectorate. During their occupation of Chumbi Valley, the British troops controlled the administrative, financial, and judicial powers of the region and planned a long-term presence to secure Tibetan payment of indemnity. After repeated negotiations, British troops withdrew from the valley in February 1908. In addition, they successfully drove a wedge between Tibetan local government and the Chinese central authorities, which engineered a hidden danger for the "issue of Tibet."

The Qing dynasty's actual administration of Tibet waned considerably with its gradual weakening in the nineteenth century. To strengthen its governance capacity, the Qing throne decided to extend the "New Policies" to the frontier province. Historically known as the "Late Qing Reform," the "New Policies" were a series of political, economic, military, cultural and educational policies implemented in the last decade of the Qing Empire to keep the dynasty in power after the humiliating

---

[32]Candler (1989b): 182.

[33]Liang J. *The Great Britain and Tibet: 1774–1904*, p. 308.

defeat of the Boxer Rebellion. Yintang Zhang, the Qing high commissioner stationed in Tibet during the last years of the Qing dynasty, implemented a series of policies, such as taking a survey of rent accounts, building a business center, reorganizing the Tibetan Army, reducing punishments, rejuvenating education and reforming habits and customs. These measures, however, did not bring industrial development to Tibet and had even less effect on the traditional Tibetan power structure.

From the eighteenth century to the early twentieth century, Tibet had been described by the Westerners as a land of backwardness and ignorance. Evariste Regis Huc, a French Catholic priest and traveler who was tasked with a mission to Lhasa in 1864, recounted: "As the supreme political and religious leader, the Dalai Lama dictates the legislative, judicial and administrative powers of Tibet. Moreover, the exercise of his power depends entirely on his moment of interest and pleasure, with neither a charter nor a constitution to check his abuse of power."[34] Four decades later, the war correspondent Edmund Candler recounted his personal experience while visiting the Potala Palace, the residence of the Dalai Lama: "the splendid and mythical abode of the spiritual leader, who portrays himself as the reincarnation of Buddha, has witnessed more massacres and cruelties than the most bloodshed castle in medieval Europe."[35] Apparently, we can read the colonists' long-established sense of superiority from the accounts of Candler. At the same time, his recollections did expose the entrenched social ills of Tibet. "Such backwardness and ignorance of the Tibetans were permeated in all aspects of their lives, including antiquated polity, idol worship, lynching, witchcraft and soul reincarnation. I bet the sudden exposure of the stubbornness and darkness of Tibet to the enlightenment of modern science is unprecedented in the history of the world."[36] These Westerners had witnessed medieval Europe's cruelty and darkness in the theocratic society of Tibet. Therefore, whatever is the purpose of the British aggression against Tibet, the dark reality of Tibet, which is all a far cry from modern society, will inevitably change with the political upheaval in China in the first half of the twentieth century.

2.5   The Borderland Crises of China After the Xinhai Revolution

The year of 1911 coincides with the Xinhai stem-branch in the sexagenary cycle of the Chinese traditional calendar. Therefore, the Revolution of 1911 is commonly named the Xinhai Revolution. As the Qing endeavors proved insincere and discriminatory against the Han people, the revolutionaries gained increasing support from young intellectuals, secret societies, and overseas Chinese communities. The Xinhai Revolution actually consisted of many revolts and uprisings. The turning point was the Wuchang Uprising on October 10. The revolution ended with the abdication of

---

[34] Huc (1991): 509–510.

[35] Candler (1989b): 186.

[36] Ibid.

the six-year-old "Last Emperor" of the Qing dynasty, marking the end of 2000 years of imperial rule and the beginning of China's early republican era. Among this kind of revolution in the modern history of the world, the most representative and influential was undoubtedly the French Revolution, a period of far-reaching social and political upheaval in France that lasted from 1789 until 1799. Inspired by liberal and radical ideas, the French Revolution profoundly altered the course of modern history, triggering the global decline of absolute monarchies while replacing them with republics and liberal democracies. Eric Hobsbawm commented: "in addition to providing the first great prototype and concept for nationalism, the French Revolution brought the thoughts of the modern world to the ancient civilizations of Asia, which for a very long time have defied the penetration of European ideologies."[37] The Xinhai Revolution and Sun Yat-sen's "Three Principles of the People"[38] were the results of such ideological infiltration.

The Wuchang Uprising, which was assisted by the New Army in a coup against the Qing government, served as the catalyst of the Xinhai Revolution. The New Army rebels met little resistance and had complete control of the city by noon on October 10, 1911. The rapidity of the success from the uprising to the establishment of the Republic of China on January 1, 1912, has been rarely equaled by any other great revolutions of the world. Therefore, the uprising itself was by no means a tough and brutal war; rather, it was, in a sense, accomplished without the least difficulty. However, behind the easily acquired success were the Qing government's decadence and the fomented anti-Manchu sentiments among the Han people.

From the middle of the nineteenth century, Chinese history was largely one continuous record of national humiliation. The long list of unequal treaties from *the Treaty of Nanking* in 1842 to the *Boxer Protocol* of 1901, the loss of the tributary states in the 1880s and the 1890s, and the lack of vigor in domestic administration have testified the Qing government's inability to defend China's honor in the modern world. What formerly had been the proud "Celestial Empire" was now reduced to a lamentable semi-colony. The Manchu people, who had controlled the Chinese central power since 1644 as conquerors, completely lost face before the Chinese public. Chosen by Empress Dowager Cixi, Puyi became emperor at the age of three after the Guangxu Emperor died. The decadent Qing royal family became more conservative against the backdrop of the overwhelming anti-Manchu mentality. Under the political pressure of the constitutionalists, the Qing court appointed the "Imperial Cabinet" in May 1911. It dismayed constitutionalists as the Cabinet was not answerable to the National Assembly and contained seven Manchu imperial kinsmen with only four Han Chinese among its 13 members, breaking the long-standing policy of appointing equal numbers of both ethnicities. More power was concentrated in the hands of the Manchu minority than at any time since the Qing dynasty's early years. The Chinese public became increasingly convinced that genuine constitutionalism was

---

[37] Hobsbawm (1999b): 70.

[38] "Three Principles of the People" include: a nationalistic revolution to overthrow the Manchu dynasty and the imperial institution, a democratic revolution to establish a republic and popular sovereignty, and a social revolution to equalize land rights and to prevent the ills of capitalism.

impossible under Manchu leadership. Such a flagrant show of discrimination amidst rapid dynastic decline exacerbated opposition from the ruled. Disillusion and disappointment generated mounting anti-Manchu sentiment and swung public feeling toward the revolutionary cause.

At the time, the Qing authorities were under the financial pressure of having to pay back huge debts under the terms of *the Boxer Protocol*. In early May 1911, the Qing government ordered the nationalization of all locally controlled railway projects and signed a loan agreement with the Four Powers Consortium in exchange for a loan of 10 million British pounds. The railway nationalization decree infuriated many businessmen who invested heavily in rail, and they were told that they would be compensated with only a portion of the amount they invested. This alienated many bourgeoisie and gentry and turned them toward revolution. They started the Railway Protection Movement to oppose the Qing government's decree of railway nationalization. The movement, centered in Sichuan province, expressed mass discontent with Qing rule, galvanized anti-Qing groups and contributed to the outbreak of the Xinhai Revolution.

The mobilization of imperial troops from neighboring Hubei province to suppress the Railway Protection Movement created the opportunity for revolutionaries in Wuhan to launch the Wuchang Uprising, which triggered the revolution that overthrew the Qing dynasty and established the Republic of China. After the Wuchang Uprising, the revolutionaries sent messengers to other provinces, calling for concerted actions to topple the Qing dynasty. What was most encouraging for them was the rapid succession of declarations of independence by the provinces and important municipalities. Within a month and a half, fifteen provinces, or two-thirds of all China, seceded from Qing rule. Just like the autumn wind wiping out the withered leaves, the Xinhai Revolution swept the Qing dynasty into the oblivion of history.

In November 1911, representatives of the revolutionaries convened in Wuchang and decided to establish the Republic of China (ROC), with its capital to be in Nanjing. At the time, Sun Yat-sen had no direct involvement in the Wuchang Uprising as he was still in exile. Upon learning of the successful rebellion against the Qing Emperor from press reports, he returned to China from the USA. On December 29, a meeting of representatives from provinces elected Sun Yat-sen as the ROC's provisional president. In the late Qing dynasty, the expulsion of the Manchus was the most powerful slogan of the bourgeois nationalist revolutionary movement. However, the leader of this revolution, Sun Yat-sen, soon realized that overthrowing the Qing dynasty was not a national revolution, but a political revolution. His nationalist ideology, based on the perception of Chinese multi-ethnic history, described the state building target in terms of a republic of "five ethnicities," including Han, Manchu, Mongolian, Hui, and Tibetan. On New Year's Day 1912, as provisional president, he declared that "the base of the country lies in the people, and in uniting the Han, Manchu, Mongolian, Hui, and Tibetan into one state; uniting these people—this is called national unification. The unification of territory means the concerted actions of all the nationalities and provinces, not going astray under the leadership of the center and extending its rule to the four boundaries."[39] Although the republic of "five ethnicities," with regard to China's history and especially the historical unification of China's multi-ethnic state, is very limited, it broke through the narrow perception of the earlier unitary Han state. In fact, Sun Yat-sen realized, "we actually have far more than five ethnicities, and we should meld all the ethnicities into a Chinese nation."

Responding actively to the Xinhai Revolution, the Qing garrisons in Lhasa staged a coup in November 1911, overthrowing the rule of the Qing imperial resident in Tibet. However, the internal strife of the Qing Army ended up with the garrisons struggling against each other, and Tibet fell into a state of anarchy. The situation turned worse as Xikang, one of the neighboring provinces of Tibet, fell into turmoil as well. As a result, the Dalai Lama, who had long been living in exile in India, returned to Lhasa as the sole administrator of the region. During the Xinhai Revolution, the region of Outer Mongolia declared to be independence from the Qing dynasty. The Jebtsundamba Khutughtu, the spiritual leader of the Gelug school of Tibetan Buddhism in Outer Mongolia, was elevated to theocratic ruler of the newly established Mongolian state, called "Bogd Khan," and argued that the contract of Mongolian submission to the Manchu had become invalid after the fall of the Qing dynasty. Thereafter, the Outer Mongols deported the Qing garrisons and the Imperial Commissioner of the Qing throne in Urga. It was, as a matter of fact, a natural product of Tsarist Russia's longtime patronage to the Mongol secessionists to achieve the goal of establishing its own preeminence in Mongolia. Taking advantage of China's internal chaos in the wake of the 1911 revolution, Russia flagrantly instigated the independence of Outer Mongolia by fostering pro-Russian forces among the Mongol nobilities.

Though Sun Yat-sen was recommended as the ROC's provisional president after the Xinhai Revolution, he faced a shortage of military support with which to topple the Qing Empire. At that time, Shikai Yuan, a general of the previous imperial Qing government who made a political alliance with the Empress Dowager Cixi during the Hundred Days' Reform in 1898, reserved the dominance of the military power of China. Yuan arranged for the abdication of the last emperor of the Qing dynasty in return for being granted the position of President of the ROC. In his inaugural speech, Yuan declared: "Mongolia, Tibet and Xinjiang are integral parts of China. All the people inhabited in these regions are Chinese nationals of equal rights." In *Message to the Mongols and Tibetans*, Yuan reiterated his stance of ethnic equality: "this administration solemnly promises to eradicate the former autocracies of the imperial Qing and guarantee the equal rights of all Chinese ethnic groups." Then, the Bureau of Mongolian and Tibetan Affairs was instituted to replace the Qing dynasty's *Lifanyuan* (literally "Board for the Administration of Outlying Regions"), which supervised the Qing dynasty's frontier Inner Asia regions, including Mongolia and Tibet.[40] It demonstrated the strong determination of the Chinese central authorities to safeguard national sovereignty and territorial integrity.

After that, Shikai Yuan telegrammed to Jebtsundamba Khutughtu, urging him to renounce the independence of Outer Mongolia, for "Mongolia is, and must remain,

---

[39] Sun (1982): 2.
[40] Zhou and Zhou (2015): 3–6.

an integral part of China for the newly founded Republic of China is the successor of the Qing Empire." It was, as a matter of course, defied by Outer Mongolia authorities. In addition, the Outer Mongols were tireless in their efforts to attract international recognition of their independence. At that time, Russia had already drafted the *Mongolia–Russia Agreement*, making further unreasonable demands in Outer Mongolia.[41] After making a representation to the Russian government, the ROC government was compelled to negotiate with Russia regarding the political status of Outer Mongolia. Over the same period, the British government instigated the 13th Dalai Lama to discourage the Chinese troops' garrison in Tibet. London reiterated that China had only "suzerainty", rather than sovereignty, over Tibet. The concept of "suzerainty" found its first appearance in the *Anglo-Russian Entente* concluded in 1907.[42]

In this context, the 13th Dalai Lama returned to Lhasa from Darjeeling of India, where he had been living in exile for the past decade, and assumed control of Lhasa authorities. In February 1913, he issued *A Proclamation to All Tibetans,* declaring that China had no sovereignty over Tibet. By denying the historical fact that Tibet is part of China, he attempted to redefine the political ties between Tibet and Chinese central government as a rapport of "almsgiving," similar to the relationship between the Roman Empire and the Holy See. It attached, by its very nature, a religious label for the British colonists' conspiracy to separate Tibet from China.[43] In saying so, the Dalai Lama tried to seek a Western "regulation" for the "legitimacy" of the "issue of Tibet." Therefore, the Dalai Lama's 1913 proclamation was acclaimed by the Tibetan separatists as the "independence declaration of Tibet." However, advertising the proclamation as an "independence declaration" would be a self-renunciation of the so-called rapport of "almsgiving."

As a matter of fact, the following historical facts during the reigns of the Yuan, Ming, and Qing dynasties will suffice to refute this far-fetched comparison of the Tibetan separatists. In the Yuan dynasty (1271–1368), the central government established the Supreme Control Commission of Buddhism (later renamed the Commission for Buddhist and Tibetan Affairs), and set up in Tibet the Chief Military Command under the Pacification Commissioner's Office to directly manage the region's political and military affairs. The Yuan court stationed troops in Tibet and sent officials to Tibet three times to conduct census. The Ming dynasty (1368–1644) generally followed the Yuan administrative system for Tibet. Politically, the Ming court implemented a policy of multiple enfeoffment, conferring the titles "Prince of Dharma" and "Imperial Empowerments Master" upon religious leaders in Tibet. In the Qing dynasty (1644–1911), the Ministry of Tribal Affairs took charge of Tibetan affairs. In 1653 and 1713, the Qing Emperors established the system of lot-drawing from the golden urn to confirm the reincarnated soul boy of a deceased Living Buddha. In 1727, the Qing government started to station grand ministers resident (Amban)

---

[41]Liu (2001): 20–24.

[42]Liang J. *The Britons and the Tibet of China: 1774–1904*, p. 342.

[43]Zhou W. & Zhou Y. *The Comprehensive History of Tibet*: 1912–1949, p. 19.

in Tibet. In 1793, *the 29-Article Imperial Decree for Better Governing in Tibet* was promulgated to enhance the Qing court's administration of Tibet.

After the collapse of the Qing dynasty in 1911, both Tibet and Outer Mongolia declared their independence under theocratic heads of states, but both failed to gain recognition from the newly established Republic of China. In January 1913, the 13th Dalai Lama appointed Agvan Dorjiev, a Russian-born monk of the Gelug school of Tibetan Buddhism, as his emissary to negotiate the conclusion of the *Treaty of Friendship and Alliance between Outer Mongolia and Tibet*. Its major provisions included: the Dalai Lama and Tibet to recognize the independence of Outer Mongolia; the Outer Mongolian government to recognize Tibet as a sovereign state and the Dalai Lama as the religious leader of Tibet. Due to the negative effects of *the Mongolia–Tibet Treaty* on British interests, the Tibetan government refused to sign it for fear of offending the British government. At the same time, the Lhasa authorities headed by the 13th Dalai Lama also denied that Agvan Dorjiev who had been authorized to negotiate political issues of Tibet. In any case, the independence of Tibet and Mongolia continued not to be recognized by the imperialist powers, which acknowledged at least the suzerainty of China over the two regions. Even the Russians and British were more comfortable with formally recognizing China's suzerainty and keeping an ambivalent position toward the political status of Mongolia and Tibet. In addition, there was a concern among the Russians and British that acknowledging the independence of Tibet and Mongolia would allow these areas to come under the influence of other powers. Therefore, the status quo, namely a nominal control over Tibet and Mongolia by China, was in conformity with the maximum interests of the British and Russian governments.

Under domestic pressure to oppose separatism and safeguard national unity, the ROC government headed by Shikai Yuan held intermittent negotiations with Russia, which resulted in the conclusions of *the Russo-Chinese Agreement* in November 1913 and *Treaty of Kyakhta* in June 1915. Accordingly, China recognized Outer Mongolia's autonomy; Russia acknowledged China's suzerainty over Outer Mongolia, which had no right to conclude treaties with foreign countries regarding political and territorial issues. As a consequence, Russia deepened its control over Outer Mongolia with the signing of these treaties.[44] While the ROC government and Tsarist Russia were holding talks regarding the political status of Outer Mongolia, the British government convened a conference at Simla in India to discuss the issue of Tibet in October 1913. The conference was attended by representatives of Britain, the newly founded Republic of China and the Tibetan government. Henry McMahon, foreign secretary of British India and chief negotiator of the British government, proposed the division of "Inner Tibet" and "Outer Tibet": the former, including parts of Qinghai, Gansu, Sichuan, and Yunnan inhabited by Tibetans would be under the jurisdiction of the Chinese government; the latter, referring approximately to the whole of modern-day Tibet, would enjoy a high degree of autonomy. The Tibetan government would

---

[44]Liu X. *The Issue of Outer Mongolia*, pp. 25–30.

appoint all "Outer Tibet" officials, and "Outer Tibet" was not to be represented in the Chinese Parliament or any such assembly. [45]

After the Chinese plenipotentiary withdrew from the convention, the British and Tibetan representatives attached a note denying China any privileges under the agreement and signed it as *the Simla Accord*. A boundary between Tibet and British India, later called the McMahon Line, was drawn on a map referred to in the treaty. The line is regarded by India as the legal national border, but China rejects *the Simla Accord* and the McMahon Line, contending that Tibet is not a sovereign state and therefore does not have the power to conclude treaties.

After Russia's October Revolution in 1917, the newly established Soviet government declared that all privileged rights and interests that Tsarist Russia won from China should be returned to the Chinese people, which provided a favorable environment for Outer Mongolia's independence renunciation. Thereafter, the ROC government controlled by the Beiyang Warlords talked with the ruling elites of Outer Mongolia about the political status of the region. On November 22, 1919, the Beiyang government issued a decree, revoking Outer Mongolia's autonomy. In October 1920, some remnants of the "White Army," a loose confederation of anti-communist forces that fought the Bolsheviks during the Russian Civil War, captured Urga, the capital of Outer Mongolia. Roman von Ungern-Sternberg, an anti-Bolshevik lieutenant general, expelled Chinese troops from Mongolia and restored the monarchic power of the Bogd Khan. At the request of the Outer Mongols, the Soviet Union government sent its Red Army to Outer Mongolia, defeating Ungern's forces. Thereafter, the Mongolian People's Revolutionary Party declared a constitutional monarchy in Outer Mongolia, with the Jebtsundamba Khutuktu, the spiritual head of the Gelug school of Tibetan Buddhism in Mongolia, as the Bogd Khan.[46] In early 1923, the Soviet Union and Outer Mongolia concluded a secret agreement, which legalized the Soviet Army's presence in the region. After the death of Jebtsundamba, the Great Hural (Mongolian's State Congress) abolished the constitutional monarchy and established the Mongolian People's Republic. With the backing of the Soviet Union, Outer Mongolia became a de facto independent country.

2.6 Manchukuo: A Puppet State Under the Control of Japan

With the completion of the Manchurian Railway, the vast region of Manchuria, a widely used term outside China to denote the geographical and historical region of the country's northeast, fell under Russian influence. Russia's ever-increasing influence in Manchuria and Outer Mongolia offended the vested interests of Japan. From 1904 to 1905, the two imperialist powers fought in Manchuria and Korea the Russo-Japanese War. Though Russia was defeated in the armed conflict, it sought

---

[45]Guo Q. *Chronicle of Major Events of Tibet: 1912–1949*, p. 47.

[46]Hao and Du (2007): 91.

to collaborate with Japan for their common colonial interests. The two imperialist powers concluded *the 1907 Russo-Japanese Treaty* for a redistribution of their interests. Japan vowed not to acquire railroad and telegraph concessions in Russian's sphere of influence in northern Manchuria, and Russia made a reciprocal promise regarding the Japanese sphere in southern Manchuria. In addition, Japan recognized the existence of special Russian interests in Outer Mongolia and promised to refrain from any interference that might prejudice those interests.

After the Xinhai Revolution, Empress Dowager Longyu endorsed *the Imperial Edict of the Abdication of the Qing Emperor* on February 12, 1912, under a deal brokered by Prime Minister Shikai Yuan, who concurrently served as commander-in-chief of the powerful Western-style Beiyang Army established by the Qing government in the late nineteenth century, with the imperial court in Beijing and the Republicans in Southern China. Under *the Articles of Favorable Treatment of the Great Qing Emperor after His Abdication,* signed with the ROC government, the last emperor of the Qing dynasty, Puyi, was to retain his imperial title and be treated by the new regime with the protocol attached to a foreign monarch. Puyi and the imperial court were allowed to remain in the northern half of the Forbidden City as well as in the Summer Palace. The abdication ended the Qing dynasty and averted further bloodshed in the revolution. A hefty annual subsidy of four million taels of silver was granted by the republic government to the imperial household, although it was never fully paid and was scrapped after just a few years.

After the last Qing Emperor's abdication, Japan launched the Independence Movement of Manchuria, which had long been the traditional homeland for the Manchu people, by fostering pro-Japan forces among the Manchu nobilities. In the spring of 1917, the confrontation about whether to join the Allies in the First World War and declare war on Germany led to domestic political unrest in the Chinese capital. On the morning of July 1, 1917, General Xun Zhang, who was a Qing dynasty loyalist, took advantage of the unrest and entered Beijing, proclaiming the restoration of Puyi and reviving the Qing monarchy. Zhang ordered his army to keep their queues, pigtails for the Manchu males, to display loyalty to the Qing Emperor. Due to extensive opposition across China, the restoration lasted only 12 days and was quickly reversed by the Republican troops. However, the brief restoration greatly whetted Puyi's appetite for the throne. After the October Revolution, Russia's political and economic influences in China gradually declined, which provided a golden opportunity for the Japanese occupation of the vast territory of Manchuria.

In October 1924, a coup led by Yuxiang Feng, a warlord of the Republic of China, took control of Beijing. The favorable treatments accorded to Puyi, the abdicated Qing Emperor, were unilaterally curtailed. Accordingly, Puyi was expelled from the Forbidden City. After temporarily residing in the Japanese Embassy in Beijing, he moved to the Japanese Concession in Tianjin. During this period, Puyi and his advisers discussed plans to restore the Qing dynasty. On September 18, 1931, the Imperial Japanese Army launched an offensive against the Chinese garrison in Shenyang, with a full invasion that led to the occupation of Manchuria. The entire episode of events is known as the Mukden Incident.

After the Japanese invasion of Manchuria, Japanese militarists moved forward to separate the region from Chinese control. To create an air of legitimacy, Puyi was invited to come with his followers and act as the head of state for Manchukuo (literally "State of Manchuria"). The independence of Manchuria was proclaimed on February 18, 1932. The city of Changchun became the capital of the new entity. The Japanese military commander appointed Puyi as regent for the time being, stating that he would become "Emperor of Manchukuo" but could not reign using the title of "Emperor of the Great Qing Empire" as he once held.

In fact, Puyi was nothing more than a figurehead and the real authority of Manchukuo rested in the hands of the Japanese officials. Therefore, he was constantly at odds with the Japanese in private, though submissive in public, for he resented being "Chief Executive of Manchukuo" and then "Emperor of Manchukuo" rather than being fully restored as the Qing Emperor. The Kwangtung Army leadership placed Japanese vice ministers in the Manchukuo cabinet, while all Chinese advisors gradually resigned or were dismissed. In this manner, Japan formally detached Manchukuo from China during the course of the 1930s. After Japan's occupation of Manchuria in 1931, the League of Nations entrusted the Lytton Commission[47] to evaluate the Mukden Incident. *The Lytton Report* released in October 1932 stated Japan was the aggressor, arguing that the Japanese puppet state of Manchukuo should not be recognized. After that, the fully fledged Japan gave formal notice of its withdrawal from the League of Nations.[48]

Using Manchuria as a base from which to invade other parts of China, the Japanese militarist forces completely dominated the politics, economy, culture, and society of the puppet state. They colonized Manchukuo by implementing the "divide and rule" policy among the peoples of Manchu, Han, Mongol, and Korea. In addition, Tokyo drafted an ambitious plan to relocate five million Japanese citizens to Manchuria within 20 years. Statistics showed that the Japanese immigrants living in Manchukuo totaled 300,000 as of Japan's surrender in 1945.[49]

Japan used Manchukuo as a base for military expansion into China. The establishment of the puppet state actually demonstrated that Japan began to actualize its dream of world empire, the *Tanaka Memorial*, a strategic planning document in which Prime Minister Baron Tanaka Giichi laid out for Emperor Hirohito a strategy to take over the world: "in order to conquer China, the Empire of Japan needs to take over Manchuria and Mongolia." On August 8, 1945, the Soviet Union declared war on Japan, in accordance with the agreement reached at the Yalta Conference, and invaded Manchukuo from Manchuria and Outer Mongolia. Thereafter, Manchukuo's government was abolished after the defeat of Imperial Japan in the Second Sino-Japanese War. The territories formally claimed by the puppet state were first seized

---

[47]It was headed by Victor Bulwer-Lytton, the second Earl of Lytton of Great Britain.

[48]Hsü I. *The Rise of China:1600–2000*, p. 442.

[49]Jiang N. *The History of Manchukuo*, pp. 342–345.

in the Soviet invasion of Manchuria, and then formally transferred to Chinese administration in the following year. For years, academia outside China has been haunted by the viewpoint that "Manchuria and Inner Mongolia are not Chinese territories"; with that, the Chinese people shall remain vigilant at all times to these people's ill-intentioned purpose.

2.7   East Turkistan: The Uyghur Separatist Movement in Xinjiang

The Tarim and Dzungaria regions were known as the "Western Regions" or "Xiyu" in Mandarin Chinese. Because of its strategic location astride the Silk Road, "Xiyu" has been historically significant since at least the third-century BC. Divided into the Dzungarian Basin in the north and the Tarim Basin in the south by the Tianshan Mountains, Xinjiang is home to a variety of ethnic groups, including Han, Kazakh, Tajik, Hui, Uyghur, Kyrgyz, Mongol, and Russian. It is also a region with diverse languages, cultures and religions. During the late Ming and early Qing dynasties, the Dzungar Khanate, an Oirat khanate on the Eurasian Steppe, controlled the region. Galdan Boshugtu Khan of the Dzungar Khanate drove the Khalkhas into the arms of the Qing dynasty and made himself a military threat to the Manchus. The Dzungar-Qing Wars, the series of armed conflicts fought between the Dzungar Khanate and the Qing Empire between 1687 and 1757, ultimately led to the incorporation of the "Western Regions" into the Qing Empire. Since then, it has been commonly referred to as "Xinjiang," meaning "old borderland newly returned."[50]

After the First Opium War in 1840, Russia coerced the Qing government into signing a series of unequal treaties, which legalized Russia's annexation of a large-sized Chinese territory. In 1865, the forces of Yaqub Beg from Kokand Khanate launched an offensive against southern Xinjiang. Six years later, Ili was captured by Russia. Thereafter, the Qing throne appointed Zongtang Zuo to supervise the military affairs of Xinjiang. Zuo successfully suppressed Yakub Beg's rebellion and helped to negotiate an end to Russian occupation of Ili. He was vocal in the debate at the Qing imperial court over what to do with the Xinjiang situation, advocating for Xinjiang to become a province. In 1884, Xinjiang was made a province, which strengthened the Qing government's rule on the northwest frontier. However, the collapse of the Qing Empire and the imperialist powers' fierce competition for the sphere of influence in Central Asia and West Asia posed new threats to Xinjiang.

After the 1911 revolution, Xinjiang acceded in name to the newly established Republic of China. Zengxin Yang, a warlord of Han ethnicity, took control of the province. Yang relied heavily on the Hui people to enforce his rule. Through Machiavellian politics and clever balancing of mixed ethnic constituencies, Yang maintained control over Xinjiang until his assassination in 1928. After Yang, the frontier

---

[50]Xiao (1979).

province was successively dominated by Shuren Jin and Shicai Sheng. During this period, penetrations of Xinjiang by the foreign powers had been intensified.

The 1880s witnessed an upsurge of the Islamic Revival Movement in central, Western, and southern Asia. Reflecting the Islamic peoples' wishes of social progress and revolution against colonial occupation, Pan-Islamism, as the Islamic world's ideological arsenal against the Western powers' aggression, was utilized as ideological weaponry by "East Turkistan" forces to split China.[51] Due to its geographical proximity to Turkey and Central Asia, Xinjiang became a target for the dissemination of Pan-Islamism and Pan-Turkism. The adherents of Pan-Turkism and Pan-Islamism implanted the radical ideology to Uyghur youths under the pretext of funding schools, organizing religious activities, printing, and distributing pamphlets. The annual Islamic pilgrimage to Mecca, the Hajj, attracted a lot of Uyghur Muslims; some of them consciously or subconsciously accepted the radical ideology. At the same time, the British Consulate in Kashgar distributed to the Uyghurs a large number of Pan-Turkism and Pan-Islamism pamphlets, in which the Governor of Mecca called on the Arabs to break away from the rule of the alien race.[52] In the aftermath of the October Revolution and the Civil War of Russia, a great many anti-Bolshevik White Russian refugees, commonly known as the white émigrés, emigrated to Xinjiang. At the same time, the central Asian regions occupied by Tsarist Russia successively joined the Soviet Union by way of "national self-determination" or "independent nation-building."[53] These factors exerted a direct impact on the situation of Xinjiang.

In 1926, the Nationalist Party of China (Kuomingtang or KMT), the ruling party of the Republic of China, founded its first branch in Xinjiang. As the guiding ideology of the KMT, the "Three Principles of the People", a political program developed by Sun Yat-sen as part of a philosophy to make China a free, prosperous, and powerful nation began to be disseminated in Xinjiang. Nominally pledging allegiance to the Nationalist government based in Nanjing, the Xinjiang governor Zengxin Yang maintained a firm control on all important affairs of the province.[54] After Yang was killed in a coup attempt in July 1928, Shuren Jin, a Han warlord born in Gansu, became the new governor. Lacking the resources to oust Jin, the Nationalist government headed by Kai-shek Chiang recognized his succession to the governorship. Jin's half-decade rule of Xinjiang was characterized by frequent strife caused by chaos and corruption. In 1931, the troops led by Zhongying Ma, a Hui Muslim warlord entered Xinjiang under the pretext of "liberating Islam." It triggered a series of Muslim riots due to the awakened religious and national consciousness, as well as the intensified conflicts between the Uyghurs and the Han people. Autocratic, corrupt, and ineffective at managing the province's development, Jin further antagonized the populace by prohibiting participation in the Hajj and bringing in Han officials to replace local

---

[51] Wu and Zhou (2000): 146.
[52] Zhou (2001): 105.
[53] The Nation-state Building History of the Soviet Union (1997).
[54] Zhou H. *Xinjiang Society during the Republic of China*, p. 119.

leaders. As a result, scattered revolts, mobs, and resistance movements mushroomed throughout Xinjiang.

As mentioned earlier, a large number of anti-Bolshevik White Russian refugees emigrated to Xinjiang in the wake of the October Revolution. They were conscripted into the local forces by Shuren Jin to crush the riots. In April 1933, the military commanders of the White Russian troops changed allegiance and engineered a coup, which ended Jin's reign. Shicai Sheng, a Han warlord who was marshaling the provincial forces in eastern Xinjiang, returned to Ürümqi to seize power in the midst of the chaos. Without consulting the central government, the coup leaders appointed Sheng as Military Governor of Xinjiang. At that time, the Nationalist Government of China had inadequate military capacity and resources to attend the unrest of the frontier province. Therefore, Shicai Sheng turned to the Soviet Union for assistance, which provided a good opportunity for Moscow's interference in the affairs of Xinjiang.

Following insurgencies against the brutal rule of Shuren Jin, a rebellion in Kashgar led to the establishment of the short-lived First East Turkistan Republic (First ETR) on November 12, 1933.

The ETR claimed authority over territory stretching from Aksu along the northern rim of the Tarim Basin to Khotan in the south. The rebels released constitution and policy agenda, proclaiming "East Turkistan" was an "independent state" for the Uyghurs. The separatists employed Turkish citizens as military advisors and ran periodicals to advertise their ideologies of independence and holy war.[55] At that time, Shicai Sheng, the newly appointed governor of Xinjiang, had already reached an agreement with the Soviet Union, which vowed to provide military assistance in suppressing the riots in Xinjiang. In January 1934, the White Russian troops of Shicai Sheng, assisted by the Red Army of the Soviet Union, defeated the rebel forces commanded by Zhongying Ma. During their retreat to southern Xinjiang, Ma's remaining troops attacked Kashgar, the base of the East Turkistan Republic. The first ETR was effectively eliminated. By establishing a pro-Soviet regime headed by Shicai Sheng, Moscow regained its control over Xinjiang. Stalin believed the frontier province of China would be an effective buffer region against Japan's military expansion for Tokyo had long been coveting the vast territories of northwest China after annexing Manchuria. As a consequence, the Soviet Union won a battle in its enduring geopolitical competition with Japan.

Under Shicai Sheng's rule, Xinjiang was a part of China in name only. The province was considered a "Soviet Satellite," being under total Soviet control. Admittedly, some policies implemented by Sheng's regime, such as championing ethnic equality and providing assistance with the social undertakings of ethnic minorities, were beneficial to the rapprochement between the Uyghurs and the Han people. In 1934, Sheng's Xinjiang Provincial government promulgated a decree, banning the use of the derogatory "chantou" (literally "rag head") to address the Uyghurs. The pro-Soviet stance of Shicai Sheng also created a favorable environment for the Chinese Communist Party's presence in Xinjiang. The Eighth Route Army established

---

[55]Li (2003).

a liaison office in Urumqi, which symbolized the westward extension of the united front tactic advocated by the Chinese Communists.

Under the patronage of the Soviet Union, Shicai Sheng stabilized the situation of Xinjiang. Though Sheng joined the Soviet Union Communist Party at Stalin's request, he was not happy with Moscow's virtual control. Distrustful and suspicious of everyone else, he was concerned about how to maintain his authoritarian rule. During the Second World War, the Nationalist Government of China headed by Kai-shek Chiang sought to undermine the Soviet presence in Xinjiang and retake the province from Soviet control. Chiang worked with the Hui Muslim warlord of Qinghai to build up the KMT government's military forces around Xinjiang and increase the pressure on Shicai Sheng and the Soviet Union.

Following the German invasion of the Soviet Union in June 1941, and the entry of the USA into Second World War in December 1941, the Soviet Union became a far less attractive patron for Sheng than the Nationalist Government of China. By 1943, Sheng switched his allegiance to the Kuomintang after major Soviet defeats at the hands of the Germans in Second World War. After that, all Soviet military forces and political officers residing in Xinjiang were expelled, and the Kuomingtang's National Revolutionary Army took control of the province. Thus, more than one decade of Sheng's reign over Xinjiang came to an end. After taking over the governance of Xinjiang, the Nationalist government appointed Zhongxin Wu as a governor of the frontier province and garrisoned a large number of troops there. However, the newly appointed governor had increasing trouble maintaining local order due to the long-accumulated anti-Han sentiment among the ethnic minorities.

To re-assert Soviet influence in Xinjiang, Moscow decided to establish a pro-Soviet regime in the region, which became the underlying driving force for the Ili Rebellion, a Soviet-backed revolt against the Kuomintang government.[56] The rebels assaulted Yining on November 7, 1944 and rapidly took over parts of the city, massacring the KMT troops and Han civilians. The Soviet Army assisted the rebels in capturing several towns and airbases. The creation of the "Provisional Government of East Turkestan Republic" was declared on November 12, 1944. The rebels proclaimed that they would "sweep away Han Chinese," threatening to extract a "blood debt" from the Han people. In spite of their proclamation of fighting against the authoritarian rule of the local warlord and the KMT government, the Ili Rebellion and the subsequent establishment of the "East Turkestan Republic" carried on the national secession stance, marking the development of the East Turkistan separatist forces.

---

[56]Shen (2007a).

2.8 The Historical "Legacies" Created by Imperialist Powers' Invasions of China

While competing with the ancient societies of Asia and Africa, the colonial forces equipped with sophisticated weaponry had absolute superiority. In addition to forced assimilation, expulsion, segregation, or even genocide, the imperialists resorted to some other tactics, such as "divide and rule," "repelling one nation with the other," and "driving a wedge between nations," to weaken the resistance of the colonized peoples. By fomenting ethnic, religious or regional clashes, they then offered to be arbitrators of these conflicts. At the same time, the imperialist powers carved up their spheres of influence by partitioning sovereign states, creating enclaves or setting up new states in their colonies or semi-colonies. The geometric contour of the national borders of Africa is the natural result of these strategies. It is no exaggeration to say that the roots for most of the ethno-national issues, religious conflicts, and territorial disputes of the contemporary world should be traced to the colonial era. Therefore, the ethno-national issues in the broad sense, including race, ethnicity, religion, and language, are historical "legacies" created by the imperialist powers. Of course, China also inherited such negative assets.

With a history of more than 5000 years, the Chinese nation created a splendid civilization and made remarkable contributions to mankind. But with the Opium War, China was plunged into the darkness of successive foreign invasions. Throughout the colonial era, the destiny of China, due to its weak composite strength, had been dominated by the "Law of the Jungle." From the British invasion of Tibet in the late nineteenth century to the Japanese invasion of northeast China in the twentieth century, imperialist forces have conducted activities to split China. China's north-east, north, north-west, and south-west border areas have faced the threat of fragmentation by the foreign powers. During the First World War, the Chinese government controlled by the Beiyang Warlords supported the Allies on condition that the Kiautschou Bay concession on the Shandong peninsula, which had belonged to the German Empire prior to its occupation by Japan in 1914, would be returned to China. However, *the Treaty of Versailles* concluded in 1919 officially transferred Shandong to Japan instead of returning its sovereign to China. Toward the end of the Second Sino-Japanese War, the Chinese people were once again unfairly treated by the imperialists. In spite of its great contribution to the anti-fascist war at the cost of large casualties, China was obliged to acknowledge the independence of Outer Mongolia.

In February 1945, the heads of government of the USA, the UK, and the Soviet Union, for the purpose of defeating German and Japanese fascists, convened a secret conference in Yalta. In the clauses regarding their joint combat against Japan, *the Yalta Agreement* provided: "The leaders of the three powers have agreed that 'in two or three months after Germany has surrendered and the war in Europe is terminated', the Soviet Union shall enter into war against Japan on the side of the Allies on condition that: the status quo in Outer Mongolia shall be preserved." It added that: "it is understood that the agreement concerning Outer Mongolia and the ports and railroads referred to above will require the concurrence of Generalissimo Kai-shek Chiang of China." As a political deal made by the three powers without the knowledge of the Chinese government, *the Yalta Agreement* seriously undermined the sovereignty of China. However, the Nationalist government of China had to swallow this bitter pill for it was in a desperate plight of external aggression and domestic unrest.

In late June of 1945, representatives of China and the Soviet Union held talks on *the Sino-Soviet Treaty of Friendship and League* in Moscow, the status of Outer Mongolia being one of the thorny issues. The Yalta Conference provided for the Soviet Union's participation in the Pacific War. One of the Soviet conditions for its participation, put forward at Yalta, was that after the war Outer Mongolia would retain its "status quo." The precise meaning of this "status quo" became a bone of contention at the Sino-Soviet talks. Stalin insisted on China's recognition of Outer Mongolia's independence, something that it already enjoyed de facto even as it remained a part of China de jure. Kai-shek Chiang at first resisted the idea but eventually gave in. China was forced to acknowledge the independence of Outer Mongolia after the Soviet Union's entering into war against Japan on the side of the Allies. In return, Moscow made several commitments, such as safeguarding the sovereignty and territorial integrity of China, no assistance to the forces of the Chinese Communists, and non-interference in the affairs of Xinjiang.[57] Thus, the Sino-Soviet Treaty guaranteed Outer Mongolia's independence. In a declaration made in connection with the treaty, China acknowledged the independence of Outer Mongolia within its previous borders, provided that a referendum on the issue be held and that the Soviet Union ceased aiding the Chinese Communists. On October 20, 1945, a referendum was held in Outer Mongolia. China sent a delegation to "observe" the referendum.[58] On January 5, 1946, the Nationalist government of China officially recognized the Mongolia People's Republic.[59]

The *Sino-Soviet Treaty* granted the Soviet Union a range of concessions that the USA promised at the Yalta Conference. This ended overt Soviet support for the East Turkistan separatist forces, which created a favorable international climate for the peaceful solution to the "Second East Turkestan Republic" (SETR), a Soviet-backed revolt against the Government of the Republic of China (ROC) in 1944 in the three northern districts of Xinjiang: Ili, Tarbaghatai, and Altai. Through Moscow's mediation, the ROC government reached an agreement with the leaders of the SETR in June 1946. The three districts were incorporated into the newly founded Xinjiang coalition government.[60] However, the hangover effect of the two separatist regimes, including the First East Turkestan Republic founded in 1933 with its base in Kashgar and the Second East Turkestan Republic established in northern Xinjiang in 1944, continued to influence modern Uyghur nationalist support for the creation of an independent East Turkistan in Xinjiang.

---

[57] Shen (2007b).

[58] Li (1986).

[59] Liu X. *The Issue of Outer Mongolia*, p. 85.

[60] Li S. *Xinjiang: History and Current Situation*, p. 206.

In August 1945, following the unconditional surrender of Japan at the end of Second World War, the Allied Forces handed the territorial sovereignty and administrative control of Taiwan to the Republic of China, thus ending 50 years of Japanese colonial rule. On the eve of the ROC government's taking control of Taiwan, Japanese militarists and some Taiwanese gentry conspired to launch the "independence movement of Taiwan."[61] Although this incident was aborted, support for "Taiwan's independence" appeared on the island. The flashpoint came on February 27, 1947, in Taipei, when a dispute between a cigarette vendor and an officer of the Office of Monopoly triggered civil disorder and an open rebellion that lasted for days. The uprising was violently put down by the military of the KMT government the following day. As one of the most important events in Taiwan's modern history, this anti-government uprising was commonly referred to as the "February 28 Incident." It became a critical impetus for the independence movement of Taiwan. Prior to that, some Taiwanese had petitioned the US Congress, demanding that "Taiwan should not be incorporated into China." After the "February 28 Incident," various political organizations seeking Taiwan's independence were successively founded. On February 28, 1948, the "Alliance for Taiwan's Re-liberation" was established in Hong Kong. After relocating the headquarters to Japan in 1950, the organization renamed itself the "Taiwan Democratic Independence Party."[62] With the formation of the "Taiwan Independence Alliance" around the 1970s, the USA became the new base for the independence campaign of the island.[63] Therefore, the ferment and development of Taiwan's independence movement have long been connected with the instigation and backing of the imperialist powers.

The Soviet Union was the first socialist country to put Marxism–Leninism into practice. However, the post-Lenin Soviet Union, during its competition with imperialist powers and practice of "exporting proletarian revolution," failed to overcome the hegemonic mentality characteristic of Tsarist Russia. To some extent, the domestic and foreign policies of the Soviet Union during Stalin's reign, because of a high degree of centralization and personality cult, fell back onto the old path of Tsarist Russia. It led to Moscow's hegemony acts while handling its domestic ethno-national issues and international affairs. For the purposes of engineering potential trouble for the Nationalist government of China headed by Kai-shek Chiang, and taking revenge on the Xinjiang governor Shicai Sheng's betrayal, Stalin at one time overtly supported the "Second Eastern Turkistan Republic." In Stalin's mind, China at that time was in the sphere of influence of the USA. He did not believe the Communist Party of China, whose forces were compelled to retreat to Yan'an, an isolated mountainous town in northern Shaanxi, could become the ultimate winner of the Chinese Revolution. Therefore, Moscow insisted that the Chinese Communists should fight for their future by parliamentary politics instead of launching armed rebellions after the Second Sino-Japanese War.[64] Stalin did not expect that the Soviet-backed "Second

---

[61] Chen (1998).

[62] Sun (2007).

[63] Chen (1998).

[64] Shen Z. *The History of Sino-Soviet Relations*, p. 80.

East Turkestan Republic," like the historical legacies created by imperialist powers' invasion of China, would become one of the major problems that the Chinese Communists would face after the founding of the People's Republic of China in 1949.

For a unified multi-ethnic country like China, the national division is tantamount to the dividing of the Chinese nation. Therefore, the independence campaigns of Taiwan, Tibet, or Xinjiang are of the same nature, namely splitting China and dividing the Chinese nation. In other words, separatist forces in China are not confined to ethnic minorities, for the main body of the separatist elements advocating "Taiwan independence" is made up of the Han people. In this sense, advocates of the independence of any Chinese territory, be it Taiwan, Tibet, or Xinjiang, shall be defined as separatists. Formed in the century of foreign powers' aggression of China between 1840 and 1949, these separatist forces are closely related to the patronage of imperialists and power politics. For a solution to the ethno-national issues of China and realization of the rejuvenation of the Chinese nation, China must eradicate these historical "legacies" left behind by imperialist powers. Chinese President Xi Jinping declared: "We stand firm in safeguarding China's sovereignty and territorial integrity, and will never allow the historical tragedy of national division to repeat itself. Any separatist activity is certain to meet with the resolute opposition of the Chinese people. We will never allow anyone, any organization, or any political party, at any time or in any form, to separate any part of Chinese territory from China."

References

Candler, E. (1989a). *The unveiling of Lhasa*. Lhasa: Tibet People's Press.
Candler, E. (1989b). *The unveiling of Lhasa*. In Yin J. & Su P. (Eds.), Trans. Lhasa: Tibet People's Press.
Chen, J. (1998). *History of Taiwan independence movement*. Taipei: Qianwei Press.
Desideri, I. (2004). *An account of Tibet: The travels of Ippolito Desideri of Pistoia*. Lhasa: Tibet People's Press.
Feng, T. (2001). *Japanese Samurai's Observations of China in 1862*. Beijing: The Commercial Press.
Hao, S., & Chen, J. (2012). *The ethno-national issues of Taiwan: from "Barbarians" to "Aborigines"*. Beijing: Social Science Academic Press.
Hao, S., & Du, S. (2007). *The history of outer Mongolia*. Beijing: Social Science Academic Press.
Hobsbawm, E. (1999a). *The age of empire: 1875–1914*. Nanjing: Jiangsu People's Press.
Hobsbawm, E. (1999b). *The age of revolution: Europe 1789–1848*. Nanjing: Jiangsu People's Press.
Hu, S. (1981). *From the opium war to the may fourth movement*. Beijing: People's Press.
Huc, E. R. (1991). *Travels in Tartary, Tibet, and China during the Years 1844-5-6* (pp. 509–510). Beijing: China Tibetology Press.
Li, A. (1986). *Research on Kai-shek Chiang* (Vol. 2, p. 133). Taipei: Taiwan Tianyuan Book Company.
Li, S. (2003). *Xinjiang: History and current situation*. Urumqi: Xinjiang People's Press.
Liang, J. (2012). *The British empire and Tibet (1774–1904)* (pp. 38–40). Lanzhou: Lanzhou University Press.
Liu, X. (2001). *The issue of outer Mongolia* (pp. 20–24). Taipei: Nantian Book Company.

Shen, Z. (2007a). *A brief history of sino-soviet history*. Beijing: Xinhua Press.

Shen, Z. (2007b). *A brief history of sino-soviet relations*. Beijing: Xinhua Press.

Shen, Z., & Liu, S. (2014). *Tibet and Tibetans*. Beijing: China Tibetology Press.

Stavrianos, L. (1992). *A global history: The world after 1500*. Shanghai: Press of Shanghai Social Sciences Academy.

Sun, Y. (1982). *The collected works of Yat-sen Sun* (Vol. 2, p. 2). Beijing: Zhonghua Book Company.

Sun, Y. (2007). *Theories and Ideologies for "Taiwan Independence"*. Beijing: Jiuzhou Press.

Sun, Z. (2003). *Map scaling and territory formation during the reigns of Kangxi, Yongzheng and Qianlong* (pp. 37–44). Beijing: Press of Renmin University of China.

Taylor, M. (1995). *Discovering Tibet*. Beijing: China Tibetology Press.

The Nation-state Building History of the Soviet Union. (1997). (Vol. 1, pp. 318–320). Beijing: The Commercial Press

Turner, S. (2004). *Tashilhunpo monastery of Tibet*. Lhasa: Tibet People's Press.

Wang, X. (2000). *Modern history of sino-japanese cultural exchange*. Beijing: Zhonghua Book Company.

Wright, M. C. (2002). *The last stand of Chinese conservatism: The Tongzhi restoration 1862–1874*. Beijing: China Social Sciences Press.

Wu, Y., & Zhou, X. (2000). *Modern Islamic thoughts and movement*. Beijing: Social Science Academic Press.

Xiao, Z. (1979). The several "Xinjiangs" in the Qing dynasty. *Chinese Journal of History* (8).

Yoda, Y. (2004). *The foundations of Japan's modernization: A comparison with China's path towards modernization*. Shanghai: Shanghai Far East Publishing House.

Zhou, H. (2001). *Xinjiang society during the republic of China*. Urumqi: Xinjiang University Press.

Zhou, W., & Zhou, Y. (2015). *History of Tibet* (Vol. 1, pp. 3–6). Beijing: China Tibetology Press.

Zou, Z. (2000). *Western geography in the late qing dynasty: A case study of the dissemination of western geography between 1815–1911*. Shanghai: Shanghai Press for Ancient Books.

Chapter 3
The Chinese Nation: A Pluralistic Integration

In the early twentieth century, the Chinese concept of *zhonghua minzu* (Chinese nation) began frequently to appear in the media of China. It has become a key political term that is entwined with the modern Chinese history of nation-building. Although both *zhonghua* (Chinese) and *minzu* (nation) are inherent terms in ancient China, the combination of the two is an important symbol for the country's emergence as a modern nation state. The series of juxtaposed concepts in Chinese, including *huaxia* (the Han people) and *siyi* ("four Barbarians"), the North China Plain and frontier regions, *huanei* (domestic areas), and *huawai* (foreign areas), as well as the paired concepts appeared in the early days of the Republic of China (1912–1949), such as "China Proper" and "foreign regions," "Chinese nation" and "ethnic minorities," all had important impacts on the construction of a modern nation state. How, then, can the western concept of "one nation, one state" be realized in time-honored China? How can the unified multi-ethnic state structure, which has been established and maintained since the dynasties of Qin (221–207 BC) and Han (202 BC–220 AD), can be evolved into a modern nation state? These questions are closely related to the interpretation and definition of "Chinese nation," which gives modern significance to the ancient state-governance philosophy of China.

3.1 "The Five Ethnicities" Entering the Modern Era

As are the most ancient written languages, Chinese characters constitute the oldest continuously used system of writing in the world. Yirong Wang (1845–1900), a scholar-official of the Qing Imperial Academy, was the first to recognize the symbols inscribed on animal bones or turtle plastrons used in the late 2nd millennium BC. Commonly known as Oracle bone script, and these symbols were the earliest form of Chinese writing. Some other ancient scripts of the world, such as the cuneiform text of the Sumerians and the hieroglyphs of the Egyptians and the Indians, have already been buried in the dust of history. It was not until modern times that these ancient writing systems were decoded by paleographers. However, the current languages

© China Social Sciences Press 2020

S. Hao, *China's Solution to Its Ethno-national Issues*, China Insights,
https://doi.org/10.1007/978-981-32-9519-3_3

of Iraq, Egypt, and India have no inherited ties with these ancient scripts. Widely established as an important symbol of the enduring Chinese civilization, Oracle bone script has experienced an uninterrupted development of three millennia. Chinese culture, the sum of the cultures of all the ethnic groups of China, is recorded in the heritage system of Chinese characters.

In Oracle bone script, the ideographic structure of the Chinese character 族 (zu), meaning "nation," is composed of a flag and an arrow, symbolizing a military unit in the early clan society. The forms of social organizations of human groups have experienced an evolution from primitive groups, families, and clans to tribes. The most notable features of these human organizations are kinship ties and common cultural characteristics, among which language is the most prominent. At the same time, we can discover a tendency of population growth and territorial expansion in the progression of the above-mentioned human organization forms. A pyramid-style concentration process for power and social status can be discovered in their hierarchical system, ranking from patriarch, tribal chief, and king to emperor. The basis for such power centralization and elevated social status is their possession and distribution of wealth, which brought about class differentiation. In the formation process of tribe and state due to common geographical ties, the militia of the clan society became the standing armed forces of the ruling classes. While losing its referential meaning of "military unit," the Chinese ideograph *zu* highlighted the significance of classifying things and human groups, forming the earliest specification for taxonomy. "Nation" in English can be approximately translated as *minzu* in Chinese, which is defined as a collective of people with common attributes, such as blood tie, family name, language, customs, social attribution, and residential area. It is a cultural-political community that has become conscious of its autonomy, unity, and particular interests.

These human groups with different characteristics embrace not only "self-identity" but also "otherness identity," which contributes to the dichotomy between "my nation" and "the other nation." This concept is bound to occur in the course of human society, in particular, during the contact among different human groups. Of course, the scope of "my nation" is also specified while defining "the other nation." As a result, the recognition of "my nation" and "the other nations" has always been a two-way course. A human society with a writing system can record the ideas expressed in this "naming process," which can be passed down to the future generations. However, human groups without a writing system can only resort to oral transmission, which is highly likely to result in the loss of information. Therefore, when Christopher Columbus discovered the "New World" and was faced with the natives of the American Caribbean islands, he recorded the grotesque physical appearances of these islanders and labeled them as "eccentrics." However, the Caribbean islanders' "oddball" cognizance of these Spanish explorers was not known to the outside world due to their absence of a script.

In the history of the Chinese ancients' interactions and engagements, the employment of the term *minzu* (the equivalent of "nation" in English) had not been as prevalent as that of "clan," "tribe" or "race." Therefore, we can retrieve no entry of *minzu* in the established Chinese dictionaries, including the first comprehensive thesaurus of Chinese characters, *Shuowen Jiezi* (literally "explaining graphs and analyzing characters") compiled by Shen Xu in the Eastern Han dynasty (25–189), and *the Kangxi Dictionary* finished during the reign of the Kangxi Emperor of the Qing dynasty. Rixiu Pi, a poet in the Tang dynasty (618–907), wrote in a verse, "the *Nanman* people have lived in Guangdong from time immemorial."[1] Here, the *nanman*, or "Southern Barbarians," was a historical pejorative term given by the Han people to the indigenous inhabitants living in Southern China. The four directional appellations for the various human groups bordering the Han people, including *dongyi, xirong, nanman* and *beidi* (eastern, western, southern, and northern Barbarians, respectively), and , were collectively referred to in the Chinese classics as *siyi* (Four Barbarians), a general designation for the barbarian tribes in ancient China. Their respective social organizations were at divergent development stages, ranging from blood-tied clan or tribe and geographic-based tribe alliance to tight-knit state coalition or nomadic empire. The state capacity of the nomadic empire may have become powerful enough to challenge the Chinese central dynasty based in North China Plain. In this case, the self-appellations of the nomadic empires, such as the Hun, Xianbei, Turkic, Tubo, Huihe, Khitan, Jurchen, Mongol, and Manchu peoples, naturally found their way into the official historical records of China.

Minzu in ancient Chinese text obviously transcends the above-mentioned limitations of value judgment, demonstrating its universal sense as a cultural-political community. In other words, the idea of *minzu* consists of not only the Han people but also the ethnic minorities. In comparison with the traditional Western knowledge system, the connotation of *minzu* in Chinese is similar to the referents of "ethnos" in Greek and "nasci" in Latin, namely, a collective of people with common characteristics attributed to them, such as language, traditions, places of birth, folkways, and customs.

The term *minzu* found its initial occurrence in 1837 in *the Eastern Western Monthly Magazine*, the inaugural Modern-Age Chinese language magazine first published in 1833 in Canton (today's Guangzhou) by the Prussian protestant missionary Karl Gützlaff at a time when foreign missionaries risked strangulation or deportation.[2] The Israelites in the Bible were described by Gützlaff as "Israeli nation," which referred to a historical Israeli nation, rather than the modern Israeli people who emerged with the Zionism Movement decades later. The King James Bible, an English translation of the Christian Bible for the Church of England, has widely adopted the term "nation," whose initial meaning, "a collective of foreigners sharing the same place of origin," is similar to that of "people," symbolizing the formation of the idea of "a sovereign people."[3] The ideas of "nation" and its subsequent formation of "nationalism" were diffused from the British Isles to France, Germany, and Russia, and then to North America, creating a nation state era in Europe and North America.

Against the backdrop of "eastward transmission of western sciences" after the First Opium War in 1840, Chinese intellectuals began to understand the significance

---

[1]Pi R. *The Collected Works of Rixiu Pi*. Volume I.
[2]Collected Articles of Eastern Western Monthly Magazine (1997): 271.
[3]Greenfeld (2010): 2–8.

of modern nation and state. With regard to this, the result of Japan's cultural integration between the East and the West provides a shortcut. The term 民族 (*minzu* in
Romanized Pinyin) frequently found occurrence in Japan after the Meiji Restoration.
Yoichi Komori, a famous critic of Japanese modern literature, pointed out: "a large
number of disyllabic Chinese phrases have been created since the Meiji Restoration."[4] This argument was, however, inconsistent with reality. Rather than a coinage
by the Japanese, *minzu* is an inherent concept in ancient Chinese. It was vested with
modern significance and new interpretations during the Meiji Restoration. The relatively singular national structure of Japan prompted the Japanese elites to accept the
Germanic concept of "nation"; that is, the Yamato people are composed of "people
of the same race." It had a direct impact on the Chinese intellectuals who travelled to
Japan to learn the way of nation-building after the aborted "Hundred Days' Reform"
in the late Qing dynasty. The Chinese term 民族 was endowed with meaning corresponding to the western concept of state and nation, and influenced China's path in
exploring the modern nation-state. The modern meaning of the concept of nation and
the theoretical discourse of nationalism spread to China. The extensive application of
民族 was directly correlated with China's historical process of establishing a modern
nation-state.

The word "nation" in the West can be traced to "natio" in Latin, meaning "birth"
or "origin." In ancient Rome, "natio" referred to foreign nationals whose social status
was lower than that of Roman citizens. During the Middle Ages, "nation" referred
to a student association in the several universities shared by the Christian world.
For example, "L'honorable nation de France" was composed of all the students
from France, Italy, and Spain, with the meaning of "a unified community." In the
late thirteenth century, the term "nation", with its connotation of "a community
of opinions", referred to the "representatives of the secular and religious rulers,"
namely, "seigneurs" and "bishops" in the writings of Montesquieu. In the sixteenth
century, "nation" was adopted to refer to all the inhabitants of England, with the
implication of the people.[5] After it was introduced to France, the idea of "nation"
represented by the "Third Estate," including peasants and bourgeoisie, replaced the
King of France as "the source of identity and focus of social solidarity." Therefore,
the term "nation" in English was vested with the implication of a cultural-political
community that has become conscious of its autonomy, unity, and particular interests.
With the expansion of Western colonization, this concept was propagated throughout
the world with extreme rapidity.

The message contained in the Chinese term *minzu* has not experienced such a
complicated evolution. However, China was on the eve of a revolution toward a
modern state when Qichao Liang (1873–1929), a Chinese philosopher and reformist
who inspired Chinese scholars with his writings and reform movements, put forward
the term "Chinese nation" in 1902. As the most populous country with a diversity of
ethnic groups, China abounds with appellations for these peoples. This phenomenon
is also very common in the historical literature of the Western world. Against the

---

[4]Yōichi (2003): 106.

[5]Greenfeld L. *Nationalism: Five Roads to Modernity*, pp. 2–5.

backdrop of the global colonial expansion, one of the most important factors in the formation of modern nations in Western Europe is the highlighted boundary between "self-nation" and "other-nation" in the process of establishing modern nation-states in these countries. Dominated by the "law of the jungle," the strong "self-nation" consciousness enhanced the identity of the colonists as rulers; at the same time, it minimized the significance of the diverse structure of nationals within the territories of the imperialist powers at a certain historical stage. In this respect, the Britain can be defined as one of the most typical examples. Acclaimed as a global empire on which "the sun never sets," the outstanding renown of the British Empire in its prime time concealed the wide multi-ethnic identity divergences among its subjects.

Taking advantage of the multi-ethnic national structure of China, the imperialist powers employed the time-tested "divide and rule" strategy to dissolve its political tradition. Therefore, integrating the diverse historical ethnic groups into a modern "Chinese nation" became a top priority in transforming China from a feudal dynasty to a modern sovereign. The establishment of the modern nation concept is a complex process in the context of China's thousands of years of interaction among the "five ethnicities." China first faced the question of how to define China and the Chinese nation-state. How could the western "one nation, one state" theory explain the continued interaction of "five ethnicities" in the history of China? Could the concept of "Chinese nation" become the "identity source" for state unity, territorial unification, and ethnicity integration? The Chinese society needed to address these problems from the ideological perspective.

3.2 "A Republic of Five Ethnicities": The Building of a Nation-State After the Xinhai Revolution

With the Opium War of 1840, China was plunged into the darkness of domestic turmoil and foreign aggression; its people, ravaged by war, saw their homeland torn apart and lived in poverty and despair. In the years when China suffered aggression from imperialist powers, some influential Chinese people expressed bitter hatred toward the timid Qing government, which ceded territory and paid indemnities and committed other humiliating acts. Through political reform they sought to make the nation stronger, overthrowing the political orientation of Qing rule; Evolutionary theories of struggle for survival by the law of natural selection, and survival of the fittest formed the basis of a renewal of the Han ethnic group traditions and eliminated the Manchu ethnic minority rule. The nationalist movement led to the expulsion of the Manchus as the representative ideology. In the late Qing dynasty, expulsion of the Manchus was the most powerful slogan of the bourgeois nationalist revolutionary movement.

Under the influence of Western society's evolutionism, the banner of "ousting the Manchu barbarians" was held high among Han intellectuals. Therefore, the anti-Machu mentality, as the core concept of Sun Yat-sen's nationalism, was influential among the radical revolutionaries at that time. In addition, the anti-Manchu mentality was accepted by Han elites as the key to the survival of the Han people in the first decade of the twentieth century. Thus, "to oust the Manchus from power and rejuvenate the Han people" was popularized as a catchphrase by the Chinese media at that time.[6] Influenced by the traditional Sino-centrism and the reality of being ruled by the Manchu "barbarians," a diversity of race-nationalism ideologies began to take shape among Han intellectuals. For example, by infusing kinship terms into racial rhetoric, some concluded that the Han people were actually a large family and that the Yellow Emperor, one of the legendary Chinese sovereigns and cultural heroes included among the mytho-historical Three Sovereigns and Five Emperors was the great ancestor; others maintained that the uncivilized Manchu ethnic group was a culturally inferior race in comparison with the time-honored Han people, who resided in "an area of illustrious prosperity and culture"; others even traced the origin of the early Chinese civilization to the Western countries. These theories inspired the revolutionaries to topple the weak and incompetent Qing dynasty and establish a Western-style nation-state in China.

As the first proponent of the "Chinese nation," Qichao Liang, a philosopher and reformist who lived during the late Qing dynasty and the early Republic of China, was a keen advocate of the modern nationalist movement in China. He believed that the Han people's anti-Manchu nationalism was actually a restrictive view of the ethnic nation-state, or "minor nationalism." It would result in the loss of large parts of imperial territory for the collapse of the Qing dynasty inevitably led to controversy about the status of territories in Tibet and Mongolia.[7] The national crisis of China could only be desisted by integrating all the Chinese ethnic groups into the Chinese nation, Liang asserted. Liang's proposition of forming the "Chinese nation," consisting of the various ethnic groups of China, exerted a direct effect on Sun Yat-sen's nationalist ideology.

In the late Qing dynasty, expulsion of the Manchus was the most powerful slogan of the bourgeois nationalist revolutionary movement. However, the leader of this revolution, Sun Yat-sen, soon realized that overthrowing the Qing dynasty was not a national revolution, but a political revolution. His "Three People's Principles"—nationalism, democracy, and the "people's livelihood"—were changed in the struggle to overthrow the Qing dynasty. His nationalist ideology, based on the perception of Chinese multi-ethnic history, described the state building target in terms of a "republic of five ethnicities"—Han, Manchu, Mongolian, Hui, and Tibetan. On New Year's Day 1912, as provisional president, he declared that "the base of the country lies in the people, and in uniting the Han, Manchu, Mongolian, Hui, and Tibetan into one state; uniting these people—this is called national unification."[8] Although the republic of five ethnicities, with regard to China's history and especially the historical unification of China's multi-ethnic state, is very limited, it broke through the narrow perception of the earlier unitary Han state. It made a political declaration on the

[6]Feng (1999): 99.
[7]Liang (1989): 76.
[8]Sun (1982): 2.

ethnic unity of the infant republic. However, the "ethnic unity" within a "republic of five ethnicities" failed to provide an answer to the concrete constituents of the "Chinese nation".

Following the Xinhai Revolution and the founding of the ROC government, the southern provinces subsequently declared their independence from the Qing dynasty, but the Beiyang Army controlled by the powerful warlord Shikai Yuan refused to take a clear stance for or against the rebellion. Both the Qing court and Yuan were fully aware that the Beiyang Army, which functioned as the centerpiece in the Qing Empire's military system, was the only imperial Qing force powerful enough to quell the rebel. After repeated pleas by the Qing throne, Yuan agreed and eventually left his hometown for Beijing, becoming Prime Minister of the Qing Cabinet. Meanwhile, in the Battle of Yangxia, Yuan's forces recaptured Hankou and Hanyang from the revolutionaries. Yuan knew that complete suppression of the revolution would end his usefulness to the Qing regime. Instead of attacking Wuchang, the base of the rebels, he began to negotiate with the revolutionaries. At that time, the revolutionaries elected Sun Yat-sen as Provisional President of the newly-established Republic of China. However, Sun Yat-sen was in a weak position militarily, so he negotiated with the Qing government, using Shikai Yuan as an intermediary. Yuan arranged for the abdication of the last Qing emperor in return for being granted the position of ROC President.

On February 12, 1912, after being persuaded and pressured by Shikai Yuan and other ministers, Empress Dowager Longyu accepted the terms for the Imperial family's abdication, issuing an imperial edict announcing the abdication of the Xuantong Emperor. The edict read: "It is now evident that the hearts of the majority of the people are in favor of a republican form of government: the provinces of the South were the first to espouse the cause, and the generals of the North have since pledged their support. From the preference of the people's hearts, the Will of Heaven can be discerned. How could we then bear to oppose the will of the millions for the glory of one family! Therefore, observing the tendencies of the age on the one hand and studying the opinions of the people on the other, we and His Majesty the Emperor hereby vest the sovereignty in the people and decide in favor of a republican form of constitutional government. Thus, we would gratify on the one hand the desires of the whole nation who, tired of anarchy, are desirous of peace, and on the other hand would follow in the footsteps of the Ancient Sages, who regarded the Throne as the sacred trust of the Nation."[9]

Thus, the 267-year Qing rule of China came to an end and with it ended a 2000-year-old system of imperial governance in the country. After Shikai Yuan delivered a speech in favor of the republic system, Sun Yat-sen resigned his post of ROC Provisional President, which indicated the end of the short-lived ROC Nanjing Government. *The ROC Constitution* issued in March 1912 reiterated that "The territory of the Republic of China will comply with all the territory of the former Empire, including Inner and Outer Mongolia, Tibet, Qinghai and Xinjiang," and "The nationals of the Republic of China will be equal before the law regardless of their races, classes

---

[9]Yang (2014).

or religions." Facing the imminent independence of Outer Mongolia from China, Shikai Yuan stated: "Outer Mongolia is part of *zhonghua minzu* (Chinese nation) and has been of one family for centuries." Though the proposition of building "a republic of five ethnicities" failed to reflect the history and reality of China's multi-ethnic structure of nationals, it redefined the territorial scope and national structure of the country. Therefore, it transcended the demerits of building an ethnic nation-state exclusively for the Han people, which would have covered only the 18 provinces in China Proper.

3.3   A Melting Pot of All the Chinese Ethnic Groups: Sun Yat-Sen's Proposition of "State-Nation"

The "one out of many" or "melting pot" structure of the US nationals has always been Sun Yat-sen's ideal nation-building model. To prevent civil war and possible foreign intervention from undermining the fledgling Republic of China, he agreed to Shikai Yuan's demand for China to be united under a Beijing government. On March 10, 1912, Yuan was sworn in as the ROC President. In August, Sun Yat-sen founded the Nationalist Party of China (Kuomintang or KMT for short). Yuan's use of violence dashed the Kuomintang's hope of achieving reforms and political goals through electoral means. Devoid of a strong and unified government, China was thrust into a period of warlordism. At that time, Yuan's power "was not much different from the emperor of Imperial China."[10] Nonetheless, Yuan claimed the "Mandate of Heaven" to assume the role of emperor for he had long coveted the absolute power of a governing emperor. "As Napoleon III did in France, Yuan was fully prepared to betray the republic system by 1915."[11] At the same time, many of Yuan's supporters advocated a revival of the monarchy and asked Yuan to ascend the throne. The imperialist powers also asserted that "despotism should be continued in China" for the Chinese people were not mature enough for a democratic form of government.[12] In November 1915, Yuan held a specially convened "Constituent Assembly", which voted unanimously to offer Yuan the throne. On December 12, he "accepted" the invitation and proclaimed himself Emperor of the Chinese Empire under the era name of "Hongxian" (literally "constitutional abundance").

Yuan had expected widespread domestic and international support for his reign. However, he and his supporters had badly miscalculated. Many of the emperor's closest supporters abandoned him, and the solidarity of his Beiyang clique dissolved. There were open protests throughout the country denouncing Yuan. The foreign powers, including Japan, proved suddenly indifferent or openly hostile to him, not giving him the recognition anticipated. Sun Yat-sen, who had fled to Tokyo and set up a base there, actively organized efforts to overthrow the Hongxian Emperor. Faced

---

[10]Zhang Y. *The Building of a New Nation: 1911–1917*, p. 158.

[11]Immanuel C. Y. Hsü. *The Rise of Modern China*: 1600–2000, p. 382.

[12]Fairbank J. K. *The Great Chinese Revolution: 1800–1985*, 2. p. 10.

with widespread opposition, Yuan repeatedly delayed the accession rite in order to appease his foes, but his prestige was irreparably damaged and one province after another continued to voice disapproval. On December 25, the military leaders of Yunnan declared their independence and launched expeditions against the Hongxian Emperor. Yuan's army experienced several defeats which led other provinces in the South to declare independence as well. The armed conflict was historically termed the National Protection War, also known as Anti-Monarchy War. Eventually, under immense pressure from the entire nation, Yuan was forced to abdicate on March 22. This was not enough for his enemies, who called for his resignation as President of the Republic of China. More provinces rebelled until Yuan died in June 1916. In the following 12 years, China was left without any generally recognized central authority, and the nation's army quickly fragmented into forces of competing warlords.

During this period, Sun Yat-sen released "Three Principles of the People", a political philosophy to make China a free, prosperous, and powerful nation, including nationalism, democracy, and the livelihood of the people.[13] Sun Yat-sen's nationalism can be traced to the anti-Manchu mentality advocated during the Xinhai Revolution. The toppling of the Qing dynasty, in spite of its accomplishment of "ousting the Manchu rulers," failed to realized Sun Yat-sen's dream of "national, territorial, and administrational unity." When serving as the ROC Provisional President, he advanced the proposition of "a republic of five ethnicities", which was apparently a large step forward in comparison with the anti-Manchu mentality. Therefore, the idea of "a republic of five ethnicities" was widely established as a commendable nation-building ideology by future generations. However, Sun Yat-sen later abandoned this proposition for its non-compliance with the nationalism principle of "one nation, one state" and its contradiction with his ideal of preserving the territorial integrity of China. In a speech titled *specific solutions to the Three Principles of the People* in 1921, Sun Yat-sen declared: "The Chinese nation still fails to stand independently among the nations of the world although the Qing dynasty was overthrown. What's the reason for that? I am convinced that it should be ascribed to our strayed ethnic policy. After the success of the Xinhai Revolution and restoration of the central power to the Han people, some hereditary bureaucrats, obstinate reformists, feudal monarchy restoration forces improvised the so-called 'five races under one union', which found its expression in the colored stripes of the Five-Colored Flag during the Wuchang Uprising. However, its demerits of "warlord despotism" inherited from the Qing dynasty led to the disintegration of Chinese territory."[14] Sun Yat-sen added: "Some people insist we will have no further need of nationalism after the overthrow of the Qing dynasty. This statement is absolutely mistaken. At present we speak of unifying the 'five races' (Han, Manchu, Mongol, Hui, and Tibetan) under one union, yet surely China has far more than five races. My stand is that we should unite all the ethnic groups of China into one Chinese nation and develop that nation into an advanced, civilized nation; only then will nationalism be finished".[15]

---

[13]Sun (2000): 1.

[14]Ibid.

[15]Sun (1985a): 394.

However, we should keep in mind that Sun Yat-sen's political abandonment of "five races under one union" was not for the aim of acknowledging the multi-ethnic structure of Chinese nationals; rather, it was a reversion to the race-nationalism for the Han people. Sun Yat-sen asserted: "With a population of more than 400 million, the Han people are not able to create an independent sovereign state of their own, which is really a disgrace on the culturally advanced Han ethnicity. The populations of the Manchus, the Mongols, the Hui, and the Tibetans, are relatively small in comparison with that of the Han people. Therefore, the Han people should provide assistance to the ethnic minorities. As the ruling party of China, the Kuomingtang shall work to achieve the unfulfilled nationalism mission by assimilating the ethnic minorities in the Han people and founding a common state by holding high the banner of nationalism."[16] To this end, the promotion of "five races under one union" and "ethnic unity" is far from adequate in a multi-ethnic country like China; rather, all the ethnic groups of China must be integrated to form the Chinese nation as a whole. "Due to their absolute majority in the total population of China, the Han people shall be the only core for the ultimate state-nation formation."[17] Strongly endorsing the "one out of many" or "melting pot" nation-state construction model of the USA, Sun Yat-sen declared: "The 100 million American people are the result of assimilating the blacks, Britons, the Dutch, Germans, French and others, which fully testifies to the great effect of nationalism. Therefore, we should abandon the biased notion of 'five races under one union' and transform the Han people into the Chinese nation by assimilating the various minority ethnic groups."[18] This is the "positive nationalism" advocated by Sun Yat-sen, namely, the "Chinese nation" with the Han people as the "state nation."

On the basis of Western nationalism's principle of "one nation, one state", Sun Yat-sen's nationalism ideology complied with the US-style "melting pot" model. At that time, the political ideology of Sun Yat-sen included both racial and ancestral identity in the biological sense and the legitimacy of inheriting the territory of the Qing dynasty. From a historical perspective, there are inherent contradictions between the territorial integrity of China and the identity of the Chinese nation emphasized by Sun Yat-sen, including "commonalities of blood ties, languages, religion, folkways and customs."

As a matter of fact, both safeguarding territorial integrity and constructing the identity of the Chinese nation were closely related to addressing the ethno-national issues of China. Of course, Sun Yat-sen was also cognizant of this. He asked his countrymen: "Are the Mongols, the Hui People and Tibetans willing to participate in the nationalism and self-determination of the Han people?"[19] In regard to this, Sun Yat-sen argued that all the Chinese nationals can be collectively classified as the Han people for the population of ethnic minorities was "less than 10 million" among the total 400 million. Due to the absolute majority of the Han people in the total Chinese

---

[16]Sun (1985a): 473.
[17]Sun (2000): 1.
[18]Sun (1985b): 1.
[19]Sun (2000): 261.

population, the Han ethnicity ought to be the only core for the ultimate national formation. Therefore, Sun Yat-sen and his successors embraced an ethnicity-based nation state, which led to their ethnic assimilation ideal in terms of building a nation state in China.

In addition to drawing on the insights of Western nationalism, Sun Yat-sen incorporated the Chinese intellectuals' interpretations and arguments on race, ethnicity, nationalism, nationals and statism while elaborating his "Three Principles of the People". In spite of its ambiguity and vagueness, Sun Yat-sen's nationalism doctrine was adopted as the guiding principle for the ethno-national policies of the Nationalist government, exerting an "enduring effect on Chinese politics."[20]

From the perspective of the nation state formation of Western countries, the principle of "one nation, one state" has its justified modern significance. However, the essence of so-called one nation, one state refers to the identity of a state-nation that embodies the independent will of state sovereignty in international relations. In the modern nation-state pattern, there are very rare cases in which the identity of "one nation" formed in history coincides with the territory of a modern nation-state. After entering the era of modern nation state, the ancient unified multi-ethnic countries either fragmented into many states, or established a sovereign state of "one nation," which, however, contained a diversity of ethnic groups. The so-called nation-state has the characteristics of sovereign independence, territorial integrity and conversion from "subjects" loyal to the emperor to modern citizens loyal to the country. The traditional concept of nationalism emphasized a single and unitary composition of nationals, and pursued the principle of unified language and region—'one nation, one state'. However, this principle is almost impossible to put into practice because the majority of former nation-states form a multi-ethnic group, multi-lingual, and multi-religious. As far as China is concerned, the "one nation" here refers to the "Chinese nation," the collective of all the Chinese ethnic groups. However, if we equate the Chinese nation with the Han people and ignore the identity of ethnic minorities from the perspectives of history, population, language, and culture, it would go against the historical process of China's unified multi-ethnic state and intensify the conflict between the Han people and the minority ethnic groups.

In the bourgeois-democratic revolution of the colonies and semi-colonies, nationalism played an irreplaceable role in mobilizing the public, resisting foreign aggression and fighting for national independence and liberation. For this reason, Sun Yat-sen regarded nationalism as a magic elixir for all the social problems of China. However, Sun Yat-sen's theoretical declaration of solving China's ethno-national issues was aimed at forging a "coin" of the "Chinese nation": one side for "ousting the Manchu barbarians from central power", the other for "rejuvenating the Han people." The Xinhai Revolution and the subsequent founding of the Republic of China symbolized the accomplishment of the former task. However, Sun Yat-sen's endorsements of "Han people's self-determination" and "assimilating the ethnic minorities into the Han People" obscure the deserved rights and interests of the ethnic minorities in the framework of "civil rights."

---

[20]Feng K. *Racial Ideas in Modern China*, pp. 112–113.

In short, Sun Yat-sen's proposition of creating the "Chinese nation" by simulating the "one out of many" model of the USA completely ignored the different national conditions of the two countries, in that China has been a unified multi-ethnic state since ancient times, while the USA, with a history of merely a few hundred years, is a nation of immigrants. In spite of having theoretical or empirical backings from Western ideology, the nationalism of Sun Yat-sen failed to solve the ethno-national issues of China for it was divorced from the basic national conditions of the country. The Chinese Revolution of 1911 terminated the history of China's feudal dynasties and established the Republic of China. The road explored by Sun Yat-sen, the federal system of the "republic of five ethnicities" included elements that emulated the Soviet Union, and was not aligned with the history and national conditions of China. When imperialism, disintegration, and aggression encroached on Chinese border areas, China implemented federation state building, which signified divisions within the nation. John King Fairbank commented: "During the early days of the Republic of China, many foreign ideas were imported to China. However, few of them survived on Chinese soil."[21]

3.4   The Defining of the Chinese Nation by the Communist Party of China

During the First World War, the European powers were locked in prolonged battles and chaos. After gaining a large sphere of interests in Northern China and Manchuria through its victories in the First Sino-Japanese War and the Russo-Japanese War, Japan joined the ranks of the European imperialist powers in their scramble to establish political and economic domination over China. With the overthrow of the Qing dynasty in the Xinhai Revolution and the establishment of the Chinese central authority under Shikai Yuan, Japan saw an opportunity to expand its sphere of influence in China. To greatly extend Japanese control of Manchuria and of the Chinese economy, Tokyo presented a list of demands, known as *the Twenty-One Demands,* to Shikai Yuan on January 8, 1915, with warnings of dire consequences if China were to reject them.

The Chinese people responded with a spontaneous nationwide boycott of Japanese goods. In 1915, the movement of rejecting Japanese goods and encouraging the consumption of domestically produced daily necessities, such as soaps, towels, matches, cotton cloth, shoes, hats, umbrellas and candles, and gathered momentum. It greatly motivated Chinese nationals' patriotic consciousness.

This anti-imperialist patriotic movement transcended the narrowness of domestic racial-nationalism, symbolizing that "the Chinese people are ready to produce, define and accept expressions of new nationalism and anti-imperialism."[22] The patriotic

---

[21]Fairbank (2000): 197.

[22]Gerth K. *Manufacturing China: Consumer Culture and the Establishment of Nation-state,* pp. 144–145.

struggle of the Chinese people, which got off the ground with economic nationalism, was focused on imperialist powers. Different from the old-style merchants and virtually self-sufficient farmers, the national industry and industrial-commercial classes formed under the oppression of imperialists were "extremely sensitive to the plight of China," with a strong determination to defend national interests.[23] Therefore, they had an extremely keen desire for new ideas and ideologies.

In 1915, Duxiu Chen, a famous revolutionary socialist, educator, and philosopher, founded *the Youth Magazine* in Shanghai. Highly critical of Confucianism, Chen used the publication to promote democracy, science, and vernacular writing at the expense of traditional Confucian writing conventions. The following year, the name of the periodical was changed to *the New Youth*, which quickly became the most popular and widely distributed publication in the 1910s and 1920s. Dedicated to arousing the youth of the country to destroy the stagnant old traditions and forge a new culture, it became a banner for the ideological awakening of China, playing an important role in initiating the New Culture Movement and spreading the influence of the May Fourth Movement. The contributors of *the New Youth* launched an all-out attack on the bastions of traditionalism: old literature, old ethics, old human relations, and Confucianism.

After Russia's October Revolution in 1917, *the New Youth* began to cover the theory of Marxism–Leninism, motivating the founding of Marxist study groups in China. Scholars like Duxiu Chen, Yuanpei Cai, Dazhao Li, and Xun Lu, who had classical educations but began to lead a revolt against Chinese traditional culture, called for the creation of a new Chinese culture based on global and Western standards, especially democracy and science. They launched a wave of literary and intellectual campaigns known as the New Culture Movement, which sprang from the disillusionment with the traditional Chinese culture. "The salvoes of the October Revolution brought Marxism–Leninism to China." The October Revolution put Marxism into practice for the first time, providing an alternative path to China's national independence and self-strengthening other than the nation-building models of Western Europe, the USA, and Japan. In the scientific truth of Marxism–Leninism, Chinese progressives saw a solution to China's problems. In addition, the new world order dominated by Western powers after the conclusion of the First World War left no room for China's national self-determination and standing on its own.

In January 1919, the Versailles Peace Conference was convened in Paris. In this conference, the envoy of the Chinese Beiyang government put forth the following requests: abolishing all privileges of foreign powers in China; canceling the "*Twenty-One Demands*" with the Japanese; the territory of Shandong, which Japan had taken from Germany during First World War , to be returned to China. However, the Western Allies refused China's requests and transferred the German concessions to Japan instead, which aroused widespread public indignation and protests in China. The Chinese people's fantasy of the Western powers' ostensible declaration of "fair victory" was smashed. Just as Lenin said, "*the Treaty of Versailles* is nothing but

---

[23] Hsu I. C. Y. *The Rise of Modern China: 1600–2000*, 395.

an act of violence imposed on the weak countries by the Western democracies in a brutal and despicable manner."[24]

On the afternoon of May 4th, over 3000 students of Peking University and other schools gathered in the center of Beijing. Chanting slogans like "struggling for the sovereignty externally, getting rid of the national traitors at home," "doing away with the *'Twenty-One Demands'*," and "rejecting *the Versailles Treaty*," they voiced their fury at the Western powers' betrayal of China, denounced the Chinese government's spineless inability to protect Chinese interests, and called for a boycott of Japanese products.[25] This anti-imperialist and patriotic movement growing out of student participants in Beijing was commonly known as the May Fourth Movement. The next day, students in Beijing as a whole went on strike and in the larger cities across China, students, merchants and workers joined protests. From early June, workers and businessmen in Shanghai also went on strike as the center of the movement shifted from Beijing to Shanghai. Newspapers, magazines, civil societies, and chambers of commerce offered support for the students. Merchants threatened to withhold tax payments if the Chinese government remained obstinate. In Shanghai, a general strike of merchants and workers nearly devastated the entire Chinese economy. Under intense public pressure, the Chinese representative to the Versailles Peace Conference refused to sign the peace treaty. As a result, the May Fourth Movement won an initial victory, which was, however, primarily symbolic since Japan for the moment retained control of the Shandong Peninsula. Still, the partial success of the movement exhibited the ability of China's social classes across the country to collaborate given proper motivation and leadership. The movement marked the upsurge of Chinese nationalism, a shift toward political mobilization and a populist base rather than the intellectual elite. As spiritual power for Chinese people's mind emancipation, the New Culture Movement represented by *the New Youth* exposed the essence of capitalism. Marxism became the mainstream ideology of the Chinese Revolution. Thus, to take a path of the Russian-style "October Revolution" and to establish a socialist state became the historical choice of China.

As early as 1913, Lenin specified two tendencies of ethno-national issues in the capitalist era, "fighting against all forms of national oppression and creating a nation-state"[26] being one of them. "Nation-states, as a compulsory stage in the growth of capitalism, provide necessary basis for the development of productive forces at a certain stage of capitalism,"[27] he added. Thus, be it in Western Europe or the whole world at large, the nation state is "a typical and normal form of state in the capitalist era".[28] Upon analyzing the Proletarian Revolution and nationalist liberation movement of the colonies and semi-colonies, Lenin put forward a guiding prophecy: "in India and China, the proletariats with political consciousness can only take the road of the nationalist movement, for these two countries have not yet evolved into

---

[24]Lenin (2009): 253.

[25]Gerth K. *Manufacturing China: Consumer Culture and the Establishment of Nation-state*, p. 153.

[26]Lenin (2009): 290.

[27]Lenin (2009): 88.

[28]Lenin (1995): 371.

nation states."[29] Though such kind of nation state is categorized as the state form of the capitalist era, independent sovereignty, territorial integrity, and national unity are its basic characteristics. The colonial and semi-colonial peoples must establish their own nation states before casting off the imperialists' aggression, yoke and enslavement, for "the world order created and dominated by Western powers accepts the nation state as the only legitimate polity."[30]

As one of the most prominent pioneers to seek a modern nation-building path for China, Sun Yat-sen dedicated his whole life to subverting the Manchu-controlled Qing dynasty and establishing a Western-style nation state in China. After Russia's October Revolution, Sun Yat-sen amended his iconic doctrine, "the Three Principles of the People", including nationalism, democracy, and the livelihood of the people, by drawing on Marxism–Leninism. He declared: "the principle of the livelihood of the people is tantamount to socialism and communism, in spite of their divergent approaches to realization."[31] However, his "nationalism" has never transcended the demerits of "linking race and enlightenment history to nation state." Such kind of sublimation can only be accomplished by the "awakened proletariats," for "all the proletarians are created without ethnic prejudice."[32] During the May Fourth Movement, the strike of workers throughout the major cities of China symbolized the "awakened proletariats" taking to the stage of history. In the scientific truth of Marxism–Leninism, Chinese progressives saw a solution to China's problems.

It was in the midst of this, in 1921, as Marxism–Leninism was integrated with the Chinese workers' movement, that the Communist Party of China was born, which unfolded the historical process of the new democratic revolution in China. From that moment on, the Chinese people have had in the Party a backbone for their pursuit of national independence and liberation, of a stronger and more prosperous country, and of their own happiness; and the mindset of the Chinese people has changed, from passivity to taking the initiative. In *the Communist Manifesto*, Marx and Engels came to two conclusions: the first, "the eradication of national profiteering will be followed by a society free of human exploitation"; the second, "the hostile relationship between nations will be eliminated with the disappearance of intra-nation class antagonism."[33] With regard to solutions to the ethno-national issues, the Chinese Communists are convinced of their truth. Therefore, "the elimination of inequality among ethnic groups," which was regarded by Sun Yat-sen as a target of "negative nationalism," is exactly a goal pursued by the CPC for the eradication of class repression and ethnic oppression. The core of the goal is to achieve equality among people of all ethnic groups, which is also the basis of ethnic unity. In this sense, the "positive nationalism" of Sun Yat-sen, namely, "assimilating the ethnic

[29]Lenin V. *The Collected works of Lenin*, p. 89.

[30]Duara (2003): 59.

[31]Sun Y. *the Three Principles of the People*, p. 199.

[32]Marx and Friedrich (1957): 665.

[33]*The Complete Works of Marx and Engels*, p. 50.

minorities into the Han People," in spite of its good intention of "uniting all Chinese ethnic groups,"[34] simply cannot be achieved for its inherent lack of ethnic equality.

Acknowledging China's multi-ethnic national condition, the CPC upholds the political proposition that all ethnic groups of China are on an equal footing. After the epic Long March, a military retreat undertaken by the CPC's Red Army to evade the pursuit of the Kuomintang (KMT) army, the Chinese Communists arrived at Yan'an, an isolated town in northern Shaanxi. Against the backdrop of Japan's full-scale war of aggression against China, the CPC advocated the most extensive anti-Japanese national united front to resist Japanese aggression. At this specific historical stage, the idea that China has long been a unified multi-ethnic state was cognized by the CPC. In *the Chinese Revolution and the Communist Party of China* written in 1939, Mao Zedong proclaimed: "China has a population of 450 million, which accounts for almost a quarter of the world's total. Of the Chinese populaces, more than 90% are of the Han ethnicity. In addition to the majority Han people, there are dozens of ethnic minorities, such as the Mongols, Hui, Tibetans, Uighurs, Miao, Yi, Zhuang, Koreans and so on. In spite of their non-synchronous economic, social and cultural developments, all the Chinese ethnic groups boast a time-honored history. Therefore, China is a populous country with a diversity of ethnic groups."[35] It was the first public formulation on the multi-ethnic structure of Chinese nationals by a political party of China since the 1911 Revolution.

The CPC's historical cognition and realistic acknowledgement of the multi-ethnic national condition of China are directly related to the fundamental problem of realizing the state and ethnic unity in the anti-imperialism and anti-feudalism democratic revolution, that is, the problem of how to construct the Chinese nation. In this regard, the CPC put forward a brand-new outlook on nation: "as a collective term for all the Chinese ethnic groups, the Chinese nation, with 450 million people as compatriots of the common motherland, is a community of shared future."[36] Therefore, the concept of "one nation, one state" understood by the CPC is characterized by the following qualities: Chinese people of all ethnic groups are the "compatriots of the common motherland"; the Chinese nation is their common identity; the aggression of the Japanese imperialists and the brutal oppression of the feudal classes are their common enemies. Ethnic solidarity and state unity become the common goals of people of all ethnic groups. By defining "the Chinese nation," the CPC vests its political program with the essence of Chinese nationalism, that is, the CPC not only stands for workers and peasants but people of all ethnic groups as well."[37] As a consequence, the dedicated proposition of the CPC was transformed from "establishing a government for workers and peasants" to "inaugurating a 'people's republic' for the people of all ethnic groups"; the latter integrated people's democratic revolution and the Chinese nation's revolution into an organic whole.

---

[34] Sun (1985c): 1, 3.

[35] Mao (1991b): 622.

[36] The United Front Department of the CCP Central Committee. *Selected documents on the ethnic issues of China*, 808.

[37] Mao (1991a): 156.

In 1936, Japanese imperialists continuously expanded their invasion of China, but the ruling Nationalist Government headed by Kai-shek Chiang adhered to the non-resistance policy and continued the civil war. After the Xi'an Incident, Chiang agreed to end the ongoing civil war against the CPC and began actively preparing for the impending war with Japan. Widely accepted as an important turning point in the Chinese modern history, the incident led to a truce between the KMT and the CPC, forming a united front against the threat posed by Japan. It halted China's civil war and united the Kuomintang and the Communist Party, who together turned their guns against the Japanese invaders. Mao Zedong pointed out: "the anti-Japanese national united front opened up a new era in the history of the Chinese revolution and played a decisive role in overthrowing the Japanese imperialists. It was 'a national front' by its nature, for it was participated not only by the various political parties and social strata of China but also by the people of all ethnic groups." The Marco Polo Bridge Incident, a battle between China's National Revolutionary Army and the Imperial Japanese Army on July 7, 1937, heralded the start of the Second Sino-Japanese War. Therefore, mobilizing the Chinese people of all ethnic groups to jointly fight against Japan became the most urgent task at that time.

Against this background, the Sixth Plenary Session of the Sixth CPC Central Committee was held in Yan'an, the headquarters of the CPC. Mao Zedong addressed the conference: "On the premise of safeguarding state unity, the minority ethnic groups are entitled to manage their own affairs. At the same time, the Chinese people of all ethnic groups shall jointly establish a unified country."[38] In short, the CPC's basic ethno-national policies during its time based in Yan'an (1935–1948) included: equality of all ethnic groups as constituents of the Chinese nation; minority ethnic groups to have the right of autonomy; all ethnic groups to jointly establish a unified state. More than merely theoretical declarations, these policy concepts were put into practice in the Shaan-Gan-Ning Border Region, which was created by the CPC in agreement with the Kuomintang as a part of the Second United Front policy.

The CPC's new interpretations on the "Chinese nation" overcome the demerits of the various nationalist ideologies proposed by the Chinese elites from the late Qing dynasty to the early period of the Republic of China; in addition, they transcended the singleness of countrymen structure embodied in the Western nationalism's "one nation, one state". The CPC's advocacy of building a unified Chinese nation in a multi-ethnic country can be defined as the integration of nationals on the basis of vesting all ethnic groups with equal rights. It was both a theoretical inception to abandon the Soviet Union's federalist nation-building model and a political choice that conformed to the national conditions and popular feeling of China. The identity of the Chinese nation on the basis of acknowledging and respecting the distinctions among various ethnic groups established the Chinese people's self-reliance and sense of state belonging. These theoretical judgments and conceptual innovation indicated that the CPC had mastered the discourse initiative of interpreting Chinese history, confronting the reality, and looking forward to the future. The Chinese nation had become the carrier of the national will for the establishment of a new China in which

---

[38] Mao Zedong. *The Selected Works of Mao Zedong*. Volume I. Beijing: People's Press, p. 595.

all ethnic groups were on an equal footing. Under the leadership of the CPC, China would usher in the Chinese nation's self-determination, the founding of the People's Republic of China in 1949 being the symbol.[39]

3.5   Ethnic Recognition After the Founding of the People's Republic of China

During a history of more than 5000 years, the Chinese nation created a splendid civilization. But with the Opium War of 1840, China was plunged into the darkness of domestic turmoil and foreign aggression. The century of national humiliation, referring to the period of intervention and aggression by foreign powers in China between 1840 and 1949, shows that it is impossible for any ethnic group, including the Han people, to achieve national self-determination on the basis of inheriting the "grand unity" of the country. The history of China is written and inherited by Chinese people of all ethnic groups. Therefore, the historical legacy of the country as a unified multi-ethnic state must be maintained and carried on by the whole Chinese nation; otherwise, the country would be fragmented. In the 7th National Congress of the Communist Party of China held in Yan'an in 1945, Mao Zedong declared: "the unity of the Chinese nation indicates that we shall transform a disunited China into a unified country, which is the historical task to be fulfilled by the Chinese people."[40]

In 1937, the Marco Polo Bridge Incident, a dispute between Japanese and Chinese troops, escalated into the Second Sino-Japanese War, a large-scale military conflict between the two Asian countries. To the Chinese, the war is commonly known as the War of Resistance against Japan. Under the banner of the national united front, the Chinese Nationalist Party (the KMT) and the Communist Party of China (CPC) agreed to form an alliance to resist the Japanese invasion. Reorganized as the New Fourth Army and the Eighth Route Army, the CPC's armed forces fought alongside the KMT forces. In 1945, the war ended with the unconditional surrender of Japan. It did not, however, bring peace to the Chinese people. After the war with the Japanese ended, Kai-shek Chiang quickly moved the KMT troops to the newly liberated areas to prevent the Communist forces from receiving the Japanese surrender. In July 1946, Chiang launched a full blown assault on the Communist-controlled areas with 1.6 million troops. As a major turning point in modern Chinese history, it marked the final phase of the Chinese Civil War, with the CPC gaining control of almost the entirety of mainland China. In 1947, the People's Government of the Inner Mongolia Autonomous Region was established as part of the regional ethnic autonomy system. The system combined ethnic and regional factors in ethnic minority communities within a concentrated and unified state power structure.

In this context, the CPC organized a "Chinese People's Political Consultative Conference" (CPPCC) to prepare for the establishment of an administration to replace

---

[39]Ulanhu (1999): 359.

[40]Mao (1991c): 1071.

the KMT-dominated Republic of China government. The first meeting of the CPPCC adopted *the Common Program*, which effectively acted as an interim constitution of the new administration. After the end of the conference, the People's Republic of China (PRC) was proclaimed on October 1, 1949. The *Common Program* clearly stipulated that regional autonomy be implemented in the ethnic minority regions. Then, which areas could be defined as compact communities of ethnic minorities? How many ethnic groups were there in China? These problems had to be addressed before the full implementation of regional autonomy for ethnic minorities.

For China, ethnic minorities refer to various ethnic groups relative to the populous Han Chinese. The ethnic minorities have a significantly smaller population than the Han Chinese, and mostly inhabit the border areas, which are essentially underdeveloped regions that lag behind in economic, cultural, and social life due to geographical, historical, and cultural characteristics. The fundamental task of the regional ethnic autonomy system is to achieve equity of all ethnic minorities through national legal, institutional, and policy guarantees, especially ensuring that ethnic minorities enjoy equal development rights in economic, cultural, and social life.

Before the establishment of the People's Republic of China, China recognized its status as a unified multi-ethnic state and classified the meaning of the Chinese nation. However, how many members there are in the Chinese family of ethnic groups and nationalities is not completely certain. In China's very long historical process, the pre-Qin dynasty "five ethnicities' and their descendants appeared with numerous "self-titles" and "titles by others." In their evolution, they mixed, restructured, migrated, and scattered, and told historical stories of culturally diverse group interaction, absorption, and integration. The populous Han and some influential ethnic minorities gradually stabilized, and their ethnic titles became more stable and unified. However, due to the closed natural geographical environment and the constrained social development environment, many cultural diversity groups still lacked internal integration. Such groups were evolving in language and culture, economic life, social customs and habits, and self-titles and existed in a frequent state of mobility, transformation, and many kinds of overlapping titles.

Believing that there were many more than merely five ethnic groups in China, Sun Yat-sen, in his later revolutionary career, renounced the concept of "a republic of five ethnicities," one of the major principles upon which the Republic of China was founded in 1911. The "five ethnicities" here refer to the five major ethnic groups of China, including the Han, Manchu, Mongols, Hui, and Tibetans. While establishing the concept of the Chinese nation, the Chinese Communists believed that there were "dozens of ethnic groups" in addition to the above-mentioned five major ones. However, the exact number needed to be determined by systematic and scientific field investigations. As early as 1937, the Chinese ethnologist Yingliang Jiang pointed out: "only after we have a thorough and clear understanding of all ethnicities in the Chinese territory can we say that we have a good understanding of ourselves, and embark on the road of nation rejuvenation."[41] During the Second Sino-Japanese War, Chinese academia conducted a series of quantitative investigations into the

---

[41] Jiang (1937).

history, language, religious beliefs, folkways, and customs of the borderland ethnic minorities. These activities played an important role in stimulating Chinese people's national, territorial, and frontier consciousnesses against the wartime background. In addition, these researches provided invaluable academic information for the ethnic classification after the founding of the People's Republic of China.

With the goals of promoting the ethno-national policies of the newly-established regime and understanding the economic and social development status of the ethnic minority regions, the State Council dispatched several delegations to inspect the compact communities of ethnic minorities in 1950. While meeting with the delegates, Deng Xiaoping, who was then serving as head of the Southwest Greater Administrative Area, spoke frankly: "in terms of ethnic minority affairs, I am still a pupil in that we are in the dark about the exact number of minority ethnic groups living in the Southwest provinces. For example, we even mistakenly classified the Dong People into the Miao ethnicity in spite of their distinctive languages and historical backgrounds. Therefore, a lot of work needs to be done in our management of ethnic minority affairs."[42]

Based on keeping abreast of the historical and actual conditions of the country, the CPC established the policy of implementing regional autonomy in the compact communities of ethnic minorities in the period of the New Democratic Revolution (1919–1949). To put it into practice, the government must, first of all, guarantee the equal status of all ethnic groups, that is, acknowledging and respecting the equal status of ethnic minorities as constituents of the Chinese nation. In the modernization process of Western countries, the emphasis on the notion of "an egalitarian society" actually obscured the group differences or even economic and social development discrepancies that widely existed among different ethnic groups, races, and immigrant groups. It led to the two controversial paradoxes in the field of racial relations: the first was the legal doctrine of "separate but equal," which means, as long as the facilities provided to each race were equal, state and local governments could require that services, facilities, public accommodations, housing, medical care, education, employment, and transportation be segregated by race; the second was "the de facto inequality in spite of the theoretical proposition that "all men are created equal" in the American constitutional practices.[43] These triggered the Civil Rights Movement in the 1960s and the ensuing "affirmative action" with the impetus of redressing the disadvantages associated with the past and present discrimination, including government-mandated and voluntary private programs that tended to focus on access to education and employment, specifically granting special considerations to historically excluded groups such as racial or ethnic minorities. In this regard, China's policy and practice of acknowledging and safeguarding the equal status of ethnic minorities are forward looking.

In 1953, China carried out its first census. The results showed that the population of the country totalled 601 million, in which the Han people and minority nationalities accounted for 93.94% and 6.06%, respectively. Among the ethnic minorities, the

---

[42]Deng (1994): 161–162.
[43]Pole (2007): 203.

populations of ten exceeded a million, including the Zhuang (6.61 million), the Uighurs (3.64 million), the Hui (3.55 million), the Yi (3.25 million), the Tibetans (2.77 million), the Miao (2.51 million), the Manchu (2.41 million), the Mongols (1.46 million), the Buyi (1.24 million), and the Koreans (1.12 million). The self-titles reported by ethnic minorities reached over 400. It was, thus, almost impossible for the social management system, which relied on administrative regions with a certain population size, to establish the autonomous regions. The development of ethnic minority identification and the confirmation of ethnic minority identity and group belonging became at that time an important issue for the Chinese government.

These different ethnonyms, which were further complicated by the diversity of geographical conditions, family names, dialects, customs, and traditions, actually demonstrated their asynchronous social and historical developments while forming stable communities: some groups still retained the characteristics of kindred clan society; some were in the stage of tribal alliance; the remaining were integrating with other ethnic groups due to ever-increasing communications and interactions. At the same time, the most populous Han people also formed different subgroups because of their distinctive settlements, dialects, production modes, and lifestyles. Therefore, for a country as large as China, ethnic classification was an extremely complex social project.

Then, which human group can be defined as a *minzu* (nation)? Chinese historical documents did not provide a clear definition of the term. However, we can still chalk up some basic elements from the Chinese ancient texts. The *Records of the Grand Historian* describes China as a state jointly created by the "five ethnicities," including the Han People based in the North China Plain, and the ethnic minorities in the four cardinal directions. At first, the group properties, folkways and customs for the "five ethnicities" were dissimilar due to their divergent geographical environments; secondly, their residences, diet, and clothing were made from different materials and of divergent shapes or forms; and thirdly, they had communication barriers due to their dissimilar languages. These elements construe to a large extent the characteristics of "nation." Their diverse means of subsistence, such as farming, animal husbandry, fishing, hunting or food collection, on the one hand reflect their divergent geographical environments; on the other hand, they demonstrate the different stages of social development for each ethnic group. These could be regarded as China's indigenous resources for the definition of "nation." With the introduction of Western learning to China in the modern era, the various interpretations on the characteristics of "nation" by Western academia had exerted a significant impact on Chinese intellectuals, who also put forward their interpretations of "nation." We can see salient elements of blood ties or ancestral worship in these definitions due to the influence of race-nationalism ideology. However, the racial feature was not a yardstick for China's ethnic classification.

Among the proponents of Marxism–Leninism, Stalin's definition of "nation," namely, "a historically formed stable community which shares a common language, geographic location, economic life, and a psychological quality that is expressed in a common culture,"[44] provided important theoretical guidance for the ethnic classification of China. In other words, the commonalities of language, geographical location, economic life, and culture constitute a nation. To be sure, the "stable community" defined by Stalin refers to the nation in the era of nation-state, that is, the various constituent republics of the Soviet Union are construed as "nations." Those human groups without all the above-mentioned "indispensable" elements were categorized as "tribes" in the Soviet Union.

Though Stalin's definition of "nation" was regarded as the most important theoretical basis, China's ethnic classification to the largest extent considered the national conditions of the country, in particular, its historical formation and development process as a unified multi-ethnic state. In this regard, Zhou Enlai proclaimed: "we shall never copy Stalin's definition of 'nation,' for it fails to account for the complex problems which existed in the various stages of the pre-capitalist era; rather, we shall take the historical and actual national conditions of China into consideration while acknowledging the cultural differences of all ethnic groups and respecting their ethnic self-consciousness."[45]

While determining a collective identity of an ethnic minority in the practice of ethnic recognition, we shall consider not only their common grounds of economic mode but their religious belief, folkways, and customs as well. The ethnic recognition of the Hui people is a good case in point. Found throughout China, the Hui, an ethnic group composed predominantly of adherents of the Muslim faith, are concentrated mainly in the northwestern provinces. In spite of the absence of their own language, they are devout adherents of Islam, which has shaped their customs, economic life, cultural and psychological commonalities. Therefore, China's ethnic classification did not follow dogmatically Stalin's definition of "nation," which emphasized the indispensability of common language, geographical location, economic life, cultural, and psychological aspects; rather, it fully considered the historical processes, literature records, cultural characteristics, and economic life of various ethnic groups.

In the 1950s, the central government dispatched missions to the north-west, south-west, south, north-east, Inner Mongolia, and other ethnic minority areas, to promote ethnic policy and carry out social investigation. A large number of scientific workers were organized, especially in anthropology, ethnology, sociology, history, linguistics, and other disciplines, and they launched a large-scale minority language script and social historical investigation. This unprecedented scientific activity was a most comprehensive understanding of China's multi-ethnic, multi-lingual, multi-cultural, and multi-religious conditions, and provided a scientific basis for ethnic identification in China. Complex scientific research was carried out of the "self-titles" based on full respect for the will of minorities and the principle of "naming after the master." This was more difficult for ethnic minorities with no script. Carrying out deep and comprehensive investigations into social, historical, linguistic, cultural, and economic life, customs and other aspects can accurately reflect the origin, similarities and differences of these groups, and provide scientific advice for their affiliation. In

---

[44]Stalin (1979): 64.
[45]The CCP leaders' Writings on the Ethno-national Issues (1994): 151.

this investigation, the central government identified and approved ethnic minority titles. As of 1954, 20-plus ethnic groups, such as the people of Zhuang, Buyi, Dong, Bai, and Kazakhstan, had been added to the official list of the Chinese minority ethnic groups. In the following decade, the central government organized a series of nationwide field investigations on the society, history, spoken, and written languages of the frontier regions. In this period, 15 ethnic minorities, including the people of Tujia, She, Daur, Blang, Achang, and Hezhe, were recognized, adding the total number of minority nationalities to 53. By 1965, China had confirmed the identification of 54 ethnic minorities including the Tibet Lhoba. The Cultural Revolution began in 1966 and its ten years of political, economic, and social disorder forced the ethnic identification work and scientific research to be shut down.

We should note that the ethnic recognition of China is not for the purpose of knowing the exact number of ethnic groups in the history of the country. After longtime engagement and evolution, almost every nation contains elements of other ethnic groups, the most populous Han people being the most typical. This kind of integration and mutual learning are the civil foundations for the creation of a unified multi-ethnic state. The prevalent existence of group differences in reality does not equate to the division of their historical origins. As a matter of fact, the widespread phenomena of "one source with multiple branches" and "confluence of all tributaries" are the basic logic for China's ethnic classification. Therefore, the small-populous ethnic minorities, such as the people of Oroqen, Derung, Hezhen, Gaoshan, Lhoba, and Tatars, were not merged into other ethnic groups because they had only a few thousand people; likewise, nations with relatively large populations were not divided into divergent ethnic groups. Since reform and opening up, China has confirmed the Yunnan Jino ethnic group, and by 1979 completed the ethnic identification work, bringing the number of ethnic groups to the current 56. At the same time, the field survey data collected were preserved in the forms of ethnography, language annals or documentary, becoming valuable materials for ethnology researchers.

China's ethnic identification is a state-led scientific practice. There is a basic requirement to give ethnic minorities political status to co-govern the country, the autonomy to develop economy and culture and other social undertakings in accordance with the ethnic and local realities in their inhabited areas. The ethnic identification of China, due to its due respect for Chinese history as a unified multi-ethnic country and conforming to the popular feeling, was warmly lauded by the public. In the construction of a modern state, China established the Chinese nation as the state-nation. Meanwhile, the ethnic identification regularized the appellations of each historical nation. This means that the state has provided institutional and policy guarantees for the rights and interests of ethnic minorities. The removal of discriminatory ethnonyms left over from history reflected the concrete practice of China's ethnic policy in realizing ethnic equality. For example, the "Guihua people" (literally "naturalized people"), referring to the Russians who migrated to Xinjiang during the early days of the Republic of China (1912–1949), were renamed as "the ethnic Russians" in the ethnic classification process, becoming one of the 55 national minorities of China.[46] If they were to be classified in accordance with the Western countries' theory and practice of dealing with foreign immigrants, the Russians who migrated to Xinjiang would only have the status of "ethnic group" within the framework of multi-culturalism.

After the Second World War, the international community began to attach more importance to the rights of ethnic minorities. At the same time, a succession of relevant resolutions and declarations adopted by the United Nations highlighted the ethnic minorities' equal human rights. To guarantee the equal rights of ethnic minorities, we must recognize their social existence and give equal social status to them. In this regard, one of the most important agendas for the fledgling People's Republic of China was to carry out ethnic classification and implement regional autonomy in the compact communities of ethnic minorities. Though the economy of China at that time was extremely underdeveloped after the enduring civil war, the ethnic policy and practice of the country were at the forefront of the world in terms of recognizing and protecting the equal rights of ethnic minorities. More importantly, China's efforts to recognize the group rights of ethnic minorities was aimed at guaranteeing state unity and forging the identity of the Chinese nation, which, in turn, contributes to the cherished goal of "diversity in unity," or "harmony without uniformity."

3.6   The Chinese Nation: A Large Family of 56 Ethnic Groups

When coerced into inking land sale agreements with the white settlers in 1854, Chief Seattle (1786–1866), a native American tribe chief, delivered a widely publicized speech, *This Land is Sacred,* in which he argued in favor of ecological responsibility and respect for Native Americans' land rights. The Indian chief concluded his speech passionately: "All things are connected like the blood which unites one family. Even the white man, whose God walks and talks with him as friend to friend, cannot be exempt from the common destiny. We may be brothers after all. We shall see."[47] More than 140 years later, the descendants of Chief Seattle still couldn't feel the warmth of "brothers of common destiny" in American society. However, Chief Seattle's good wish of harmonious coexistence among people of all ethnic groups within a sovereign state has been achieved on the other side of the Pacific Ocean. In China, the ethnic minorities are addressed as "brotherly nations" and the unified multi-ethnic country is acclaimed as "an extended family established on the basis of equal, mutual-benefit and win-win cooperation among people of all ethnic groups." Zhou Enlai (1898–1976), the first Premier of the PRC, pointed out: "rather than monopolized by any constituent of the Chinese nation, the People's Republic of China is shared by all the Chinese ethnic groups." As equal members of the Chinese nation, the 56 ethnic

---

[46]Huang and Shi (2005): 81.
[47]The Collected Speeches of Chief Seattle (2001): 31.

groups share "the Chinese nation" as their common family name whilst having their respective given names, which was summarized by Mr. Xiaotong Fei, a pioneering Chinese researcher of sociology and anthropology, as "the pluralistic integration of the Chinese nation."[48]

Within the components of the Chinese nation, we can still find widespread economic and social development gaps, which impede the ethnic minorities' equal access to the achievements of China's reform and opening up. It is an objective reality that history has left to China. Therefore, the state must provide necessary assistance to the development of the minority ethnic groups while respecting their customs and traditions, which can be construed as a "family regulation." Its purpose is to narrow the developmental disparity among the various ethnic groups, which will, in turn, lead to their mutual respect, reciprocal assistance and win-win cooperation for the common prosperity of the Chinese nation. From the academic point of view, the goal of building the Chinese nation is to achieve state unity among the diversified composition of Chinese nationals. It is a totally different nation-state building approach from the Western countries.

In the history of nation-state construction, the integration of nationals was usually effectuated by establishing institutionalized identity, such as a national language used by the people at large or a national religion. Will Kymlicka, a Canadian political philosopher, pointed out: "the Western countries have used a variety of tactics, including promulgating laws on citizenship, naturalization, education and language, as well as implementing policies regarding public service personnel recruitment, military service system and national communication media, to realize the uniformity of language and social systems." The purpose of these policies is to achieve a cultural "homogeneity" by eliminating the "heterogeneity" in the constituents of nationals.[49] The policy practices with the goal of ethnic assimilation had been prevalent until the first half of the twentieth century. These include: racial, ethnic, religious or language cleansing, forced assimilation, and migration, resident swaps between countries and Nazi Germany's genocide atrocities. As a result, the theories and practices of racism, chauvinism, nationalism and fascism all originate from Western societies' modern state construction process.

Michael Mann, a British-born professor of sociology, proclaimed: "though the countries in Europe and North America have experienced the horrible history of ethnic cleansing while constructing their nation-states, they are, at least theoretically, upholding multiculturalism." The outbreak of the Civil Rights Movement in Western countries in the 1960s symbolized the failures of policies like the "melting pot" in the USA, "integration" in Western Europe and "assimilation" in Northern Europe. As a response, the USA, Canada, and Australia began to resort to the multi-cultural "affirmative action", the policy of favoring members of a disadvantaged group who suffer or have suffered from discrimination for historical reasons within a culture. Historically and internationally, support for "affirmative action" has sought to achieve goals such as bridging inequalities in employment and pay, increasing access to education,

---

[48]The Collected Documents on the Governance of Xinjiang: 1949–2010 (2012): 180.
[49]Kymlicka (2004): 1.

promoting diversity, and redressing apparent past wrongs, harms or hindrances. On the basis of recognizing cultural differences and economic development discrepancies among the various constituents of nationals, "affirmative action" affected the European countries and a large number of capitalist developing countries beyond Europe. Michael Mann arrived at an optimistic conclusion: "after experiencing ethnic cleansing and the democratization process, Europe is approaching the final stage of the nation-state construction."[50] However, the seemingly fruitful nation-state construction in Western countries is confronted with many inherent contradictions and irreconcilable plights in the "democratization system", the conflict between the values of individual freedom and the rights of minority groups being the most prominent.

In the current world, very few countries take the initiative to recognize, respect, and guarantee the equal rights of ethnic minorities. Many countries, including those in Western developed society, played down or even wrote off the group rights of ethnic minorities and indigenous peoples on the pretext of the individual rights of liberalism, such as "all men are created equal," or "civic society," for the purpose of building a nation-state in accordance with the principle of "one nation, one state". This ostensibly indiscriminate social integration policy is essentially a denial of the rights of "heterogeneous" groups under the disguise of highlighting the justified facade of "equal opportunity for all.".The so-called "heterogeneity" of national constituents within a unified country is not tantamount to differences in social class, stratum or occupation among the nationals; rather, it often refers to the minority groups who represent the non-mainstream traditional culture within a particular society. The minority groups' conscious identification and integration with the larger social environment can by no means be achieved instantly by proclaiming nominally that "all men are created equal" or "all men have equal access to the opportunity of upward social mobility." The American Dream, as one of the ethos of the United States, advocates individual freedom, including the opportunity for prosperity and success, and an upward social mobility for the family and children achieved through hard work in a society with few barriers. In fact, it reinforces the situation in which some minority groups are generally at the bottom or on the margins of the American society.

Some highly emotive issues, including American conservatism's severe criticism of multi-culturalism, street atrocities committed by racial "hatred groups" and new fascist organizations, resurgence of the far-right politics, which is often associated with Nazism, neo-Nazism, fascism, neo-fascism, and other ideologies or organizations that feature extreme nationalist, chauvinist, xenophobic, racist or reactionary views, and intensification of regional-national separatist movement in Europe, have always accompanied with the processes of Western society's transformation from assimilationism to multi-culturalism and recognizing the rights of ethnic minorities. Theoretically speaking, the Western societies were not short of enlightened and rational understandings in dealing with such problems. Will Kymlicka asserted: "If the existence of nation-state construction policy contributes to the legalization of ethnic minorities' rights and interests, this formula can also be justified in the other direction, that is, the protection of ethic minorities' rights and interests promotes the

---

[50]Mann (2015): 635.

legalization of nation-state construction."[51] A case in point is the Cornish national-ism, a cultural, political, and social movement that seeks the recognition of Cornwall, which forms the westernmost part of the south-west peninsula of the British Isles, as a nation distinct from England. The Cornish people can trace their roots to the ancient Britons who inhabited southern and central Great Britain before the Roman conquest. Just before the independence referendum of Scotland in 2014, the British government officially recognized the Cornish people as one of the national minorities of the country. Therefore, we have to admit that the anticipated goal of the nation-state construction of Western countries has still a long way to go even though it is approaching its "final stage".

The building of a state-nation in a multi-ethnic state demands "unity in diversity" and "harmony without uniformity," which has always been and will be a protracted and formidable task. Although the nation-state model created by Western Europe has undergone a history of several hundred years, we cannot arbitrarily conclude that it has produced universal successful experiences. To some extent, it contributed to the dictum of Benedict Anderson, namely, "nation is an imagined political community, and imagined as both inherently limited and sovereign," in which the political sci-entist depicts a nation as a socially constructed community imagined by the people who perceive themselves as part of that group.[52] For Anderson, the idea of the "na-tion" is relatively new and is a product of various socio-material forces. As Anderson puts it, a nation "is imagined because the members of even the smallest nation will never know most of their fellow-members, meet them, or even hear of them, yet in the minds of each lives the image of their communion". According to Anderson, a nation is a community because "regardless of the actual inequality and exploitation that may prevail in each, the nation is always conceived as a deep, horizontal com-radeship." The prevalence of Andersons' definition of "nation" can be accounted for from the following aspects: first of all, it extricates itself from the controversy over the constituent elements of "nation"; secondly, it demonstrates the widespread perplexing problems in the nation-state construction. Admittedly, the concept of the "Chinese nation" was non-existent in the ancient history of China. However, this does not mean that this notion is an "imagined product"; rather, the unique course of Chinese history and the special experiences of the Chinese people of various ethnic groups consummated the Chinese nation. In his address to the deputies of the National People's Congress in 2013, the Chinese President Xi Jinping declared: "over the course of several thousand years, what have closely bound us together, the 56 ethnic groups of China's 1.3-billion-plus people, are our indomitable struggles, the beautiful homeland we have built together and the national spirit we have nur-tured together. Running through it all, most importantly, are the ideals and vision that we share and hold dear."[53] As a result, we shall take to the road of socialism with Chinese characteristics and achieve the rejuvenation of the Chinese nation.

---

[51] Kymlicka (2004): 1.

[52] Andersons (2003): 5.

[53] Xi (2014): 39.

In terms of understanding the development model of China, including the answer to its ethno-national issues, the "Soviet model" was once established as a magic elixir for all socialist states. Therefore, it's hardly surprising that some Western politicians and intellectuals would arrive at the conclusion that "all the socialist multi-ethnic states are destined to collapse" after the disintegration of the Soviet Union. Believing the "Soviet model" as the only standard for all socialist countries, the adherents of cold-war mentality completely ignored the Chinese people's initiative in exploring their own development model. At the same time, some scholars enumerated the "crimes" of the Soviet Union's ethno-national policies, for example, recognizing the status of the diverse ethnic minorities, giving non-Russian peoples the right to establish their own republics, implementing the "ethnic segregation" system within the union and vesting the constituent republics with the right to withdraw from the union. Following this line of reasoning, they groundlessly concluded that China's ethnic classification and regional autonomy for ethnic minorities were nothing more than parodies of the ethno-national policies of the Soviet Union. In accordance with this simplified political logic, both the European Union's recognition of its member states' sovereign independence and the EU Constitution's provision of the member states' right of withdrawal from the union would also lead to the disintegration of the EU.

At one time, Moscow also purported the Soviet Union was a family composed of ethnically diverse republics. In the Brezhnev era, the Kremlin even declared that "a new historical community, that is, the Soviet people, has already taken shape," believing that the ethno-national issues of the union had been resolved once and for all.[54] Established on the so-called "integration," during which the highly centralized regime in Moscow superseded the legal rights and interests of the constituent republics, this sanguine assessment was based on the firm conviction that the Soviet Union had already built a developed and mature socialism. While nominally a union of equals, the Soviet Union was actually dominated by the ethnic Russians to such an extent that for most of the Soviet Union's existence, it was commonly referred to as "Russia". It was for this reason that the people of the Soviet Union were often referred to as the "Russians," rather than the "Soviets," in that "the Russian culture dominates the cultural interaction among the various constituent republics" and "Russia has been widely accepted as a common language for the diverse ethnic groups of the union."[55] The idea of equating Russia with the Soviet Union was so deep-rooted that Mikhail Gorbachev, General Secretary of the Communist Party of the Soviet Union from 1985 until 1991, involuntarily blurted out in a toast: "Russia, what I mean is the Soviet Union, is a fortress for all the Soviet citizens."[56] In just a few years, this "fortress" collapsed with the disintegration of the Soviet Union.

Some western politicians predicted that the dissolution of the Soviet Union would set off a chain of similar events in other countries; China was the next obvious candidate. However, the "domino effect" prophesied and encouraged by Western

---

[54]The Soviet Union Academy of Sciences (1997): 610.

[55]The Soviet Union Academy of Sciences (1997): 749.

[56]Brzezinski (1988): 116.

society did not occur in China. A country's development path, as well as the solution to its ethno-national issues, must conform to its own national conditions. Xi Jinping pointed out: "there are no two leaves exactly alike on earth. A nation and country must know who they are, where they came from and where they are heading. Keep on going toward the goal when you have made your choice."[57] For China, this goal is the great rejuvenation of the Chinese nation, whose driving force comes from the unity and concerted efforts of the Chinese people of all ethnic groups. The 56 ethnic groups of China are vested with equal status, which is aimed at forging the integration of the Chinese nation. Of course, its accomplishment will be an enduring process. The socialism with Chinese characteristics in China is at the initial stage of scientific socialism. China's efforts to solve all its social problems, including its ethno-national issues, can by no means go beyond the basic features of this development phase. We must bear this in mind while comparing China's solution to its social problems with those of the developed countries.

Labeling the ethno-national policies of China as the "Soviet model," some Western elites concluded that China's solution to its ethno-national issues would be a dead end due to the existence of national secessionism, extreme religious forces, and violent terrorism. By equating the "Soviet model" to scientific socialism, these people rigidly and dogmatically interpreted socialism with Chinese characteristics. Ignoring the serious racial and religious conflicts in the USA, India and Brazil, they strongly suggested that the "melting pot" or ethnic assimilation models of these countries be imported to China. In fact, such importation would certainly lead China down the erroneous path of changing its political direction.

Chinese nationalism, which asserts that the 56 ethnic groups are equal components of Chinese nation and promotes the cultural and national unity among the Chinese nationals, is characteristic of unity in diversity. Recognizing the diversity of the 56 constituents of the Chinese nation and respecting for the rights of ethnic minorities shall by no means deny the legal rights of citizens; rather, the widespread regional development gap and the cultural particularities of the minority nationalities require special attention and practical support. China's pursuit of state unity and forging the identity of the Chinese nation are aimed at integration during the accelerated economic and social development of ethnic minority regions. Just like Xi Jinping said: "to meet our development goals, we must enrich ourselves not only materially but culturally and ethically as well. The people of all ethnic groups in the country should strive to realize the rejuvenation of the Chinese nation with a sense of urgency."[58] In terms of the solution to the ethno-national issues of China, the system of regional ethnic autonomy is an institutional guarantee for the equal rights of ethnic minorities.

---

[57] Xi Jinping. *The Governance of China*, p. 171.

[58] Xi Jinping. *The Governance of China*, p. 46.

References

Andersons, B. (2003). *Imagined communities: Reflections on the origin and spread of nationalism.* Shanghai: Shanghai People's Press.

Brzezinski, Z. (1988). *Competitive plan: A geopolitical strategy for US-soviet competition.* Beijing: China Translation Corporation.

Collected articles of Eastern Western monthly magazine. Beijing: Zhonghua Book Company (1997).

Deng, X. (1994). *The collected works of Deng Xiaoping* (Vol. I). Beijing: People's Press.

Duara, P. (2003). *Rescuing history from the nation: Questioning narratives of modern China.* Beijing: Social Science Academic Press.

Fairbank, J. (2000). *The great Chinese revolution:1800–1985.* Beijing: World Affairs Press.

Feng, K. (1999). *The concept of race in Modern China.* Nanjing: Jiangsu People's Press.

Greenfeld, L. (2010). *Nationalism: Five roads to modernity.* Shanghai: The SDX Joint Publishing Company.

Huang, G., & Shi, L. (2005). *Ethnicity classification of China: The origin of 56 ethnic groups.* Beijing: The Ethnic Publishing House.

Jiang, Y. (1937). The history of the ethnic Yao people in Guandong. *Journal of Folkways and Customs.*

Kymlicka, W. (2004). *Politics in the vernacular: Nationalism, multiculturalism and citizenship.* Taipei: Left Bank Culture Press.

Lenin, V. (1995). *The collected works of Lenin* (Vol. II). Beijing: People's Press.

Lenin, V. (2009). *The collected works of Lenin.* Beijing: People's Press.

Liang, Q. (1989). *The selected works of Qichao Liang* (Vol. XIII). Beijing: Zhonghua Book Company.

Mann, M. (2015).*The dark side of democracy: Explaining ethnic cleansing.* Beijing: Central Compilation & Translation Press.

Mao, Z. (1991a). *The selected works of Mao Zedong* (Vol. I). Beijing: People's Press.

Mao, Z. (1991b). *The selected works of Mao Zedong* (Vol. II). Beijing: People's Press.

Mao, Z. (1991c). *The selected works of Mao Zedong* (Vol. III). Beijing: People's Press.

Marx, K., & Friedrich, E. (1957). *The complete works of Marx and Engels.* Beijing: People's Press.

Pole, J. (2007). *The pursuit of equality in American history.* Beijing: The Commercial Press.

Stalin, J. (1979). *The selected works of Stalin* (Vol. I). Beijing: People's Press.

Sun, Y. (1982). *The completed works of Sun Yat-sen* (Vol. II). Beijing: Zhonghua Book Company.

Sun, Y. (1985a). *The collected works of Sun Yat-sen* (Vol. V). Beijing: Zhonghua Book Company.

Sun, Y. (1985b). *The selected works of Sun Yat-sen* (Vol. VII). Beijing: Zhonghua Book Company.

Sun, Y. (1985c). *The works of Yat-sen Sun* (Vol. VII). Beijing: The Zhonghua Book Company.

Sun, Y. (2000). *Three principles of the people.* Changsha: Yuelu Book Company.

The CCP leaders' writings on the ethno-national issues. Beijing: The Ethnic Publishing House (1994).

The collected documents on the Governance of Xinjiang: 1949–2010. Beijing: People's Press (2012).

The collected speeches of chief seattle. Hong Kong: The Facebook Press (2001).

The Soviet Union Academy of Sciences. (1997). *The nation-state building history of the Soviet Union.* Beijing: The Commercial Press.

Ulanhu. (1999). *The selected works of Ulanhu. Volume I.* Beijing: The Central Document Publishing House.

Xi, J. (2014). *The governance of China.* Beijing: Foreign Languages Press.

Yang, T. (2014). The abdication of the last Qing emperor and the "Republic of Five Races". *Journal of Modern Chinese History,* (2), 16–19.

Yōichi, K. (2003). *Criticism of modern Japanese.* Changchun: Jilin People's Press.

Chapter 4
Regional Autonomy: An Institutional Arrangement for Solving Ethno-national Issues

The State Constitution of China stipulates: "The People's Republic of China is a unitary multi-national state created jointly by the people of all its nationalities. Regional autonomy is practiced in areas where people of minority nationalities live in concentrated communities; in these areas, organs of self-government are established to exercise the power of autonomy. All autonomous areas for ethnic minorities are integral parts of China". In accordance with this principle, *the Law on Regional Autonomy for Ethnic Minorities* declares: "Regional autonomy is the basic policy adopted by the Communist Party of China for the solution of ethno-national issues through its application of Marxism–Leninism; it is a basic political system of the state". In the national conference on ethnic minority affairs convened in 2014, Xi Jinping pointed out: "practice has testified that regional ethnic autonomy is in line with China's national conditions. It plays an important role in safeguarding state unity and territorial integrity, strengthening ethnic unity, and equality, promoting the development of ethnic minority areas and enhancing the cohesion of the Chinese nation".[1] The system is the inevitable course that China must take to solve its ethno-national issues for it respects the historical development of the Chinese nation and conforms to the national conditions of the country.

4.1 Regional Ethnic Autonomy: A Basic Policy of the State Based on the History and National Conditions of China

Upon establishing the nation-state model, the Western European countries, driven by the Industrial Revolution and overseas expansion, constructed a worldwide colonial system and international rules. The imperialist powers' military conquest, colonial rule, and institutional transplantation almost completely transformed the developmental course of the ancient societies in Asia, Africa, and South America. Naturally, these oppressed states and nations aspired to set up their own nation-states by actively

---

[1] Angben (2014).

© China Social Sciences Press 2020
S. Hao, *China's Solution to Its Ethno-national Issues*, China Insights,
https://doi.org/10.1007/978-981-32-9519-3_4

or passively adapting to the international regulations created by the Western world. Thus, the number of modern nation-states has shown an ever-increasing tendency after the two world wars. This process was accompanied by the collapse of continental imperial hegemony and the marine colonial system. Human societies entered the nation-state era with the disintegration of ancient traditional empires and modern colonial empires.

In this course, several thousand ancient peoples, respectively, came under the jurisdiction of several hundred sovereign states. As a consequence, the composition of nationals in the vast majority of modern countries is characterized by a multitude of ethnicities, cultures, religions, and races. The formation of this sovereign state pattern was, on the one hand, ascribed to national division or unification in ancient times; on the other, as the result of colonial division, empire hegemony and power politics in the modern era. Entering the twentieth century, the international order framed by the two world wars justified the concepts of sovereign independence, territorial integrity, and national self-determination, which fundamentally accelerated the tide of state independence and national liberation; at the same time, the imperialist powers' struggle, compromise, and deal for colonial interests continued to dominate patterns of state formation around the world.

After the conclusion of the First World War, the peoples in Central and Eastern Europe set off a nationalist movement within the former territories of the fragmented Ottoman Empire and Austro-Hungarian Empire. However, *the Treaty of Versailles* administered by the Western powers left infinite troubles for territorial disputes and ethnic conflicts. Thus, 16.8 million people became ethnic minorities in foreign lands. As Lloyd George, one of the founders of the Versailles System who served as the British Prime Minister during and immediately after the First World War, lamented: "There was only one issue of Alsace-Lorraine in Europe before the First World War. However, dozens of similar problems came into being after *the Treaty of Versailles* re-delimited state boundaries".[2] The national liberation movement in Asia, Africa, and Latin American after the Second World War smashed the global rule of the colonial empire. Nonetheless, the newly created nation-states were compelled to inherit or accept the legacies of the colonial era, resulting in ceaseless territorial disputes, national strife, and religious conflicts. Therefore, almost all the countries of the world needed to face up to the ethno-national issues in the broad sense.

From a historical point of view, the remedies prescribed by the colonial powers for addressing racial conflicts and coordinating cultural diversity fit into the following categories: divide and rule, forced assimilation, and apartheid and racial genocide. In general, these therapies took three different paths, including nationalism for the goal of "one nation, one state",[3] racism advocating "white people first", and fascism proposing the extermination of "inferior races". While revealing the demerits of capitalist society and explaining the developmental trajectory of human society, Marx put forward his insightful solutions to the ethno-national issues, the right of self-

---

[2]Vyigotski (1979): 285.

[3]The traditional concept of nationalism emphasized a single and unitary composition of nationals and pursued the principle of unified language and region.

determination for the oppressed nations and states under the imperialist colonial rule being one of them. In a speech delivered to the US Congress on January 8, 1918, *the Fourteen Points*, President Woodrow Wilson drew on Lenin's thoughts about national self-determination. However, Wilson's exposition on self-determination was based on his narrow bourgeois stance of "one nation, one state". It contributed to the emergence of dozens of "issues of Alsace-Lorraine" during state reorganization in Europe after the First World War.[4]

Based on the basic position of fighting against imperialist oppression and colonial rule, the national self-determination of Marxism–Leninism disapproves of the tenet of "one nation, one state" due to its secession tendency. At the same time, Marxism–Leninism advocates that the equal rights and interests of ethnic minorities be protected in the unified multi-ethnic state. Therefore, the Soviet Union founded after the First World War, as well as the socialist states in Eastern Europe, China, and Vietnam established after the Second World War, are all multi-ethnic sovereign countries. In fact, the majority of the Western developed economies and a large number of newly established developing countries are also characterized by multiple races, nations, and religions. In this sense, how to properly handle the generalized ethnonational issues, including race, ethnicity, language, culture, and religion, become important affairs for virtually all the countries of the world. To maintain the political requirement of state unity and realize the integration of nationals, we must appropriately address the relationship between diverse ethnic groups and heterogeneous social cultures, which can be defined as a dialectical relationship between "unity" and "diversity". Therefore, a variety of government forms, including federalism, regional autonomy for ethnic minorities and national autonomy, came into being.

After Russia's October Revolution, Lenin intended to establish a centralized and unified socialist state. However, the legacy inherited by the Bolsheviks rendered it impossible to establish a unified Russia. According to the statistics of 1897, "only 43% of the subjects of the Russian Empire identified the Russian language as their mother tongue".[5] The February Revolution ended with the abdication of Tsar Nicholas II and the Romanov Dynasty, which inspired the national liberation movement of the various nationalities within the Russian Empire. Similar to the circumstances of the Austro-Hungarian Empire, ethnic and territorial disintegration appeared in Russia. To make things more complicated, the Soviet regime founded by the Bolsheviks after the October Revolution was confronted with foreign powers' threat of armed interventions.

To effectuate a union for the proletariats of all nations and states, Lenin suggested that a nation-state be established on the basis of the national self-determination of the various peoples under the leadership of the proletarian party. The realization of such a union could only resort to federalism as the form of government under the historical conditions at that time. Nikolai Rizhkov later commented: "Lenin had no alternative at the time, for an immediate architecture of a unitary nation state would

---

[4]Bai (1999): 7.
[5]The Soviet Academy of Sciences (1977): 16.

inevitably render it impossible to establish".[6] In fact, the Soviet Union was nominally a supranational union of nation-states under the leadership of the proletarian party.

The federal system of government originated in the USA as the product of the 13 North American colonies' rebellion against the British Empire. "American federalism is the division of sovereignty or ultimate dominion between the central authority and local governments".[7] However, the national self-determination of the USA is only self-determination for the white immigrants. Described as "one out of many" for the White race on the basis of national and local decentralization, the US federal system, which combines the federal power with regional governments in a single political system, cannot be defined as multi-ethnic or multi-racial federalism. The civil rights and "the inalienable natural human rights" advocated by the founding fathers of the USA excluded the blacks, the Native Americans and even women. Rather than the state governments of the USA in which they are physically located, the reservation system in the USA is a legal designation for an area of land managed by a Native American tribe under the Bureau of Indian Affairs. As a marginalized system separated from mainstream American society, the reservation system for the segregated Native American Indian tribes is endowed with an autonomous nature.

The federal system of the USA and the Soviet Union have affected to varying degrees the Chinese elite's explorations of governmental modes, from the inauguration of the Republic of China (ROC) on the basis of "five races under one union" initiated by Dr. Sun Yat-sen, to the establishment of a unified people's state by the Chinese Communists, then to the implementation of regional autonomy in the compact communities of ethnic minorities. While designing the governance model for the newly established ROC government, Sun Yat-sen, who served as the interim president after the success of the Xinhai Revolution, not only drew on the Anglo-American state systems but also accepted and developed the principle of "one nation, one state" embodied in western nationalism. Both the Chinese Soviet Republic founded by the Communist Party of China in 1931 and the Red Army's political declaration of establishing a federal republic in China en route to the Long March can be identified as the Chinese Communists' early attempts to inaugurate a federal republic in China. However, these symbolic advocacies and practices were unable to be realized due to their incompatibility with the national conditions of China.

Historical facts have testified that neither the American-style "one out of many" federalism nor the Soviet-style "union of constituent socialist republics" applies to China due to its unique ancient historical process and modern historical experience. Therefore, maintaining state unity and respect for diversity have been upheld as a national commitment by the people of all ethnic groups due to China's time-honored history as a unified multi-ethnic state. Toward the modern era of China, which was heralded by the First Opium War in 1840, the state unity, political unification, ethnic solidarity, and territorial integrity of the country were seriously threatened and undermined by the foreign powers' aggression. Neither the social conditions for Bourgeois Revolution nor the backbone forces for launching Proletarian Revolution were exis-

---

[6]Rizhkov (2008): 384.
[7]Patterson (2007): 77.

tent in Mongolia, Tibet or Xinjiang at that time. If these regions were factitiously facilitated for "national self-determination" and founding independent states, they would inevitably be reduced as imperialist powers' colonies or spheres of influence. In addition, the Versailles Peace Conference in the wake of the First World War permitted no space for China's national self-determination. Therefore, federalism is only a fantasy for China; it would only lead to national and state disintegration.

China's historical circumstances show that the national self-determination of the country can only be achieved by the common will of all ethnic groups; only after ousting all imperialist forces could the state independence of China be realized. After the "Marco Polo Bridge Incident", the Second United Front, a brief alliance between the Chinese Nationalist Party (KMT) and the Communist Party of China (CPC) to resist the Japanese invasion, was formed. The ruling KMT, except for the nominal vow of "union of five races", refused to recognize the diversity and equality of ethnic minorities in its governance practices. By highlighting the notion of "state-nation", the KMT government turned a blind eye to the multi-ethnic reality of China and implemented ethnic assimilation policy, which incurred a strong resentment from the ethnic minorities.

The ethnic policy advocated by the CPC set the goal of founding a unified country upon winning the War of Chinese People's Resistance against Japanese Aggression. On the eve of the founding of the People's Republic of China, the first session of the Chinese People's Political Consultative Conference (CPPCC) was convened in September 1949. At the suggestion of the CPC, deputies of different ethnic groups and political parties held consultations and decided to proclaim the establishment of the People's Republic of China as a united multi-ethnic state. The conference also adopted *the Common Program*, which actually served as a provisional constitution of the new regime. A chapter in *the Common Program* specially expounded on New China's ethno-national policies and clearly defined regional ethnic autonomy as a basic policy of the state. The widespread establishment of regional ethnic autonomy in the compact communities of ethnic minorities laid a solid foundation for the maintenance of state unity and territorial integrity. The self-determination aspiration of all Chinese ethnic groups was thus sublimated to the self-determination consciousness of the Chinese nation, that is, to cast off the enslavement of imperialist forces and inaugurate a new regime for the Chinese nation.

The Chinese Communists believe in Marxism–Leninism and respect the status of the Soviet Union as a prototype for the socialist state; nevertheless, this does not mean that China's socialism must mechanically copy the experiences of the Soviet Union in terms of state institution, system design, and policy formulation. Marxism–Leninism believes that regional ethnic autonomy is an approach to solving the ethno-national issues. Lenin stated: "we shall consider the ethnic composition, economic mode and living habits of local residents while determining the scope of autonomous regions for ethnic minorities".[8] China's regional ethnic autonomy is not the result of indiscriminately imitating the Soviet Union's federalism; rather, it is the combination of the basic principles of Marxism and China's national conditions.

---

[8]Lenin (1990a): 61.

Marxism argues that any social problem must be analyzed and understood in a certain historical time and space. Stalin pointed out: "While addressing the ethnonational issues of a country, we must take the specific national conditions of that country into consideration".[9] The federalism form of government tallies with the reality of the Russian Revolution at that time; however, it does not mean that the Soviet-style union of constituent republics is the only form of government for all the socialist states. Some federated states of Eastern Europe founded after the Second World War, for example, Czechoslovakia and Yugoslavia, successively collapsed after the dissolution of the Soviet Union. It was, fundamentally speaking, the inevitable result of divorcing from their corresponding national conditions. Although the reasons for the fiasco of socialist construction in these countries were varied, it was true that they failed to shake off the fetter of the Soviet model. While deciding the developmental path for a country, we should keep it in mind that our most fundamental foothold is in conformity with national conditions and people's wishes. It has repeatedly been testified by history. With the establishment of Inner Mongolia Autonomous Government in May 1947 as the starting point, regional ethnic autonomy was put into practice by the Chinese Communists in the compact communities of the ethnic minorities.

In comparison, it was after experiencing a series of social upheavals represented by the US Civil Rights Movement in the 1970s that the western developed countries began to explore and implement regional autonomy for ethnic minorities. The autonomous communities of Catalonia and Basque in Spain, the Sami Parliament in the Nordic countries, and the Scottish Parliament of Britain were some typical examples. Based on his investigations into ethnic conflicts around the world, the Canadian political philosopher Will Kymlicka concluded: "autonomy for ethnic minorities helps, rather than threatens, political stability".[10] Although this understanding in western academia is far from a prophetic vision, it verifies the universality of regional ethnic autonomy expounded by Marx and Lenin.

4.2 Regional Ethnic Autonomy: Comply with the Aspirations of the People

As post-war negotiations between the Nationalist Government in Nanjing and the Communist Party failed, the civil war between these two parties resumed. Major combat in the Chinese Civil War ended in 1949 with the Communist Party in control of most of Chinese mainland, and the Kuomintang retreating offshore, reducing the Nationalist Government's territory to only Taiwan, Hainan, and their surrounding islands. On September 21, the Chinese Communists organized the Chinese People's Political Consultative Conference (CPPCC), inviting delegates from various political parties to attend and discuss the establishment of a new state. In the opening speech, Mao Zedong solemnly declared: "the convening of the conference signifies the rising

---

[9] Stalin (1979): 81.
[10] Kymlicka (2004): 96.

up of the Chinese people; it symbolizes the birth of a new era".[11] The first meeting of the CPPCC adopted *the Common Program*, specifying the structure of the new government and determining the name and symbols of the new state. It also elected the leaders of the central government. Therefore, *the Common Program* effectively served as an interim constitution. On October 1, 1949, Mao Zedong proclaimed the establishment of the People's Republic of China (PRC), with its capital at Beiping, which was renamed back to Beijing.

In addressing the first session of the CPPCC, Premier Zhou Enlai stated: "China is a multi-ethnic country in which the ethnic minorities make up less than 10% of the total population. Of course, all the ethnic groups, regardless of their population sizes and levels of economic development are on an equal footing. The Han people should respect the religious beliefs, languages, folkways, and customs of ethnic minorities. We advocate regional ethnic autonomy under the pre-condition of maintaining the territorial integrity of the country. Any ethnic group is undoubtedly entitled to the endowed right of self-determination. But today, the imperialists intend to divide China by fomenting the independence of Tibet, Taiwan or even Xinjiang. Against this backdrop, we hope people of all ethnic groups will not be incited by the provocations of the ill-conceived imperialist forces. For this very reason, the name of our new administration is called the People's Republic of China, rather than the federal republic. We shall implement regional autonomy in the concentrated communities of ethnic minorities to ensure their right of autonomy". Zhou Enlai added: "the policy of regional ethnic autonomy, by means of ethnic cooperation and assistance, aims to achieve a common development and prosperity of all ethnic groups. It will, in turn, contribute to a prosperous, culturally advanced and unified China".[12]

The Common Program officially established regional ethnic autonomy as one of the basic political systems of the state. It stipulated: "regional autonomy shall be implemented in areas where the minority ethnic groups live in compact communities and set up organs of self-government for the exercise of the power of autonomy". With regard to this, Ulanhu, the founding Chairman of the Inner Mongolia Autonomous Government, concluded: "this policy is not only suitable for the Mongols, but for other minority ethnic groups as well. It has become a program that we must comply with".[13] The system of regional ethnic autonomy combines the basic principle of Marxism–Leninism and the distribution pattern of ethnic minorities, namely, the pattern of living together over vast areas while some live in individual compact communities in small areas. Therefore, China's regional ethnic autonomy integrates ethnic autonomy and regional self-government. It guarantees the unified state leadership and uniformity of legal decrees, and economic and social systems. Therefore, the unitary system of government, in which the central government is ultimately supreme and any administrative divisions exercise only powers that the central government chooses to delegate, entails the particularity of regional ethnic

---

[11] *The Founding of the People's Republic of China*. Beijing: China Literature and History Publishing House, 2009: 10, 20.

[12] *Selected Documents on the Administration of Xinjiang: 1949–2010*, p. 3.

[13] Ulanhu (2013): 104.

autonomy. The practice of regional ethnic autonomy within a unified country was conducive to the achievement of ethnic equality due to its conforming to the actual situations of China.

The implementation of regional ethnic autonomy is a special form of maintaining state unity in China, a vast country with complex ethnic composition. The organic combination of "state unity" and "regional autonomy" is an important practice of historical materialism and dialectical materialism. Therefore, the centralization of the state and the autonomy of the ethnic minority regions have become one of the characteristics of China's democratic centralism, in which the division of functions and powers between the central and local state organs is guided by the principle of giving full play to the initiative and enthusiasm of local authorities under the unified leadership of the central government. The right of autonomy delegated by the central government to the concentrated communities of minority ethnic groups is an institutional arrangement to guarantee the equality of all ethnic groups, which epitomizes the merits of the socialist democratic system with Chinese characteristics. As one of the connotations of democratic politics, regional autonomy takes into account the rights and interests of ethnic minorities, and those of all ethnic groups, emphasizing an equal cooperation among people of all ethnic groups within the autonomous region; in addition, it highlights the mutually beneficial cooperative relations between autonomous regions and other administrative divisions under the centralized and unified leadership of the state.

By comparing the historical conditions and developmental path of China with those of the Soviet Union, Zhou Enlai expounded the reasons why the Chinese government established the system of regional ethnic autonomy as a basic political system: "Historical conditions and the revolutionary movement development have provided a sound basis for ethnic cooperation in China; therefore, regional ethnic autonomy conforms to the national conditions of China". Zhou Enlai added: "in addition to their obvious different appellations, the regional autonomy of China and the federalism of the Soviet Union are basically different; the former is an administrative division under unified state leadership, while the latter is a loosely-connected union of constituent republics, which are essentially ethnically-based proto-states."[14]

When meeting with Janos Kadar, General Secretary of the Hungarian Socialist Workers' Party in Oct. 1987, Deng Xiaoping asserted: "We can neither copy the paths of the western capitalist countries nor indiscriminately imitate the models of the socialist states in the Soviet Union or Eastern Europe. Regional ethnic autonomy, due to its pertinence to the national conditions of China, is contributive to addressing the ethno-national issues of the country".[15] One of the important backgrounds of Deng Xiaoping's statement was Kazakhstan's "Jeltoqsan Incident", in which riots took place in Almaty, Kazakhstan's capital city, at the end of 1986, in response to General Secretary Mikhail Gorbachev's dismissal of Dinmukhamed Kunayev, an ethnic Kazakh and the First Secretary of the Communist Party of Kazakhstan, and his appointment of Gennady Kolbin, an outsider from Russia. In the context of the

---

[14]*Selected Documents on the Administration of Xinjiang: 1949–2010*, pp. 190, 185.

[15]Deng Xiaoping. *The Selected Works of Deng Xiaoping*, Volume III, p. 257.

Soviet Union's turbulent reforms, Deng Xiaoping's remarks showed that China would firmly commit to its own way of development. Upholding and improving regional ethnic autonomy has become a political choice for the construction of socialism with Chinese characteristics.

4.3 Structural Hierarchy for Ethnic Autonomous Areas

The establishment of autonomous areas has a direct bearing on multi-faceted factors, including history, reality, politics, economy, ethnicity, and geographical location; in addition, some concrete conditions of the ethnic minorities, such as population size, geographical area, and administrative status, must be taken into consideration. In a speech delivered in 1950, Mao Zedong stated: "We must coordinate our efforts towards the implementation of regional ethnic autonomy, which involves a wide range of issues".[16] Among these, one of the most important and pressing agendas was to determine the subjects of regional autonomy and scopes for their compact communities. Therefore, the full implementation of regional autonomy for the ethnic minorities ran parallel to ethnicity recognition, a series of scientific investigations on the basis of history, appellation, language, culture, customs, economic life, religious belief, geographical distribution, and demographics of the various ethnic minorities.

As mentioned earlier, the long existence of a united multi-ethnic state and the patriotic spirit formed during their common fight against foreign invasions in modern times are, respectively, the historical basis and political foundation for practicing regional ethnic autonomy. In their long historical development, the various ethnic groups moved frequently from one place to another and gradually formed the pattern of living together over vast areas while some live in individual compact communities in small areas. The Han people, which constitute approximately 92% of the total population, are the majority in every province, municipality, and autonomous region except for Xinjiang and Tibet, where Uighurs and Tibetans are the majority, respectively.

The populations of the 55 ethnic minorities are relatively small and most of them live in the frontier areas. Still, they can be found in all the administrative regions above county level in the hinterland. Many ethnic minorities, such as the Hui, who are predominantly adherents of the Muslim faith, are found throughout China, though they are concentrated mainly in the northwestern provinces. The Mongols have concentrated distributions in Inner Mongolia, Qinghai, Xinjiang, Jilin, Liaoning, Hebei, Henan, and Yunnan. As of the 2014 census, there are 2.2 million Tibetans living in the Tibet Autonomous Region and ten Tibetan Autonomous Prefectures in Yunnan, Gansu, Qinghai, and Sichuan. The southwest provinces, in particular Yunnan and Guizhou, are reputed to be the most ethnically diverse regions of China, with ethnic minorities accounting for 34% and 37% of their respective total populations.

---

[16]Mao Zedong. *The Collected Works of Mao Zedong*, p. 29.

In China, it is quite common for people of one single ethnic group to live in different administrative regions, while in a single administrative region there can be many different ethnic groups. With the widespread phenomenon of embedded ethnic distribution, the compact communities of ethnic minorities are not clearly demarcated.[17] In addition, the disparities between different areas in access to natural resources and stage of development make it pragmatic to adopt the policy of regional autonomy for ethnic minorities.

As of 1952, 130 autonomous administrative divisions, which were of various sizes and populations, had been established throughout the country. According to *the Constitution of China* issued in 1954, autonomous areas for ethnic minorities were classified into three hierarchies, including autonomous regions (provincial-level), autonomous prefectures (subprovincial level), and autonomous counties or autonomous banners (subprefecture level). The nomenclature of autonomous areas highlighted the dual factors of ethnicity and geographical location by linking the appellations of a geographical area, the predominant ethnic minority or minorities and a type of administrative division. Some autonomous areas have more than one specified minority, which tend to be listed in the name of autonomous prefectures, leading to rather long names.

The founding of autonomous regions in China not only considered the compact community size of ethnic minorities within a particular autonomous administrative division but also took the historical distribution of compact settlements into account. For example, the League banner system, referring to the administrative division of the Qing Dynasty into which all Manchu households were placed primarily for military purposes, experienced a variety of transformations with the full introduction of the provincial system during the Republic of China (1912–1949). As a consequence, some banners were incorporated into adjacent provinces, while others were merged into newly established provinces, such as Chahar, Rehe, and Suiyuan.

After its inception in 1947 by the Communist Party of China, the Inner Mongolia Autonomous Region successively incorporated the territories of Suiyuan, Chahar, Rehe, Liaobei, and Xing'an, along with the northern parts of Gansu and Ningxia. It is currently the third-largest subdivision of China, covering approximately 1,200,000 km^2, or 12% of the total land area of the country. Therefore, it can be concluded that a unified autonomy of the Mongols has been achieved in Inner Mongolia. As a matter of fact, it was a commitment made by the Chinese Communists to the Mongols as early as 1935: "The territories of Chahar, Rehe and Suiyuan shall be merged with Inner Mongolia autonomous government to be established. Any other ethnic group, including the Han people, shall never occupy or deprive the land of the Inner Mongols under any pretext".[18] Therefore, the system of regional ethnic autonomy advocated by the CPC is a sincere policy practice instead of an expedient measure.

Besides the Mongols, the residents of Inner Mongolia Autonomous Region include the peoples of Han, Daur, Ewenki, and Oroqen. They jointly exercise the

---

[17]Ulanhu (2013): 145.
[18]United Front Department of the CCP (1991): 323.

local power of the autonomous region. To guarantee the right of autonomy for ethnic minorities, the Chinese government established Oroqen Autonomous Banner, Evenk Autonomous Banner, and Morin Dawa Daur Autonomous Banner within their compact communities, each with a designated ethnic majority other than the Mongols. Therefore, Inner Mongolia contains different hierarchies of autonomous administrative divisions, which can also be found in the other provincial-level autonomous regions. To guarantee the right of autonomy for the Mongols living outside of Inner Mongolia, the Central Authorities established autonomous prefectures or autonomous counties in these compact communities of the Mongols.

To sum up, China's autonomous areas for ethnic minorities can be categorized into three hierarchies: The first is the five provincial-level autonomous regions, including Guangxi Zhuang Autonomous Region designated to the Zhuang people, Inner Mongolia Autonomous Region to the Mongols, Tibet Autonomous Region to the Tibetans, Xinjiang Uyghur Autonomous Region to the Uyghurs, and Ningxia Hui Autonomous Region to the Hui People. The second is the autonomous prefecture or autonomous county (banner) designated to one ethnic minority according to its population size and geographical distribution, such as Gansu Linxia Autonomous Prefecture designated to the Hui people, Jilin Yanbian Autonomous Prefecture to the Koreans, and Sichuan Liangshan Autonomous Prefecture to the Yi people. The third is the autonomous prefecture or autonomous county (banner) designated to two or more ethnic minorities, such as Guizhou Qiandongnan Autonomous Prefecture designated to the peoples of Miao and Dong, Guangxi Longsheng Autonomous County to the Peoples of Dong, Yao, and Miao.

As one of the five provincial-level autonomous regions, Xinjiang, which spans over 1.6 million square kilometers, is the largest administrative division of China and home to 13 ethnic groups, including the Uyghur, Han, Kazakhs, Tajiks, Hui, Kyrgyz, Mongols, and Russians, of which the Uyghurs account for over 70%. Upon its peaceful liberation in September 1949, a coalition government was established. The preparation of setting up Xinjiang autonomous region went largely smoothly except for divided opinions on its nomenclature. After much debate, the various ethnic groups agreed to name the autonomous region "Xinjiang Uyghur Autonomous Region" to recognize its significant ethnic Uyghur population.[19]

The establishment process of autonomous areas for the ethnic minorities lasted for decades, the founding of Guangxi Gongcheng Yao Autonomous County in 1990 marking its completion. Such a long duration can be expounded from the following aspects. Firstly, setting up autonomous areas was closely related to ethnic recognition. The development of ethnic minority identification and the confirmation of ethnic minority identity and group belonging became at that time an important issue for the Chinese government. It was not accomplished until 1979 when the Chinese government officially recognized the Jino people as the 55th ethnic minority of the country. Secondly, the class and religious privileges formed in the history of ethnic minorities needed to be abolished by social reform, for the establishment of organs of self-government in ethnic autonomous regions must reflect the basic

---

[19] *The Selected Documents on the Administration of Xinjiang: 1949–2010*, p. 131.

socialist attributes, namely, the people being masters of their own destiny. Finally, the sociopolitical movements launched by the CPC leadership, in particular, the Great Leap Forward (1958–1962) and the Cultural Revolution (1966–1976), paralyzed China politically and negatively affected the country's economy and society to a significant degree.

As of 1990, China had established 155 autonomous administrative divisions, including 5 autonomous regions, 30 autonomous prefectures, and 120 autonomous counties, which are designated to 44 minority ethnic groups. In addition to their sporadic distribution in some of the interior or coastal provinces, these autonomous areas, whose areas account for 64% of the total area of China, are mainly located in the western provinces. In other words, regional ethnic autonomy, as a basic political system of China, has an extensive geographical coverage. To guarantee the autonomous rights of the 11 ethnic minorities not covered by regional autonomy, the Chinese government established 1248 ethnic townships throughout the country. Although, they are not considered to be autonomous divisions and do not enjoy the self-government rights pertaining to the larger autonomous areas, the widespread founding of ethnic townships marks the extension of the principle of regional autonomy into the "micro settlement" community of ethnic minorities.

In this sense, the system design of regional autonomy is well established, showing an extensive coverage of protecting the equal rights of ethnic minorities. It also highlights the nation-building foundation of China, namely, the equality of all ethnic groups. Zhou Enlai concluded: "Regional ethnic autonomy appropriately combines regional autonomy and ethnic self-governance by integrating economic and political factors. All ethnic minorities, be they large or small in size, are given the right to exercise the right of autonomy. Such a system is an unprecedented endeavor in the history of China".[20] Therefore, regional ethnic autonomy is the institutional guarantee for China's answer to its ethno-national issues.

4.4   Regional Autonomy for the Common Development of All Ethnic Groups

China's regional ethnic autonomy integrates the unified state leadership and self-governance of minority ethnic groups. The organs of self-government established within the jurisdiction of the autonomous regions, including local legislative and administrative organizations, government agencies and social organizations, operate in accordance with state constitution. The ethnic minorities' autonomous rights are at first reflected in their equal political participation in the unified state institution. In the local congress of an autonomous administrative division, in addition to the deputies from the ethnic group exercising regional autonomy in the administrative area, the other ethnic groups inhabiting the area are also entitled to appropriate representation. The chairman of an autonomous region, the prefect of an autonomous prefecture and

---

[20] *The Selected Documents on the Administration of Xinjiang: 1949–2010*, p. 188.

the head of an autonomous county must be a citizen of the nationality exercising regional autonomy in the area concerned. Other posts in the local government of an autonomous region, an autonomous prefecture and an autonomous county must rationally be assumed by people of the nationality exercising regional autonomy and of other minority nationalities in the area concerned.

The organs of self-government in ethnic autonomous areas perform the functions of local state organs as prescribed in the Constitution. They exercise the right of self-governance provided for in the *Constitution, the Law on Regional Ethnic Autonomy* and other laws, and of carrying out and implementing state laws and policies in the light of specific local conditions. The state organs at higher levels guarantee that organs of self-government in ethnic autonomous areas exercise their rights, including independently managing the ethnic group's internal affairs in its autonomous area; formulating self-government regulations and separate regulations; using and developing spoken and written languages of ethnic groups; respecting and guaranteeing the freedom of religious belief of ethnic minorities; retaining or altering the folkways and customs of ethnic groups; independently arranging, managing, and developing economic construction; independently developing educational, scientific, technological, and cultural undertakings. In addition to being political requirements for guaranteeing the rights of the ethnic minorities to be masters of the country, the above-mentioned rights of self-government for the ethnic minorities are internal mechanisms for the combination of "state unity" and "regional autonomy for ethnic minorities".

In ethnic minority communities within a concentrated and unified state power structure, the regional ethnic autonomy system combines history and reality, ethnic and regional factors, as well as politics and economy. The first is the combination between history and reality. It means we must consider the historical and current national conditions of China as a unified multi-ethnic state, including the compact communities of ethnic minorities and their traditional living areas, population distribution of various ethnic groups and their mutual relationship when deciding the territorial scope and administrative hierarchy of autonomous areas. The second is the combination between ethnic and regional factors. People of the designated ethnic minority of an autonomous area are entitled to administer their internal affairs, while people of all ethnic groups in the autonomous area enjoy the right to jointly manage the local affairs. The third is the combination between politics and economy. That is to say, to be masters of the ethnic minorities' own affairs politically is closely linked to the economic development and prosperity of the ethnic minority regions. This is the most critical point and the basis for the system of regional ethnic autonomy. In this regard, Deng Xiaoping's comment is concise and to the point: "Regional autonomy for ethnic minorities with the absence of economic development is tantamount to paying lip service".[21]

As a matter of fact, there has been a sharp discrepancy between the advanced system design and an underdeveloped economic and social basis from the outset of China's socialist construction. It can be expounded from the following two perspec-

---

[21] Xiaoping (1994): 167.

tives: firstly, the social revolution led by superstructure has promoted economic and social development through transforming the system of ownership and emancipating productive forces; secondly, the backward economic basis restricted the advantages of the superstructure system. Such incompatibility was more prominent in the ethnic minority regions. One of the basic national conditions of China was its unbalanced regional development, which found its fullest expression in the developmental discrepancy between the ethnic minority areas and coastal provinces.

In the New Democratic Revolution (1919–1949), the revolution of workers and peasants led the peasantry's struggle against the feudal landlords. Therefore, in the compact communities of the Han people, the policy of "land to the tillers", that is, confiscating landlords' farmlands and distributing them freely among peasants became an effective strategy to mobilize the poverty-stricken farmers to participate in the revolution. Due to the long-standing ethnic oppression and the induced ethnic conflicts in the old society, such radical land revolution could not, however, be rigidly applied to the ethnic minority areas in which the upper ruling classes of the ethnic minorities were serving as spokesmen of their national interests. In addition, the endorsement of ethnic minority elites was a pre-condition for the successful implementation of any social reforms to be carried out in the compact communities of ethnic minorities. Therefore, some enlightened ethnic minority personages needed to be recruited to the newly established democratic coalition government in implementing the system of regional autonomy. It could be defined as a development of the CPC's united front policy under the new historical conditions.

The democratic reform and implementation of regional ethnic autonomy abolished the vested privileges of the ruling classes and eliminated the oppression systems, which not only effectively redistributed means of production but fundamentally emancipated productive forces as well. These were necessary requirements and basic conditions of establishing socialism, a range of economic and social systems characterized by social ownership and democratic control of the means of production, in the compact communities of the ethnic minorities. Nevertheless, the inauguration of autonomous governments did not mean that the backward economic foundation of the ethnic minority regions could be changed overnight for the huge regional developmental disparity cannot be narrowed in a short time. Such a gap in development not only highlighted the contradiction between superstructure and economic base but also manifested the inconsistency between the idea of ethnic equality and the "de facto economic and social development inequality". Therefore, narrowing and to the largest extent eliminating this regional development gap is the basic focus in China's solution to its ethno-national issues. In Deng Xiaoping's words, "economic development is the master key to all social problems".[22]

China's regional ethnic autonomy is, in its essence, completely different from the Indian Reservation, which is actually a legal designation for an area of land managed by the Native American tribe under the US Bureau of Indian Affairs; it is also dissimilar to the "national autonomy" of the Sami People, an indigenous Finno-Ugric people inhabiting the Arctic area of the Nordic countries.

---

[22]Deng Xiaoping. *The Selected Documents on the Governance of Xinjiang: 1949–2010*, p. 104.

The implementation of regional autonomy in the ethnic minority regions has experienced a complicated process in that both the geographical scope of ethnic minorities' traditional compact communities, and more importantly, the various conditions conducive to the economic and social development of the autonomous areas, such as population, natural conditions, mineral resources, transportation, business conditions, urban layout, and industrial base, must be taken into consideration. While establishing the five provincial-level autonomous regions, the Chinese government not only considered the favorable conditions for development within the autonomous region but also the economic ties between the autonomous region and its neighboring provinces.

Although most of the ethnic minority areas are located in the underdeveloped Western provinces or border areas, the newly established autonomous regions must combine the administrative division adjustment as much as possible with economic elements, including agricultural basis, industrial layout, and existing infrastructure facilities. For example, Guisui (today's Hohhot) and Baotou, which enjoyed favorable conditions for business and industrial development, were included to the jurisdiction of Inner Mongolia Autonomous Region in 1954 to enhance its self-development capacity. After incorporating the territories of Suiyuan, Chahar, Rehe, Liaobei, and Xing'an, Inner Mongolia became the third largest subdivision of China, covering approximately 1,200,000 km^2. In terms of population size and ethnic composition, the administrative division layout of Inner Mongolia embodies the historically formed ethnic distribution pattern of China, that is, "living together over vast areas while some live in individual compact communities in small areas"; in addition, it creates a colossal stage for the common prosperity for people of all ethnic groups.

With a population of around 18 million, the Zhuang is the largest ethnic minority in China. While most Zhuang communities are concentrated in a compact area in Guangxi, the others are scattered over places shared by other ethnic groups such as Han, Yao, Miao, Dong, Mulao, Maonan, and Shui. Guangxi had been established as a province after the founding of the People's Republic of China. The Zhuang are found largely in the western two-thirds of the region, while the Han are concentrated in the eastern third. In 1958, Guangxi was converted into an autonomous region for the Zhuang in an effort to satisfy local aspirations. This decision was made because the Zhuang are the largest minority group in China and are mostly concentrated in the province. In addition to the compact communities of the Zhuang in the western part of Guangxi, the concentrated settlements of the Han people in the eastern part was also incorporated into the newly founded autonomous region for the Zhuang.

As a matter of fact, it is impossible for any ethnic group to realize a modernized development under a single resource structure and an isolated geographical environment. To this day, in some corners of the world, such as the Amazon rainforest, we can still find primitive tribes who are living in an uncivilized society. Their subsistence is obtained by hunting wild animals or gathering roots, nuts, and fruits. But of course, rather than being evolutionary latecomers, stragglers in the transition from ape to human, they have experienced all the years of modern human evolution. Their confined life, though we don't know whether such isolation is out of their active choice or passive endurance, contribute to stagnation in their social development.

The social progress of an ethnic group requires extensive contacts and exchanges with the outside world. The win-win cooperation arising from equal exchanges and mutual aids is exactly the most important development condition needed for the construction and guarantee of China's regional autonomy for ethnic minorities. In this regard, the creation of Ningxia Hui Autonomous Region is another case in point. With a size of 70,000 km^2, Ningxia is vested with an encouraging economic development layout. Facing the Yellow River in the east, Yinchuan, the capital city of Ningxia, enjoys favorable conditions for agriculture and has long earned fame as a "riverside city in the northwest China" and "land of fish and rice". The Plain of Wuzhong has the traditional advantages of water conservancy and irrigation systems. At the same time, there are vast grasslands within the autonomous region, which is helpful to the development of the traditional animal husbandry of the Hui people. The abundant coal reserves and dozens of other mineral resources provide supportive conditions for industrial development.[23]

Under the historical conditions at that time, the Chinese government fully considered conditions beneficial to local economic development while establishing autonomous regions for ethnic minorities, for "economic development is the most important pre-condition for ethnic equality".[24] Let us cite the administrative division adjustments of Yining and Xichang to further illustrate this point. Located along Ili River Valley, Yining, also known as Ghulja or Kulja, is characterized by a mild climate and rich grazing land. In 1954, the city was included into the Ili Kazakh Autonomous Prefecture, becoming the local political, economic, and cultural center.[25] Xichang, a relatively developed city in the far south of Sichuan, was merged into Liangshan Yi Autonomous Prefecture to enhance its self-development capacity.

Invested with the CPC's basic concepts and policy practices in addressing the ethno-national issues of the country, regional ethnic autonomy is neither an aerial castle in the superstructure nor an empty promise. It integrates the compact communities of the ethnic minorities into the unified political and social systems of China. However, the principle of ethnic equality should not only be reflected in the ethnic minorities' equal political status but in economic, cultural, and social development parities as well. As Zhou Enlai said in 1957, "none of the Chinese ethnic groups shall be left behind by socialist modernization, for the essence of socialism is common prosperity for all".[26] Therefore, highlighting the economic foundation conducive to regional economic cooperation is the core content of the administrative division adjustment of the autonomous regions.

After the founding of the new China in 1949, the implementation of regional autonomy in the compact communities of ethnic minorities was built on democratic reform and socialist transformation. As an integral part of the socialist system of China, the system of regional autonomy gives ethnic minorities the right to manage

---

[23] *Publicity Outline for the Establishment of Ningxia Hui Autonomous Region.* Gansu Daily, published on July 23, 1957.

[24] *The Selected Documents on the Administration of Xinjiang: 1949–2010*, p. 145.

[25] Ibid., p. 99.

[26] *The Selected Documents on the Administration of Xinjiang: 1949–2010*, p. 197.

their own affairs. However, it does not mean that the traditional social system and economic life of the ethnic minorities will be left intact; rather, the economic base sustaining the out-dated class repression within the ethnic minority society will be abolished by gradual democratic reform. The backward economic and social development of the ethnic minority regions could never be changed without transforming the old society with the new system. In this respect, the process of implementing regional autonomy in Tibet represents the most typical case.

4.5   The Arduous Course of Building a New Tibet

The establishment of Tibet Autonomous Region was delayed till 1965 due to a series of complicated factors. Among them, the impact of foreign imperialists' aggression toward Tibet since the start of the modern era was the most important. These elements rendered it extremely difficult for Tibet to be integrated into the constructional endeavors of the new China. After the Simla conference, the Britons and the Tibetan separatist forces attempted to engineer a "Tibet state" that could be embraced by the western world. Even in the 1950s, Tibet was still a society ruled by feudal serfdom under a theocracy. It was thus a most backward mode of human society under which the people had no democratic, economic, social or cultural rights, and their basic human rights were not protected. Old Tibet was a far cry from modern civilization. Under feudal serfdom, serfs suffered cruel political oppression and had no personal freedom or fundamental rights. Living a life of extreme poverty, the Tibetan people paid a huge price for carrying on the heavy religious traditions totally divorced from reality and the loss of personal freedom stretching back many generations. Attaching the label of "Tibet state" to the region can never obscure the essence of feudal theocracy serfdom.

As a matter of fact, "no trace of statism can be observed in the Tibetans' self-image since the decline of the ancient Tibetan Empire. It is consistent with the historical facts of Tibet".[27] Therefore, "neither the Western powers nor Tibetan secessionists have sufficient grounds to assert the independence of Tibet" even in the global tide of national self-determination inspired by the two world wars.[28] Even so, after the Second World War, the USA and some hostile Western forces attempted to utilize Tibet as a buffer to resist the Soviet Union's influence in the South Asian subcontinent, or "check the southward expansion of Communism".

After the Chinese Communists proclaimed the founding of the People's Republic of China in 1949, Tibet's Kashag, the governing council of Tibet during the rule of the Qing Dynasty and post-Qing period until the 1950s, stepped up its secession activities. Catering to the western powers' concern for the spread of Communism, or, "in view of the success of Communism in China, the impending danger is that Tibet will become its next prey", the Tibetan separatists pleaded with the UK and the USA

---

[27]Ekwa. R. B. *The Self-image of the Tibetans*. Beijing: China Tibetology Research Center, p. 497.
[28]Stein (1999): 103.

for help.[29] If the British Empire's invasion of Tibet was out of its need to expand its sphere of influence during the era of colonialism, then the Western powers' concern and conspiracy over the "issue of Tibet", as well as their vigorous backing of the 14th Dalai Lama after the conclusion of the Second World War, in particular after the "loss of China", were for the sake of the competition between different ideologies and social systems. The Tibetan separatists headed by the Dalai Lama, which had long been considered by the Westerners to be a conservative and xenophobic force, catered to the Western powers' Cold War mentality by vesting the "issue of Tibet" with an implication of anti-Communism.

Toward the end of the Second Chinese Civil War fought between Kai-shek Chiang's ruling Nationalist Government forces and Mao Zedong's Communist Army, the CPC gained control of most of Mainland China. In July 1949, the Lhasa authorities, via its radio station in Kalimpong, India, demanded that "the delegates of the Chinese Mission to Lhasa immediately leave Tibet to avert Communist riots". Soon after that, the Kashag government expelled all Chinese officials from Tibet despite protests from both the Kuomintang and the Communists. On October 1, 1949, the Chinese Communists established the People's Republic of China (PRC) in Beijing after gaining control of almost the entirety of mainland China. After the founding of the PRC, ousting all imperialist forces and liberating Tibet were perfectly justified to guarantee state sovereignty, territorial integrity, and national unification. Therefore, the presence of the People's Liberation Army in Tibet became an inevitable condition for the liberation of the whole China. As a response to the Western world's intimidation that "the crisis of Tibet is tantamount to disaster of the free world", Mao Zedong declared: "no matter the Tibetan Kashag is willing to negotiate with the Chinese central authorities or not, and whatever the outcome of the negotiations, the Chinese Army has full confidence and capacity to liberate all the territories of Tibet".[30]

By October 1949, the People's Liberation Army had consolidated control over most of eastern China and sought to bring peripheral areas such as Tibet back into the fold. Mao Zedong sought to resolve Tibet's political status by peaceful negotiations. Like two sides of a coin, Tibet's peaceful liberation and the PLA's garrison in the region solved the problems of state unification and ethnic solidarity. Of course, any attempt or action to oppose state unity, resist the Chinese troop's presence in Tibet and engineer ethnic conflicts was nothing to do with peace.

The pro-British Tibetan government stalled and delayed negotiations while bolstering its army. With the assistance of British training and equipment, the Tibetan Army served as the de facto armed forces of the Dalai Lama government. The main force was deployed in the strategic Qamdo region to obstruct the advance of the PLA. After months of wars of words between the Chinese Communists and the Kashag, the PLA won the Battle of Qamdo in October 1950.[31] The loss of Qamdo resulted in an internal division within the leadership of the Lhasa authorities. The 3rd Taktra

---

[29]Shakya (2011): 43.
[30]Zhang (2009): 139.
[31]Wang (2009): 179.

Rinpoche, Regent of Tibet, and a "pro-Britain and pro-slavery separatist", was forced to resign. Supported by the ecclesiastical and secular Tibetans, the adolescent Dalai Lama assumed full political duties.[32]

In April 1951, the Tibetan local government sent a five-member delegation to Beijing, with Ngapoi Ngawang Jigme as chief delegate, to talk with the central people's government on matters regarding the peaceful liberation of Tibet. As the central people's government gave full consideration to national policy and took on board the opinions of the Tibetan delegates, the negotiations were carried out smoothly, culminating in the signing of an agreement on the peaceful liberation of Tibet on May 23. In a speech commemorating the sealing of the agreement, Mao Zedong declared: "the Dalai Lama, the Panchen Lama and the Chinese central government have come to a common consensus in the governance of Tibet. Based on this grand unity, we are fully confident that Tibet will see fundamental progress in all respects".[33] The inking of the agreement established the "inherent status and authority" of the 10th Panchen Lama in the political and religious affairs of Tibet; in addition, it bridged the piled-up grievances between the sects of the Dalai Lama and the Panchen Lama.[34] Upon the conclusion of the agreement, the Panchen Lama sent a congratulatory letter to the Dalai Lama. In response, the Dalai Lama acknowledged the Panchen Lama's legitimacy in Tibet.[35]

The agreement was widely applauded by the ecclesiastical and secular people of Tibet. In September 1951, the Tibetan local government called a meeting, which was attended by 300 delegates from all walks of life. The conference unanimously endorsed the agreement. On October 24, the Dalai Lama sent a letter to Mao Zedong, which read: "The Tibetan Kashag and the ecclesiastical and secular Tibetans fully support *the 17-Article Agreement*, and, under the leadership of Chairman Mao and the Central People's Government, will actively assist the PLA troops entering Tibet to consolidate national defense, ousting imperialist influences from Tibet and safeguarding the unification of the territory and the sovereignty of the motherland".[36] Article three of *the 17-Article Agreement* provides: "In accordance with the ethnic policy laid down in the Common Program, the Tibetans have the right to exercise regional autonomy under the unified leadership of the Central Government".[37] This marked the promising future of Tibet after its peaceful liberation. However, the realization of this social transformation must be based on the actual situation of Tibet.

Caricatured by British missionaries as an isolated place of ignorance and superstition that placed the word of religious authorities over personal experience and rational activity, Tibet had long been a dark theocracy run by Buddhist monks. Of course, this backward and outmoded social system had to be terminated after the founding of the People's Republic of China. Due to the deep-rooted influence of the

---

[32]Lama (1990): 63.

[33]Mao Zedong. *the Selected Works of Mao Zedong*, p. 43.

[34]Gyatso (2011): 211.

[35]Ya (1987): 322.

[36]Huang (1995): 337.

[37]Wang X. *The Governance of Tibet by the People's Republic of China: 1949–2009*, p. 60.

theocratic rule, the ecclesiastical and secular people of Tibet unconsciously defended the political power and serfdom while venerating the religious authority of the Dalai Lama. Therefore, the secular reform of divorcing religion from politics was bound to encounter tremendous challenges from complex and sensitive social psychology. Any social reform in Tibet had to conform to the wishes of the Tibetans; more importantly, it required conscious cooperation from the local political and religious elites. In view of the unique social background of Tibet, *the 17-Article Agreement* emphasized the following principles: the existing political system in Tibet should not be altered; any major reforms in Tibet would be carried out by the local government of Tibet of its own accord; the central government will not impose social reform on Tibet. While meeting with the Dalai Lama, Mao Zedong declared: "An essential pre-condition for the reform of Tibet is the endorsement of the senior officials of the Tibetan local government and the abbots of Tibetan Buddhist monasteries".[38]

In the first National People's Congress convened in 1954, the Dalai Lama was anointed as vice chairman of the top legislature of China. He stated at the conference that "the policies of regional autonomy, ethnic equality and national unity stipulated in the State Constitution are supported wholeheartedly by all Tibetans".[39] Prior to that, the representatives of the Dalai Lama and the Panchen Lama had reached an agreement, resolving the long-standing discord between the two major sects of Tibetan Buddhism.

On March 9, 1955, the seventh plenary session of the State Council adopted *the Resolution on the Establishment of the Preparatory Committee of the Tibet Autonomous Region*. Among the 51 members of the preparatory committee, 46 were Tibetans, with the Dalai Lama and Panchen Lama serving as chairman and deputy chairman, respectively.[40] The composition of the preparatory committee, with its wide representation of different religious sects and social strata, laid a sound foundation for ethnic unity and cooperation.[41] On April 22, 1956, the committee held its inauguration conference, symbolizing the realization of regional, political, and religious unity within Tibet. In the opening ceremony, the Dalai Lama solemnly declared: "to satisfy the common aspirations of the broad public, we will carry out a phased democratic reform and social transformation. The Tibetan people will be united to build a unified autonomous region in the near future".[42] Also in 1956, the socialist transformations of agricultural cooperation, handicraft industry cooperation, and the public–private partnership of industry and commerce were completed in the communities of the Han people, which symbolized the basic establishment of the socialist system in China. However, Tibet was still in the stage of creating conditions for socialist reform.

With the central government's increasing support for the economic and social development of Tibet, such as running schools, founding clinics, building roads and

---

[38]Mao Zedong. *The Collected Works of Mao Zedong*, p. 110.

[39]Gyatso (2011): 211.

[40]Ibid.

[41]Mao Zedong. *The Collected Works of Mao Zedong*, p. 132.

[42]Gyatso (2011): 211.

bridges, assisting disaster relief, promoting ethnic equality, and respect for the local religious beliefs, the Chinese Communists and the garrisoned People's Liberation Army gradually won the trust of the Tibetans. A strong desire for social reform was observed among the Tibetan serfs, who accounted for 95% of the local population. Therefore, the CPC Tibet Committee launched a pilot social reform scheme in Qamdo and Shigatse in June 1956. However, the reform immediately led to a rebellion in some parts of Qamdo. In response, Mao Zedong immediately demanded the termination of the pilot reform and reiterated that "any important policy regarding Tibet must be endorsed by the Tibetan upper classes".[43]

Evidently, the central government has always adopted a very prudent policy on the social reform of Tibet considering the unique political, economic, and social systems of the region. In February 1957, Mao Zedong further stated: "In matters relating to the reform of Tibet, there will be no compulsion on the part of the central authorities in accordance with *the 17-Article Agreement*. The local government of Tibet shall carry out reforms of its own accord. When the people of Tibet raise demands for such reform, they shall be acted upon in consultation with senior officials of the Tibetan Kashag and religious elites".[44]

As a unifying symbol of Tibet, the Dalai Lama represents Buddhist values and traditions above any specific religious school. Therefore, he did enjoy a large political and religious influence in Tibet. After taking over the reins of government in 1950, he came to the conclusion that the social system of Tibet was "hopelessly obsolete". Accordingly, he strongly advocated the abolition of the "inherited debts", lambasting it as "the root of all evils in Tibetan society".[45] If these were his very thoughts at that time, there would be no resistance to the democratic reform in Tibet. But that was not the case. Instead of acknowledging the ruthlessness and cruelty of the dark theocracy of Tibet, he clung to the old system to maintain the vested interests of serf owners, which accounted for a mere 5% of the Tibetan population. Even after the creation of the Preparatory Committee for the Tibet Autonomous Region and his appointment as its head, he still refused to push forward the democratic reform.

However, a small incident that touched off public concern prompted the Chinese central authorities to take a step forward toward social reform. In 1957, an estate holder in Gyantse cruelly tortured one of his "nangzans", the hereditary household slaves who were deprived of any means of production and personal freedom, for the "nangzan" took part in public service at the cost of neglecting the corvee labor, a broad term covering not only corvee, but taxes and levies, and rents for land and livestock. As a matter of fact, such cold-blooded atrocities against serfs had been prevalent in the old Tibet.

To liberate the serfs from the personal bondage and enslavement of the inhuman feudal serfdom, the Preparatory Committee for Tibet Autonomous Region adopted a

---

[43] *Chronicles of Major Events for the CPC Tibet Committee*. Lhasa: Tibet People's Press. 1995: 75.

[44] Mao Zedong. *The Selected Works of Mao Zedong*, p. 160.

[45] Dalai Lama. *The Autobiography of the 14th Dalai Lama*. Beijing: the Commercial Press, pp. 93–94.

resolution, abrogating the corvee labor imposed on the Tibetan serfs.[46] It was widely accepted as a breakthrough with the sense of "human emancipation" in Tibet's endogenous democratic reform, for the personal liberation of the serfs meant the collapse of the feudal serfdom, which sustained the dark theocracy in old Tibet. Therefore, the Tibetan upper class, including the hereditary nobility and high government and monk officials, were bound to resist and boycott the democratic reform and regional autonomy for the purpose of maintaining their vested interests.

During his 1956 trip to India to celebrate the 2500th anniversary of Shakya Muni's nirvana, the Dalai Lama asked Jawaharlal Nehru, the Prime Minister of India, if New Delhi would agree to his request for political asylum should he choose to stay. Nehru discouraged this as a provocation against peace and reminded him of the Indian Government's non-interventionist stance agreed upon in its 1954 treaty with China. After that, the Dalai Lama returned to Lhasa in early 1957.

At the same time, Gyalo Thondup, the second-eldest brother of the Dalai Lama, sent six Tibetan youths to the Tibetan Program sponsored by the US Central Intelligence Agency (CIA), with the purpose of training Tibetan resistance fighters against the People's Liberation Army of China.[47] In May 1957, Chushi Gangdruk, commonly known as "Four Rivers and Six Ranges", which was actually an organization of Tibetan guerrilla fighters, was founded in Lhasa. Eventually, the CIA provided the group with material assistance and aid, including arms and ammunition, as well as training to members of Tibetan guerrilla groups at Camp Hale, a US Army training facility in Colorado. During this period, 27 armed rebel forces of varying sizes were founded in Tibet. In October, Tibetan secret services trained by the CIA were airdropped in Shannan and Qamdo. All of this meant that the Tibetan secessionists were ready to start their preparations to launch an armed rebellion.

Fundamentally speaking, these incidents were the inevitable results of the conflict between the theocratic feudal serfdom of Tibet and the newly established Chinese socialist system. If democratic reforms could be gradually carried out in accordance with *the 17-Article Agreement*, such institutional conflict would have been completely resolved and concluded in a peaceful manner. However, the Dalai Lama and his followers, placing their hopes on the foreign powers' backing of Tibetan independence, declined to honor their commitment. Moreover, they even attempted to boycott the social reform by fomenting and launching armed rebellions. Against this backdrop, Mao Zedong declared: "There must be a showdown before we can solve the issue of Tibet completely".[48] The changing domestic political environment served as a catalyst in accelerating the arrival of such a "showdown".

In May 1958, the CPC publicized its general guideline for the Second Five-year Plan, with the target of catching up with Britain in terms of major industrial products in 15 years or less. Mao Zedong called for "grassroots socialism" in order to speed up his plan for turning China into a modern industrialized state. In this spirit, Mao Zedong launched the "Great Leap Forward", established People's Communes in the

---

[46]Chinese Tibetology Research Center (2009): 101.

[47]Li (2010): 55.

[48]Mao Zedong. *The Selected Works of Mao Zedong on the Affairs of Tibet*, p. 170.

countryside, and began the mass mobilization of the people into collectives. All the ethnic minority areas, except Tibet, were involved in this movement.

The climaxes of the "Great Leap Forward" and "People's Communes Movement" were quickly popularized in China. The basic idea behind these social campaigns was that rapid development of China's agricultural and industrial sectors should take place in parallel. The hope was to industrialize the country by making use of the massive supply of cheap labor. The management system and distribution forms of the People's Communes dampened the production enthusiasm of farmers of all ethnic groups. Uneducated farmers attempted to produce steel on a massive scale, partially relying on backyard furnaces to achieve the production targets set by local officials. The steel produced was, however, low quality and largely useless. "The Great Leap Forward" reduced harvest sizes and led to a decline in the production of most goods except substandard pig iron and steel. The policy, characterized by highly impractical indexes, arbitrary direction and extreme equalitarianism, had serious detrimental impacts on the economic development and people's livelihood in ethnic minority areas. In accordance with the supreme directive that "farming is the top priority among all economic sectors", large-sized pastorals were reclaimed, causing serious ecological calamities. Such a radical political and social environment provided a golden opportunity for the Tibetan separatists to launch an armed rebellion.

In early 1959, frequent social unrest began to appear in Lhasa and other Tibetan regions. On 10 March, several thousand Tibetans surrounded the Norbulingka Palace, which served as the traditional summer residence of the successive Dalai Lamas from the 1780s up until the 14th Dalai Lama's exile in 1959, in response to a rumor that the Chinese Communists were planning to arrest the religious leader when he went to a cultural performance at the PLA's headquarters to celebrate his completion of Lharampa Geshe, the highest Tibetan Buddhist academic degree for monks and nuns. This marked the beginning of the 1959 Tibetan Uprising. At first, the violence was directed at Tibetan officials perceived not to have protected the Dalai Lama or to be pro-Chinese. Attacks on the Han people started later. One of the first casualties of the mob was a senior Lama who worked with the Chinese government as a member of the Preparatory Committee of the Tibetan Autonomous Region.

Two days later, protesters took to the streets of Lhasa. Tibetan rebel forces began to fortify positions within and around Lhasa in preparation for the upcoming conflict. A petition of support for the rebels outside the city was taken up, and an appeal for assistance was made to the Indian Consul. The armed rebels, chanting slogans like "Tibet is an independent state", and "Drive the Han Chinese out of Tibet", gradually built up in Lhasa. It greatly encouraged the Tibetan ecclesiastical and secular upper classes. They convened the so-called Tibetan People's Congress, declaring: "From this day on, the Tibetans stand up and break away from Chinese rule. We shall fight for the independence of our sacred land". After that, the rebels burned the Chinese national flag and effigies of Mao Zedong in front of the Potala Palace.

In 1960, the exiled Dalai Lama set aside the date of March 10 as the "Tibetan Uprising Day", which was often accompanied by the release of a statement. In fact, the so-called Tibetan Uprising Day was only a sign of their armed rebellion and unilateral breach of *the 17-Article Agreement* concluded between the Tibetan Kashag (the ruling council of Tibet) and the Chinese central authorities. Soon after the rebellion, the Tibetan Kashag convened the "People's Congress of Tibet", giving orders of "armed revolution" and submitting "declaration of the independence of Tibet" to the consulates of India and Nepal in Lhasa.[49] In his letter to the acting representative of the central government, the spiritual leader of Tibet wrote, "Reactionary and evil elements are carrying out secessionary activities on the pretext of ensuring my safety. I am taking steps to calm things down. The unlawful activities of the reactionary clique cause me endless worry and sorrow. As to the incidents of yesterday and the day before, which were brought about on the pretext of ensuring my safety and have seriously estranged relations between the Central People's Government and the Tibet local authorities, I am making every possible effort to deal with them". In the second letter, he stated that he had "severely criticized" officials of the Tibetan Kashag.[50] In fact, the Dalai Lama was more than happy to see the chaos and unrest in Tibet.

The Central People's Government was deeply concerned about the chaotic situation in Tibet. On March 15, Mao Zedong wrote to the Dalai Lama, demanding that he abide by the principles stipulated in the *17-Article Agreement* and take immediate measures to stop the Tibetan rebels' military provocations.[51] On the evening of March 17, the Dalai Lama, attired as a servant, slipped out of the Norbulinka, his summer residence in Lhasa, and began his flight to India.

At the beginning of the rebellion, the Dalai Lama disguised himself as an involuntary victim in his three letters to the representative of the central government. On leaving Lhasa, he could hardly wait to reveal his true separatist stance by authoring *a Message to all Tibetans*, calling on the Tibetans to make sacrifices for "the independence of Tibet". The Dalai Lama's fleeing abroad symbolized that he was politically broken with the Chinese central government. As vice-chairperson of the National People's Congress and director of the Preparatory Committee of Tibet Autonomous Region, he breached the *17-Article Agreement* and betrayed his historical responsibility of leading the socialist reform and establishing Tibet Autonomous Region. On the early morning of March 20, 1959, the armed rebels launched an offensive against the PLA garrisons and the central government agencies in Tibet. Subsequently, the PLA and militia began to strike back. Within two days, the rebellion in Lhasa was suppressed. However, the remnants of the rebel forces, due to the CIA's military backing, were not wiped out until late 1961.

The Chinese people will forever bear in mind the heroic undertakings of the First American Volunteer Group (AVG) during the Second Sino-Japanese War. Composed of pilots from the US Army Air Corps, Navy, and Marine Corps, the AVG, nicknamed "the Flying Tigers", flew military transport aircraft from India to China between 1941 and 1942 to resupply the Chinese war effort at a time when flying over the Himalayas was extremely dangerous and made more difficult by a lack of reliable charts, an absence of radio navigation aids, and a dearth of weather information. However, we must never forget the CIA's inglorious role in the Tibetan rebellion. "From 1957 to

---

[49]*The Suppression of the 1959 Tibetan Uprising*, p. 22.

[50]Ibid., p. 21.

[51]Mao Zedong. *The Selected Works of Mao Zedong on the Affairs of Tibet*, p. 171.

1961, the CIA airlifted 250 tons of equipment, weapons, munitions, radios, medical equipments, military gears, and manual printers to the Tibetan rebels".[52] In addition to training the first group of Tibetan agents in Saipan, the CIA opened a secret facility in 1958 at Camp Hale near Leadville, Colorado, training up a large number of Tibetan recruits. Thus, China's suppression of Tibetan insurgency involved an indirect contest with the CIA.

On March 28, 1959, the State Council of the People's Republic of China issued a decree dissolving the local Tibetan government. The Preparatory Committee of the Tibet Autonomous Region, with the 10th Panchen Lama as acting head, was authorized to exercise administrational power in Tibet for the time being. Under the leadership of the CPC, all the ethnic groups in Tibet launched a magnificent democratic reform movement, eliminating the feudal land ownership system and the attachment of the serfs to their owners existing in old Tibet.

The major policies at the first stage included: reducing serfs' land rents paid to the landlords and abolishing the slavery system. In the farming and pastoral areas, the harvests whose landlord had participated in the 1959 rebellion went to the tenanted farmers or herdsmen; the landlords or ranchers who had not taken part in the insurgency kept 20% of the farming or animal husbandry yields, with the remaining 80% distributed among the tenants. Meanwhile, the personal attachment slavery system was abolished. The second move was confiscating the production means owned by the landlords who had played a part in the rebellion and then allocating these production means among farmers and herdsmen. To those landlords who had not partaken in the armed rebellion, the local authorities purchased their production means and then gave them out to farmers and herdsmen free of charge. At the same time, these landlords were allowed to keep some of their means of production.

These measures received a hearty welcome among the poverty-stricken Tibetan serfs and slaves. As of late 1960, the land reform had almost been accomplished in Tibet. With the abolishment of the feudal ownership system, the serfs and slaves, who had been treated as "talking beasts" in the old Tibet for thousands of years, became human beings in the true sense and masters of their own destiny. With the completion of the land reform, the million serfs of Tibet were totally liberated in terms of politics, economics, and intellectual, cultural, and ideological matters, the productive forces of society were greatly liberated and all the ethnic groups in Tibet truly made the historical leap from feudal serfdom to socialist society and started out on the new road of socialist modernization.

In September 1965, the Tibetan People's Congress announced the founding of the Tibet Autonomous Region, with Ngapoi Ngawang Jigme, a Tibetan senior official who assumed various military and political responsibilities both before and after 1951, as Chairman of the Tibet People's Committee. Among the total 301 delegates in the general assembly, Tibetans accounted for more than 80%. The establishment of the Tibet Autonomous Region laid a solid foundation for the development and prosperity of the region.[53] In September 2015, a grand celebration was held to com-

---

[52] Knaus J. *Orphans of the Cold war: America and the Tibetan Struggle for Survival*, p. 169.

[53] *1959–2009: Democratic Reform in Tibet and the Dalai Lama's Exile*, p. 150.

memorate the 50th anniversary of the region, showing the tremendous changes of Tibet in the past five decades. The most important guarantee for the great achievements is the implementation of *the Law on Regional Ethnic Autonomy*.

4.6 Regional Ethnic Autonomy: Legal Norms and Practices

In August 1952, *the Program on Implementing Regional Ethnic Autonomy* (hereinafter referred to as the program) was submitted to the State Council for consideration, which marked the preliminary legislative effort to carry out the system. Its promulgation provides a legal framework for the full implementation of regional autonomy in China. It defines the nature of autonomous regions in China: "Autonomous regions shall be subordinated to the unified state leadership; in addition, they shall be subjected to the governance of higher-level government". The program embodies the basic requirements of autonomous regions as inseparable parts of China and the centralized and unified autonomous power. At the same time, this document stipulates the structure of the organs of self-government, the power of autonomy, ethnic relations within an autonomous area and leadership from state organs at higher levels. The promulgation and implementation of the program as China's first administrative statute on regional ethnic autonomy represent an important step forward in its effort to promote the rule of law in ethnic minority affairs. At the same time, it provided a favorable reference for the legislation of *the 1954 Constitution*.

Adopted and enacted through the first National People's Congress, *the 1954 Constitution* makes principled provisions on the self-government powers of the autonomous areas. It also guarantees a range of rights, including the requirement that the head of government of each autonomous area be of the ethnic group as specified by the autonomous area; self-regulation of finance, economic planning, science, and culture; the administering of their local public security forces in accordance with the military system of the state; drawing up statutes governing the exercise of autonomy or separate regulations suited to the political, economic, and cultural characteristic of the nationality or nationalities in a given area; employment of the spoken and written language by the organs of self-government. Among these provisions, the power of drafting autonomous statutes or separate regulations is the key to the specification of the power of autonomy.

Marxism–Leninism believes that the multi-ethnic socialist state, in addition to formulating state laws, should elaborate and develop the nationwide law by drafting special decrees applicable to a given area.[54] In the discourse of China, it means that we should "act according to circumstances". Zhou Enlai pointed out: "it is totally impossible to set uniform provisions on the right of autonomy for all the autonomous regions due to their divergent local conditions. The experiences and approaches applicable to the compact communities of the Han people shall not be mechanically

---

[54]Lenin (1990b): 147.

copied to autonomous areas for ethnic minorities; likewise, those suitable to a certain autonomous area shall not be indiscriminately imitated in another".[55]

In fact, it is easier to implement a uniform and nationwide policy than draft corresponding measures applicable to the specific conditions of a given area. Therefore, the promulgation of autonomous statutes or separate regulations must be based on grasping the local conditions in a realistic way while understanding the unifying principle of the nationwide policy. All these need to be explored step by step in the process of building the autonomous areas.

The Great Leap Forward (1958–1961), an economic and social campaign aimed at rapidly transforming China from an agrarian economy into a socialist society through expeditious industrialization and collectivization, interrupted this exploration process. The deficiency of legal mechanisms to put the ethnic autonomous laws and regulations into force in such radical social atmosphere not only resulted in limited exercise of the autonomous power but also, in some extreme cases, threatened the entire existence of the ethnic minority autonomous areas. During the Cultural Revolution (1966–1976), some established ethnic autonomous regions were arbitrarily split or abolished without any legal process.[56]

During the Great Leap Forward and Cultural Revolution, minority rights were largely ignored. The system meant to protect minority rights turned out too vulnerable to political movements and party politics. *The 1975 Constitution* reduced the entire six article section titled "Autonomous Institution of the Minority Autonomous Region" to one article, abolishing all autonomous powers. It further omitted a former provision that granted minorities "the right to keep and reform their custom and habits". These absurd constitutional changes clearly demonstrate the historical shortage of legal guarantees of ethnic minority autonomous powers. The reform and opening up of China must address the following major problems: what is socialism and how to build it? What is the system of regional ethnic autonomy? How should the system be implemented in a multi-ethnic state like China?

In 1980, the CPC Central Committee put forward a motion to the fifth National People's Congress, suggesting regional autonomy for ethnic minorities be added in the new state constitution.[57] During his tour of investigation in Xinjiang in August 1981, Deng Xiaoping declared: "regional autonomy is the only way out for the ethno-national issues of Xinjiang and other ethnic minority regions. It shall be stipulated as a basic political system of China".[58] In June 1981, the Sixth Plenary Session of the Eleventh Central Committee of the Communist Party of China adopted *the Resolution on Certain Questions in the History of Our Party since the Founding of the People's Republic of China*, which condemned the wrong policies and practices of the "Cultural Revolution". It confessed that "on the issue of the ethnic minority, in the past, especially during the 'Cultural Revolution', we made a serious mistake magnifying the class battle, harmed many minority cadres and people, and failed

---

[55]*The Selected Documents on the Affairs of Xinjiang: 1949–2010*, p. 199.

[56]Huang G. *The Ethnic Affairs of Contemporary China*, p. 218.

[57]Deng Xiaoping. *The Collected Works of Deng Xiaoping*, p. 339.

[58]*The Collected Documents on the Governance of Xinjiang: 1949–2010*, p. 252.

to pay enough respect to the autonomous rights of ethnic minorities". In addition, the resolution clearly provided: "We must upheld and firmly implement regional ethnic autonomy, and guarantee the ethnic minorities' right to govern themselves in accordance with the actual conditions".

The 1982 State Constitution rehabilitated the provision of regional autonomy for ethnic minorities. Moreover, it clearly stipulated the power of autonomy for autonomous areas by stating that "the state fully respects and guarantees the democratic rights of the minority nationalities to manage their own affairs".[59] These provide a sound legal basis for the formulation of the law on regional ethnic autonomy.

After a series of procedures, *the Law on Regional Ethnic Autonomy* was formally adopted at the Second Session of the Sixth National People's Congress and effective as of October 1, 1984. The law summarized experiences and policies since the implementation of the system, and development requirements of China's reform and opening up, and provided legal guarantees for the development and improvement of regional ethnic autonomy. Upon giving an explicit definition to regional autonomy for ethnic minorities, *the preface* points out that the establishment of autonomous areas is determined by ethnic relations, economic development, and other conditions, with reference to historical background; *part one* provides the general principles and basic contents of regional ethnic autonomy; *part two* prescribes the establishment of ethnic autonomous areas and the structure of the self-government organs; *part three* defines the autonomous power of the self-government organs; *part four* stipulates the nature and competence of the People's Courts and People's Procuratorates of autonomous areas; *part five* elaborates on the relations among ethnic groups within an ethnic autonomous area; *part six* specifies the leadership and assistance from state organs at higher levels; *part seven* details some supplementary provisions.

It can be said that the law on regional ethnic autonomy incarnates the Chinese Communists' ethnic policy principles developed over a long historical period. When meeting with Kádár János, General Secretary of Hungarian Socialist Workers' Party in October 1987, Deng Xiaoping said: "the system of regional ethnic autonomy, due to its pertinence to the national realities of China, is conductive to addressing the problems of the ethnic minorities". Deng Xiaoping added: "As for the harm done to ethnic minorities during the Cultural Revolution, that sort of thing can't be used as evidence that we discriminate against them. In those years it was not just the minorities that suffered; it was the Han people that were hit hardest. Tibet has tremendous development potential. Many of China's natural resources are located in ethnic minority areas, including Tibet and Xinjiang. If these areas can begin to develop, their future will be bright. It is our unshakable policy to help them do that". Thereafter, the successive leadership of the CPC restated this position in different situations. Xi Jinping concluded: "The system of regional ethnic autonomy is the source of our ethno-national policies".[60]

With the gradual establishment of a socialist market economic system in China, some of the provisions of *the Law on Regional Ethnic Autonomy* could no longer

[59]Huang G. *The Ethnic Affairs in Contemporary China*, p. 219.
[60]Hao (2015).

meet the needs of economic reform and Western development. Therefore, it was imperative to amend the law to adapt to the changing situations. Adopted at the Second Session of the Sixth National People's Congress, the 2001 Amendment to the law stipulates that: "regional ethnic autonomy is the basic policy adopted by the Communist Party of China for the solution of the ethno-national problems of China through its application of Marxism–Leninism". The system of regional ethnic autonomy is established as a basic political system of the State. In addition, the amendment adds the following clauses: the guidance of Deng Xiaoping Theory; to uphold and improve the system of regional ethnic autonomy; to persevere in the policy of reform and opening up to the outside world; to develop the socialist market economy; to enhance the socialist democracy and legal system construction.[61]

The changes have been rightly recognized as necessary to provide surety for the nation's progress by advancing law-based governance and upholding and developing socialism with Chinese characteristics in the new era. The revisions enshrine what the ruling Communist Party of China has accomplished in the recent development of its praxis and theory. They are of great significance to ensuring prosperity and the lasting security of the nation. By stipulating that the coastal provinces shall provide pairing-up assistance to the development of ethnic autonomous regions, the amendment highlights the importance of the accelerated development of ethnic minority areas. The successful practice has proved and will continue to prove that China's regional ethnic autonomy is a system based on fairness and justice. It leads the world in the system design and legal norms in guaranteeing political equality, economic development, cultural prosperity, and social progress for ethnic minorities.

At the same time, the progressiveness and superiority of the system design need to be displayed in practice. The most fundamental condition is to ensure that all ethnic groups are equal and the basic factor for achieving ethnic equality is to promote the economic and social development of the ethnic minority regions. As the most important legal norm for regional ethnic autonomy, *the Law on the Regional Ethnic Autonomy*, on the one hand, prescribes a series of preferential policies for the accelerated development of autonomous regions; on the other hand, it formulates regulations for the state organs to actively support the development of ethnic autonomous regions. The aim is to continuously narrow the de facto regional development gap and achieve the common prosperity of all ethnic groups. At the current stage, we must lay emphasis on the economic and social development of the ethnic minority regions while implementing regional ethnic autonomy. The 2014 national conference on the ethnic minority affairs emphasized: "the key to the implementation of the regional ethnic autonomy is to help the autonomous regions develop their economy and improve the people's livelihood".[62]

In addition to enacting and amending *the Law on Regional Ethnic Autonomy*, the legal system construction in the field of ethnic minority affairs was also demonstrated in the formulation of self-governing regulations by autonomous areas at different levels in light of their specific conditions. *The 1982 State Constitution* restored and

---

[61] *The Collected Documents on the Governance of Xinjiang: 1949–2010*, p. 263.
[62] Hao (2015).

improved the legislative power of ethnic autonomous areas, which created a favorable environment for the promulgation of self-governing regulations.

China's regional ethnic autonomy system uses fairness and justice as its basic principles. Its institutional design and legal norms in political equality, economic development, cultural prosperity, and social security are advanced. China's ethnic autonomous regions are, however, mostly socio-economically underdeveloped areas. Advanced institutional arrangements and a backward economic base constitute the first contradiction that must be solved if China is to uphold and improve the regional ethnic autonomy system. The fundamental task of China's ethnic affairs is to speed up the economic and social development of minorities and their inhabited areas, and gradually reduce and eliminate interethnic economic, cultural, and social life developmental differences, so that people of all ethnicities in ethnic autonomous regions and across China can enjoy common prosperity.

China's ethnic affairs, through regional national autonomy, and the political, economic, cultural, and social aspects of various ethnic minority policies, has to coordinate the relationship between the 56 ethnic groups, particularly the relationship between the Han and minority ethnicities; and to enable ethnic equality, solidarity, mutual assistance, and harmony between ethnic minorities. The fundamental task of achieving this goal is speeding up the economic and social development of ethnic minorities and their inhabited areas, and to gradually reduce and eliminate the various developmental differences between ethnic minorities in terms of their economic, cultural, and social lives.

References

Angben, D. *Taking to the path of Chinese characteristic solution to the ethno-national issues of China*. China Ethnic News. December 15, 2014.

Bai, G. (1999). *National self-determination in the international law*. Beijing: The Chinese Overseas Publishing House.

Chinese Tibetology Research Center. (2009). *The democratic reform in Tibet and the Dalai Lama's Exile*. Beijing: People's Press.

Gyatso, J. (2011). *Zhou Enlai and the peaceful liberation of Tibet*. Beijing: China Social Sciences Academic Press.

Hao, S. (2015). *Regional autonomy for the ethnic minorities: New formulations on the national conference on ethnic affairs*. Journal of the Minzu University of China, (2).

Huang, Y. (1995). *The history of the relationship between Tibet and the Chinese Central Government*. Lhasa: Tibet People's Press.

Kymlicka, W. (2004). *Rights of minorities: Nationalism, multiculturalism and citizenship*. Taipei: Left Bank Culture Press.

Lama, D. (1990). *Autobiography of the 14th Dalai Lama*. Taipei: Linking Publishing Services.

Lenin, V. (1990a). *The selected works of Lenin* (Vol. XXIII). Beijing: People's Press.

Lenin. V. (1990b). *The collected works of Lenin*. Beijing: People's Press.

Li, J. (2010). *1959: The 14th Dalai Lama's fleeing to India*. Taipei: Lianjing Publishing House.

Patterson, T. (2007). *The political culture of the US*. Beijing: the Orient Publishing House.

Rizhkov, N. (2008). *The tragedy of the great power: The disintegration of the Soviet Union*. Beijing: Xinhua Publishing House.

Shakya, T. (2011). *The Dragon in the land of snows: A history of modern Tibet since 1947*. Taibei: Left Bank Culture Press.

Stalin, J. (1979). *The selected works of Stalin* (Vol. 1). Beijing: People's Press.

Stein, R. (1999). *Civilizations of Tibet*. Beijing: China Tibetology Press.

The Soviet Academy of Sciences. (1977). *History of nation-state construction in the Soviet Union*. Beijing: The Commercial Press.

Ulanhu. (2013). *The collected works of Ulanhu*. Beijing: Central Press on the CPC's Documents.

Ulanhu. (2013). *The collected works of Ulanhu*. Beijing: China Central Wenxian Press.

United Front Department of the CCP. (1991). *Collected CCP documents on ethno-national issues*. Beijing: The Press of the CCP Party School.

Vyigotski, L. (1979). *Diplomatic history*. Beijing: The SDX Joint Publishing Company.

Wang, X. (2009). *The governance of Tibet by the People's Republic of China: 1949–2009*. Beijing: People's Press.

Xiaoping, D. (1994). *The collected works of Deng Xiaoping*. Beijing: People's Press.

Ya, H. (1987). *The biography of the 10th Panchen Lama*. Lhasa: Tibet People's Press.

Zhang, Z. (2009). *The US-China relations and Tibet: Historical evolution and decision analysis*. Beijing: Chinese Literature and Art Publishing House.

Chapter 5
Reducing the Interethnic Developmental Gap: A Road to Common Prosperity and Development

With a land area of 9.6 million square kilometers and a population of over 1.3 billion, China is the world's second-largest state by size and the most populous country. One objective of Chinese President Xi Jinping's "Chinese Dream" is to achieve a "moderately well-off country" by 2021 when the Chinese Communist Party celebrates its centenary. Realizing the dream, according to Xi, requires a second phase of transformative economic reform. During this process, China is tasked with narrowing and eliminating the interethnic developmental gap. As mentioned earlier, the ethnic minorities have a significantly smaller population than the Han Chinese, and mostly inhabit the border areas, which are essentially underdeveloped regions that lag behind in economic, cultural, and social terms due to geographical, historical, and cultural characteristics. Therefore, the regional development discrepancy also highlights the delayed economic growth of autonomous regions for ethnic minorities. Accelerating the growth of the western provinces and realizing the common prosperity of all ethnic groups are the essential requirements of socialism with Chinese characteristics and the only way to true equality of all ethnic groups.

5.1 Solution to the Plight of the "Hu Line" Effect

Much more than a mere geographical location, the "western region," which has become a widely used phrase in the Chinese media, is also a concept of economic geography. Defined as a regional category, economic geography combines natural geographical conditions and economic development level. A specific economic-geographical area is reflected in its position in the whole and its relationship with surrounding areas, including innate endowments (geographical features, climatic conditions, and natural resources) and acquired characteristics (population distribution, economic life, and transportation). The scientific cognition of economic-geographical features of the "western region" was put forward by Huanyong Hu (1901–1998), a forefather of modern Chinese demography and founder of China's population geography. In a paper published in 1935 titled *Distribution of China's*

© China Social Sciences Press 2020
S. Hao, *China's Solution to Its Ethno-national Issues*, China Insights,
https://doi.org/10.1007/978-981-32-9519-3_5

Population, he first postulated the term of the "Heihe-Tengchong Line." Known in international academia as the "Hu Line," it was an imaginary geo-demographic demarcation line stretching from Heihe in northeast China's Heilongjiang province to Tengchong in southwest Yunnan province, diagonally across the country. The line divides China into two roughly equal segments. Statistics of 1935 showed that the eastern part fed 94% of the Chinese population with only appropriately 43% of the total land, while the western part was sparsely populated in spite of its vastness.

The Hu Line, which was proposed on the basis of population density, inspired a series of systematic investigations into the unbalanced distribution of natural and geographical factors along the line. The results show that the Hu Line to a large extent overlaps with the distribution of rainfall, topography, and natural landscape features, thus forming contrasting attributes between the eastern and western regions, for instance, humid versus arid, lowland versus plateau, farming agriculture versus nomadic herding, and cultivated land versus desert. In addition to the unbalanced distributions of population density and economic development, the line largely reflects the ethnic spatial dispersion of China, with the western part and eastern part being the compact communities for the ethnic minorities and the Han, respectively. Therefore, the line is also of great significance in understanding the divergent humanistic elements of the two parts, such as language, culture, religion, folkways, and customs. In this sense, the value of the Hu Line in the understanding of China's national conditions should not be underestimated. It accounts, to a large extent, for the enduring effect of the line. Studies of meteorological geography show that the existence of the Hu Line phenomenon was closely related to climate change in ancient times. The dropping temperature, reduced rainfall, and frequent natural disasters in Western China contributed to its declining agricultural yields. Therefore, a large number of poverty-stricken farmers of western provinces were compelled to migrate eastward to seek a livelihood.

Most of the historical capitals of China, such as Luoyang in the dynasties of Xia, Shang and Zhou, Xi'an in the dynasties of Qin, Han and Tang, as well as the cities of Kaifeng, Zhengzhou and Anyang, were all economic and cultural cosmopolitans of the world at that time. In terms of their geographical distribution, all these cities are located to the west of the Hu Line. This fully testifies the non-existence of this division's effects at that time. As the cradle of ancient Chinese civilization, the hinterland of "Zhongyuan" (North China Plain), based on the deposits of the Yellow River and the relatively developed agriculture technology, sustained a large population. Therefore, the population density of the North China Plain was much higher than that of the eastern region in ancient times. Studies show that the population density of Chang'an (today's Xi'an) was more than 1000 per square kilometer during the Western Han Dynasty (206 BC–9AD). The population of north China, referring to the regions to the north of the Qinling Mountains and Huaihe River, accounted for 80% of the total of China at that time.[1] Due to climatic change, frequent natural disasters and armed conflicts in north China, as well as ceaseless invasions by the northern nomads, the farmers of the Huanghe River Basin fled to the Yangtze River

---

[1]Ge (1997): 56.

Valley and southeast China, thus forming three migration climaxes respectively in the last years of the Western Jin (266–316), Tang (618–907), and Northern Song dynasties (960–1127).[2] These migration upsurges coincided with three destructive armed conflicts, including the Sixteen Kingdoms (304–439), Five Dynasties and Ten Kingdoms (907–960), and the Jingkang Incident (1126–1127). The node of sudden climatic change in China was observed around 1260, in which Kublai Khan founded the Yuan Dynasty. The timeline also overlapped with the end of the Medieval Warm Period (950–1250), also known as the Medieval Climatic Anomaly.

The sudden climate change led to the continuous evolution of the ecological geomorphology in the terrain of China, forming vastly different population distributions between the eastern and western parts. This feature was ingeniously marked by the Hu Line, which to a large extent coincides with the annual rainfall catchment area of 400 mm. The relatively developed agriculture in the eastern part sustained a rapid growth in transportation, urban development, and industries, in particular, the sectors of textiles and porcelain. However, the ever-increasing desertification and drought in the western part led to low agriculture and animal husbandry yields, which fundamentally limited its population growth. Though the successive Chinese central dynasties greatly encouraged land reclamations in the western provinces. It, nonetheless, had a very limited impact on the development of the vast western region. As mentioned earlier, the area to the west of the Hu Line has long been compact communities of ethnic minorities. Most of their traditional societies were in a closed state. Due to geographical isolation, underdeveloped traffic conditions, and sparse population, a great amount of natural resources were not able to be exploited. Therefore, the economic and social forms of many ethnic minorities were stagnated. The developmental gap between the eastern and western parts became increasingly prominent, which remained so until China crossed the watershed of the modern era in the mid-1800s. It seemed that the population density distribution rule of China established by the Hu Line would become an eternal truth.

Since 1949, the Chinese government has carried out six censuses. The statistics from the first to the fifth revealed that the population distribution pattern embodied in the Hu Line remained unaltered though the total population of the country already broke a ceiling of 1 billion in 2000. By the 2010 census, the Chinese population had increased to 1.3 billion. The pattern of population distribution in the eastern and western parts demarcated by the Hu Line began to change. Then, China's reform and opening-up was evincing a new synchronous regional development pattern, including the Western Development, the rise of the central provinces, the revitalization of the old industrial bases in Northeast China, and the accelerating development of the coastal provinces. It seems that the long-standing Hu Line effect was invalidated in terms of the population distribution shares of these regions. However, in comparison with the population distribution of 2000, the proportion of the eastern provinces in 2010 increased by 2.41%, while percentages of the central, western, and northeastern provinces were observed in a declining tendency, the reduction rate of the western region reaching 1.11%. The ascending and descending inclinations of these regions'

---

[2]Ibid., p. 246.

population proportions, with rural-to-urban migrant workers as the predominant feature, highlight the geographical advantages of coastal provinces, which to a large extent testify the economic appeal of the Hu Line effect.

While visiting a human habitat exhibition in the National Museum on November 27, 2014, Chinese Premier Keqiang Li attentively read the introductory texts of a map of China marked with the Hu Line. Directing against the distinction between "livable areas" and "unlivable areas" along the line, Li prescribed his solution to the plight of the Hu Line effect. He pointed out that China, as a multi-ethnic country with a vast territory, must make an overall plan on its regional development so that people of the central and western provinces might have equal access to the benefits of modernization at their doorstep. In other words, the realization of a moderately well-off society in China does not mean that people of the central and western provinces must leave their homeland for employment in the coastal provinces; rather, the Chinese government should divert more resources to accelerate the development of central and western regions. The Western Development Strategy initiated in 2000 is a great practice to solve this historical problem.

5.2   The Phased Development Strategy: From Coastal Areas to Interior Provinces

Since the founding of the People's Republic of China in 1949, the central government has attached great importance to the economic and social development of ethnic minority regions. By implementing regional autonomy for ethnic minorities, the economic conditions of mutual assistance and cooperative development among people of all ethnic groups have been basically established in the compact communities of ethnic minorities. In addition to giving the supports of manpower, material, and financial resources, the central authorities formulated preferential policies to speed up the development of autonomous regions. In *the First Five-year Plan*, the series of social and economic development initiatives implemented between 1953 and 1957, the state gave priorities to the development of agriculture, animal husbandry, trade, and transportation of these areas. In the layout of the national industrial base and transportation network, construction of industrial base, railway, and highway in the ethnic minority areas also witnessed unprecedented progress. A huge number of large-sized industrial enterprises, including Baotou Iron and Steel Plant, Karamay Oilfield, Qingtongxia Hydropower Station, and Gejiu Tin Company, were put into production. During this period, the transportation facilities of the ethnic minority regions have witnessed great progress. Among the newly built eight railways, five were located in or connected with these regions. It was also during this period that the highways of Xikang–Tibet, Qinghai–Tibet, and Xinjiang–Tibet were completed.[3]

The ethnic minority regions have experienced rapid economic growth during this period though the majority of them were in the stage of establishing autonomous

---

[3]Huang G, *The Ethnic Minority Affairs of Contemporary China*, p. 120.

governments. The agriculture yields of the autonomous areas in 1957 increased by 62.9% and the number of livestock by 14.1% in comparison with that of 1949. Industrial output rose fivefold with the creation of a large number of small and medium-sized plants. Correspondingly, the occupation composition of the minority population experienced an unprecedented change. The number of ethnic minority populaces engaged in industrial production increased from 46,000 in 1949 to 820,000 in 1957.[4]

At that time, the Chinese government's basic policy in autonomous areas was to assist in their economic development and cultural progress. However, the Anti-Rightist Movement, a reaction against the "Hundred Flowers Campaign" during which the Communist Party of China encouraged Chinese citizens to openly express their opinions of the regime, and the subsequent movements of "Great Leap Forward" and People's Communes created a mentality of unreasoning impetuosity. In May 1958, the CPC Central Committee released its general guideline for the Second Five-year Plan, with a romantic target of catching up with Britain in terms of major industrial products in 15 years or a shorter period of time. The basic idea behind the "Great Leap Forward" was that rapid development of China's agricultural and industrial sectors should take place in parallel. The hope was to industrialize the country by making use of the massive supply of cheap labor and avoid having to import heavy machinery. The People's Communes, the highest of three administrative levels in the rural areas between 1958 and 1983, were formed in support of the "Great Leap Forward" and remained an inseparable part of the campaign.

The radical social movement reduced harvest sizes and led to a decline in the production of most goods except substandard pig iron and steel. Meanwhile, local leaders were pressured into falsely reporting ever-higher grain production figures to their political superiors. Participants at political meetings remembered production figures being inflated up to ten times of the actual production amounts in the race to please superiors and win plaudits.[5] The ethnic minority regions were no exception against the fanatic social environment throughout the country. To name just two examples, in September 1958, a farm in Qinghai purported to achieve a "miracle" wheat yield of 64.5 tons per hectare. Also during this year, a People's Commune of Guangxi fabricated an astronomical rice yield of 975 tons per hectare. The inflated agricultural yields brought about serious detrimental effects on the economic growth of ethnic minority regions. For example, the total grain output of Guangxi Zhuang Autonomous Region in 1960 was lower than that of 1952.[6] Likewise, traditional animal husbandry and fledgling industry were also subject to the impact of the fraud atmosphere.

The ensuing incidents, including the 1959 Tibetan Rebellion, the collapse of the Sino-Soviet alliance, and the Sino-Indian Border Conflict in 1962, complicated the already-strained domestic ethnic relations. These events became motivating forces for the Cultural Revolution, a nationwide social-political movement from 1966 until

---

[4]Ibid., p. 121.

[5]Jin (2009): 876.

[6]Huang G, *The Ethnic Minority Affairs of Contemporary China*, p. 130.

1976.[7] Initiated by Mao Zedong, then Chairman of the CPC, its stated goal was to preserve true Communist ideology in the country by purging remnants of capitalist and traditional elements from Chinese society, and to reimpose Maoist thought as the dominant ideology within the Party. During the Cultural Revolution, much economic activity was halted, with "revolution," regardless of interpretation, being the primary objective of the country. Because of the anarchic political environment, local governments lacked organization and stability, if they existed at all. Measures to invigorate the rural economy, such as rural fairs, self-financing mechanisms, and household responsibility system, were discouraged or strictly prohibited. For the purpose of increasing grain production, the overly zealous reclamation of grasslands was not uncommon, resulting in a devastating disappearance of large-sized pastures.

The 3rd Plenary Session of the 11th Central Committee of the CPC in late 1978 marked the beginning of the wholesale repudiation of Mao Zedong's Cultural Revolution policies and set China on the course for economic reforms. Trying to distance itself from the former practice of putting politics before economy, the new CPC leadership headed by Deng Xiaoping decreed that greater attention be diverted to economic construction. The "four modernizations" of industry, agriculture, national defense, and science-technology were considered the Party's key tasks for the new period. The ethnic minority areas, like other parts of China, have witnessed rapid development since the introduction of economic reform policies. To accelerate the development of the compact communities of ethnic minorities, the central authorities released a series of preferential policies, such as granting financial subsidies with the annually increasing rate of 10% from 1980 to 1988, appropriating education and construction allowances for frontier regions, implementing policies of tax reduction or exemption, increasing the purchasing prices of agriculture, animal husbandry, sideline, and native products, as well as encouraging rural fair trade and border trade, etc.

Since the first national symposium on the work of frontier regions in 1979, the Chinese government has put into effect a policy of pairing-up support for ethnic minority regions, where the economically developed coastal provinces or municipalities, including Beijing, Hebei, Jiangsu, Shandong, Tianjin, and Shanghai, have been paired up with providing assistance to frontier regions and ethnic minority regions. Later, this pairing-up support policy was expanded exclusively for Tibet. Accordingly, 60 central state organs, 18 provinces, and 17 centrally managed state-owned in enterprises have been paired up with specific regions of Tibet. After that, the scope and forms of the pairing-up assistance testified an expansion during the implementation process. In 1980, the central government set up an exclusive fund to support the development of the least-developed provinces.

The coastal provinces' pairing-up support for ethnic minority regions is of great significance to speeding up the development of ethnic minorities. Against the general layout of the reform and opening-up of China, these preferential policies given to the ethnic minority regions were aimed at achieving the common prosperity of all Chinese nationals by minimizing the regional development gap. Deng Xiaoping

---

[7]Shen Z, *The History of Sino-Soviet Relations: 1917–1991*, pp. 311–312.

pointed out: "common prosperity is both the fundamental quality of socialism and a primary goal of China's reform and opening up." For a unified multi-ethnic country like China, poverty elimination and common prosperity are two cornerstones of state unity and ethnic equality.

China's ethno-national policies themselves are essentially arrangements of adapting to diversity based on guaranteeing state unity. From the aspect of ethnicity, the preferential treatments are accorded merely to the 55 ethnic minorities; in terms of geographical location, these favored policies are only given to the autonomous regions of ethnic minorities, including five provincial-level autonomous regions, 30 autonomous prefectures, 117 autonomous counties, and three autonomous banners. In addition, these measures have been continuously enriched and strengthened since 1978. For example, financial subsidy to ethnic minority areas provided an effective way to increase the financial self-sufficiency rate of ethnic minority regions.

Due to the escalating development disparity between ethnic minority regions and the remaining parts of China, the autonomous regions must be supported by special policies to eliminate poverty as early as possible. Poverty is a widespread phenomenon in the concentrated communities of ethnic minorities. In 1986, the State Council set up the Steering Group for the Economic Development of Poverty-stricken Areas, which marked the beginning of a nationwide poverty alleviation campaign. In the same year, the central government listed 331 underdeveloped counties, in which 143 were compact communities of ethnic minorities.[8] All of the 74 counties of Tibet are included in the coverage of the national poverty alleviation campaign, which fully testifies that the problem of poverty eradication of ethnic minority areas has become the focus of the countrywide poverty alleviation. Against this backdrop, it was impossible for ethnic minority regions to achieve a synchronous development with the central and coastal provinces. Due to China's weak composite national strength and inadequate financial resources in the 1980s, a breakthrough for the reform and opening-up must rely on the eastern provinces, which boast relatively developed infrastructure and favorable economic base.

If the reform and opening-up of China is likened to a "game of chess," the pieces must be phased in at the early stage. In 1988, Deng Xiaoping proposed that "where conditions permit, some areas may develop faster than others; those that develop faster can help promote the progress of those that lag behind, until all become prosperous." He added: "The coastal areas, which comprise a vast region with a population of 200 million, should accelerate their opening to the outside world, and we should help them develop rapidly first; afterwards they can promote the development of the interior. The development of the coastal areas is of overriding importance, and the interior provinces should subordinate themselves to it. When the coastal areas have developed to a certain extent, they will be required to give still more help to the interior. Then, the development of the interior provinces will be of overriding importance, and the coastal areas will have to subordinate themselves to it."[9]

---

[8] *The Poverty Alleviation in China's Rural Areas*. People's Daily, dated on Oct. 16, 2001.

[9] Deng Xiaoping, *The collected works of Deng Xiaoping*. Volume III, p. 277.

In accordance with this development strategy, the ethnic minority areas were placed in the posterior stage for these regions promised a smaller profit margin to investors than coastal provinces. Since 1980, China has established special economic zones in Shenzhen, Zhuhai, and Shantou in Guangdong Province and Xiamen in Fujian Province, and designated the entire province of Hainan as a special economic zone. With the special economic zones, which offer tax and business incentives to attract foreign investment and technology, as the vanguards, the coastal provinces experienced a long period of high-speed growth thanks to their leverages of economy, education, technology, market, and labor force. In 1984, China opened a further 14 coastal cities to overseas investment: Dalian, Qinhuangdao, Tianjin, Yantai, Qingdao, Lianyungang, Nantong, Shanghai, Ningbo, Wenzhou, Fuzhou, Guangzhou, Zhanjiang, and Beihai. This development, on the one hand, further widened the gap between the coastal region and the western provinces; on the other hand, it swiftly expanded the total economy of China and enhanced the country's composite national strength. This, in turn, created necessary conditions for the development of other parts of China.

In the process of the coastal regions' leading development, Deng Xiaoping was deliberating over the second move of the reform and opening-up, that is, the development of the western and central provinces. He believed that "it will be a big problem to find ways for the coastal areas to assist the interior provinces." As to the ever-growing regional development disparity, Deng Xiaoping pointed out: "we can have one coastal province help one or two interior provinces. Nevertheless, we should not lay too heavy burden on the coastal areas all at once. During the initial period, they can just transfer certain technologies to the interior. Since the very beginning of the reform, we have been emphasizing the need for common prosperity; that will surely be the central issue someday. Socialism does not mean allowing a few people to grow rich while the overwhelming majority live in poverty. The greatest superiority of socialism is that it enables all the people to prosper, and common prosperity is the essence of socialism. If polarization occurred, things would be different. The contradictions between various ethnic groups, regions and classes would become sharper and, accordingly, the contradictions between the central and local authorities would also be intensified. That would lead to disturbances."[10]

Therefore, while encouraging the coastal provinces to forge ahead and speed up their development momentum, the Chinese government steadily upgraded the preferential policies to the ethnic minority regions. In 1992, the state established the Fund for Ethnic Minority Development, which was mainly used to deal with special difficulties encountered in the development of ethnic autonomous areas. In 1994, the allocation ratio for mineral resource compensation fee between the central government and provincial-level autonomous regions was adjusted from 5:5 to 4:6. The move was beneficial to enhancing the self-development capacity of the autonomous regions. In addition, the state encourages better-off areas and ethnic groups to help those that are not well-off yet, and attain common prosperity this way. Since the end of the 1970s, the Chinese government has organized the more developed areas

---

[10]Deng Xiaoping, *The Collected Works of Deng Xiaoping. Volume III*, p. 364.

along the eastern coast to provide corresponding aid to western areas, helping ethnic minority areas develop their economies and public services. In 1996, corresponding assistance was made more specific: Beijing is to assist Inner Mongolia; Shandong, Xinjiang; Fujian, Ningxia; and Guangdong, Guangxi. As regards Tibet, it receives assistance from all the other areas of the country.

From 1994 to 2000, the state invested 43.553 billion RMB in Inner Mongolia, Guangxi, Tibet, Ningxia, Xinjian, Guizhou, Yunnan, and Qinghai, accounting for 38.4% of the total investment in the whole country. Since 2000, the Chinese government has pursued a drive known as "More Prosperous Frontiers and Better-off People," adopting special measures to assist the 22 ethnic minority groups each with a population of less than 100,000. These favored policies indicated that the focus of China's economic development was gradually shifted to the interior provinces.

5.3 The Western Development Strategy: For the Accelerated Development of the Western Provinces

In the spring of 1992, Deng Xiaoping made his famous southern tour, visiting Guangzhou, Shenzhen, and Zhuhai and spending the New Year in Shanghai, using his travels as a method of reasserting his economic policy after his retirement from office. Deng Xiaoping reiterated that "some areas must get rich before others," and asserted that the wealth from coastal regions will eventually be transferred to aid economic construction inland. During this tour, Deng Xiaoping clearly put forward a timetable for the "second overall situation," that is, the development of the interior provinces. He declared: "we shall solve this problem at the end of this century when we will have accomplished the target of building a relatively well-off society in China."[11] At the national conference on ethnic minority affairs in 1999, Zeming Jiang, who was then serving as the CPC General Secretary and President of the country, proclaimed: "the implementation of the Western Development Strategy is a necessary condition both for maintaining a sustained, healthy national economy and achieving the third strategic goal of modernization, that is, to build China into a moderately well-off society by 2020."[12] The resolution adopted in this conference pointed out: "the purpose for Western Development is to accelerate economic and social growth of ethnic minority regions, which is of great significance to the national economic revitalization and common prosperity of all ethnic groups."[13] Obviously, the goal of the strategy is to completely eradicate the developmental gap between ethnic minority regions and coastal provinces, which is one of the basic conditions to achieve true equality of all ethnic groups.

---

[11] Deng Xiaoping, *The Collected Works of Deng Xiaoping*. Volume III, p. 375.

[12] *The Collected Documents on the Ethnic Affairs of China: 1990–2002*, p. 213.

[13] Ibid., p. 222.

In 2000, the Chinese government officially launched the Western Development Strategy. From a geographical point of view, the western region covers six provinces (Gansu, Guizhou, Qinghai, Shaanxi, Sichuan, and Yunnan), five autonomous regions (Guangxi, Inner Mongolia, Ningxia, Tibet, and Xinjiang), and one municipality (Chongqing). This region contains 71.4% of mainland China's area, but only 28.8% of its population. The majority of China's autonomous regions for ethnic minorities, including five provincial-level autonomous regions, 27 autonomous prefectures, and 83 autonomous counties, are located in the western provinces. In other words, the "western region" in China's Western Development Strategy is basically the compact communities of ethnic minorities.

Since the introduction of the reform and opening-up policy in the late 1970s, China has attracted worldwide attention, created modernization miracles, and demonstrated a leading economic output in the world. However, from the perspective of China's comprehensive, coordinated, and sustainable development, it is still faced with economic and social issues in vast less developed regions, and the social construction task of joint development, prosperity, and progress of all ethnicities. The Western Development Strategy is the most formidable task in China's modernization, and also an onerous task for resolving China's ethnic issues, achieving fairness and justice, building a harmonious society and creating a solid material foundation. Western Development is not a simple economic act, but carries the purpose of constructing a peaceful and prosperous society and realizing China's modernization. Its most important aim is to solve ethnic issues by developing the western regions and to speed up economic and social development of minorities and their inhabited areas.

The regional ethnic autonomous regions of China, in addition to their concentrated distribution in the western region, are also sporadically scattered in the central and eastern provinces, including three autonomous prefectures and 37 autonomous counties. Although these 40 autonomous administrative divisions are located outside of western provinces, their development shares economic-geographical features with the western region. As a consequence, the Chinese government decreed that the three autonomous prefectures and 15 autonomous counties in the central provinces be included in the coverage of the Western Development. Thus, we can conclude that the "western region" designated in the Western Development Strategy may be categorized as a concept in economic geography. In 2005, the remaining 22 autonomous counties not included in the scope of the Western Development Strategy were given various preferential policies according to the western region. These measures fully show that the initiative of Western Development is directly aimed at the accelerated development of compact communities of ethnic minorities.

The main components of the Western Development Strategy include infrastructure development (transport, hydropower plants, energy, and telecommunications), foreign investment enticement, ecological protection, improvement of social undertakings (education, culture, health services, and science), and retention of talent flowing to richer provinces. In 2000, the Chinese government decided that as for the foreign-funded enterprises in Western China whose development is encouraged, within three years after the termination of the implementation period of the existing preferential tax policy, their income tax will be collected at a reduced rate of 15%; and that for enterprises whose products are for export taxes shall be waived or reduced, with a tax rate of 10% at the lowest. In addition, the provinces, autonomous regions, and municipality in the western region enjoy the limits of authority equivalent to those of the coastal provinces and municipalities.

As of 2006, a total of one trillion Yuan had been spent building infrastructure in Western China. The Western Development bureau affiliated to the State Council released a list of 10 major projects to launch in 2008, with a combined budget of 436 billion RMB. These projects included new railway lines connecting Guiyang and Guangzhou, Lanzhou and Chongqing, and Kashgar and Hotan in Xinjiang; highways between Wanyuan and Dazhou in Sichuan province, Shuikou and Duyun in Guizhou Province; airport expansion projects in Chengdu, Chongqing, and Xi'an. They also include the building of hydropower stations, coal mines, gas and oil transmission tube lines as well as public utilities projects in western regions. By the end of 2007, China had started 92 key construction projects in western regions, with a total investment of more than 1.3 trillion Yuan.

However, it is impractical to accomplish the move within a short period of time for the Western Development involves all aspects of economic development and social undertakings in a vast area. To give full play to the effect of national policy, local authorities must come up with specific policies and measures while implementing the principled policies. At the same time, the state also needs to constantly adjust and formulate new policies to adapt to the changing circumstances. In the national conference on ethnic minority affairs held in 1999, Chinese Premier Rongji Zhu commented: "we must fully realize that the Western Development is a long-term task, which merits hard yet meticulous work to fundamentally change the backwardness of the western provinces. Therefore, we must take on new responsibilities to speed up the development of ethnic minority areas. In addition, we should also proceed from reality and act in accordance with objective laws."[14] Accordingly, it is inappropriate to adopt a "one size fits all" approach; rather, we must creatively carry out state policies in light of specific conditions of each administrative division and each ethnic group. Meanwhile, we shall neither simplify the development process nor indiscriminately copy the successful experiences of the coastal provinces.

The western provinces are characterized by an underdeveloped economy and traffic facilities, a relatively lower literacy rate, a high proportion of farming and husbandry-based population, a diversity of natural geography, ecological environment, climatic conditions, and cultural life. In this complex and diverse development environment, the Western Development Strategy reflects regional disparities between coastal provinces and western regions; at the same time, it contains special policy practices aimed at particular geographical locations and ethnic groups. Among them, the drives of "prosperous frontiers and better-off people" and "assisting the development of small-populated minority ethnic groups" are two of the most representative cases.

---

[14] *The Collected Documents on the Ethnic Affairs of China: 1990–2002*, p. 222.

5.4   The Drives of "Prosperous Frontiers and Better-off People" and "Assisting the Development of Small-Population Minority Ethnic Groups"

The Chinese borderlands, with a size of 2.12 million square kilometers and a population of 20.5 million, cover 136 counties. Among these counties, 107 are concentrated communities of ethnic minorities, whose land area and population account for 92 and 51% in the total frontier regions of China. In addition, the 30-plus minority ethnic groups living in the Chinese borderlands share homologous economic and cultural ties with the various peoples of the neighboring countries. In brief, of China's 22,000-km land border, about 19,000 km belong to autonomous regions for ethnic minorities. As the borderland of the country, national defense security is undoubtedly the top priority. In addition, the economic growth of frontier regions tends to be marginalized due to their sparse population and underdeveloped infrastructures. Therefore, the borderlands more saliently highlight the economic and social characteristics of Western China.

In the process of China's economic reform, the opening-up of the coastal areas has produced tremendous economic benefits. The border areas function as the frontline of opening-up to the neighboring countries of China. The development of frontier regions, therefore, bears not only on the consolidation of national defense but also on good-neighborly relations with nearby countries. In 1999, the State Ethnic Affairs Commission, the National Development and Reform Commission, and the Ministry of Finance jointly launched the drive of "prosperous frontiers and better-off people", a development program designated exclusively for border areas. With goals of "enriching border area residents, enhancing national defense, developing good-neighborly relations with nearby countries," it is a "linear" plan along the borderland.

Playing a special role in China's Western Development, the drive is directly related to the opening-up of nine provinces or autonomous regions, including Liaoning, Jilin, Heilongjiang, Inner Mongolia, Gansu, Xinjiang, Tibet, Yunnan, and Guangxi. In 2000, China launched the drive to support the development of the border region. A two-day work conference focusing on the drive was convened in Beijing at the end of that year. In the conference, Chinese Premier Jiabao Wen called for more efforts to promote the development of the nation's border regions. Wen joined officials from central government departments and officials from the country's nine border provinces and regions at the meeting. Public services should be improved and provided equally to people in the border regions, with more efforts being made to improve poverty alleviation work, housing, health, and education, Wen said. He also called for better infrastructure, environmental protection, industrial structure adjustment, and ethnic unity. In 2006, the drive was included in the supporting scope of the "Ethnic Minority Development Fund," with goals of improving infrastructure facilities (drinking water, electricity, fuels for cooking, roads, and housing), promoting applicable production techniques, developing crop farming, livestock breeding, and agricultural products processing industry, as well as supporting handicraft and tourism industries.

In 2007, to comprehensively promote the economic growth of border areas, the State Council formulated the 11th Five-year-plan for the drive, which covers 136 borderland counties and 58 settlements of Xinjiang Production and Construction Corps, a unique economic and paramilitary organization in the Xinjiang Uyghur Autonomous Region. Through special-purpose transfer payments from the exchequer and other methods, the central government has increased the financial input in border areas to promote their self-development capacity. In 2009, the main economic indicators of the 136 border counties increased threefold in comparison with those of 2000. Among these indicators, the GDP and the general budget of local fiscal revenue grew by 342.2 and 340.3%, respectively.

In 2011, the State Council issued the 12th Five-year-plan for the drive, which gave priority to the improvement of border residents' livelihood. The new round of drive put forward the following goals: further improvement of infrastructure development; marked betterment of borderland residents' living standards; great progress in social undertakings; significant expansion of borderland opening-up; rapid development of advantageous industries; enhanced ethnic unity and national defense.

As of 2014, the central government's transfer payments to the border areas totaled 27.75 billion Yuan. The ever-increasing capital investments brought about fundamental changes to the economic and social outlook of frontier regions. The GDP of border areas amounted to 809.7 billion Yuan in 2013, with an annual growth rate of 16% between 2010 and 2013. The per capita disposable income of urban and rural residents reached 19,168 and 7589 Yuan, respectively.[15] Such speedy growth rates were unrivaled throughout the rest of the country. At the same time, the border areas' opening-up to the neighboring countries of China has also witnessed an expansion, with a total of 121 border ports and 421 border trade markets by 2014. As these open areas adopt different preferential policies, they play the dual roles of "windows" in developing the foreign-oriented economy, generating foreign exchanges through exporting products and importing advanced technologies and of "radiators" in accelerating inland economic development. The economic capacity growth of border areas brought about an overall progress in their social undertakings, with a full coverage of rural cooperative medical system and rural subsistence security system. Fundamental changes have taken place in the once destitute and isolated border areas.

Like the drive of "prosperous frontiers and better-off people", the action of "assisting the development of small-populated minority ethnic groups" constitutes a combination effect of the Western Development Strategy. As of 2010, the population of the 55 Chinese ethnic minorities added up to 100 million, which comprised 8.49% of the population of mainland China. In addition, the population sizes of ethnic minorities vary greatly, ranging from the Zhuang, with more than 10 million the largest, to the Lhoba, who only number 2000. Most of the small-population ethnic minorities are in a less competitive position in terms of their economic conditions, human resources, and traditional industry, with the widespread phenomenon of underdeveloped economic and social development.

---

[15]*Great Achievements of China's Initiative of Rejuvenating Border Areas.* Xinhua News Agency, Sep. 23, 2014.

In 2001, the development of small-population ethnic minorities was included as one of the top agendas for the Western Development Strategy. Four years later, the State Council issued a development program for 22 small-population ethnic minorities. With a total population of 630,000, these ethnic groups included the Maonan, Salar, Blang, Tajik, Achang, Pumi, Ewenk, Nu, Jing, Keno, De'ang, Bonan, Russian, Yugur, Uzbek, Monba, Oroqen, Derung, Tatars, Hezhen, Gaoshan, and Lhoba peoples. They were living in 640 rural communities in Inner Mongolia, Heilongjiang, Fujian, Guangxi, Guizhou, Yunnan, Tibet, Gansu, Qinghai, and Xinjiang. In 2003, their per capita net income was only 884 Yuan, which was only one-third of the average per capita rural net income over the same period. Among the inhabitants of these villages, the poverty-stricken population was calculated to be 190,000.

These villages had extremely backward production and living conditions. Some remote hamlets had no access to electricity, telephone, postal services, clean water supply, and TV signals. 46,346 households were thatched cottages or shanties. In such destitute environments, the education level of the school-aged children was extremely low, the average illiteracy rate reaching 42.3%. At the same time, endemics and infectious diseases were common occurrences due to backward medical facilities.[16] Apparently, these grassroots villages had not experienced fundamental progress in changing their underdeveloped economic and social landscape since the founding of the People's Republic of China. Therefore, it is imperative to accelerate the development of the small-populated ethnic minorities and their settlements.

The specific measures of the action include infrastructure construction, financial support, credit funds, social undertakings development, human resources cultivation, and pairing-up support. The development goals are succinctly summarized as "four accesses" (to road traffic, electricity, water, radio, and television), "five haves" (basic housing, primary schools, village clinics, safe drinking water, and stable-yield farmlands), and "three reaches", which means the per capita net income, per capita grain consumption, and nine-year compulsory education popularization rate reaching the average national standard. These targets are reflected in 80-plus indicators.

In addition to its self-evident purpose of poverty alleviation, the drive has its special significance in that these 22 small-populated ethnic minorities account for 40% in the total number of Chinese ethnic groups. Therefore, the core of this policy is to achieve equality among all ethnic groups. It is the institutional guarantee for the Chinese governments' solemn promise that "none of the constituents of the Chinese nation shall be left behind in realizing two centenary goals." Between 1999 and 2005, a total amount of 3.751 billion RMB had been invested in 11,168 projects, with the basic accomplishment of anticipated targets and the fundamental improvement of the local people's living conditions.[17]

In 2011, the State Ethnic Affairs Commission, the National Development and Reform Commission, the Ministry of Finance, the People's Bank of China, and

---

[16] *The Collected Documents on the Ethnic Affairs of China: 2003–2009.* Beijing: Central Press for the CCP's documents. 2010, pp. 119–121.

[17] *Reflections on the Chinese Government's Policy of Assisting the Development of Small-populated Ethnic Minorities.* Journal of Guangxi Ethno-national Studies. 2011 (4), pp. 67–69.

the State Poverty Alleviation Office jointly issued *the Development Plan for the Small-population Ethnic Minorities: 2011–2015,* which became a new driving force for the accelerated growth of ethnic minority regions. In comparison with the plan released in 2005, the new one redefined the "small-population ethnic minorities" from the former scope of 100,000 to the current 300,000. Therefore, in addition to the aforementioned 22 small-populated minority ethnic groups, the new version covers six more, including the Jingpo, Daur, Kirgiz, Xibo, Mulao, and Tu. With a total population of 1.695 million, these 28 ethnic minorities are distributed in 2119 villages throughout China.

The coverage expansion for the action is mainly due to the comparative effect of economic and social development during China's 11th Five-Year Plan. Firstly, the poverty line for the destitute population has experienced a corresponding increase with rising per capita income. Secondly, the overall development of the 22 small-populated ethnic minorities has reached or even surpassed the newly added six ones after the first round of accelerated growth. As of the end of 2009, the impoverished population among the 28 small-populated ethnic minorities added up to 891,000, the impoverishment rate reaching 32.7%, which was much higher than that of the average national level (3.8%). Among the 2119 impoverished villages, those without electricity, clean drinking water, and basic clinic facilities accounted for 11.0, 35.2 and 30.7%, respectively. The average per capita net income of local farmers and herdsmen was only 2591 Yuan, only half of the national average.[18] Therefore, consolidating the effect of poverty alleviation and improving the self-development capacity of the small-population ethnic minorities are a protracted and complicated process. At the same time, we must make every effort to give full play to the functions of the completed projects. For example, a large number of built-up village clinics are short of medical services and supplies. To make things worse, 43.8% of these clinics are lacking in qualified medical staff.

5.5   Development-Oriented Poverty Reduction in Ethnic Minority Regions

As components of the Western Development Strategy, the drives of "prosperous frontiers and better-off people" and "assisting the development of small-populated minority ethnic groups" are important policy practices of addressing the development problems of border areas and small-populated ethnic minorities. However, the policies and measures stipulated in the two drives, in spite of their noteworthy achievements, have limited beneficiary areas if we take the vast territory of the western region into consideration. That is to say, such "linear" development in the frontier regions and "dotted" growth in the compact communities of small-populated ethnic minorities cannot be sustained without the overall progress of the western provinces.

---

[18] *The Development Plan for the Small-populated Ethnic Minorities: 2011–2015.* www.gov.cn. Dated on July 1, 2011.

We must therefore ensure that people of all ethnic groups have access to the achievements of China's economic reform. As a result, poverty alleviation becomes the most pressing agenda in ethnic minority regions. It is and has always been a goal and a basic right of all Chinese nationals in their pursuit of a happy life. Over the years, based on the prevailing national conditions, the Chinese government has remained committed to a development concept that puts people's rights to subsistence and to develop first. Committed to reducing and eliminating poverty, China has endeavored to guarantee and improve people's well-being, and developed a full range of social undertakings, to ensure that the results of development benefit all the people in a fairer way and that all enjoy the rights to equal development.

Since the introduction of reform and opening-up in the late 1970s, the Chinese government has worked without fail to alleviate poverty, establishing special poverty-relief institutions, determining targeted areas and population, allocating specialized funds, formulating poverty standards and special preferential policies adapted to China's national conditions, and steering its policy of poverty alleviation through development. The government has carried out large-scale development-oriented poverty eradication programs across the country in a planned and organized way, and implemented a series of medium- and long-term projects which include *the Seven-Year Program for Lifting 80 Million People Out of Poverty (1994–2000), the Outline for Development-Oriented Poverty Alleviation for China's Rural Areas (2001–2010)* and *the Outline for Development-Oriented Poverty Alleviation for China's Rural Areas (2011–2020)*. Poverty reduction has become an important component of China's national strategy.

Over the past 30 years or more since the launch of reform and opening-up, 660 million Chinese people have been lifted from poverty. With the most people lifted out of poverty, China has led other countries to realize *the UN Millennium Development Goal* and made an enormous contribution to poverty reduction worldwide. Its endeavors have been widely hailed by the international community. However, the Chinese government is fully aware that the fight remains tough as the country still has a large population living in poverty, and the solutions to their problems are becoming increasingly costly and complex. By the end of 2013, 82.49 million people, the equivalent of the entire population of a medium-sized country, were living below the 6.3 Yuan-a-day poverty line. These poverty-stricken people are concentrated in the 14 contiguous impoverished areas. Among them, 11 are autonomous regions for ethnic minorities, including Tibet and Tibetan-inhabited areas in Sichuan, Yunnan, Gansu, and Qinghai provinces, as well as the three prefectures in the south of Xinjiang. The data released by the National Bureau of Statistics showed that, as of 2015, there were 70.17 million poverty-stricken rural residents, of which the destitute populaces in the ethnic minority areas constituted about one-third. Among the 10 desperately impoverished areas, nine were concentrated communities of ethnic minorities.[19] Therefore, China has entered the crucial stage of poverty reduction. Most of the targets of China's poverty reduction efforts are now those living in

---

[19]*The Investigation Report of China's Poverty Alleviation.* http://www.xinhuanet.com/. June 22, 2015.

extreme poverty, and this poses formidable problems for the country. The first problem is the nature of the challenge: the increasing cost and complexity resulting from an extreme degree of poverty afflicting the majority of these people, and their weak capacity for development.

Though China's success in reducing poverty over the last three decades has been remarkable and is well recognized globally, the remaining poor are harder to reach as they are less concentrated in a specific location and are more dispersed in remote and inaccessible areas. Most of the remaining absolute poor are rural inhabitants, and about 80% of these poor reside in the western and central provinces. In addition, there is less responsiveness of poverty reduction to economic growth. It is becoming more costly to reduce poverty further using conventional approaches. Ethnic minority groups and people with disabilities are known to represent a highly disproportionate share of the rural poor. Ethnic minority groups make up less than 9% of the total population, but were believed to account for about 40% of the remaining absolute poor at the time of project appraisal, and often lived in the deepest poverty. Similarly, people with disabilities and households with disabled members represented a large and rising share of the poor. It was believed that people with disabilities comprised about one-third of the remaining rural poor. In poor areas, there was a mutually reinforcing relationship between poverty and disability.

The second problem is time pressure. China has set itself the goal of lifting 10 million people out of poverty every year from 2016. The third is the high risk of a return to poverty. A large number of poor households struggle to remain free of poverty and can be pushed back into poverty as a result of factors such as natural disaster, illness, or issues involving education, marriage, and housing; they, therefore, rejoin the existing impoverished population.

Aimed at eliminating poverty and better protecting the people's rights to live and to develop in impoverished areas, the CPC Central Committee led by General Secretary Xi Jinping has committed China to pursuing innovative, balanced, and eco-friendly development featuring openness and sharing, to making the best use of its political and institutional strengths, and to implementing the basic strategy of taking targeted measures for poverty alleviation. The central authorities are determined to mobilize the society to achieve poverty eradication by ensuring that progress in development-oriented poverty alleviation is coordinated with overall economic and social development with the following strategies: attaching equal importance to poverty alleviation and ecological protection, and integrating poverty alleviation with social security.

In 2011, the CPC Central Committee and the State Council jointly released *the Outline for Development-oriented Poverty Reduction for the Rural Areas: 2011–2020*, which mapped out 14 contiguous impoverished areas. Among the 592 key counties for national development-oriented poverty alleviation work, 263 were compact communities of ethnic minorities. At the same time, it defined overall goals of poverty alleviation for the next decade: by 2020, the impoverished rural population has stable access to adequate food, clothing, compulsory education, basic medical services, and housing; the growth rate of per capita disposable income and major indices for basic public services in 14 contiguous impoverished areas approach the national average. Without comparing unrealistically with the development indicators for the moderately well-off society in an all-around way, the above-mentioned goals are on the basis of solving the most pressing problems for the impoverished rural population. Even so, this is an extremely difficult task.

After six months' field investigations into the poverty alleviation in China's contiguous impoverished areas, a team of reporters of the Xinhua News Agency published a report, *Facing China's Impoverished Corners,* on June 22, 2015. Among the 10 samples of dire poverty areas covered in the report, nine are compact communities of ethnic minorities. The results of the investigations showed that the full realization of poverty eradication has still a long way to go. Although there are different contributors to poverty in a particular household or village, the 10 impoverished samples are very typical in the contiguous impoverished areas. Therefore, in addition to the capital and technology investments from the state and local governments, it was up to the poverty-stricken populace to take the initiative in lifting themselves out of poverty. Simply put, impoverished rural areas need not only external assistance but also internal dynamics as well.

The development-oriented poverty reduction is targeted to improve the self-development capability of poverty-stricken families, villages, and communities. To that end, impoverished population's stereotypical mentality irreconcilable with modern life must be reformed. In this regard, the so-called "able persons" who can mobilize collective support and get down to action are highly needed in rural poverty alleviation. At the 4th National Poverty Reduction Conference held on Oct. 17, 2013, a woman named Yingxiang Deng, a native of an isolated village in Luodian county, Guizhou province, took the podium and was highly lauded by the delegates for her perseverance and willpower. Deng's home village was surrounded by rugged mountains, with only a steep trail to the outside world. Refusing to surrender to the dire poverty caused by geographical obstruction, Deng and the villagers were determined to dig a tunnel through the mountains. Regarded as an exemplar of what farmers could achieve and local mass initiative, the seemingly impossible mission was achieved through 12 years of toil with only hoes and baskets. In August 2011, the tunnel, with a length of 216 m, was completed and open to traffic. The mountainous village thus embarked on a path of poverty alleviation and prosperity. Several years later, more than 80% of the villagers moved into their new homes, with a fundamental increase of their per capita net income.[20]

With the development of the national economy and the growth in financial revenue, the transfer payments from the exchequer to autonomous areas of ethnic minorities witnessed a fundamental growth, from 22.2 billion Yuan in 2010 to 43.3 billion in 2014. The poverty of the ethnic minority region was in large part attributed to the unfavorable natural conditions and backward development basis. Nevertheless, the dire poverty of some families was a result of illiteracy, outmoded mentality, or lack of labor force. Therefore, we need to do more in targeted poverty elimination for impoverished areas and people represent the field of greatest weakness we must face as we work to finish building a moderately well-off society in all respects. It is one

---

[20] 12-year Toils for the Tunneling of a Mountain. http://www.china.com.cn/. April 9, 2014.

of the basic policies of the Chinese government to innovatively improve its methods in reducing and eradicating poverty and take targeted measures to that end. Recently, through data tracking on the conditions of the impoverished population, the government analyzes the causes of their problems and offers guidance on their development needs. Targeted measures are implemented in terms of funding, projects, and recipients. Every impoverished household is guaranteed help, every village has designated officials to carry out poverty eradication measures, and goals are met within the defined standards. In the fight against poverty, China has enhanced poverty eradication effects, accelerated the speed of poverty eradication, and ensured impoverished people's right to life.

At the closure of the Central Economic Work Meeting on December 11, 2014, the central leadership floated the idea of a targeted approach to alleviating poverty. On June 18, 2015, during his visit to Guizhou Province, Xi Jinping once more raised the subject, which he believes will determine the success of the poverty alleviation drive. It has subsequently become a hot topic among the general public. In its *Proposal for Formulating the 13th Five-year Plan for National Economic and Social Development*, released in November 2015, the 18th CPC Central Committee specified targeted measures to be taken in the coming five years. Targeted efforts are designed to ensure that average income statistics would not eclipse the true living conditions of many in hardship. Such efforts require attention to detail. Greater emphasis will be laid upon identifying low-income groups in need of assistance, so that they will receive due attention and their basic standard of living will be guaranteed.

The central leadership proposed such a targeted approach at a time when China faces a daunting challenge in its efforts to eliminate the final pockets of poverty across the country. To ensure that poverty reduction efforts are fully effective, Xi Jinping called for policies and programs of assistance to be tailored for the needs of individual families in conjunction with targeted funding and village-specific expert support, and to be pursued with a results-oriented focus.

As a social problem relating to a diversity of factors, the problem of poverty means not only lack of material gains but also reflects the want of cultural services. Therefore, poverty alleviation demands active participation and support from all social sectors. To promote the development of ethnic minority areas, China has put energetic efforts into poverty reduction work in some key poverty-stricken counties in those areas, with help coming from a number of organizations, including all departments and units of the CPC Central Committee and state organs, non-governmental organizations, key large-sized state-owned enterprises, state-holding financial institutions, central committees of non-Communist parties and All-China Federation of Industry and Commerce, and state key research institutions and universities. Over the past few years, those units and organizations have provided various forms of help to their targeted recipients in such aspects as sending officials to the aided counties, helping them with infrastructure construction, industrialized operations, training of labor force and provision of labor services to other places, investment introduction, ecological construction, and medical health services. They also provide their targeted recipients with assistance in culture, education, science, and technology, in addition to aid in disaster relief.

Pairing the more developed provinces and municipalities in the east with the impoverished regions in the west in poverty reduction is a policy adopted by the Chinese government in its efforts to achieve common prosperity. Since 1996, the government has made arrangement for 15 economically more developed provinces and municipalities in the east to help 11 provinces (autonomous regions and municipalities directly under the central government) in the west get rid of poverty. The basic framework of this east-help-west cooperation is mainly comprised of government assistance, enterprise cooperation, social aid and human resource support.

Social organizations, private enterprises, and the general public also take an active part in the poverty reduction drive. In line with the actual conditions and specific requirements of the impoverished regions and people, these organizations have helped with industrial development, infrastructure construction, education and public health development, improvement of production and living conditions and ecological environment construction by pairing with the places in need of help, implementing poverty reduction projects, and holding specific aid activities. They have also mobilized public-spirited personages with professional skills to engage in volunteer work to help people out of poverty. The private enterprises have been actively fulfilling their corporate social responsibilities and engaged in poverty reduction by donating money, hiring workers, setting up businesses and training bases.

According to the new standard for poverty-stricken population, the ethnic minority region is still the focus of China's developed-oriented poverty alleviation in the next five years, for the impoverished people in the concentrated communities of the ethnic minorities added up to 25 million, accounting for about a third of the poverty-stricken population of the country. In addition, it is extremely difficult to lift the continuous impoverished areas out of destitution due to the restrictions of natural geographical conditions and traditional mode of production.

In the national conference on ethnic minority affairs held in 2014, Xi Jinping pointed out: "the ethnic minority region is the focus for China's poverty alleviation. We shall improve poverty alleviation effectiveness by combining overall advancement, implementing targeted poverty reduction and elimination measures for poor areas and people living in poverty." Xi added: "we are determined to eradicate the root of impoverishment in China," which is the final goal for China's development-oriented poverty alleviation.

5.6 The "Inner Mongolia Phenomenon": The Economic Miracle of Inner Mongolia

Since the implementation of the Western Development Strategy, the western provinces, including the five autonomous regions and the provinces of Gansu, Qinghai, Sichuan, Guizhou, and Yunnan, have experienced a constant accelerated development. The state's capital input and arrangement of major infrastructure projects in the western regions have also witnessed an unprecedented growth. From 2000 to 2012, the central government's financial transfer payments to the western region added up to 8.5 trillion Yuan. These favored policies fundamentally improved the transportation, water conservancy, and energy and communications facilities of the western provinces. The series of key projects, including the Qinghai–Tibet Railway, "West-East Natural Gas Transmission Project", "West-East Electricity Transmission Project", "North-south Coal Transmission Project", as well as the various hydropower plants along the Huanghe River and Changjiang River, laid a solid foundation for the sustainable growth of the region.

The Western Development Strategy includes both the overall policies for all western provinces and special plans for particular regions. For example, in 2007, the State Council issued *Several Opinions on Promoting the Economic and Social Development of Xinjiang*, formulating development goals of the frontier province in the next three years: the per capita GNP, basic public services and income of urban–rural residents reaching the national average, ranking at the forefront among the western provinces. Such policy arrangements were made in accordance with the conditions of particular regions, such as geological location, population, ecological environment, resource endowment, economic base, market development, featured industries, and existing problems. Also in the year of 2007, the central government released *Resolutions on Supporting the Economic and Social Development of the Tibetan-inhabited Areas in Sichuan, Yunnan, Gansu and Qinghai Provinces,* proposing an interprovincial development plan in light of their common problems.

As discussed earlier, the Hu Line divides China into two roughly equal parts, including the densely populated eastern part and the sparsely populated western one. During the widespread implementation of the development-oriented poverty alleviation, the western region was further divided into border areas, regions inhabited by small-population ethnic minorities and contiguous poverty-stricken areas. Their developments were supported by corresponding favored policies. At the same time, the State Council successively promulgated differentiated policies applicable to the five autonomous regions, including Xinjiang, Inner Mongolia, Tibet, Ningxia, and Guangxi, as well as the provinces with large ethnic minority areas, such as Gansu, Yunnan, and Guizhou.

By giving full play to the geographical and resource advantages of each administrative division, these custom-made polices contributed to the gradational development of the western provinces. In accordance with Deng Xiaoping's phased development strategy, "some areas may develop faster than others where conditions permit; those that develop faster can help promote the progress of those that lag behind, until all become prosperous." Therefore, the development of the coastal provinces gathered momentum after China introduced the reform and opening-up policy in 1978. Likewise, the development of the vast western region also demanded such a progressive approach. In other words, some ethnic minority areas take the lead in accelerating their economic growth, which, in turn, can help promote the progress of others. In this regard, the so-called "Inner Mongolia phenomenon," referring to the sustained rapid economic growth of Inner Mongolia Autonomous Region in the first round of the Western Development, with its industrialization level and GDP volume ranked the first among the 12 western provinces, is quite representative.

While meeting with the former US President Jimmy Carter in 1987, Deng Xiaoping declared: "Our policy is to focus on the development of ethnic minority areas. For example, Inner Mongolia, with its vast grasslands and sparse population, may become one of the most developed areas of China in the near future. When assessing a minority nationality area, the important thing is to see whether it has development potential. If the number of Han people is fairly large and if they are helping the local people develop the economy, that's not a bad thing. In judging a matter of this sort, one has to consider the essence and not the form."[21] Here, the "essence" emphasized by Deng Xiaoping, as the basic foothold for the regional autonomy for ethnic minorities, is the modernized development of minority ethnic groups and their compact communities. The realization of this "essence" will disrupt the imbalanced regional economic status quo and achieve the common prosperity of all ethnic groups. The "Inner Mongolia phenomenon" is the typical embodiment of this "essence."

Since the launch of economic reforms in the late 1970s, some cities and regions in China have been growing much faster than others, stimulating scholarly research on the forces underlying uneven development. In the process of China's economic reform, a good many successful development experiences have been created in the coastal areas, such as Su Nan Model and Wenzhou Model. The former refers to the rapid development of township and village enterprises in the cities of Suzhou, Wuxi, and Changzhou of Jiangsu province, while the latter relies heavily on the booming small- and medium-sized private enterprises in Wenzhou of Zhejiang Province. They fully showcase the particular advantages of these regions, such as geological location, intensive foreign investments, dynamic township and village enterprises, as well as an intensive labor force. However, Inner Mongolia, which has a small population in spite of a large territory, is devoid of these leverages. Unlike the coastal areas, its rich natural resources become a trump card for its development.

One year after the official launch of the Western Development initiative in 2001, the GDP of Inner Mongolia was only 140 billion Yuan, with a growth rate of 9.7% over the previous year. Only after a decade, the GDP of Inner Mongolia soared to 1165.5 billion Yuan, ranked 15th among the provincial-level administrative divisions of the Chinese mainland; the per capita GDP ranked 7th, taking the lead among the western provinces. Statistical information showed that the economic output discrepancy between Guangdong and Inner Mongolia shrank from 7.5 times in 2001 to 5.8 times in 2010. The high-speed economic growth of Inner Mongolia between 2000 and 2010 can be, on the one hand, attributed to the favorable external conditions, including preferential state policies, expansion of central financial input, and pairing-up support from the developed regions; on the other hand, the overall development of various economic sectors, such as industry, agriculture, animal husbandry, forestry, trade, port economy, and services has formed the motive force for the region's endogenous economic development.

The abundant natural resources of Inner Mongolia, such as coal, electricity, rare earths, cashmere, and dairy, played a vital role in accelerating the economic growth of the region. The resource-based industries of Inner Mongolia, including energy

---

[21]Deng Xiaoping, *The Collected Works of Deng Xiaoping. Volume III*, p. 246.

development and cashmere processing in Ordos, the dairy industry represented by Mengniu and Yili companies, coal and rare earth extraction in eastern Inner Mongolia and Baotou, sustain the local economic growth. Inner Mongolia has become one of the most important bases for energy, heavy chemical industry, agricultural, and livestock products. In 2014, the per capita GDP of Inner Mongolia reached 10,000 USD, being the only one among the five autonomous regions for ethnic minorities to achieve such figures.

The fast economic growth of Inner Mongolia was driven by exploiting its rich natural resources. However, this development model has its inherent weaknesses, such as single industrial structure and environmental pollution. In light of its resource advantages and existing problems, the Chinese central government put forward a new development orientation for Inner Mongolia in 2011: ecological barrier of north China, power base, production and processing base of green agricultural and livestock products, new base for chemical industry and non-ferrous metals, as well as important bridgehead for China's opening-up to Russia and the Republic of Mongolia.

As the first autonomous region for ethnic minorities, Inner Mongolia provided experiences and set an example for the construction and development of autonomous administrative divisions. During the process of realizing the leap forward development of economy and society, the "Inner Mongolia phenomenon" has produced an exemplary effect on the development of other western provinces. During its fast economic growth, Inner Mongolia was also confronted with a series of problems, including underdeveloped infrastructures, fragile ecology, single industrial structure, unbalanced regional development, and inadequate public service capacity. It will be a demanding task for Inner Mongolia to realize a sustainable and fast economic growth while adapting to the economic slowdown throughout China. At present, Inner Mongolia must complete the various mammoth undertakings, such as readjusting industrial structure, promoting industrial transformation, and improving people's livelihood.

5.7   Creating Miracles on the Qinghai–Tibet Plateau

With a length of 1956 km, the Qinghai–Tibet Railway is a high-elevation railroad that connects Qinghai to Tibet. This railway is the first that links Tibet to any other provinces of China. Tibet, due to its elevation and terrain, is the last provincial-level region in China to have a railway. The main engineering challenge, aside from oxygen shortages, is the weakness of permafrost. Therefore, the railway has been widely acclaimed to be a "sky road" for its engineering miracles. The rail link connecting Lhasa and Shigatse—an extension to the Qinghai–Tibet Railway—is now in service. The Qinghai–Tibet Plateau, reputed as "the roof of the world" due to its high elevation, also witnessed fast growth in airport construction. So far, eight high altitude airports have been open to traffic, including the world's highest civilian airport, Daocheng Yading Airport at 4411 m above sea level, and the previous record holder Qamdo Bamda Airport at 4334 m. A comprehensive transportation system including road, aviation, railway, and pipeline transportation has been gradually developed and improved, which is an important symbol of the modernization of the Qinghai–Tibet Plateau. Tibet Autonomous Region, which forms the main part of the Qinghai–Tibet Plateau, is the most special area in China's modernization process.

In its drive of modernization, Tibet has experienced an extremely arduous course. After the founding of Tibet Autonomous Region, the socialist ownership reform was started in 1966. A decade later, the transformation of private business and handicraft industry in the urban areas came to an end. This decade witnessed some growth in Tibet's transportation, agriculture, animal husbandry, and social undertakings. However, the "Cultural Revolution" wreaked much havoc in Tibet. After the conclusion of the "Cultural Revolution," a new generation of pragmatic reformers represented by Deng Xiaoping reversed the former policies almost in their entirety.

The first stage of China's economic reforms in the late 1970s and early 1980s involved the de-collectivization of agriculture, emphasizing the household responsibility system. It divided the land of the People's Communes into private plots. In December 1978, eighteen of the farmers in Xiaogang village in Fengyang County, Anhui province agreed to break the law at the time by signing a secret agreement to divide the land of the local People's Commune into family plots. Each plot was to be worked by an individual family who would turn over some of what they grew to the government and the collective while at the same time agreeing that they could keep the surplus for themselves. After this secret reform, the village produced a harvest that was larger than the previous five years combined. The discovery of Xiaogang Village's innovation was held up as a model to other rural communities across the country, which led to the abandonment of collectivized farming across China and a large increase in agricultural production. The People's Commune system, which was barely established in the Tibetan rural and pastoral areas in 1975, became a breakthrough in China's economic reform. Apparently, due to its geographical isolation and dire poverty, Tibet demanded an accelerated economic growth to catch up with the overall development momentum of China.

The reform and opening-up policy initiated by Deng Xiaoping greatly expanded China's ties with the outside world. On February 28, 1979, Gyalo Thondup, the second-eldest brother of the Dalai Lama, visited Beijing. During his meeting with Thondup, Deng Xiaoping pointed out: "Tibet is part of China, which is the only criterion for judging right or wrong. The central government is ready to talk with the Dalai Lama as long as he publicly acknowledges this fact."[22] In 1980, the CPC General Secretary Hu Yaobang presided over the first national symposium on work in Tibet, setting a series of major principles for the governance of Tibet, including: all the departments of the state to actively support Tibet's economic and social development in terms of financial, material, and technological aspects; the central budget to provide a quota subsidy to Tibet with an average yearly increase of 10%; giving greater autonomy to the enterprises of Tibet and tax reduction. To boost the economic growth of the region, the second national symposium on work in Tibet held in 1984 released more incentive policies. As an important mechanism for the governance of Tibet,

---

[22]Wang X, *The Governance of Tibet by the People's Republic of China: 1949–2009*, p. 229.

the "National Symposium on the Work in Tibet" has become the source of policy impetus, which effectively maintained social stability and speeded up the economic growth of the region.

With the full support of the central government and the generous assistance of other ethnic groups from the rest of the country, the people of Tibet have worked together to achieve widespread success. There have been substantial improvements in the quality of life. The rapid development of infrastructure facilities, from the completion of Lhasa Gonggar Airport in 1965, the opening of the Qinghai–Tibet Railway in 2006, to Daocheng Yading Airport's opening to traffic in 2013, are important symbols for the earth-shaking change in Tibet. Keeping abreast with other parts of China, Tibet has gradually evolved from being a closed type to being one that is open and market-oriented. Tibet has been fully incorporated into the national market system. While products from all over the nation and across the world flow into Tibet, the region's own characteristic products also move in large quantities to other parts of the country and further afield. In 2014, the per capita net income of farmers and herdsmen in Tibet reached 7471 Yuan, which was, however, still far behind the national average figure (9892 Yuan). In spite of that, the rapid growth of Tibet in the past three decades was still impressive in comparison with the per capita net income of the Tibetan rural residents in 1982 (200 Yuan). It was indeed a hard-earned feat.

Over the past three decades and more, the Dalai Lama clique have adjusted and altered their tactics along with changing domestic and international circumstances. With the thaw of Sino-US relations, in particular, after the establishment of diplomatic ties between China and the US, the so-called "issue of Tibet" was mothballed by the White House. The Dalai Lama's campaign for Tibet's independence by means of violence was steadily losing public support with the changing international situation. Therefore, he turned to a new strategy: constantly provoking incidents of violence to keep up the pressure on the Chinese government, while publicly proclaiming non-violence to deceive his international audience. Taking advantage of the waves of religious fanaticism and nationalism after the mid-1980s, the Dalai Lama actively sought foreign support. He made every effort to facilitate the internationalization of the "Tibet Issue." On September 21, 1987, he made a speech to the US Congress, publicly calling for Tibet's independence.[23] Six days later, in the square of Jokhang Temple in Lhasa, a group of Lamas chanted separatist slogans, attacked police, and injured many civilians. The rioters demanded the support of bystanders and threatened personal retaliation toward those who failed to join them. In spite of the apparent causal link between the Dalai Lama's provocative speech and the Lhasa riot, the Tibetan separatist forces attributed the unrest to the Chinese government's denunciation of the Dalai Lama's "peace proposals." It is, obviously, a ridiculous political logic of putting the cart before the horse.

After Mikhail Gorbachev introduced his radical domestic reforms with the purpose of reforming the stagnating economy of the Soviet Union, the White House, sniffing out the taste of "democratic socialism" from Gorbachev's "new thinking," publicly unveiled the secret of the National Endowment for Democracy (NED), a US

---

[23] The Dalai Lama (1990): 303.

non-profit soft power organization with the purported goal of "promoting democracy" abroad.[24] While attempting to effect a political transformation in the Soviet Union and Eastern Europe, the NED spared no efforts to produce a "domino effect" in Asia. The "issue of Tibet" was, therefore, utilized by the hostile western forces as an "open sesame" to infiltrate and subvert China. Thereafter, the "US Congressional Human Rights Caucus" began to interfere with the affairs of Tibet by using the "human rights of Tibetans" as leverage. In May 1987, two US congressmen put forward a motion, *the Chinese government's human rights abuses in Tibet*, to the US House of Representatives. With the intention of building an international stage for "the justified and legitimate aspirations of Tibetans," the Caucus invited the 14th Dalai Lama to speak about the situation of Tibet. It was the first formal invitation to the Dalai Lama from the US government organization.

As a response, the Chinese side promptly made serious representations with the US government through diplomatic channels to strongly protest and condemn the gross interference of the domestic affairs of China by the US Congress.[25] Immersed in the worship of the dark theocracy in which the Dalai Lama is the source from which all authority derives, the very few Tibetan Buddhist monks ingratiated themselves with the exiled 14th Dalai Lama and manufactured a series of riots in Tibet. In early March of 1989, Lhasa witnessed another commotion in which one policeman was shot dead and 40 others were injured. After three days of violence, martial law was declared on March 8, 1989. The separatist activities of the Dalai Lama and his followers provided excuses for western countries' interference in Tibetan affairs. In 1989, the Norwegian Nobel Committee awarded the Dalai Lama the Nobel Peace Prize. When it deemed necessary, the "issue of Tibet" would be utilized by the US politicians to frame "the human rights abuses" of China. To exert pressure on Beijing, the White House continued to introduce bills on the human rights of Tibetans in the United Nations Human Rights Conference. Some American media, civil society, organizations and academic institutions also provided generous support to the Dalai Lama clique through various forms. In addition to providing public opinion spaces for the campaign of "Tibet's independence," the western countries' patronage of the Dalai Lama triggered the 2008 Lhasa violence.

China's modernization program is an important component of the common development and progress of mankind. A peaceful international and domestic environment is necessary for China's development, and a prosperous and stable China in turn benefits world peace and prosperity. In terms of maintaining the stability of Tibet, China has long been confronted with two huge challenges, the sabotage of the Dalai clique and the pressure from the western hostile forces. In spite of that, economic development as the center is the key to solving all the problems of China. This fundamental principle shall not be shaken at any time. While meeting with the former US President Jimmy Carter in 1987, Deng Xiaoping reiterated the Chinese government's strong determination to assist the economic and social development of Tibet. Deng Xiaoping said: "The government has decided that all other provinces and cities should share

---

[24]Engdahl (2009): 86.
[25]Zhang (2007).

long-term responsibility for helping Tibet carry out certain development projects. Tibet has tremendous development potential. Many of China's natural resources are located in minority nationality areas, including Tibet and Xinjiang. If these areas can begin to develop, their future will be bright. It is our unshakable policy to help them do that."[26] In terms of human rights protection, the Chinese people strongly believe that the right to development is the basis for the realization of full human rights, which is also the cornerstone of China's basic position on human rights. Therefore, the Chinese government adheres to the policy of accelerating the economic and social growth of Tibet while maintaining its social stability.

Since 1994, the central government has put into effect the policy of pairing-up support for Tibet where 60 central state organs, 18 provinces or municipalities directly under the central government, and 17 centrally managed state-owned enterprises have been paired up with and made to provide assistance to specific areas of Tibet. Over the last two decades, a total of 7615 assistance projects have been carried out and 26 billion Yuan has been invested in Tibet and mainly directed at improving infrastructure and quality of life. All of this assistance has made an enormous contribution to Tibet's social and economic development. After 2010, the central government determined that the 17 provincial and municipal governments involved in the paired-up support program should provide Tibet with 0.1% of their yearly fiscal revenues as aid funds, thus establishing a mechanism to ensure a steady growth in such aiding funds.[27]

Unbalanced regional economic development within a sovereignty state is a prevalent phenomenon globally. Most of the Western developed countries also experienced a process of assisting the development of less developed regions by means of government procurement, transfer payments, tax incentives, financial preferential policies, and human resource development. However, it is virtually impossible for these countries to mobilize the developed areas or large enterprises to aid the progress of the underdeveloped regions. Moreover, the preferential policies of some Western countries given to the destitute regions even became one of the motive forces for regional separatist movements. For example, Flanders of Belgium, Catalonia and Basque of Spain, the Northern Union of Italy, Slovenia and Croatia in the former Yugoslavia, the three Baltic republics of the former Soviet Union, were the richest or relatively developed areas in their corresponding countries. At the same time, these regions were also sources of national secession campaigns in their respective countries.

In China, it is the consistent policy of the state to support the development of ethnic minority regions, border areas, and poverty-stricken areas. To help Tibet develop rapidly and get rid of poverty and backwardness, the central government has fully exploited the institutional advantages of the socialist system to pool nationwide strengths to support the construction of Tibet, and a series of preferential policies have been adopted, and great financial and material resources, as well as manpower, have been amassed to inject new impetus into its development.

---

[26]Deng Xiaoping, *The Selected Works of Deng Xiaoping*. Volume III, p. 246.

[27]*Paired-up Support Programs in Tibet: 1984–2014*. Xinhua News Agency, Aug. 24, 2014.

In addition to Tibet, the Tibetans are distributed in the 10 autonomous prefectures and two autonomous counties in Sichuan, Qinghai, Gansu, and Yunnan. Since 2008, the preferential policies for Tibet have been extended to the other Tibetan-inhabited areas. Pairing the more developed provinces and municipalities in the east with the impoverished regions in the west in poverty reduction is a policy adopted by the Chinese government in its efforts to achieve common prosperity. Since 2010, the government has made arrangements for the economically more developed provinces and municipalities in the east and key large-sized state-owned enterprises to help the 12 compact communities of Tibetans in the four western provinces to get rid of poverty. The basic framework of this east-help-west cooperation is mainly comprised of government assistance, enterprise cooperation, social aid, and human resource support.

Located in the Qinghai–Tibet Plateau, the 12 autonomous areas for the Tibetans had already integrated with the non-Tibetan communities, thus forming regional characteristics in terms of social organization, economic life, language, and culture. However, the difficulties encountered in the process of modernization by these autonomous areas are no different from those of Tibet in that the physiographic conditions of the Qinghai–Tibet Plateau pose a common restriction on their economic and social development. In this sense, the "Greater Tibet area" advocated by the Dalai Lama has never existed at any time in history. In total disregard of the fact that the Qinghai–Tibet Plateau has been a multi-ethnic region since ancient times, he denies the access of other ethnic groups to "Greater Tibet" and drives them out of regions where they have lived for generations. The concept of "Greater Tibet" is sheer fantasy, which does not conform to China's history and national conditions.

The modernization of the Qinghai–Tibet Plateau, as a region inhabited by the Tibetans and 40 other ethnic groups, is the modernization of all members of the Chinese nation living there. In 2015, the Chinese central government convened the sixth national symposium on the work of Tibet, which injected new impetus to the development of the autonomous region. The meeting called for Tibet to achieve "five combinations" in accelerating its development, including government support and market role, external aid and self-development capacity, an open policy both internationally and domestically, new urbanization and new rural construction, development and ecological protection.

While attending the ceremony for the 50th anniversary of the establishment of Tibet Autonomous Region on September 8, 2015, Zhengsheng Yu, Chairman of the Chinese People's Political Consultative Conference (CPPCC), and a member of the Politburo Standing Committee of the CPC, pointed out: "Tibet is a barrier for national security, a strategic resource reserve base, an important cultural center of the Chinese nation and a significant channel for China's opening up to South Asian subcontinent. The central government will continue to implement the preferential policies and mobilize the whole society to support the development of Tibet." Following the launch of reform and opening-up in 1978, the drive for modernization has brought extensive benefits to Tibet as much as to any other part of the country. Especially in the twenty-first century, Tibet has achieved even faster growth and further progress toward building a moderately prosperous society in an all-round way. Through more than 60 years of development, the people of Tibet have found a path of development that is both characteristically Chinese and suited to the actual prevailing conditions in Tibet. Thus, a new Tibet that is a blend of both the traditional and the modern has appeared.

5.8   The Development of Xinjiang Uyghur Autonomous Region

Since the founding of the new China in 1949, the preferential policy of supporting the economic and social development of Xinjiang has never been interrupted, for "the construction of Xinjiang is part of building a new China," a quote from De Zhu, the principal founder and one of the Ten Marshals of the People's Liberation Army, succinctly reveals that the development of Xinjiang is an indispensable part of the nation-building of China. The Chinese central government has kept intensifying efforts to support Xinjiang in the fields of economy, education, science, culture, medical services, finance, and environmental protection since the introduction of the reform and opening-up policy. At the same time, the central government and some developed provinces and cities have been providing aid to Xinjiang. To further spur the region's development and maintain local stability, the central leadership made a strategic decision in 1996 to launch the first round of large-scale aid projects. A new action plan (2011–2020) was rolled out in 2010. It called for pairing up sectoral partners to streamline and enhance aid delivery. The goal is to narrow the development gap between Xinjiang and the rest of the country to the greatest extent possible, and bring a comparable level of prosperity to the region by 2020.

   While meeting with the former US President Jimmy Carter in 1987, Deng Xiaoping pointed out: "many of China's natural resources are located in ethnic minority areas, including Tibet and Xinjiang. If these areas can begin to develop, their future will be bright. It is our unshakable policy to help them."[28] To help the development of ethnic minority regions is the natural justice of China's development. In the modernization process of China, industrialization and urbanization are two of the most important indicators. However, most of the ethnic minority areas of China are still engaging in traditional farming or animal husbandry with a low degree of urbanization, Xinjiang being no exception. At the same time, Xinjiang is endowed with abundant resources, including water, land, petroleum, natural gas, coal, cotton, and stockbreeding products, which demand to be scientifically and rationally utilized to achieve product upgrading and structural optimization. Therefore, the modernized development of Xinjiang is more than the construction of infrastructure facilities; rather, it lies in realizing the value of resource advantages in the overall development of China's reform and opening-up to the outside world. As the largest administrative division of China, Xinjiang spans over 1.6 million square kilometers. It is home to a diverse of ethnic groups, including the Uyghur, Kazakhs, Tajiks, Hui, Kyrgyz,

---

[28] See Footnote 26.

Mongols, Han, and Russians. More than a dozen autonomous prefectures and counties for the ethnic minorities have been established in Xinjiang. In addition, it borders Russia, Kazakhstan, Mongolia, Kyrgyzstan, Tajikistan, Afghanistan, Pakistan, and India. As a key region on the Silk Road Economic Belt, it functions as a major window on China's opening-up to the outside world.

Since the implementation of the Western Development initiative, Xinjiang has witnessed a rapid economic growth. Its GDP increased from 148.5 billion Yuan in 2001 to 926.41 billion in 2014; the per capita GDP rose from 7898 Yuan in 2001 to 40,707 in 2014; the per capita disposable incomes of urban and rural residents increased by 3.5 and 5.1 times, respectively. Such a fast growth has been widely acclaimed as a marvel of development in that Xinjiang, as an autonomous region for a diversity of ethnic minorities and the largest frontier province of China, is tasked with safeguarding national security, social stability, ethnic unity and religious harmony while accelerating economic growth.

Since its peaceful liberation in 1949, Xinjiang has long been haunted by the infiltrations of Pan-Islamism and Pan-Turkism; the First and Second "East Turkistan Republic" founded in 1933 and 1944, respectively are the two upsurges of the "East Turkistan" separatist forces. In the early summer of 1962, a total number of 60,000-plus residents of Ili and Tarbagatay defected to the Soviet Union under the patronage of Moscow. It was commonly referred to as the "Ili-Tarbagatay Incident." In the late 1950s and 1960s, the Soviet Union accelerated its infiltrations into Xinjiang against the backdrop of the Sino-Soviet split, which was caused by two main factors: differing national interests and various interpretations of Communist ideology. As a consequence, Xinjiang witnessed a series of demonstrations, riots, or even armed rebellions, which seriously endangered social security and national unity. After the collapse of the Soviet Union and the end of the Cold War, the nationalism and Islam revival movement in the Central Asian countries and the "Greater Turkism" in Western Asia complicated the external environment of Xinjiang. Taking advantage of the Islamic revival trend, the Pan-Islamic forces stepped up their incitement of ethnic hatred and religious fanaticism among the people of Xinjiang.

In the early 1990s, Hasan Mahsum, one of the Uyghur jihadists, founded the East Turkestan Islamic Movement (ETIM), an Islamic extremist separatist organization, whose stated goal was to create an independent state called "East Turkistan" in Xinjiang.[29] On April 5, 1990, around 200 rioters staged an anti-government demonstration in front of the office building of Baren Township, Akto County of Xinjiang. Six policemen were held hostage and slaughtered by the rioters. The next day, the rebels launched an offensive against the government building. Instead of an isolated event, this incident was closely related to the international and domestic climates at that time. It heralded the emergence of the "three evils," including terrorism, separatism and religious extremism, which are frequently used when referring to counter-terrorism operations undertaken by China, the Central Asian countries, and Russia. The "three evils" recruited terrorists, organized subversive activities, or even attempted to establish cross-border separatist regimes.

---

[29]Khan (2014): 197.

Formed in The Hague of the Netherlands in 1991, the Unrepresented Nations and Peoples Organization (UNPO) claimed to facilitate the voices of unrepresented and marginalized nations and peoples worldwide. Its members consist of nationalist political forces seeking independent statehood, including World Uyghur Congress, Taiwan Foundation for Democracy and Central Tibetan Administration. Its founding realized the long-expected goal of the US geopolitical strategists.[30] Under the control of the National Democratic Foundation of the USA, the UNPO generously funded the East Turkistan independence movement. With the upsurge of nationalism in the 1990s, the western countries, strongly believing that "nationalism will ultimately survive Communism," made every effort to promote the internationalization of the so-called "Tibet issue" and "Xinjiang issue." Therefore, a multitude of "East Turkistan" organizations mushroomed in Europe, North America, West and Central Asia, forming an East Turkistan Islamic organization system represented by the "World Uyghur Congress" (WUC), an international organization of exiled Uyghurs. Founded in Munich in 2004, the WUC claimed to "represent the collective rights and interests of the Uyghur people" both inside and outside Xinjiang. Fomenting political unrest and violence for its purported goal of seeking the "self-determination" of the Uyghurs, the "East Turkistan Islamic Movement" became one of the components of the international network of terrorism.

Calling for a concerted action to "rescue the peoples of 'East Turkistan' from the rule of the infidels," the East Turkistan separatists incited religious hatred and resentment against other religious beliefs. It seriously undermined the religious harmony and ethnic unity within Xinjiang and jeopardized the fundamental interests of the Chinese Muslims. By distorting and contravening Islamic theology, the extremists bewitch Muslims, especially teenagers, with such heretical ideas as "the shahid (martyr) engaged in jihad (holy war) can live in the garden of Paradise," thus turning some individuals into extremists and terrorists, who are manipulated to frequently perform acts of violence and terrorism and kill innocent people of all ethnic groups, even their fellow Islamic clerics and Muslims. Under the assistance of international hostile forces, they manufactured a series of commotions. On July 5, 2009, violent riots broke out in Ürümqi, which left nearly 200 people dead and thousands injured, many vehicles and buildings destroyed. The first day's rioting, which involved at least 1000 Uyghurs, began as a protest but escalated into violent attacks that mainly targeted the Han people. Ample evidence shows that the riots were fomented and planned from abroad by the WUC and its leader Rebiya Kadeer.

Most of the participants of the July 2009 Ürümqi riots were from the Tarim Basin of Xinjiang, or the three prefectures in the south of the frontier province, including Kashi, Hotan, and Kizilsu Kuoerzi (hereinafter referred to as "three prefectures"). The Tian Shan Mountains divide Xinjiang into two large basins: the Dzungarian Basin in the north and the Tarim Basin in the south. Much of the Tarim Basin is dominated by the Taklamakan Desert. Its extreme inland position, virtually in the very heartland of Asia and thousands of kilometers from any open body of water, accounts for the small precipitation and cold temperature at night. Therefore, the economy of the

---

[30]Engdahl (2009): 100.

Tarim Basin has long been dominated by small-scale oasis agriculture. At the same time, the economic stagnation of south Xinjiang is further complicated by rapid population growth, low education levels, and high unemployment rates. At the same time, nearly 60% of the Uyghur population of China lives in the three prefectures. The economic and social development of southern Xinjiang, therefore, shapes the future of the Uyghurs.

As the least-developed parts of Xinjiang, the GDP of these three prefectures, whose land area and population account for 27.6 and 30.5%, respectively of the total of Xinjiang, was only 9%. The conventional economic development indicators, such as the per capita GDP, per capita disposable income of urban and rural residents of a province or autonomous region, fail to reflect the regional disparity. Taking the year of 2010 as an example, the per capita GDP of Ürümqi, the capital city of Xinjiang, reached 43,039 Yuan, which far exceeded the average of Xinjiang as a whole (25,057 Yuan); however, the per capita GDP of Hotan Prefecture was only 5181 Yuan. Likewise, we can find similar tendencies in the statistics of per capita disposable income of urban and rural residents. Therefore, southern Xinjiang is designated as one of the 14 contiguous poverty-stricken areas in China. It is due to their widespread poverty that the three prefectures have become an ideal haven for extreme religious ideology and violent terrorists.

As a result, the poverty reduction and economic development of the three prefectures directly relate to the social stability and ethnic unity of Xinjiang and the whole country at large. Due to their widespread impoverishment, the three prefectures were given all the preferential treatments for ethnic minority regions, including the policy of development-oriented poverty alleviation, the drive of "Prosperous Frontiers and Better-off People" and the action of "Assisting the Development of Small-population Minority Nationalities."[31] *The Social and Economic Development Initiatives for the Three Prefectures in Southern Xinjiang* released in 2009 decided to leverage a total investment of 53.4 billion Yuan to the three prefectures in the next five years, with the construction of 13,910 projects.

These preferential policies have effectively contributed to the accelerated development of southern Xinjiang; however, these efforts have long been undermined by the terrorist activities of the "three evils," which seriously endanger social stability and undermine people's desire to pursue a happy life. The economic boom of the ethnic minority areas and a secure social environment will definitely enhance the local people's identification with the country; on the contrary, slow economic growth and ineffective solutions to poverty and other social problems become sources of people's discontentment, which will be utilized by the "three evils" to foment ethnic division and instigate social unrest. Fundamentally speaking, poverty reduction, economic structure transformation, improvement of educational facilities, and increasing employment rate constitute some basic conditions of traditional agricultural society's modernization, which will, in turn, affect a permanent cure to religious extremism and violent terrorism.

---

[31] *The Selected Documents on the Governance of Xinjiang: 1949–2010*, p. 693.

In 2011, the central authorities decided to pair off 19 provinces and municipalities directly under the central government with 82 counties in Xinjiang to render support to the latter. Moreover, the state has adopted a number of special policies to support the development of the region. These include: as of January 2015, ad valorem collection has been implemented for coal resources tax in Xinjiang at a rate of 6%; Xinjiang has been designated a key state-class comprehensive energy base and all-round efforts are called to improve the clean and efficient development, conversion, and utilization of its energy resources; specific provisions have been made in eight aspects concerning officials and professionals coming to support its development; a policy has been adopted to grant a two-year income tax exemption and three-year half pay for the enterprises listed in the *Catalog of Industries and Enterprises Enjoying Income Tax Preferences*; a policy covering 10 aspects of support to the two economic development zones in Kashi and Khorgos has been adopted. The state has also implemented a number of other talent training policies, such as selecting and appointing officials of ethnic minority origins to temporary posts in central government offices or in areas with better-developed economy to get training; implementing the "Program for High-Caliber Personnel from Ethnic Minorities" for the training of visiting scholars; and giving special policy support to the development of higher-learning institutions located in the ethnic minority areas or the master's and doctor's degree granting centers of ethnic colleges and universities in terms of graduate enrollment size, etc.

During his tour of inspection in Xinjiang in May 2014, Xi Jinping emphasized: "As the passkey to crack all hard nuts, development is the solution to all the problems of Xinjiang." The development achievements must, however, be utilized to improve people's livelihood and enhance self-development capacity and ethnic unity; otherwise, the development is of little significance. From the perspective of maintaining the long-term stability of Xinjiang, we must wipe out the roots of poverty, which will eradicate the "breeding soil" for religious extremism and social unrest. The statistics of 2011 shows that the impoverished population of Xinjiang is 3.29 million. Obviously, the poverty elimination of such a large number of needy people cannot be achieved in a short time. After years of trials and experimentation, China has established a "four-in-one" model of development-oriented poverty alleviation: a combination of special poverty reduction actions, industrial efforts, social involvement, and pairing assistance.

In 2013, Xinjiang Autonomous Government singled out employment as the top priority in the local economic development for the "soil" that breeds the "three evils" cannot be eradicated if people's livelihood is not effectively improved. Xinjiang is the largest cotton growing area of China, providing 60% of the cotton yields of the country. The textile, garment, and carpet-weaving industry, therefore, have long been the traditional economic sector of the region. However, the resource advantage and traditional carpet-weaving technology have not achieved an industrialized development due to the constraints of economic conditions and development environment. In May 2015, the central government released *Guidelines on Promoting the Employment of Xinjiang by Supporting the Local Textile and Garment Industries*, which is of great significance for optimizing the local economic structure, increasing employment rate, accelerating urbanization process, and promoting a long-term stability. In addition, the policy guidelines proposed that the industries with local advantages, such as garments for the Uyghur people and other ethnic minorities, handmade carpets, and embroidery, be developed.[32]

Under the firm leadership of the central government, and with the generous support of the whole nation, the people of all ethnic groups in Xinjiang have unswervingly followed the path of socialism with Chinese characteristics, pursued ethnic equality and unity, practiced the system of regional autonomy, and brought about enormous changes in all areas north and south of the Tianshan Mountains. Experience has proved that the combination of centralized national leadership with regional autonomy and the combination of ethnic factors with regional ones fully accord with the prevailing situation in China and with the realities and needs of Xinjiang. It is the basic premise behind the drive for equality, harmonious coexistence, and development of all ethnic groups in Xinjiang, and serves as an important guarantee that these goals will be realized. Today, Xinjiang is standing at a new starting point for development. As a key region on the Silk Road Economic Belt, it functions as a major window on China's opening to the west. It is a transportation hub that links the continents of Asia and Europe, and a center of business and trade, finance, cultural, and scientific exchange, and medical services. The people of all ethnic groups in Xinjiang will seize this precious opportunity to unite their efforts in pursuit of further achievements.

5.9   Development of Ethnic Minority Regions and the "Belt and Road" Initiative

Since the founding of the People's Republic of China in 1949, supporting the economic and social development of the ethnic minorities has been an unswerving policy of the Chinese government. It is also a basic principle stipulated in the State Constitution, "the state assists areas inhabited by minority ethnic groups in accelerating their economic and cultural development according to the characteristics and needs of the various ethnic groups." To achieve the goals of narrowing the development disparity between the eastern and western regions and realizing the common prosperity of all ethnic groups, China has taken a series of effective measures, such as financial subsidy, preferential policies, and free pairing-up assistance from the coastal provinces. In spite of the small population percentage of the western provinces among the total of China (27.04%), the central government's financial transfer payments to these provinces between 2000 and 2012 added up to 8.5 trillion RMB, accounting for 40% of the total amount of the country. As a result, the comprehensive strength of the western region has witnessed a significant improvement, their GDP percentage in the whole country rising from 17.9% in 1999 to 19.8% in 2012.

---

[32]General Office of the State Council. *Guidelines on Supporting the Development of the Textile and Garment Industry of Xinjiang to Promote Employment.* June 25, 2015.

The development of western provinces, in particular, the compact areas of the minority ethnic groups, is a precondition for solving the ethno-national issues of China. The theme of the ethno-national issues of China is the mismatching between the minority nationalities' urgent demand for development and their insufficient self-development capacities. This contradiction can only be solved by achieving the common development of all ethnic groups. Of course, it will be a protracted and difficult process. The economic growth of ethnic minority regions cannot be realized without the pairing-up assistance from the coastal provinces and the preferential state policies in a relative long period of time. However, this does not mean that the western region receives assistance in a unilateral manner in that the prosperity of ethnic minority regions is tantamount to the development of a unified multi-ethnic country. The coastal provinces' support to the western region is a driving force for east-west economic cooperation, which in turn contributes to the sustainable growth of the former.

Mao Zedong, the founding father of the People's Republic of China, once succinctly summarized China's basic national conditions as "a vast land with a large population and abundant resources." From the aspect of the Hu Line, we can conclude that the eastern side of the country (areas inhabited by the Han people) has a large population while the western side (compact communities of minority ethnic groups) has a vast territory and abundant resources. It was in this sense that Mao Zedong further pointed out: "the minority ethnic groups are of great help to the country and the whole Chinese nation in the fields of politics, economy and national defense. The vast territories inhabited by the ethnic minorities are blessed with rich natural resources. Therefore, the economy of ethnic minorities is an integral part of the Chinese national economy."[33] This is a conclusion drawn from the national conditions of China as a unified multi-ethnic state. At the same time, it does not mean that "the vast land and abundant resources" be exclusively monopolized by the ethnic minorities; rather, it implies that the exploitation of these resources shall be beneficial to the economic development and social progress of ethnic minorities and their communities.

While addressing the national conference on ethnic minority affairs in 2014, Xi Jinping described the ethnic minority regions as: areas with unique culture and underdeveloped economy, treasure houses of natural resources, ecological barriers, and sources of major river systems.[34] By taking a scientific and systematic stock of what we have got, including merits and demerits of development, Xi's statement expands a new horizon for a comprehensive and profound understanding of "the vast territory and abundant resources" of the western provinces. As a storehouse for natural resources, the compact communities of ethnic minorities have large reserves of forests, grasslands, coal, water, crude oil, and natural gas, and zinc, tin, nickel, titanium, vanadium, lithium, strontium, potassium salt, and sodium salt.[35] These resources are not only invaluable assets for the sustainable development of the

---

[33] Policy Institute of State Ethnic Affairs Commission (1994): 113.

[34] Ethnic Affairs Commission of China. *The Selected Readings on the Ethnic Affairs of China*, p. 20.

[35] Li and Zhang (2012).

Chinese nation and its future generations but also realistic advantages for accelerating the development of ethnic minority areas.

The Constitution of China stipulates that, "all mineral resources, waters, forests, mountains, grasslands, wasteland, beaches and other natural resources are owned by the state, that is, by the whole people, with the exception of the forests, mountains, grasslands, wasteland and beaches that are owned by collectives in accordance with the law. The state ensures the rational use of natural resources and protects rare animals and plants. Appropriation or damaging of natural resources by any organization or individual by whatever means is prohibited." Meanwhile, *the Law on Regional Ethnic Autonomy* provides that "while exploiting resources and undertaking construction in autonomous areas, the State shall give consideration to the interests of these areas, make arrangements favorable to the economic development there and pay proper attention to the productive pursuits and the life of the minority ethnic groups there. The State shall take measures to give due benefit compensation to the autonomous areas from which the natural resources are transported out." Accordingly, the organs of self-government of autonomous areas shall give priority to the rational exploitation and utilization of the natural resources that the local authorities are entitled to develop. The effectiveness of the coastal regions' pairing-up assistance to the western provinces is, as a matter of fact, closely associated with the ethnic minorities' contribution.

With their fast economic growth, the coastal provinces began to face the problem of power shortage. Inner Mongolia Autonomous Region, thanks to its plentiful coal reserve, has become one of the most important power bases for the "west-east electricity transmission project", with the target of easing the power shortage in north and northeast China. As of 2009, the electricity transmitted out of Inner Mongolia totaled 133.8 billion Kilowatt hours. As one of the leading producers for the "north-south coal transmission project", Inner Mongolia had transported 2.35 billion tons of coal to the southern provinces between 2001 and 2011, making a significant contribution to national energy security. In addition to Inner Mongolia, many of the coal reserves of the country are located in Western China, including Xinjiang, Gansu, Ningxia, Guizhou, and Yunnan.

The "west-east electricity transmission project" in the broad sense is actually composed of three channels. The first is the north channel, which transfers the hydropower of the Huanghe River and the coal-generated electric power of Shanxi and Inner Mongolia to north China; the second is the south channel, which delivers the hydropower of Guizhou, Yunnan, and Guangxi to Guangdong; the third is the middle channel, which transmits the hydropower of the Three Gorges and Jinsha River to the coastal provinces. Upon the completion of these three channels, the coal consumption of the whole country can be reduced by about 100 million tons per year.

Another national energy project, "the west-east natural gas transmission project", which was started in 2001, spans from the Tarim Basin of Xinjiang to Shanghai. With a total distance of 4000 km, the pipeline is an energy artery connecting the western region and coastal provinces. In 2008, the Chinese government launched the second phase of the natural gas transmission project. As the first strategic passageway to import natural gas from foreign countries, it stretches from Horgos of Xinjiang to

Hong Kong, with a distance of 8704 km. Four years later, the second phase of the project was kicked off, which extends from Horgos to Fuzhou in eastern China's Fujian province.

These projects are of great significance to the energy structure optimization, development mode transition, energy conservation, environmental protection, and improvement of people's living conditions of the regions along the natural gas pipeline. At the same time, "the west-east natural gas transmission project" took the lead in achieving a mutually beneficial cooperation between China and Central Asian countries, effectively promoting the economic and social development of Xinjiang. It can be said the project is the preliminary result of the Silk Road Economic Belt and the twenty-first-century Maritime Silk Road (hereinafter referred to as the Belt and Road Initiative, or BRI for short).

The concept of Silk Road Economic Belt was introduced by Chinese President Xi Jinping during his visit to Kazakhstan in September 2013. In a speech delivered at Nazarbayev University, Xi suggested that China and Central Asia cooperate to build a Silk Road Economic Belt. It was the first time the Chinese leadership mentioned the strategic vision. In October 2013, Xi proposed building a close-knit China-ASEAN community and offered guidance on constructing a twenty-first century Maritime Silk Road to promote maritime cooperation.[36] The Belt and Road routes run through the continents of Asia, Europe, and Africa, connecting the vibrant East Asia economic circle at one end and developed European economic circle at the other. On land, the Initiative will focus on jointly building a new Eurasian Land Bridge and developing China–Mongolia–Russia, China–Central Asia–West Asia, and China–Indochina Peninsula economic corridors by taking advantage of international transport routes, relying on core cities along the Belt and Road and using key economic industrial parks as cooperation platforms. At sea, the Initiative will focus on jointly building smooth, secure, and efficient transport routes connecting major seaports along the Belt and Road. The China–Pakistan Economic Corridor and the Bangladesh–China–India–Myanmar Economic Corridor are closely related to the Belt and Road Initiative, and therefore require closer cooperation and greater progress. The BRI is a way for win-win cooperation that promotes common development and prosperity and a road toward peace and friendship by enhancing mutual understanding and trust, and strengthening all-around exchanges. The Chinese government advocates peace and cooperation, openness and inclusiveness, mutual learning and mutual benefit. It promotes practical cooperation in all fields and works to build a community of shared interests, destiny, and responsibility featuring mutual political trust, economic integration, and cultural inclusiveness.

In advancing the BRI, China will fully leverage the comparative advantages of its various regions, adopt a proactive strategy of further opening-up, strengthen interaction and cooperation among the eastern, western, and central regions, and comprehensively improve the openness of the Chinese economy. We should make good use of Xinjiang's geographical advantage and its role as a window of westward opening up to deepen communication and cooperation with Central, South, and West Asian

---

[36]Xi (2014): 36.

countries, making it a key transportation, trade, logistics, culture, science, and education center, and a core area on the Silk Road Economic Belt. We should give full scope to the economic and cultural strengths of Shaanxi and Gansu provinces and the ethnic and cultural advantages of the Ningxia Hui Autonomous Region and Qinghai province, build Xi'an into a new focus of reform and opening-up in China's interior, speed up the development and opening-up of cities such as Lanzhou and Xining, and advance the building of the Ningxia Inland Opening-up Pilot Economic Zone with the goal of creating strategic channels, trade and logistics hubs and key bases for industrial and cultural exchanges opening to Central, South, and West Asian countries.

We should give full play to Inner Mongolia's proximity to the Republic of Mongolia and Russia, improve the railway links connecting Heilongjiang province with Russia and the regional railway network, strengthen cooperation between China's Heilongjiang, Jilin, and Liaoning provinces and Russia's Far East region on sea-land multimodal transport, and advance the construction of a Eurasian high-speed transport corridor linking Beijing and Moscow with the goal of building key windows opening to the north.

We should give full play to the unique advantage of Guangxi Zhuang Autonomous Region as a neighbor of ASEAN countries, speed up the opening-up and development of the Beibu Gulf Economic Zone and the Pearl River-Xijiang Economic Zone, build an international corridor opening to the ASEAN region, create new strategic anchors for the opening-up and development of the southwest and mid-south regions of China, and form an important gateway connecting the Silk Road Economic Belt and the twenty-first-century Maritime Silk Road. We should make good use of the geographical advantage of Yunnan province, advance the construction of an international transport corridor connecting China with neighboring countries, develop a new highlight of economic cooperation in the Greater Mekong Subregion, and make the region a pivot of China's opening-up to South and Southeast Asia. We should promote the border trade and tourism and culture cooperation between Tibet Autonomous Region and neighboring countries such as Nepal.

Against the backdrop of the BRI, the western regions, especially the areas inhabited by the minority ethnic groups, show a new pattern of openness and development. Xi Jinping pointed out: "the BRI is beneficial to the economic and social development of the ethnic minority areas, in particular, the border regions. We shall further implement the western development strategy and speed up the pace of the opening-up momentum of the frontier regions for the purpose of expanding new spaces for the development of China."[37] In other words, the BRI provides sustainable driving force for the economic and social development of the frontier regions, for only when these regions achieve a rapid growth can they fulfill the roles of the "opening-up channels," "development pivots," "strategic anchors," and "important gateways."

The BRI aims to promote the connectivity of the Asian, European, and African continents and their adjacent seas, establish and strengthen partnerships among the

---

[37]Ethnic Affairs Commission of China. *The Selected Readings on the Ethnic Affairs of China*, p. 194.

countries along the Belt and Road, set up all-dimensional, multi-tiered, and composite connectivity networks, and realize diversified, independent, balanced, and sustainable development in these countries. The connectivity projects of the Initiative will help align and coordinate the development strategies of the countries along the Belt and Road, tap market potential in this region, promote investment and consumption, create demands and job opportunities, enhance people-to-people and cultural exchanges, and mutual learning among the peoples of the relevant countries, and enable them to understand, trust, and respect each other and live in harmony, peace, and prosperity. Countries along the Belt and Road have their own resource advantages and their economies are mutually complementary. Therefore, there is a great potential and space for cooperation.

The core concept of the BRI is "connectivity." It has five major goals: policy coordination, facilities connectivity, unimpeded trade, financial integration, and people-to-people bond. Among the five goals, people-to-people bond provides the public support for implementing the Initiative. The spirit of friendly cooperation of the Silk Road should be carried forward by promoting extensive cultural and academic exchanges, personnel exchanges and cooperation, media cooperation, youth and women exchanges, and volunteer services, so as to win public support for deepening bilateral and multilateral cooperation.

Many ethnic minorities of China, for example, the Mongols in Inner Mongolia, the Uyghurs in Xinjiang, the Tibetans in Tibet, the Dai in Yunnan, the Jing in Guangxi, the Russians in Heilongjiang, and the Koreas in Jilin, share homologous historical and cultural ties, including language, culture, religion, and customs, with the people of the corresponding neighboring countries. These factors are favorable, convenient, and friendly natural conditions for the development of bilateral and multilateral non-governmental ties. Among the ethno-national policies of China, the protection, inheritance, and development of ethnic minority cultures, respect for religious freedom and tolerance of diversified customs are of great significance in promoting people-to-people bonds in China's opening-up to the outside world.

There are two fundamental footholds underlying the ethno-national policies of China, including narrowing the development gap between the ethnic minority regions and the rest of China, and respect for the cultural differences of the various ethnic groups. The former is targeted to the equality of economic and social life for people of all ethnic groups; the latter is for the goal of the Chinese nation's unity. The essence of these two positions is incarnated in the concepts of the BRI, such as mutual benefit, win-win cooperation, and harmonious coexistence.

China's economy is closely connected with the world economy. The country will stay committed to the basic policy of opening-up and integrate itself deeper into the world economic system. The Initiative will enable China to further expand and deepen its opening-up and to strengthen its mutually beneficial cooperation with countries in Asia, Europe, and Africa and the rest of the world. China is committed to shouldering more responsibilities and obligations within its capabilities and making greater contributions to the peace and development of mankind. In the building of the BRI, the concept of respecting for differences contained in the ethno-national policies of China is an important prop for the realization of "diplomacy as the extension of internal affairs." The effectiveness of China's ethnic policy will, in turn, affect the people-to-people bond, which is diplomacy in a broad sense.

References

Engdahl, W. (2009). *Behind the hegemony: The all-dominant strategy of the United States*. Beijing: Intellectual Publishing House.

Ge, J. (1997). *The history of internal migration in China* (Vol. 1). Fuzhou: Fujian People's Press.

Jin, C. (2009). *The history of China in the 20th Century* (Vol. 2). Beijing: Social Sciences Academic Press.

Khan, R. (2014). *Afghanistan and Pakistan: Conflict, extremism and resistance to modernity*. Beijing: Current Affairs Press.

Li, Z., & Zhang, Y. (2012). *Difficulties and countermeasures of environmental protection in Western China*. www.cet.com.cn.

Policy Institute of State Ethnic Affairs Commission. (1994). *On the Ethno-national issues of China by the major leaders of the Chinese communist party of China*. Beijing: The Ethnic Publishing House.

The Dalai Lama. (1990). *The autobiography of the 14th Dalai Lama*. Taipei: Lianjing Publishing Ltd.

Xi, J. (2014). *The governance of China*. Beijing: Foreign Languages Press.

Zhang, Z. (2007). An analysis of the congressional human rights caucus related to China. *The Chinese Journal of American Studies, 2*, 110–113.

Chapter 6
Tolerance of Diversity: Identity Integration Among People of All Ethnic Groups

As mentioned earlier, there is a widespread developmental gap between the ethnic minority regions and the rest of China due to their different natural geographical conditions and historical backgrounds. At the same time, we can also find striking cultural differences, including language, literature, art, religious belief, social psychology, folkways, and customs, as well as material carriers for these spiritual values, such as utensils, tools, traditional residences, and clothing, among people of various ethnic groups. As a response, we must show full respect for the cultural differences among ethnic groups—as Xiaotong Fei, a pioneering Chinese researcher and professor of sociology and anthropology puts it, "appreciating the values of others as one's own". It constitutes a driving force toward building a common spiritual home for all people of all ethnic groups.

In China's policy concept and social practice of solving its ethnic problems, neither material foundation nor cultural power can be dispensed with. They were likened by the Chinese President Xi Jinping to "two keys": One is utilized to shorten the regional development rift, and the other to the tolerance of cultural differences among various ethnic groups. The former is being realized and will be achieved in the near future in the process of building China into a moderately well-off society; however, the latter, achieving identity integration among people of all ethnic groups, is a more complicated and time-consuming task than the former.

6.1 Eliminating Historical Traces of Ethnic Discrimination

In a broad context, the Chinese word "Zhongyuan" ("Central Plain" or "North China Plain") refers to regions directly governed by the Chinese central dynasties. When used to describe the Chinese civilization, "Zhongyuan" often connotes the cultural dominance of the Han people. Representing the power center of feudal society, the centralized Chinese dynasties based in "Zhongyuan" enjoy political, economic, and cultural superiority in comparison with the peripheral "Siyi" (literally "four barbarians"). As a derogatory Chinese term for various peoples bordering China proper,

© China Social Sciences Press 2020
S. Hao, *China's Solution to Its Ethno-national Issues*, China Insights,
https://doi.org/10.1007/978-981-32-9519-3_6

"*Siyi*" has four components, including "*Dongyi*" (eastern barbarians), "*Nanman*" (southern barbarians), "*Xirong*" (western barbarians), and "*Beidi*" (northern barbarians).

Unlike the English language with one general word, "barbarian," meaning "uncultured or uncivilized peoples," Chinese had many specific exonyms for foreigners. According to the Chinese ancients, heaven and earth were matched with "yin" and "yang," with the heaven (yang) superior and the earth (yin) inferior; the Chinese as an entity were matched with the "inferior" ethnic groups surrounding them in the four cardinal directions so that the Han people could be valued and the barbarians could be rejected.[1] As a confederation of tribes living along the Huanghe River who were ancestors of what later became the Han people, "Huaxia" in its original sense is defined as a civilized society that stood in contrast to what was perceived as the barbaric peoples around them.

The "Sino-barbarian dichotomy," or the distinction between "Hua" and "Yi," which is actually an ancient Chinese concept that differentiated a culturally defined "*Hua*" (the Han people based in China proper or "Zhongyuan") from cultural or ethnic outsiders ("Yi" or "barbarians"), began to take shape. The Hua–Yi distinction was basically cultural, but it could take ethnic or racist overtones, in particular in times of war. In its cultural form, the distinction asserted the cultural superiority of the Han people; at the same time, it implied that the uncivilized outsiders could become "Hua" by adopting the values and customs of the Han people.

Throughout history, the Chinese frontiers had been periodically attacked by nomadic tribes from the north and west. These people were considered "barbarians" by the Han who believed themselves to be more refined and who had begun to build cities and live an urban life based on agriculture. It was in consideration of how best to deal with this threat that Confucius, the great Chinese philosopher, was prompted to formulate principles for relationships with these "barbarians." Actually, since the pre-Qin period (ca. 2000–221 BC), in particular during the Spring and Autumn period (770–476 BC) and the Warring States Period (475–221 BC), there had been frequent exchanges between the "four barbarians" and the "Huaxia."

China is a united multi-ethnic state with a long history. Almost all the central authorities of the feudal dynasties adopted a policy of "rule by custom" toward the ethnic minorities. Under this policy, the political unification of China was maintained while the ethnic minorities were allowed to preserve their own social systems and cultures. For example, the Han dynasty (202 BC–8 AD) created the Office of Protector General of the western regions in what is now the Xinjiang Uyghur Autonomous Region, and the Tang dynasty (618–907) established Anxi and Beiting Office of Protector General in the same area. These organizations administered only political and military affairs. The Qing dynasty (1644–1912) adopted different measures for governing the ethnic minority areas in accordance with local characteristics. In the areas where the Mongols lived, a league banner (prefecture–county) administrative system was exercised. In Tibet, the Qing government sent grand ministers resident in Tibet (the Qing Amban) and exercised a religion–political rule of Lamas and

---

[1]Feng (1994): 7.

nobles by granting honorific titles to the most influential sects of Tibetan Buddhism, including the lineages of the Dalai Lama and the Panchen Lama. In places where ethnic minority peoples lived in south China, a system of "Tusi," meaning "aboriginal office" literally, who were actually hereditary tribal leaders recognized as imperial officials by the Qing throne, was introduced.

Under the old social system, it is impossible for all ethnic groups to enjoy equality in the modern sense. As a result, strife, conflicts, or even wars among them were inevitable. Still, the long-standing existence of a united multi-ethnic state in Chinese history greatly enhanced the political, economic, and cultural exchanges among different ethnic groups, which constantly promoted the identification of all ethnic groups with the central government and their allegiance to it.

However, the Sino-barbarian dichotomy, as a highlighted expression of political, economic, and cultural oppression, is an inescapable result of the ethnic conflict in the feudal society. As a consequence, ethnic oppression or discrimination produces a reverse effect. After the northern nomads established central dynasties in the traditional Chinese style, such as the Yuan dynasty (1271–1368) and the Qing dynasty (1636–1912) found by the Mongols and the Manchus, respectively, the rulers made every effort to strengthen their power by weakening the political and cultural identities of the "four barbarians" and vesting the Mongols or the Manchu with superior social status.

During Kublai Khan's reign, a hierarchy of reliability, similar to the caste system of India, was introduced. It divided the population of the Yuan dynasty into four castes, including Mongols, Semu (non-Mongol foreigners from the West and Central Asia, like Buddhist Uyghurs from Turfan, and Jews, Nestorian Christians, and Muslims from Central Asia), the "Han" (all subjects of the former Jin dynasty, including the Han people, Khitans and Jurchens residing in Northern China, and Koreans), and Southerners (all subjects of the former Southern Song dynasty, such as the Han and minority native ethnic groups living in Southern China). After the conquest of Beijing and the North China Plain in 1644, the Manchu rulers tried to enhance their governance capacity by drawing on the Han culture, for example, making Beijing the dynastic capital, and keeping the bureaucracy of the Ming dynasty intact by reappointing most Ming officials. These measures helped quickly stabilize the regime and sped up the conquest of the rest of the country.

While many Han intellectuals joined the Manchu government and tacitly accepted Qing rule, a great many more remained in silent opposition. The very fact that the Qing was an alien dynasty continuously evoked the Han people's protest in the form of nationalistic–racial revolt and revolution. After the failure of the Taiping Rebellion, a large-scale civil war in China fought between the established Manchu-led Qing dynasty and the Christian millenarian movement of the Taiping Heavenly Kingdom between 1850 and 1864, the nationalistic–racial revolution again subsided into secret society activities, giving inspiration to later revolutionaries such as Dr. Sun Yat-sen.

At the turn of the twentieth century, a strong sense of nationalistic–racial consciousness increasingly gathered momentum among Han intellectuals. The revolutionaries represented by Sun Yat-sen disparaged the Manchu people as "furred barbarians" and called on the Han people "to oust the Manchus from Chinese central power and restore the usurped Chinese regime."

A string of Chinese military defeats during the First Sino-Japanese War exposed the corruption and incompetence of the Manchu rulers. The Revive China Society found by Sun Yat-sen in late 1894 forwarded the goal of establishing prosperity for China and became a platform for future revolutionary activities. Those admitted to the society swore the following oath: Expel Tatar barbarians, revive Zhonghua (Huaxia), and establish a unified government. By then, the scope of revolutionary aspirations had broadened to include a vendetta against foreign imperialism as well. With the downfall of the Qing dynasty in 1912, the original anti-Qing objective had been realized, and the nationalistic revolution turned against foreign imperialism.

Upon its founding in 1921, the Communist Party of China (CPC) endorsed the theoretical framework of Marxism that the essence of ethnic oppression was class repression. In other words, only by toppling intra-ethnic class antagonism can ethnic oppression be eradicated in a multi-ethnic state. On the basis of the historical and actual national conditions of China, the CPC established the revolutionary goal of overthrowing the rule of imperialism, feudal landlords, and bourgeoisie, advocating that all Chinese ethnic groups should be on equal footing.

To remove the long-standing prejudice and distrust between the Han people and minority nationalities, the CPC established a series of ethno-national policies during its political debut. These policies showed full respect for the language, culture, religious belief, and customs of the ethnic minorities. During the Red Army's Long March, a military retreat to evade the pursuit of the Kuomintang (KMT or Chinese Nationalist Party) army, the Chinese Communists, thanks to their great efforts in promoting ethnic unity and equality, won the support and trust of the ethnic minorities. It laid a solid foundation for the creation of the second united front, the brief alliance between the KMT and the CPC to resist the Japanese invasion during the Second Sino-Japanese War.

After the capitulation of Japan in 1945, China emerged victoriously but war-ravaged and financially drained. The continued hostility between the Chinese Communists and the ruling Kuomintang led to the resumption of civil war. Major combat of the armed conflict ended in 1949 with the Communists in control of most of mainland China and the Kuomintang retreating offshore. On October 1, 1949, Mao Zedong proclaimed the establishment of the People's Republic of China (PRC) in Beijing.

Among the appellations for the ethnic minorities, many had discriminatory or insulting connotations in that they often featured insect, animal, bird, or dog radicals, the graphical component of a Chinese character under which the character is traditionally listed in a Chinese dictionary. For example, the designation of the "Lolo" people, who live primarily in the rural areas of Sichuan, Yunnan, Guizhou, and Guangxi, usually in mountainous regions, was related to their worship of the tiger, as "lo" in their dialects means "tiger." "Lo" is also the basis for the Chinese exonym "Luoluo." The original character, with the "dog" radical and a "guo" phonetic, was a graphic pejorative, comparable to the Chinese name "guoran," meaning "a long-tailed ape."[2]

To eliminate the negative influence left over from the old society, the newly found PRC government issued a decree in 1954, declaring: "the appellations, place names, steles and plaques which the ethnic minorities find derogative or offensive shall be prohibited, amended or sealed." As a response, the appellation of the ethnic "Lolo" changed to the Yi people in the official documents and textbooks. In other words, China's ethno-national policies, in addition to establishing the principle of respecting ethnic minorities and opposing ethnic discrimination, were dedicated to wiping off the historical traces contradictory to ethnic equality and unity in the social life.

Ethnic equality is a core principle followed by the CPC and the Chinese government when handling ethnic relations. Irrespective of their size, history, or levels of development, all ethnic groups in China are equal in every aspect of life. No discrimination or oppression against any group can be tolerated. They have the right to equal participation in national and local affairs, regardless of whether their populations are concentrated or dispersed. Ethnic unity is the bedrock of China's ethno-national policies. It is reflected in harmonious, friendly interactions between different ethnic groups, whose members learn from and help each other in a spirit of mutual respect, trust, and understanding. It is built upon the notion that all ethnic groups in China, including the Han and minority groups, are interdependent: They breathe the same air, share the same future, aspire to the same goals, and work together for common prosperity.

To illustrate this point, we are going to cite two more examples. After the Tümed Mongol Leader Altan Khan found the settlement in the Tümed plain, the provincial capital of Inner Mongolia had been known as "Kuku-Khoto," meaning "blue town" in the Mongolian language. For the purpose of dissuading them from attacking the North China Plain, the Ming dynasty based in the plain at one time blockaded the Mongols' access to iron, cotton, and crop seeds, which were highly demanded by nomadic society. In 1570, Altan Khan successfully negotiated the end of the blockade by establishing a vassal–tributary relationship with the Ming Empire. Five years later, the Ming Emperor was renamed "Kuku-Khoto" as "Guihua." With an obvious disparaging implication, the new name literally meant "returning to civilization." In accordance with the 1954 state decree regarding correcting the derogative appellations for ethnic minorities, the original name of the city, "Kuku-Khoto," was restored. Ürümqi, the capital city of Xinjiang Uyghur Autonomous Region, also experienced a similar renaming process. During the reign of the Qianlong Emperor of the Qing dynasty, the city had been named "Dihua," meaning "to enlighten." After the finding of the People's Republic of China, the city's name was officially changed back to its traditional name Ürümqi, which means "beautiful pasture" in the Uyghur language.

By restoring the traditional appellations or place names of the ethnic minorities, the Chinese government abandoned the outdated Sino-barbarian dichotomy. Moreover, the relationship between the Han people and the minority nationalities was reformulated: The ethnic minorities and their compact communities are builders and

---

[2]*The Governance of Xinjiang: 1949–2010*, p. 66.

components for the formation and development of the unified multi-ethnic state, instead of the former "barbarians" in the "uncivilized land."

In its essence, this policy practice is not to write off bygone times; rather, it aims to carve out new history. The historical records or material carriers can be stored in libraries or museums for the use of scientific research, which will be beneficial to creating a harmonious social environment atmosphere for the construction of a new ethnic relationship. If the symbols for national conquest and ethnic discrimination are a part of the everyday life of a country which proclaims to champion modern civilization and uphold ethnic equality, the underlying ideas behind these material carriers will be impossible to change and erase. In this regard, there is no lack of real-life lessons.

On June 17, 2015, a white man gunned down nine blacks who were praying in a church in the city of Charlton in the state of South Carolina. As an extreme reflection of the long-standing violent law enforcement against the blacks in civil racial relations in recent years, this atrocity forced the Americans to reconsider the deep-rooted issue of racism in the US society. On July 10 of the same year, the Confederate Flag, which had been fluttering in front of the parliament building of South Carolina for 50-plus years, was lowered. Accepted as an icon of the institutional oppression and racial discrimination in the USA, the Confederate Flag, with a history of more than 150 years, symbolizes the self-proclaimed Confederacy composed of the 13 secessionist slave states during the civil war. A mark of the realistic legitimacy of institutional oppression and racial discrimination, the controversial flag reminded the Afro-Americans of the psychological trauma in their tragic past. In addition, the Ku Klux Klan, a white supremacy organization in the USA which called for the "purification" of American society, vested the flag with the message of racism.

The historical hallmarks of racism, such as the Confederate Flag, had a lasting and negative effect on US racial relations. Historical records and relics tell us about yesterday, but we are here to create today and head for tomorrow, instead of following the same old disastrous path. People need to understand the law of historical development and draw historical experiences from them, so that the wisdom accumulated by history can be sublimated in a modern way. Therefore, all the countries of the world must appropriately address the scourges which arose in the historical process, learning from the lessons and refraining from the repetition of similar tragedy. Realizing that these material symbols or habitual appellations are invested with old and decayed ideas, which would inevitably jeopardize ethnic unity, the Chinese government has been making every effort to weed out the historical traces which smear the images of ethnic minorities.[3]

Motivated by the American Civil Rights Movement, whose goals were to end racial segregation and discrimination against African Americans, to secure legal recognition and federal protection of the citizenship rights enumerated in the constitution and federal law, the US government also took measures to eliminate the social impact of racial discrimination in the 1960s. The Canadian-born American popular science author Steven Pinker concluded: "In the past 5 decades, the US has been

---

[3] *The Governance of Xinjiang: 1949–2010*, p. 66.

endeavoring to clear the deep-rooted marks of racism." Nowadays, "any derogatory racial jokes, insulting remarks about ethnic minorities, or unwitting mockery of
racial differences have become unacceptable taboos in musicals, movies, cartoons,
trademarks, advertisings, or appellations."[4]

Undoubtedly, it is a commendable progress of the US society driven by the Civil
Rights Movement. However, it does not mean the country has addressed its racial
problems once and for all. The rampancy of hate groups, referring to social groups
that advocate and practice hatred, hostility, or violence toward members of a race,
ethnicity, nation, religion, or any other designated sect of society, and an endless
stream of fresh examples of racism show that racist stigmas are still prevalent in
American society. Therefore, the elimination of the historical racist ideas and racial
discrimination in real life remains a decisive political agenda for the highly developed
US society.

With an ingrained influence of feudal society, China has gone through a recorded
history of nearly 4000 years. During the century of national humiliation between the
First Opium War (1840) and the finding of the People's Republic of China in 1949,
the racial nationalism of Western society was introduced to China. Therefore, it is
bound to be an arduous and protracted social project to eliminate the historical traces
of ethnic discrimination piled up over the years and to create a social atmosphere
in which people of all ethnic groups live in amity and make concerted efforts for
common prosperity.

With the rapid development of economy and society, the interaction and engagement among people of different ethnic groups are being observed in an ever-
increasing tendency. They need to understand and adapt to each other in the aspects
of language, culture, customs, and religious beliefs. In civil society communication,
people tend to describe the folkways or customs of other ethnic groups as bizarre.
It is, as a matter of fact, a common social mentality. However, such negative value
judgments, such as contempt, ridicule, or exclusion, will adversely affect ethnic relations or even lead to conflicts. Therefore, respecting for the customs and traditions of
ethnic minorities is of great significance in maintaining cordial ethnic relationship.

6.2   Respect for Ethnic Minority Customs and Traditions

During its long history of evolution, human society has always been confronted with
the reality of diversified cultural backgrounds and social life. Admittedly, ideas and
practices of rejecting differences and diversity are easily available in the history of the
world. As for China, the decency of the "Huaxia" civilization based in the North China
Plain, on the one hand, stood in contrast to what was perceived as the marginalized
non-Han barbaric and uncivilized peoples; on the other hand, the notion of tolerating
diversity, "governing an outlying region in accordance with its specific customs", also
has a time-honored history. The Chinese ancients interpreted the cultural diversity

---

[4]Pinker (2015): 458.

of different peoples from their diverse geographical environments, which gave rise to the saying, "in the mountains, one lives on mountain products; along the coast, on seafood," meaning to make a living with the local advantages. The divergent habitats of the Chinese ancestors contributed to their different folkways and customs, which can be defined as the rudiment "geographical environment determinism" in ancient China. It is, however, dissimilar to "geographical determinism" formed in modern Western society, which holds that climate and terrain largely determine human activity and psychology.

Due to its association with institutionalized racism and eugenics, Western geographical determinism has been widely criticized as a tool to legitimize colonialism, racism, and imperialism in Africa, the Americas, and Asia. It enabled geographers to scientifically justify the supremacy of white European races and the naturalness of imperialism. Many scholars underscore that this approach supported colonialism and Eurocentrism, and devalued human agency in non-Western societies. The global expansion of colonialism led to the cultural tragedy of many ancient civilizations and countries, "the disappearance of knowledge accumulated over several thousand years."[5]

As a Chinese saying goes, "each location has its own way of sustaining its inhabitants." The underlying inclusiveness vividly expresses the common value of different cultures from the spiritual perspective. Some contemporary Western scholars also interpreted the value of cultural diversity while reflecting the demerits of "Western centrism," a worldview centered on and biased toward Western civilization, especially in the context of decolonization and humanitarian aid offered by industrialized nations to developing countries.[6] The tolerance of cultural diversity is the key to understanding the Chinese government's policies of opposing ethnic discrimination and respecting the customs, language, culture, and religious beliefs of ethnic minorities.

Another Chinese saying, "hundred miles make folkways different, thousand miles make customs divergent," reflects the diversity of folkways and customs, including festivals, rituals, diet, clothing, tools, utensils, residences, decorations, taboos, as well as influences of folk worship and religious beliefs on people's daily life. As the self-identity statute among members of an ethnic group, folkways and customs penetrate all aspects of social life and regulate people's way of doing things. They are one of the most direct scales to measure the mutual adaptability in the interaction among various ethnic groups. Any behavior of belittling the other nation's customs or violating their taboos will inevitably lead to psychological estrangement or even ethnic conflict. Therefore, the idiom "do in Rome as the Romans do" demonstrates the importance of respecting for and adapting to different customs.

The customs are characterized by their stability by way of family inheritance, group compliance, and social maintenance. Its formation is a long-term process. At the same time, the customs of an ethnic group are by no means immutable. With the development of economic production and expansion of product exchange,

---

[5]Morin and Kern (1997): 2.
[6]Ibid., p. 50.

substitutions of tools and utensils, as well as changes in diet and clothing from the aspect of material culture, are common phenomena. The voluntary breaking with outmoded folkways is the natural outcome of ever-increasing human contact and communication. Moreover, it tends to be expanded with the development of society.

However, if people of ethnic minorities are prejudiced, oppressed, or even coerced into renouncing their customs and habits, inter-ethnic psychological grievances will naturally arise. In this case, the negative historical memory becomes a source for their dissatisfaction with reality. For example, while analyzing the underlying causes for the Scottish independence referendum, some scholars traced its root to King George II's *Dress Act 1746*, which outlawed all items of Highland dress including kilts (although an exception was made for the Highland regiments) with the intent of suppressing Highland culture. Such forced assimilation was also not uncommon in the history of China. The queue order, a series of laws violently imposed by the Qing dynasty in the seventeenth century, was a case in point.[7] It was compulsory for all males, and the penalty for non-compliance was executed for treason. The slogan adopted by the Qing throne was "don't shave your forehead and lose your head, or shave your forehead and keep it." In the early Qing dynasty, a lot of Han people resisted the order and the Qing government struck back with deadly force, massacring all who refused to obey.

Customs often produce the most direct feelings among different ethnic groups. Therefore, it is most likely that people tend to make value judgments on the heterogeneous folkways. If people of the minority ethnic groups are coerced into breaking with their customs, a counterproductive effect will follow. Therefore, Article 4 of *the 1954 Constitution of China* provides that "people of all ethnic groups have the freedom to preserve or reform their own folkways and customs."

Respecting the folkways and customs of all ethnic groups, in particular those of the ethnic minorities, is both a subtle topic in civil life communication and an important ethnic policy. In a conference on ethnic minority affairs held in 1950, Mao Zedong declared: "the customs of ethnic minority areas can only be reformed of the ethnic minorities' own accord. No state organ, social organization or individual shall coerce the ethnic minorities into breaking with their customs."[8]

Though the freedom of preserving and reforming folkways entails the dual rights of equality and development, it does not mean that all traditional customs must necessarily be kept intact. The culture and life customs of every ethnic group, in particular, those corrupt practices which impair public sanitation, jeopardize people's health, or infringe women's rights, need to be reformed with the development of society and change of life concepts. Let us cite some examples to illustrate this point. The first case is foot binding,[9] the custom of applying tight binding to the feet of young girls to modify the shape of the foot, which was adopted as a symbol of beauty

---

[7]The queue was a specifically male hairstyle worn by the Manchu people and later imposed on the Han people during the Qing dynasty. The hair on the front of the head was shaved off above the temples, and the remainder of the hair was braided into a long braid.

[8]On the Ethno-national Issues of China by the CCP Leadership (1994): 44.

[9]Foot binding became popular as a means of displaying status (women from wealthy families, who did not need their feet to work, could afford to have them bound) and was correspondingly adopted

in Han Chinese culture. The second example is teeth chiseling,[10] a corrupt custom practiced by the Gelao people living in the southwest provinces of China. Of course, such outworn customs can also be found beyond China, for example, tightlacing in Europe, which means the wearing of a tightly laced corset for the smallness of the waist, and some African countries' female circumcision, the ritual removal of some or all of the external female genitalia. These old-fashioned and irrational practices are destined to be abolished with the progress of modern civilization for they do not have any cultural significance worthy of respect.

However, the phasing-out of such customs like female circumcision will be an enduring process in spite of the orchestrated efforts of the United Nations, the World Health Organization, and the Feminist Movement Groups. Only by transforming the underlying superstitious mentality can these bad customs be eradicated. Therefore, economic growth and the accompanied improvement of literacy levels and living standards will surely contribute to people's conscious severing their emotional bonds to these corrupt traditions.

Marxists believe that the production mode of material life determines the whole social life. Therefore, the development of an ethnic group can only be achieved with the progress of economic production. Due to constraints of social history and natural conditions, quite a wide range of "bad habits" can still be found in some remote rural areas of China, such as thatched huts, shanties, narrow living space co-occupied by humans and livestock, "water cellars" in arid areas. Rather than the traditional "folkways or customs," these should be categorized as ways of life for poverty-stricken populace due to their lack of production capacity. The unhygienic conditions become breeding grounds for diseases and bacteria hazardous to the dwellers.

Respecting for the customs and traditions of ethnic minorities does not equate to our callous indifference to their plight; rather, we should assist them in developing economy and improving their living standards. This will, in turn, contribute to their doing away with these "bad habits." In this respect, any custom or tradition which is to the disadvantage of civilization progress, production development, and people's livelihood improvement, physical or mental health of citizens merits to be reformed during the construction of the new society. For example, the irrational practices of "child bride," polygamy, polyandry, and tisese[11] may be weeded out by legislation or social education. State unity has a common effect on the economic and social life of all ethnic groups; for example, the state establishes nationwide festivals. Nonetheless, it is by no means at odds with the reverence for the ethnic minorities' traditional festi-

---

as a symbol of beauty in Chinese culture. Therefore, a woman with perfect lotus feet was likely to make a more prestigious marriage. However, foot binding resulted in lifelong disabilities for its victims.

[10] According to this practice, any woman who is about to wed shall have two anterior teeth beat out to prevent damage to the husband.

[11] Tisese, meaning literally "walking marriage" in the local dialect, has long been practiced by the Mosuo people, in which heterosexual activity occurs only by mutual consent and mostly through the secret nocturnal visit. As a result, men and women of this small-population ethnic group living in the provinces of Yunnan and Sichuan are free to have multiple partners and to initiate or break off relationships when they please.

vals, which are celebrated as legal holidays in the corresponding regions. Respecting the customs and traditions of all ethnic groups is the justice of cultural understanding and tolerance.

Rather than being an abstract concept, culture permeates all aspects of social life and ideology, including conceptual infiltrations of religious beliefs and folk worship in social life, as well as rules in daily life. For example, the consumption of pork is forbidden by Muslim dietary law, a taboo that arises from perceptions of pigs' hygiene as well as from the ways pigs are slaughtered. Such taboos, with no cultural value of merits or demerits, can be categorized to be the morality of a human action in Islam. The Chinese government has been doing its utmost to guarantee the supply of halal food for the Muslims of China. Between the 1950s and the early 1980s, China introduced a peacetime rationing system due to food shortages. Even during this time of material scarcity, the Muslim urban residents' halal food supply was given preferential treatments. This practice of adapting to the Muslim adherents' dietary habits is really commendable under the historical conditions at that time.

With the rapid development of the Chinese economy since China introduced reform and the opening-up policy, a market-oriented mechanism for the supply of material and cultural needs of all ethnic groups has been formed, thus terminating the long-standing practice of food rationing. However, meeting the minority nationalities' special production and living needs is still an important task of the ethnic policy of China. Respecting the ethnic minorities' customs and traditions, including traditional festivals, dietary cultures, funeral rites, religion, or belief, has always been a policy focus of the CPC and the Chinese government. As ethnic customs are dynamic under the influence of social, economic, and scientific progress, the freedom to reform customary practices is also respected. But such reforms should always be initiated, decided upon, and executed by minorities themselves, rather than mandated or imposed from without.

6.3 Satisfying Special Production and Living Needs of Minority Ethnic Groups

From the aspects of production tools, cultural expressions, living utensils, attire, diet, residence, and transportation, the economy, culture, and social lives of the 55 ethnic minorities of China are of diverse character. The material products bearing these features are not only carriers of cultural inheritance but necessary materials for people's livelihood as well. These products, including the articles for daily use manufactured by the ethnic minorities themselves and traded commodities with the Han people, have become their life necessities during the long historical process. The "tea-horse trade" in ancient China, referring to the bartering trade between the tea produced in southwest provinces and horses of the border areas, was the most symbolic description between the agriculture-engaged Han people and the nomadic ethnic minorities. Such trade relationship has an age-old tradition in the Chinese civil society. In the dynasties of Tang (618–907) and Song (960–1279), official regulations were established by setting up special tea and horse trade management institutions. In addition to tea, the mule caravans along the ancient Tea-Horse Route carried native products, including silk, textiles, ironware, salt, fur, knitwear, dried fruits, and herbal medicines.

The large and continuous demand for tea in Tibet, Xinjiang, and Mongolia contributed to the production of compressed tea, blocks of whole or finely ground black tea, green tea, or postfermented tea leaves that were packed into molds and pressed into block form, in the tea-producing southwest provinces. Due to their density and toughness, tea bricks were consumed after they were broken into small pieces and boiled. They were preferred in trade prior to the nineteenth century in Asia since they were more compact than loose leaf tea and were also less susceptible to physical damage incurred through transportation over land by caravans on the ancient tea route. They are indispensable to the milk tea of the Mongols and Kazakhs, the butter tea of Tibetans, and the daily tea drink of the Uyghurs. Therefore, the tea-horse trade has become an important element affecting the ties between the tea-producing provinces and the borderland. To contain or punish the frontier ethnic minorities, the rulers of some Chinese central dynasties would forcibly block the supplies of compressed tea. During the Ming (1368–1644) and Qing (1636–1912) dynasties, the merchants of Shanxi Province played an important role in promoting the tea-horse trade.[12]

After the finding of the People's Republic of China in 1949, the central authorities attached great importance to the trade between the hinterland and the border areas to maximize the production and living needs of ethnic minorities. A series of measures were taken, such as incorporating state-run trade companies, founding supply and marketing cooperatives, expanding supply and acquisition markets. These policies effectively rectified the former unfair trade practice of "50 kg wool for only 1.5 pieces of brick tea".[13]

Meeting the ethnic minorities' production and living needs is an important measure to promote ethnic unity. Therefore, to develop trade among the various ethnic groups has become an integral part of China's ethnic policy. Satisfying the special needs of the small-population ethnic minorities is, however, far from an easy matter even for a vast and populous country like China. As a matter of fact, these products have a very small market share due to their diverse range and high transportation costs. The production and distribution of these products can be considered an economic activity for only a small percentage of the population. If measured by economic value, the manufacturing of these special necessities for the ethnic minorities' production and living needs (hereinafter referred to as special necessities) is not a profitable business for enterprises. But for the traditional production and living of the ethnic minorities, it is a major issue in relation to their right to subsistence and development.

---

[12]Deng (2000): 173–174.

[13]Huang G. *The Ethnic Affairs of Contemporary China*. volume I. 73–74.

With the development of economy and society, the standardization of daily necessities has become increasingly prominent, with more and more traditional products being substituted by standardized commodities. In the process of product upgrading and consumption convergence, the production and supply of these special necessities have the de facto custom-designed essence, which is characterized by high cost from the aspect of economy and marketing.

In the practice of China's ethnic policy, the production and supply of these special necessities are given privileged treatments. In the early 1960s, the state government introduced preferential policies for ethnic minority enterprises in profit retention, self-owned funds, and price subsidies, which effectively guaranteed the price stability and enhanced the initiative of the enterprises. However, the nationwide campaign to destroy the "Four Olds," including "Old Customs," "Old Culture," "Old Habits," and "Old Ideas," shortly after the launch of the Cultural Revolution, affected the production and supply of these special necessities. In the radical social atmosphere, these products were labeled "Old Customs," which were believed to be moribund. During the 10 chaotic years of the Cultural Revolution, these goods, including woks for the ethnic Koreans, iron tripod pots for the Miao people, frying pots, porcelain bowls, knives and hats for the Tibetans, swords, pails, and wool scissors for the Mongols, doppa, satins, lace as well as gold and silver ornaments for the Uyghurs, had been in serious short supply.

After China introduced economic reform, the former preferential policies for the ethnic minorities' special necessities, including profit retention, self-owned funds, and price subsidies, were restored. Tax concession policies for the production and trading enterprises for these products were also introduced. In June 1997, the state promulgated a new favored policy for the trade and production of these necessities. It provided that, during the period of the Ninth Five-Year Plan (1996–2000), the People's Bank of China would set aside 100 million yuan every year for loans with discounted interest for the construction of trade networks for ethnic minorities and technological renovation of enterprises designated to turn out necessities for ethnic minorities. It also stipulated that state-owned trade businesses and grassroots supply and marketing cooperatives below the county level would be exempt from value-added tax in ethnic minority areas.

At the same time, the State Ethnic Affairs Commission of China issued *the Catalog of Special Necessities for Ethnic Minorities*, which classified these products into ten major categories, including knitted fabrics and textiles, clothing and costumes, shoes and headgears, everyday utensils, furniture, recreational and sporting goods, art and craft supplies, medicine and herbs, production tools, and tea brick (compressed tea). In 2001, the catalog was amended to meet the standardized productions of these products, with the addition of a series of modern tools and gadgets, such as grinders, rice mills for mountainous area, miniature hydrogenerators, hay mowers, hay rakes, micro-solar plants, wind power stations' plastic film for pasturing areas, portable sprinkler irrigation equipment for domestic pasture, mobile sheepcotes, railing nets, shearing machines, and milk separators. The production and trade for these diverse commodities reflect the Chinese government's respect for the customs, religious beliefs, and cultural expressions of the ethnic minorities.

In 2003, the halal food was added to the catalog, which meant that halal food processing enterprises could also benefit from the tax concession and other preferential policies. By the end of 2003, there were 1378 designated manufacturers of special necessities for ethnic minorities, which enjoyed preferential policies concerning working capital loan rates, technological renovation loans with discounted interest, and reduction or exemption from taxes. Considering the importance of brick tea in the everyday life of some minority ethnic groups, the state established a brick-tea reserve system during the period of the Eighth Five-Year Plan (1991–1995) to guarantee its stable supply. In 2002, *the Measures for Administration of National Brick-Tea Reserve* was formulated, providing for the management of the reserve of brick-tea raw materials and products, and credit support to enterprises that store the relevant materials. It also provided that the central exchequer should pay the interest on loans used for the reserve of brick-tea materials.

In addition to meeting the livelihood needs of the ethnic minorities, the manufacturing, supply, and marketing of these special necessities have been integrated into the domestic market. A diversity of products, such as handicrafts, knitting, batik, accessories, costumes, daily utensils, cheese, dried meat, fried rice, and milk tea powder, have achieved industrialized development. The policy practice of catering for the needs of the small-population ethnic minorities is generating an identification effect among a large population, which has opened up a broader market for the manufacturing enterprises of the special necessities. Some products have been exported to the overseas market, becoming well-known brands of China. At the same time, the materials, techniques, and processing skills for these goods contain an abundance of historical knowledge and expertise, whose inheritance and development, in addition to guaranteeing the shape, structure, quality, and function of these products, have become necessary conditions for protecting ethnic minority cultures.

With the progress of the processing industry and diverse exploitation of raw materials, many manual techniques and locally available raw material usage are faced with the predicaments of loss or replacement. However, such process was not as spontaneous as the straight substitution of electrical lights for oil lamps and that of motor vehicles for oxcarts in that the living traditions and customs of many special necessities incarnate plenty of cultural contents and professional skills. Their cultural values and artistic originality are not only the unique contribution of an ethnic group to the human society but precious cultural resources as well.

To preserve these precious cultural resources, the State Ethnic Affairs Commission cooperated with the Chinese academic community on collecting and compiling the traditional crafts and techniques for these special necessities, for example, the embroidery and textiles of the peoples of Yao, Li, Tujia, and Zhuang, and the traditional attires of the peoples of She, Jing, Maonan, Gaoshan, and Yao. Measures for protecting and developing the ethnic minority cultures were also put forward on the basis of the inheritance vitality of traditional craftsmanship in the civil society.

6.4 Respect for and Development of Languages of Minority Ethnic Groups

The renminbi (literally "people's currency") is the legal tender of China. In addition to the official Romanization system for standard Chinese, "Zhongguo Renmin Yinhang," the denomination and the words "People's Bank of China" on banknotes are also printed in the Mongolian, Tibetan, Uyghur, and Zhuang scripts. This practice of marking the languages of minority ethnic groups on the banknote is very rare among the currencies of the world. It incarnates the basic principle of *the Constitution of China*: People of all ethnic groups have the freedom to use and develop their own spoken and written languages. The renminbi, as the banknote of China, serves as the "business card" of the country due to its implied cultural connotation. Apparently, the intention of marking the languages of the four minority ethnic groups on the renminbi is not for the convenience of circulation, for it is by no means applicable to mark the banknote with all the existing scripts of the 56 ethnic groups; rather, this nicety of expression transmits to the whole society that China is a unified multi-ethnic state, thus highlighting the equal rights and cultural status of ethnic minorities.

As the most important communication tool and knowledge carrier of mankind, spoken and written languages constitute the basic elements of culture and power for cultural inheritance and expression. Hanyu, or Chinese, is a group of related but in many cases mutually unintelligible language varieties, forming a branch of the Sino-Tibetan language family. It is spoken by the Han majority and many other ethnic groups in China. Nearly, 1.2 billion people (around 16% of the world's population) speak some form of Chinese as their first language. Standard Chinese, or Putonghua, is a standardized form of spoken Chinese based on the Beijing dialect of Mandarin. The written form of the standard language, based on the logograms known as Chinese characters (hanzi), is shared by literate speakers of otherwise unintelligible dialects. It constitutes the oldest continuously used system of writing in the world. However, the spoken and written languages used by most of the 55 ethnic minorities are different from Putonghua and hanzi. Therefore, China is endowed with bountiful resources of languages.

The Chinese government popularizes Putonghua and hanzi as the standard spoken and written Chinese language, which embodies the requirements of state unity and the integration of Chinese nation. *The Law on the Standard Spoken and Written Chinese Language* issued in 2000 stipulates: "All citizens shall have the right to learn and use the standard spoken and written Chinese language. The state provides citizens with the conditions for learning and using the standard spoken and written Chinese language. Local people's governments at various levels and the relevant departments under them shall take measures to popularize Putonghua and the standardized Chinese characters." The standard spoken and written Chinese language is, in a manner of speaking, the "mother tongue" of the Chinese nation, which is seen as an all-encompassing category consisting of people within the borders of China. At the same time, the law reiterates the constitutional principle: "People of all ethnic groups shall have the freedom to use and develop their own spoken and written languages." In other words, the spoken and written languages of every member of the Chinese nation, and the various dialects of spoken Chinese and the traditional Chinese characters, shall be protected, used, and inherited. "The right of learning and using the standard Chinese language" and "the freedom of using and developing their own languages" are two non-contradictory rights of Chinese citizens. Respecting all ethnic groups' freedom of using their own languages is a policy of language equality based on the principle of ethnic equality, reflecting the Chinese government's deference to and protection of language diversity.

Since the 1920s, Chinese academia has launched a succession of surveys on the ethnic minority languages and the various dialects of spoken Chinese. In 1950, the Chinese Academy of Social Sciences (CASS), the premier and the most comprehensive academic research organization and national center in China for study in the fields of philosophy and social sciences, set up the Institute of Linguistics. It represented the institutional construction of the Chinese government in terms of national language policy. In the late 1950s, the CASS carried out an extensive field investigation on the languages of ethnic minorities. This effort was directly related to the ethnicity recognition and implementation of regional autonomy in the compact communities of ethnic minorities. Although language is an important earmark of an ethnic group, it is not the only criterion for ethnicity identification due to the historically formed complicated language relationships. These include: Homologous ethnic groups speak different languages; heterogeneous ethnic groups use the same language; many languages penetrate each other; different languages are interwoven with the diverse dialects of a particular language. These phenomena showcase the frequent communication and interaction among the various ethnic groups in the history of China.

Through a continuous and in-depth language survey, Chinese linguists put the 129 languages of China into different language families. The current situation of each language is described in the *Languages of China*, a monumental work published in 2007.[14] The complexity and diversity of Chinese language pedigree are fully embodied in the 128 ethnic minority languages. In addition, dozens of these languages are defined as "endangered languages" in accordance with the established international standard for their users' number below 1000. It is generally agreed that, among the existing 6000 languages of the world, only one hundred are frequently or widely used by the vast majority of people, more than 2500 languages being on the brink of extinction. In this regard, China has made significant efforts to protect ethnic minority languages by the continuous investigation, collection, recording, description, and establishment of language database (including sound files).

During their long evolution, the Chinese ethnic minorities have created dozens of written languages, which can be classified into alphabetic writings, syllabic writings, hieroglyphs, and Latin texts. Some of them are mainly used in religious activities. At the same time, many ethnic minority spoken languages lack written forms. In modern society, the spoken languages without writing systems cannot be employed in the social education system. As a consequence, to create writing systems for those ethnic

---

[14] Sun and Hu (2007): 13.

minorities without scripts becomes an important policy practice for the protection, inheritance, and development of the ethnic minority languages.

As symbols of recording ideas and disseminating knowledge, written script is a carrier transcending the restrictions of time and space. Paleographers can decipher, read, and date historical manuscripts created several thousand years ago. However, the written language recorded by these ancient texts cannot be restored. In this sense, the creation of writing systems for the spoken languages of ethnic minorities has a beneficial effect on enhancing the transmission vitality and expression regularization of the particular language. In addition, it is conducive to improving the self-esteem and confidence of the given ethnic group in its modernization development. Since 1954, twelve ethnic minorities, including the peoples of Zhuang, Buyi, Miao, Yi, Li, Naxi, Lisu, Hani, Wa, Dong, Jingpo, and Tu, have developed their own alphabetic writings with the assistance of the state. The efforts of creating or standardizing the scripts for the ethnic minority languages greatly benefited illiteracy elimination, school education, knowledge popularization, news broadcast, and literary creation of the ethnic minority regions.

The creation of ethnic minority languages is a sophisticated social project, requiring continuous exploration and experimentation. The acceptance and popularization of the newly created alphabetic scripts among the relevant ethnic minorities were confronted with a multitude of factors. Due to the divergent phonemes and lexicons in the multi-dialect environment, some people find it rather difficult to acquire the new script. In some areas of dialect, the acquisition of the new writing system is tantamount to learning another language. Therefore, it was by no means an easy task to fully implement the newly created scripts in the corresponding ethnic minority regions. At the same time, some ethnic minorities, such as the peoples of Zhuang, Buyi, Dong, Shui, Bai, Hani, Yi, Lisu, Miao, and Yao, had already created their own ideographic writing systems by simulating the form and structure of Chinese characters. Shared by literate speakers of otherwise unintelligible dialects, these ancient scripts still have strong vitality in local civil life. Therefore, we must reconsider the pros and cons of Lain alphabetic writing and ideographic script while formulating writing systems for the ethnic minorities. The pilot trial of the newly created scripts showed that their introduction and promotion have not achieved desirable results, which can be accounted for by the following two reasons: On the one hand, the new writing systems themselves have inherent technical problems; on the other hand, the new scripts are inconsistent with the language usage habits of the locals.

During this period, the existing scripts of some ethnic minorities have undergone a process of improvement or reformation. For example, the Uyghur language and the Kazakh script, which had been created by their ancestors by adopting the Arabic alphabet, were reformed on the basis of the Latin alphabet and widely implemented in their corresponding communities in 1976; however, the amended versions were rejected by the Uyghurs and Kazakhs, which led to the restoration of their traditional writing systems six years later. Similarly, the Romanized Yi script, a standardized syllabic language derived from the classic script, failed to obtain popular recognition after more than 20 years of teaching experiment. However, the reformation programs for the Tai Nüa language for the Dai people, as well as the scripts of the peoples of Jingpo and Lahu, due to their basically keeping the form and structure of their traditional writing systems, were widely endorsed by the public.[15] Therefore, we can conclude that the creation and improvement of the writing systems for some minority ethnic groups must respect the objective laws and wishes of the local people.

Assisting the creation or improvement of scripts for ethnic minorities is the responsibility of the state to fulfill the constitutional principle that "all the nationalities shall have the freedom to use and develop their own spoken and written languages." Article 21 of *the Law of China on Regional Autonomy for Ethnic Minorities* stipulates: "While performing its functions, the organs of self-government of an autonomous area shall, in accordance with the regulations on the exercise of autonomy of the area, use one or several languages commonly used in the locality; where several commonly used languages are used for the performance of such functions, the language of the ethnic group exercising regional autonomy may be used as the main language." In addition, Article 134 of *the Constitution of China* states: "Citizens of all China's ethnic groups have the right to use their native spoken and written languages in court proceedings. The people's courts and people's procuratorates should provide translation for any party to the court proceedings who is not familiar with the spoken or written languages commonly used in the locality. In an area where people of a minority ethnic group live in a concentrated community or where a number of ethnic groups live together, court hearings should be conducted in the language or languages commonly used in the locality; indictments, judgments, notices and other documents should be written, according to actual needs, in the language or languages commonly used in the locality." In social life, the spoken and written languages of the ethnic minorities have been widely used in school education, newspaper and book publishing, the Internet, radio and television broadcasting. Moreover, they are penetrated in people's daily life, such as commodity logos and packaging. Therefore, protecting the ethnic minorities' rights of using and developing their own spoken and written languages demonstrates the inclusiveness of China's ethnic policy.

Any language needs to be widely applied, promoted, inherited, and developed by the modern education system. The education of ethnic minorities is an important part of the national education system of China. "Bilingual education," which involves teaching academic content in two languages, including the ethnic minorities' own languages and Chinese, is an important approach to guaranteeing their "right to learn and use the standard spoken and written Chinese language" and "freedom to use and develop their own spoken and written languages." Bilingual teaching should be executed gradually in a proper sequence. Article 37 of *the Law of China on Regional Autonomy for Ethnic Minorities* provides the basic principle for bilingual education in ethnic minority regions: "Schools (classes and grades) and other institutions of education where most of the students come from minority ethnic groups shall, whenever possible, use textbooks in their own languages and use their languages as the media of instruction. Classes for the teaching of Chinese (the Han language) shall, where possible, be opened for junior or senior grades of primary schools to popularize Putonghua and standard Chinese characters."

---

[15]Huang G. *The Ethnic Affairs in Contemporary China. Volume II*. 307–308.

With the widespread founding of public primary schools and secondary schools in ethnic minority regions, in particular, boarding schools in pastoral areas, economically underdeveloped, sparsely populated mountain areas, as well as a large number of secondary vocational education facilities and higher education institutions, a relatively complete educational system for ethnic minorities has been formed, with remarkable ensuing progress in bilingual teaching. However, due to the widespread backward economic and social development of the ethnic minority regions, their education has been confronted with many difficulties, including outdated educational concepts, delayed reform process, weak foundations, understaffed schools, and insufficient funding. Among these demerits, the shortage of qualified bilingual teachers has become a bottleneck in education development.

Since China implemented the Western Development Strategy, the educational facilities and conditions of the ethnic minority regions have testified a constant and fundamental improvement. At the same time, the state has attached ever-increasing importance to the scale and quality of bilingual education in ethnic minority regions. The series of measures, such as training qualified teachers, compiling textbooks, and increasing the proportion of bilingual courses in accordance with local conditions, effectively promoted the popularization of bilingual teaching in these areas. The fast development of bilingual teaching in Tibet is a good case in point. As of late 2014, all the primary and middle schools in the autonomous region use both Tibetan and Chinese in teaching, but mostly Tibetan for major courses. In the national college entrance exams, Tibetan students are allowed to answer questions using Tibetan script.[16]

At the same time, the state has also implemented a series of preferential policies to speed up the educational development of Tibet and Xinjiang. In recent years, 32 "Tibet classes" and 120 "Xinjiang classes," which enrolled only ethnic minority students of Tibet and Xinjiang, respectively, have been established in inland provinces. Both Chinese and ethnic minority languages are used as languages of instruction in these classes, which effectively improved the ethnic minority students' Chinese language proficiency and consolidated their native languages. The practice in the past 30 odd years has proved that the students of "Tibet classes" and "Xinjiang classes" have significantly improved their academic performances while enhancing their confidence in contributing to the construction of their hometown. After graduation, the vast majority of them chose to return to Tibet or Xinjiang.

The successful practice of bilingual education in the ethnic minority regions shows that the organic integration of Chinese and the ethnic minority languages opened a broad social space for the minority ethnic groups. In this sense, the ethnic minorities of China have no psychological resistance to the learning and using of the Chinese language. Similarly, people of all ethnic groups will cherish and value their own spoken and written languages, including the strong determination and efforts of the Han people to protect the diverse Chinese dialects and traditional Chinese characters.

While preserving and developing the languages of ethnic minorities, the state also popularizes standard spoken and written Chinese throughout the country to promote

---

[16]Bianba (2015).

economic and cultural exchanges among the various ethnic groups and regions. At the same time, the state attaches great importance to the protection of ethnic minorities' rights and interests of using and developing their own languages against the backdrop of the ever-increasing influence of the standard Chinese language.

China's goal of building a moderately well-off society in a well-rounded way by 2020 includes the anticipated target of "the universal use of the standard Chinese language and the elimination of language barriers throughout the country." In fact, it will be an enduring process. *The medium- and long-term national program for the reform and development of spoken and written languages* (2012–2020) jointly issued by the Ministry of Education and the State Language Commission reiterated that "people of all ethnic groups shall have the freedom to use and develop their own spoken and written languages," demanding that the whole of society should reach a consensus that the languages of all ethnic groups are precious cultural resources.[17] The program also elaborated measures for the protection of the languages of all ethnic groups, such as construction of audio databases, development of standard specifications for ethnic minority languages, construction of corpus on the ethnic minority languages and cultures, and investigation and protection on the 20 endangered ethnic minority languages. The roles of spoken and written languages, including inheriting and carrying forward culture, are sublimed to the height of "constructing a common cultural community for the Chinese nation," which entrusts more profound significance to the protection of ethnic minority languages.

6.5   Respect for and Protection of Ethnic Minorities' Freedom of Religious Beliefs

As a country with a sophisticated belief system, China has long been a cradle and host to a variety of the world's most enduring religious and philosophical traditions. Confucianism, Taoism, and Buddhism constitute the "three teachings" that have shaped Chinese culture. There are no clear boundaries between these intertwined religious systems, which do not claim to be exclusive, and elements of each enrich popular or folk religion. Described as a tradition, a philosophy, a religion, a humanistic or rationalistic religion, a way of governing, or simply a way of life, Confucianism has an unshakable position in the ideological system of China. The inclusiveness and mutual reconciliation of Confucianism, Taoism, and Buddhism are the mainstream political thought and folk consciousness throughout the Chinese history. To some extent, it explains the nonexistence of any protracted religious conflicts in China in spite of several fierce debates and competitions among the "three teachings." Confucianism is considered by some scholars to be a religion and by others an ethical or spiritual tradition. Broadly speaking, however, scholars agree that it is an ethical–political system developed from the teachings of Confucius (551–479 BC). Originating

---

[17] *The Medium and Long Term National Program for the Reform and Development of the Spoken and Written Languages (2012–2020)*. www.Chinanews.com. January 6, 2013.

during the Spring and Autumn period (770–476 BC) and developing metaphysical and cosmological elements in the Han dynasty (202 BC–220 AD), Confucianism has evolved to become the core idea of Chinese political ideology. In addition, Chinese culture is strongly intertwined with Confucian values, which play an important role in promoting Taoism, as well as the localization of Buddhism and Islam. While preaching Catholicism in the Ming dynasty (1368–1644), some Western missionaries, such as Matteo Ricci, interpreted Catholic doctrines by using existing Chinese concepts to explain Christianity. Ricci did not explain the Catholic faith as entirely foreign or new; instead, he held that the Chinese culture and people always believed in God and that Christianity was simply the completion of their faith. He borrowed a Chinese term, "Lord of Heaven," to use as the name for God.[18]

In his travelogue, William Rubruck, a French missionary and explorer in the mid-thirteenth century, recounted the peaceful coexistence of a Buddhist monastery, Taoist temple, mosque, and Christian church in Karakorum, which served as the capital of the Mongol Empire between 1235 and 1260. "In the city center, we saw 12 idol temples worshipped by the various races of the Mongol Empire, as well as two mosques, which chant the scriptures of Islam. Moreover, there is a Christian church at the far end of the city." The "idol temples" here referred to the Buddhist monasteries and Taoist temples.[19] Due to their expertise in astronomy, geographical survey, painting, architecture, and firearm manufacturing, the Western missionaries were highly revered by the emperors of the Ming and Qing dynasties. It, in turn, provided space for their missionary activities in China. After the Dutch colonists' occupation of Taiwan in 1624, the Western powers' expansion of their spheres of influence was followed by Protestant missions, who entered China at a time of the British East India Company's growing power.[20] Initially, they were restricted from living and traveling in China except for the limited area of the Thirteen Factories in Guangzhou and Macau. In accordance with *the Treaty of Nanking*, an unequal treaty concluded between the UK and the Chinese Qing dynasty on August 29, 1842, missionaries were granted the right to live and work in the five coastal cities, including Guangzhou, Xiamen, Fuzhou, Ningbo, and Shanghai. In 1860, the treaties ending the Second Opium War with the French and British opened up the entire country to the Westerners' mission and conversion.

The ubiquitous influence of Christianity even inspired the Taiping Rebellion, a massive civil war in China that lasted from 1850 to 1864 fought between the established Manchu-led Qing dynasty and the millenarian movement of the "Heavenly Kingdom of Peace." Due to the ever-expanding conflict between the Christian missionary activities and Chinese traditional political, cultural, and social ethics, proto-nationalist sentiments and opposition to imperialist expansion were accumulated among the Chinese people, which motivated the Boxer Rebellion, a violent anti-foreign and anti-Christian uprising that took place in China between 1899 and

---

[18] Gu (2004): 17.

[19] Rubruck (1985): 292.

[20] Hao S. & Chen J. *The Ethno-national Issue of Taiwan: from "Barbarians" to "Aboriginals,"* p. 36.

1901, toward the end of the Qing dynasty. It took place against a background of severe drought and the disruption caused by the growth of foreign spheres of influence. In the summer of 1900, when the international legations in Beijing came under attack by Boxer rebels supported by the Qing government, the Eight-Nation Alliance dispatched their armed forces, in the name of "humanitarian intervention," to defend their respective nations' citizens, as well as a number of Chinese Christians who had taken shelter in the legations. The incident ended with a coalition victory and the signing of *the Boxer Protocol*, which provided for the execution of government officials who had supported the Boxers, provisions for foreign troops to be stationed in Beijing, and 450 million taels of silver, which was more than the Qing government's annual tax revenue, to be paid as indemnity over the course of the next thirty-nine years to the eight powers involved. Therefore, the Christian mission in modern China was achieved against the backdrop of the Western powers' invasion of the country, which is the most serious conflict between the interaction of foreign religion and the traditional Chinese society.

After the Xinhai Revolution in 1911, the newly found Republic of China declared a secular state, with definite distinction between church and state bodies. The spread of Catholicism and Christianity also tended to be localized. On the one hand, the Christian mission was met by a challenge from the emerging ideologies of China at that time, such as the New Cultural Movement, nationalism, and the anti-imperialist patriotic movement; on the other hand, a series of events occurred in China, including the end of the Confucian ideology in the modern state construction, the abortion of the "Confucianism movement," and the Chinese elites' attempts to transplant the Western systems into the Chinese society, which provided favorable opportunities for the Catholic and Protestant missionaries in China. In addition to taking the initiative to adapt to Chinese etiquette, architectural style, and discourse system, the Christian church sponsored a variety of charities in China, such as hospitals, orphanages, schools, and disaster reliefs, which exerted positive effects on the Chinese urban and rural civil societies.

After the suppression of the Boxer Rebellion by a foreign alliance including the USA, the ruling Qing dynasty was required to pay indemnities to alliance members. Part of the indemnity payment funded the establishment of the Tsinghua College, a preparatory school in Peking for the Chinese graduates pursuing further studies at American universities. Arthur Henderson Smith, an American missionary, helped persuade US President Roosevelt to use the indemnity payment for education.[21] These charitable activities won wider space for the Christian church's missionary work in the Chinese land.

The Communist Party of China believes in Marxism–Leninism, and the members of the Party are atheists. As the ruling party of a multi-ethnic state with pluralistic faiths, the CPC has been confronting the challenge of uniting people of all ethnic groups for the great rejuvenation of the Chinese nation, which is a major issue related to the vital interests of all the Chinese nationals. The basic idea of respecting the freedom of religious belief was established as early as the Chinese Communists'

---

[21]Gu (2004): 17.

political debut. With its capital in Ruijing of Jiangxi Province, the Chinese Soviet Republic (CSR), established in 1931, advocates that the working classes of the CSR, regardless of ethnic group, gender, and religious beliefs, are equal. The "working classes" here excluded the religious upper stratum, whose vested powers included class oppression, economic exploitation, and interference in politics. In addition, the basic principles of "the separation of politics and religion" and "free faith of all citizens" were emphasized. In the theocratic system, the religious upper class was an integral part and important force of the ruling elites, which was particularly prominent in Tibetan Buddhism.

Therefore, abolishing the vested privileges of the religious upper class was the first problem to be addressed in the field of religious affairs by the fledging People's Republic of China in the 1950s. However, it did not equate to antagonizing the conservative religious establishment; rather, their authority and influence among the adherents should be respected for the realization of ethnic unity. It was also a basic principle of the national united front advocated by the CPC during the Second Sino-Japanese War, namely, "to unite with the patriotic religious upper class for the common fight against Japanese aggression." Throughout the history of the CPC, there has been an ideological antagonism between materialism and idealism in the perception of the phenomenon of religious belief. Karl Marx holds that the demise of religion, which boasts a time-honored history in the development of human society, is a distant topic of the future.

During the democratic reform of the ethnic minority regions in the 1950s, some CPC cadres went so far as to suggest that ethnic minorities' religious practices should be banned, equating religious faith with the widespread feudal superstition in society. Zhou Enlai, the first Premier of China who served from 1949 until his death in 1976, severely criticized this misconception. He concluded: "The religious beliefs of ethnic minorities should be respected by the Han People and the whole of society…. The social reality makes banning religion unthinkable. For some ethnic minorities, for example the Uyghurs, who primarily practice Islam, religion has a greater impact on family and social relations. The policy of religious freedom is a practical reality in China."[22] *The Constitution of China* stipulates: "no state organ, public organization or individual may compel citizens to believe in, or not to believe in, any religion; nor may they discriminate against citizens who believe in, or do not believe in, any religion." Therefore, the Chinese citizens' rights of religious faith, and that of having no faith, are guaranteed by the State Constitution. The religious adherents and atheists, with no distinction of lowliness or nobleness in value judgment, must respect each other and live side by side in harmony.

In contemporary China, Buddhism, Taoism, Islam, Catholicism, and Christianity (Protestant and Orthodox) are the five officially sanctioned religions. The coexistence of many religions in China, in particular, the concurrence of diverse religions among the various ethnic groups, adds complicatedness to the management of religious affairs. As an important part of people's spiritual life, religious belief permeates folk culture, customs, and habits. The intersection of multi-ethnicity and pluralistic

---

[22] *The Collected Documents of the CCP on the Affairs of Xinjiang: 1949–2010*, p. 145.

faiths contributes to the widespread presence of the following phenomena: People of the same ethnic group believe in different religions; people of different ethnic groups are adherents of the same faith; people of the same ethnic group and people of different ethnic groups believe in the divergent sects of the same religion. In the compact communities of the Han people, Buddhism and Taoism have entrenched an extensive influence. The indigenous Taoism shares aspects of being a philosophy or a religion, resulting in a culture of tolerance and syncretism, where multiple religions or belief systems are often practiced in concert with local customs and traditions. At the same time, Catholicism and Christianity have also gained a firm foothold among the Han people. The five major religions of China have varying degrees of influences on the spiritual life of ethnic minorities. After many years of contact and exchange, some of China's ethnic groups have spread over vast areas, while others live in individual concentrated communities in small areas. In China, it is quite common that people of one single ethnic group live in different locations, while in a single administrative district there can be many different ethnic groups, which led to the regional distribution of a particular religion and the intertwined coexistence of different faiths within a region. At the same time, many primitive religious forms, which involve the worship of various figures in Chinese mythology, folk heroes, mythological creatures, or ancestors, have been retained in all ethnic groups, in particular, the ethnic minorities.

Among the various denominations of Buddhism in China, Han Chinese Buddhism, with a large number of adherents among the peoples of Bai, Manchu, Yi, Korea, Zhuang, Yao, Tujia, Jing, Li, Buyi, Dong, Lahu, Gaoshan, Maonan, Mulao, and She, has a prevalent impact on the ethnic minorities. The traditional influences of some other branches of Buddhism, including Tibetan Buddhism and Mahayana Buddhism, are concentrated in certain areas and related ethnic minorities. With its devotees concentrated in Tibet, Inner Mongolia, Sichuan, Qinghai, Yunnan, Gansu, and Xinjiang, Tibetan Buddhism is worshipped widely among the Tibetans, Mongols, and the peoples of Tu, Yugu, Menba, Loba, and Pumi. Among the various sects of Tibetan Buddhism, the Gelug is the preeminent school. The peoples of Dai, Blang, Achang, Wa, and Lahu in Yunnan Province are adherents of Mahayana Buddhism. At the same time, other faiths, including Taoism, Catholicism, and Christianity, are worshipped among the minority nationalities.

Comparatively speaking, the singleness of religious belief is the most prominent feature among the ethnic minority Muslims, who are distributed throughout China. The highest concentrations are found in the northwest provinces of Xinjiang, Gansu, and Ningxia, with significant populations also found in Yunnan and Henan. Of China's 55 officially recognized minority peoples, ten are predominantly Muslims. The largest groups in descending order are Hui, Uyghur, Kazakh, Dongxiang, Kyrgyz, Uzbek, Salar, Tajik, Bonan, and Tatar. Except the Tajiks and a very small percentage of the Uyghurs, who are devotees of Shia Islam, the vast majority of Chinese Muslims are Sunnis. Under the influence of Sufism, or "the phenomenon of mysticism within Islam," four Sufi groups, including Khafiya, Jahriyya, Qadiriyya, and Kubrawiyya, began to take shape during the Qing dynasty (1644–1912). The religious power of each Sufi group infiltrated the local secular life, forming many sub-branches by means of mosques, parishes, and Qadim system.

The Christian faith among Chinese ethnic minorities emerged with the reintroduction of Western religion in the modern era. After the occupation of Taiwan in 1624, the Dutch colonists tried to convert the aboriginals by force, which could be described as a painful experience for the Chinese ethnic minorities. However, the missionary activities of Samuel Pollard (1864–1915) in the mountainous villages in Guizhou left warm memories among the locals. Known in Chinese as Bo Geli, the British Methodist missionary traveled to the isolated southwest China in 1887 and remained there as a missionary, until his death from typhoid. He converted many of the local people to Christianity and created a Miao script that is still in use today. During his mission, he traveled extensively, finding churches, training other missionaries, performing the role of language examiner, and arguing the causes of Miao Christians. Under the chaotic and fragmented social environment of China at that time, these Western missionaries made commendable contributions to the social development of the remote ethnic minority regions. Of course, it is also an important reason for the entrenchment of Christianity in the Chinese civil society from the late Qing dynasty to the Republic of China (1912–1949). Although the Western missionaries converted some Miao people to Christianity, they failed to change the pluralistic faiths of the locals.

As a matter of fact, the coexistence of multiple religious beliefs is very common in isolated ethnic minority regions. For example, in addition to the devotees of Tibetan Buddhism, there are Muslim groups and Catholic adherents in Tibet; within Inner Mongolia, the Hui and Mongol Muslims live side by side with Tibetan Buddhists. Sometimes, we can even find worshipers of different religions among residents of the same village or even among family members. The existence of the only Catholic Church in Shangyanjing village, Naxi Township, Changdu Prefecture of Tibet, is a unique occurrence among the multitudinous Buddhist monasteries throughout Tibet. Among the 800-plus residents in 149 households, 80% are devout followers of Catholicism. In the residence of a villager, both the portrait of the Blessed Virgin Mary and that of the living Buddha of Tibetan Buddhism are enshrined, symbolizing the different religious beliefs of the family.[23] It is a miniature of the diverse religions' harmonious coexistence throughout China.

The history of the People's Republic of China, as a process of creating a new chronicle for the country, has experienced many setbacks; among them, the "Cultural Revolution" inflicted serious harms on the ethnic minorities' freedom of religious beliefs. Between 1966 and 1976, Chinese society experienced a decade of turmoil, the Cultural Revolution. It paralyzed China politically and significantly affected the country economically and socially. During the revolution, much economic activity was halted, with "revolution," regardless of interpretation, being the primary objective of the country. It wreaked much havoc on the culture of the ethnic minorities. Regional autonomy given to the ethnic minorities was affected as part of the Red Guards' attack on the "Four Olds," including "Old Customs," "Old Culture," "Old

---

[23] *Voyage to the Only Catholic Church in Tibet*. www.xinhuanet.com, July 22, 2014.

Habits," and "Old Ideas." The destruction of Buddhist monasteries in Tibet was often conducted with the complicity of local ethnic Tibetan Red Guards.

As a decisive turning point in post-1949 Chinese history, the Third Plenary Session of the 11th CPC Central Committee held in 1978 marked the beginning of the wholesale repudiation of the Cultural Revolution policies and set China on the course for economic reforms. After this conference, a comprehensive cleanup of the errors made in the Cultural Revolution was conducted, including restoring the chaotic ethnic minority and religious affairs management to order. In 1982, the CPC Central Committee released *The Basic Viewpoint and Policy on the Religious Issue during Our Country's Socialist Period*, which comprehensively expounded the religious policies of the CPC since its founding. "The basic policy the Party has adopted toward the religious question is that of respect for and protection of the freedom of religious belief. This is a long-term policy, one which must be continually carried out until that future time when religion will itself disappear."

Since then, respect for freedom of religious belief has been part of China's basic policy. In accordance with Chinese laws and policies on religion, citizens of China have the freedom to believe or not to believe in any particular religion, or to affiliate with any particular denomination of a religion; non-believers may choose to become believers, and believers may cease to be believers at any time. No state organ, public organization, or individual may compel citizens to believe in, or reject, any religion, nor may they discriminate against citizens who believe in, or do not believe in, any religion. Freedom of religion or belief is to be enjoyed under the premise that religion is practiced within the scope of the rights and obligations prescribed by the constitution and laws, and that religious activities do not disrupt social stability, people's work, or their daily life.[24]

The management of religious affairs in accordance with law is a general practice in the contemporary world. Although only a few countries have enacted a special law on religious affairs, it is a common practice to guarantee citizens' freedom of religious belief in the State Constitution. The separation of church and state is also a universal principle. Promoting the rule of law in religious affairs is an important principle guiding the government's approach to religion, as part of its overall strategy to promote the rule of law in all spheres of life. To improve the management of religious affairs, the State Council formulated *Regulations on Religious Affairs* in 2004. It aims to protect citizens' freedom of religion or belief, safeguard religious and social harmony, and ensure proper regulation of religious affairs, or in other words to protect lawful activities and punish illegal or criminal acts.

The reincarnation of Living Buddha is a succession system unique to Tibetan Buddhism and is respected by the state. Tibetan Buddhists believe lamas and other religious figures can consciously influence how they are reborn and often are reborn many times so they can continue their religious pursuits. To further institutionalize the reincarnation of Living Buddha, *Rules Governing the Reincarnation of Tibetan Living Buddhas* was adopted by the State Administration for Religious Affairs in 2007. This document codifies reincarnation practices of Tibetan Buddhism, specifying the

---

[24]The Collected Documents on the Ethnic Affairs of China (1990): 161.

way in which the section of reincarnations is administered. The document explains its purposes and lays out principles and conditions for reincarnation, review and approval procedures, duties and responsibilities of religious groups, and penalties for violations.[25] It was enacted on the basis of respect for religious rituals and historical conventions, as a measure to ensure freedom of religion or belief. Its implementation facilitates the process of reincarnation and accommodates the wishes of Tibetan Buddhist clerics and worshippers. It represents an important effort to promote the rule of law in general and handle religious affairs according to the law in particular.

The promulgation of the decree effectively guarantees normal religious activities of Tibetan Buddhism and protects the religious belief of adherents. Since democratic reform in Tibet, over 60 Living Buddha candidates have been confirmed through historical conventions and traditional religious rituals. In 1989, the 10th Panchen Lama died suddenly in Shigatse. A committee composed of senior lamas began the process of searching for the reincarnation of the deceased. The six-year search effort in the areas inhabited by Tibetans located three candidates. By drawing lottery numbers from the Golden Urn, the search committee announced Gyancain Norbu as the only reincarnation, who was enthroned as the 11th Panchen Lama with the approval of the State Council on November 1995.

Following more than fifty years' concerted efforts by the peoples of all its ethnic groups, Tibet has embarked on a path of development conforming to the times and the people's fundamental interests. However, in their pursuit of "the independence of Tibet," the 14th Dalai Lama and his followers have always turned a blind eye to Tibet's development and progress, denying the achievements made by the people of Tibet and rejecting the sound path that Tibet has taken. As a leading incarnation in the hierarchy of the Gelug Sect of Tibetan Buddhism, the Dalai Lama's historical status and influence have been closely associated with conferment by the central government. In 1793, the Qing throne enacted *the 29-Article Authorized Regulations for the Better Governance of Tibet*. These regulations established the system of drawing lots from a Golden Urn in relation to the authenticity of the reincarnation of Living Buddha.

In September 2011, the exiled spiritual leader suggested he would not be reincarnated after his death. By its very nature, the Dalai Lama attempted to pursue his political end of promoting "the independence of Tibet" by taking advantage of his religious influence among the Tibetans. Therefore, China's practice of guaranteeing Tibetan Buddhist's freedom of worship has always been boycotted by the Dalai Lama clique. At the 2010 National People's Congress, Head of Tibet's regional congress, Padma Choling, announced that the choice of the 15th Dalai Lama would abide by the "requirements of Tibetan Buddhist tradition," including approval by the government, instead of being the choice of the 14th Dalai Lama. Padma Choling added: "Whether the Dalai Lama wants to cease reincarnation or not, this decision is not up to him. When he became the 14th Dalai Lama, it was not his decision. He was

---

[25] *The Measures on the Management of the Reincarnation of Living Buddhas of Tibetan Buddhism.* July 18, 2007.

chosen following a strict ritual dictated by religious rules and historical tradition and also with the approval of the central government."[26]

Except for the indigenous Taoism, the other four major religions of China, including Buddhism, Catholicism, Protestantism, and Islam, boast international backgrounds of dissemination. At the same time, Taoism also gained global influence with the worldwide distribution of Chinese diaspora. As nationwide religious groups that independently run their own theological affairs, China's religious organizations, including the Buddhist Association of China, Chinese Taoist Association, Islamic Association of China, Three-Self Patriotic Movement, and Chinese Patriotic Catholic Association, are windows for contacts with religious groups around the world. The Chinese Association for Religious and Cultural Exchanges found in 2005 provided a good platform for the Chinese religious circles' engagement with their international counterparts on the basis of equal exchanges, mutual respect, peaceful cooperation, and harmonious coexistence. *The Constitution of China* provides that "religious bodies and religious affairs are not subject to any foreign domination." Religious independence means freedom from foreign domination or control. Management of religious affairs remains the exclusive responsibility of followers of religions in China.

Religious independence, a choice by China's religious believers themselves, has been and remains a key principle that guides China's religious organizations in handling relations with their foreign counterparts. Friendly interactions between China's religious groups and their overseas counterparts on the basis of equality and mutual respect are encouraged. Therefore, the Chinese religious community neither interferes with the religious affairs of other countries nor accepts any outside meddling. At the same time, the international exchange of religious circles is also an important guarantee to meet the spiritual needs of religious adherents. For example, one of the primary tasks for the Islamic Association of China is to organize the adherents to fulfill their Hajj, an annual Islamic pilgrimage to Mecca.

In the first Asian–African Conference held in Bandung of Indonesia in 1955, the Chinese delegation headed by Premier Zhou Enlai reached an agreement with the Saudi Arabian government regarding the issue of Chinese Muslims' pilgrimage to Mecca. Since the 1980s, the number of Chinese Muslim pilgrims has witnessed a rising tendency, reaching 14,500 in 2015. It reflects both the realization extent of Chinese citizens' freedom of religious belief and the positive effect of the rule of law in religious affairs. The growing number of pilgrims poses a logistic challenge for the government of Saudi Arabia, which therefore sets quotas for various countries to keep the pilgrims' number at a manageable level. To meet the pilgrimage desire of the Chinese Muslims in a fair and reasonable manner, the Islamic Association of China and the State Administration of Religious Affairs jointly formulated *the Registration and Queuing Approach for Chinese Muslims' Mecca pilgrimage.*

As independent and open belief systems, the various religions of China are not subjected to foreign influence or domination. The illegal missionaries of foreign civil societies or individuals are strictly prohibited in China. At the same time, the Chi-

---

[26]Baima (2005).

nese government is determined to crack down on all kinds of "evil cults." It is the state responsibility for safeguarding the legitimate rights and interests of religions, as well as guaranteeing the citizens' freedom of religious belief. Since 1978, China has witnessed the emergence of some "cult" organizations, among which were some originating from outside the country. In contemporary China, the most serious challenge for the management of ethnic minority and religious affairs of China is Islamic extremism's infiltrations into Xinjiang. Religious extremism seeks political goals by distorting religious doctrines and perpetuating violent terrors. Religious extremists, in the name of religion, spread radical and extremist views, and take extremist means to try to establish a theocracy. In fact, religious extremism is not religion in the real sense, but tries to make use of religion. It is by nature antihuman, anti-society, anti-civilization, and anti-religion, and is an important ideological foundation for violent and terrorist activities. To realize their premeditated goals of "East Turkestan independence," the forces of terrorism, separatism, and religious extremism, which are collectively known as "the Three Evils," have engineered and organized terror campaigns in Xinjiang. Binding their political goals and extreme acts with a certain ethnic minority and religious belief, they purported to be the spokesperson for the Uyghurs and Chinese Muslims.

As the core organization for "the Three Evils," the World Uyghur Congress (WUC), which was found in April 2004 at a meeting in Munich, Germany, as a collection of various exiled Uyghur groups, including the World Uyghur Youth Congress and East Turkestan National Congress, aspires to "represent the collective interests of the Uyghur people" inside and outside Xinjiang. According to the WUC, its main aim is to "promote the right of the Uyghurs to use peaceful, nonviolent, and democratic means to determine the political future of East Turkestan." However, the WUC and its affiliated groups attempted to fabricate a legitimate cover for their illegal motives to separate China. With generous funding from some Western countries, the WUC President Rebiya Kadeer conspired with separatists and religious extremists to foment terror attacks in Xinjiang. After 1999, Tablighi Jamaat, a globally influential movement encouraging the orthodox practice of Islam, was applied by the separatists and religious extremists to instill "jihad" and separatist ideology to Chinese Muslims. By setting up religious schools and unauthorized preaching locations, Tablighi Jamaat supported violent attacks by training terrorists. The religious extremists of Xinjiang advertised that the belief in Allah was incompatible with all forms of government. Harboring political purposes of ethnic division and national separatism, they called for concerted action toward "the creation of an Islamic state" and "the salvation of East Turkestan from the brutal rule of the infidels."

The extremists bewitch Muslims, especially teenagers, with heretical ideas such as "the shahid (martyr) engaged in jihad (holy war) can live in the garden of Paradise," thus turning some individuals into terrorists. These people are manipulated to frequently perform acts of violence and terrorism and kill innocent people of all ethnic groups, even their fellow Islamic clerics and Muslims.[27] The religious extremists deny all fruits of modern civilizations, including mobile phones, computers, the

---

[27] Islam and Terrorism (2006): 5.

Internet, TV, radio, and books. In addition, they impose the so-called orthodox folk-ways and dress code, for example, beard-growing for men and burqa for women, on the ethnic Uyghurs. These phenomena seriously jeopardize the freedom of religious belief and everyday life of Muslims.

Many facts have revealed that religious extremism has developed into a real risk that endangers national unity and ethnic solidarity. Suppressing religious extremism in accordance with the law is just a move that protects the fundamental interests of the state and the people, including the Chinese Muslims themselves, and is also an important part of the international response to religious extremism. At a conference on religious affairs held in Beijing in April 2016, Xi Jinping promised to "fully implement the policy of religious freedom," but added that religious groups "must support the socialist system and socialism with Chinese characteristics." He called upon them to "merge religious doctrines with Chinese culture" and urged that "we must resolutely guard against overseas infiltrations via religious means and prevent ideological infringement by extremists."

6.6   Protection and Development of Ethnic Minority Cultures

On the morning of October 1, 2015, which coincided with the 60th anniversary of the finding of Xinjiang Uyghur Autonomous Region, large crowds of people congregated in a public square in Urumqi, the capital city of Xinjiang, for a show of "square dancing." As a routine exercise performed to music in public places, such as squares, plazas, or parks, square dancing is popular with middle-aged and retired women who have been referred to as "dancing grannies" in the English-language media. Due to its low cost and ease of participation, it has a large number of practitioners. As symbols of local culture, the art forms of ethnic minorities are the most prominent hallmarks for the engagement, communication, and integration among people of various ethnic groups. On festive days or at gatherings of friends and relatives, the Uyghurs, who are known for their special endowments in such activities, love to sing and dance. Their lively dances demonstrate diligence, bravery, openness, and optimism. Uyghur folk dances are distinguished by head and wrist movements. Their clever coordination is enhanced by the typical posture of tilted head, thrust chest, and erect waist. The dances, Sanam in particular, express the Uyghurs' feelings and character.

In August 2015, a video of a "gymnastics-style folk dance performed by the high school students of Urumqi" went viral among Chinese netizens. Since its release, the video has attained great popularity in cyberspace, making it a widespread Internet meme and a hit, with parodies and flash mobs emerging in response. Integrating the artistic elements of the Mongols, Uyghurs, Kazakhs, and Tajiks, the 4-minute folk dance fully demonstrates the multicultural elements. The wide popularity of this video won a wave of undivided admiration for the diverse ethnic minority cultures of

Xinjiang. Obviously, this art form is totally different from pop music or dance, such as the 18th K-pop single by the South Korean musician Psy, "Gangnam style." Deeply rooted in the multicultural background of Xinjiang, such folk dances can be acclaimed as the "Xinjiang style" with modern vitality. It is not only the most effective riposte from civil society in resisting religious extremism's rejection and suppression of the cultural tradition of Xinjiang but also a modern response to inheriting and developing the traditional cultures of ethnic minorities.

The Chinese culture is composed of the culture of the Han people and that of the ethnic minorities; the former is characteristic of its time-honored history, profoundness, and sophistication, and the latter of its diversity and luster. Xi Jinping pointed out that the compact communities of the minority ethnic groups are "regions of cultural diversity." In the general cultural contact, we tend to perceive that people of ethnic minorities are good at singing and dancing, which is, however, only a spillover characterization for their cultural qualities. There are divided opinions as to the definition of "culture." When used as a countable noun, "a culture" is the set of customs, traditions, and values of a society or community. In this sense, multiculturalism is a concept that values the peaceful coexistence and mutual respect between different cultures inhabiting the same planet. As a defining aspect of what it means to be human, culture encompasses the range of phenomena that are transmitted through social learning in human societies. The term "culture" is used in a general sense as the evolved ability to categorize and represent experiences with symbols and to act imaginatively and creatively.[28]

The attitude toward cultural differences, which leads to the moral judgment of cultural values, has been a controversial topic throughout the ages. It is also a problem that has a bearing on "cultural conflict" or even "clash of civilizations" in the modern era. Though the distinction between the culturally defined "Huaxia" and the ethnic minorities, who are termed the "four barbarians" in the ancient Chinese classical texts, is not a solidified political boundary, it apparently incarnates the value judgment of cultural merits and demerits. The ethnocentrism of Han society and culture which despises or belittles the cultures of the ethnic minorities had been popular among the Han elites up to the Qing dynasty (1644–1912). Admittedly, the agricultural civilization of the Han people, which represents the relatively advanced production and living standards of the ancient society, contributed to the achievements of urban construction, commercial business, and handicraft industry. However, the ways of life formed in areas not suitable for sedentary farming, including grasslands, forests, and mountains, are also human society's cultural creations. This is the diversity quality of culture. Its significance can be likened to the existing 6000-plus languages of the world. There is no language that does not belong to human beings even though some of them have a very small number of speakers.

In the primitive ages, the cultural creation and development of human society showed similar features. With the evolution of agricultural society, the Iron Age, Industrial Revolution, and the era of science and technology, the cultural development

---

[28]Cultural Patterns and their Dissemination Modes: Proceedings on Cross-cultural Communication (2003): 7.

of human society is presenting a huge gap from the Stone Age to the Space Age. It is like the scientists of NASA, ecstatic about the images of Pluto transmitted from the space probe "New Horizons," the first probe to be launched to Pluto by human beings, while the American Indian tribes hunting in the Brazilian rain forest with arrows and spear are at a loss for the passing helicopter. However, the intellectual functions of these Indian tribes, who are obviously no less evolved, are not dissimilar to those of the NASA scientists. The concept of judging merits and demerits of different cultures by means of material development disparity led to Western society's firm conviction that Caucasians are superior to other races. It has already inflicted numerous miseries and sufferings on human society. In addition, the division of "master race" and "inferior race" is still the source of evils that affect racial, ethnic, cultural, and religious relations.

Then what is the correct attitude toward culture? How should we evaluate traditional cultures of different nations? These questions need to be answered against the backdrop of protecting the cultural diversity of the world. The tolerance and protection of cultural diversity demand tangible and long-term efforts from the public sector and individuals. What's more, people need to understand the significance and value of culture from the niceties of social life. In this regard, Jared Diamond, an American Biologist who had for a time engaged in field investigations in Papua New Guinea, vividly recounted his feelings: "…when unschooled New Guineans from remote villages visit towns, they look stupid to Westerners. Conversely, I am constantly aware of how stupid I look to New Guineans when I am with them in the jungle, displaying my incompetence at simple tasks (such as following a jungle trail or erecting a shelter) at which New Guineans have been trained since childhood and I have not."[29] An archer can pierce a willow leaf with an arrow from the distance of a hundred paces; however, a sniper can hit the target 1000 steps away from him. The strong or weak points embodied in material cultures can by no means be applied as yardsticks for defining cultural values; otherwise, the connotation and significance of "archery culture" would be underestimated or even ignored in the contemporary era. As a matter of fact, "cultural geography studies not only the various nations' material culture differences, but also their ideological distinctions. In addition, it is the power of social memory and identity that bind a nation together."[30]

The Xibe people, one of the 55 ethnic minority groups officially recognized by China, are renowned for their expertise in producing bow and arrow. With their ancestral home in Liaoning in Northeast China, the Xibe, thanks to their horsemanship and archery, were sent to garrison the Xinjiang frontiers by the Qianlong Emperor of the Qing dynasty in 1764. Due to the historical experience of their ancestors' westward migration and the eternal memory of their home place, they highly esteem their native language, skills in making and using bows and arrows, as well as their folkways and customs. *The Qapqal News*, as the only newspaper in China written in the Xibe script, plays an important role in enhancing the professional use of the endangered language. The Xibe people's historical tradition of archery, though los-

---

[29]Diamond (2000): 10.
[30]Grang (2005): 2.

ing its practical use in military and hunting, is unfolding new glamor in the modern development of ethnic culture. The time-honored archery culture, in addition to being a cultural impetus for inspiring ethnic pride and confidence, provides a solid social foundation for the development of competitive archery. The local archery school has produced a large number of excellent archers for the national archery team.

Though the inheritance and development effectiveness of the Xibe people's archery culture are merely a miniature case of China's policy practice of protecting and developing the cultures of ethnic minorities, it offers an extraordinary glimpse of the concept and practice of China's ethnic policy. Among the constituents of the Chinese nation, the Xibe, with a population of 200,000, is defined as one of the small-population ethnic minorities of China. However, their production technique of bow and arrow has been included in the list of national intangible cultural heritage. In 2012, the Museum of Chinese Archery Culture was built, displaying the traditional archery items of the Xibe Minority. It has the functions of protecting and inheriting the bow- and arrow-making techniques, as well as promoting the archery culture to the outside world. The "Western Exodus Festival", which falls on the 18th day of the fourth lunar month, is celebrated to commemorate their ancestors' exodus from Northeast China during the reign of the Qianlong Emperor in the Qing Dynasty. Both the "Western Exodus Festival" and the unique folk dance of the Xibe Minority have been included as national intangible cultural heritage elements. This kind of protection measure is widespread in the modern inheritance of the traditional cultures of Chinese ethnic minorities.

In 2003, China initiated the project of protecting its intangible cultural heritage elements in accordance with the principles of *the Convention for the Safeguarding of Intangible Cultural Heritage* adopted by the UNESCO General Conference. Among the list of the 518 national intangible cultural heritage elements authorized by the State Council in 2006, those of the minority ethnic groups added up to 166. In the subsequent two lists issued in 2008 and 2011, the cultural heritage elements of the ethnic minorities accounted for 38% and 35%, respectively, in the total numbers.

Intangible cultural heritage is often referred to as the "living fossil" of culture, which contains shades of rarity and fragility. With the development of economy and society, it is a matter of course that the escalating social life convergence is gradually replacing or changing the traditional culture from the aspect of niceties. For example, some traditional utensils have been or are being replaced by new gadgets of a range of materials, shapes, and functions. Therefore, the traditional handicrafts fail to be passed down from the past generations with the development of machinery and numerical control tools. The alternative transformations with the convergence of materialized carriers contribute to the disappearance of the diverse styles, cultural qualities, and their implied knowledge, spirit, and values. It is no doubt of tragic sense to a country, a society, and a nation. Therefore, the protection of intangible cultural heritage represents one of the most serious challenges to all the countries of the world.

The intangible cultural heritage of ethnic minorities lies mainly in their outstanding cultural value, transmission vitality, and significance of cultural identity. The "heritage" nature of intangible culture has the connotation of long-term accumulation. Among the 38 Chinese elements included in the UNESCO Intangible Cultural Heritage Lists, 14 are the cultural elements of ethnic minorities, including Uyghur Muqam music, the farmers' dance of the ethnic Koreans, the Tibetan epic of Gesar, the Grand Song of the Dong people, Hua'er folk song, the Kyrgyz Epic of Manas, Tibetan opera, traditional folk long song of the Mongols, the New Year Festival of the Qiang people, the Uyghur *meshrep* (a traditional male Uyghur gathering that typically includes poetry, music, dance, and conversation within a structural context), and *Yimakan* storytelling of the Hezhen people. Rooted in the social life of the ethnic minorities, these cultural elements constitute the fine traditional culture of the Chinese nation, thus becoming the common cultural heritage of the world.

At the same time, the state funded a series of cultural projects for the minority ethnic groups, for example, compilation of classical works, publishing of the oral literature or epics, and development of traditional medicine, music, dance, and sports. These include some large-scale cultural display activities organized by the central government, the national traditional sports games for the ethnic minorities being a typical example. Instead of aiming at athletic competition, the games are targeted to display the traditional sports of various ethnic groups and to promote their cultural exchanges, understanding, and appreciation. In August 2015, the city of Ordos in Inner Mongolia hosted the 10th games, with 178 demonstration events, such as polo, Mongolian wrestling, lion dance, and acrobatics.

In addition to the natural landscapes, cultural relics, handicrafts, and native cuisines, the traditional residences of the ethnic minorities are also invaluable cultural assets in the process of developing ethnic minority culture and tourism industry. It is for this reason that the Chinese government began to incorporate the protection and development of the traditional residences of the ethnic minorities into the national plan in 2009. With generous state funding, the protection program was piloted in the 370 ethnic minority villages distributed throughout the 28 provincial-level administrative divisions. *The protection and development plan for the traditional residences of ethnic minorities* issued by the State Ethnic Affairs Commission proposed a phased plan for the renovation of 1000 ethnic minority villages from 2011 to 2015,[31] which has important demonstration significance throughout the country.

Since China embarked on the path of reform and opening up four decades ago, the housing conditions of rural residents have undergone a constant improvement. However, the uniformity of new rural construction and the pursuit of modern amenities in residential construction have changed the cultural qualities of traditional architectural communities, which led to the rapid disappearance of traditional villages with tranquil pastoral scenes. According to a nationwide survey by the Ministry of Housing and Urban-Rural Development in 2013, the number of villages with traditional characteristics was less than 2% among the total number of administrative villages. Among the 1,561 historic villages under state protection, a large number were rural

---

[31] *The Protection and Development Plan for the Ethnic Minorities' Traditional Residences: 2011–2015*. www.gov.cn. December 10, 2012.

human settlements of ethnic minorities.[32] The rural and pastoral areas are the vitality source and fertile soil for traditional culture. However, the peasants and herdsmen who guard and inherit the cultural traditions are also entitled to a modernized development. Therefore, the protection of the traditional culture of ethnic minorities is not for the preservation of a "living fossil"; rather, it aims to expand the development space for ethnic minority cultures.

Culture is an important characteristic of an ethnic group and a source of its vitality, creativity, and cohesion. The cultures of China's ethnic minorities are a vital part of Chinese civilization and are intellectual assets owned by the entire Chinese nation. *The Constitution of the People's Republic of China* stipulates that the state helps the ethnic minorities to accelerate the development of their cultural undertakings according to their characteristics and needs. The Chinese government adopts various policies and measures to respect, protect, and support the inheritance, development, and innovation of the cultures of the various ethnic minorities, to encourage all ethnic groups to enhance their cultural exchanges and develop their cultural undertakings.

In 2009, the State Council released Several Opinions on Further promoting the *Cultural Undertakings of the Ethnic Minorities*, which outlined the Chinese government's basic theoretical stance on ethnic culture, ethnic minority culture, and Chinese culture. It declared:"culture is an important source of national vitality, cohesion and creativity; the culture of ethnic minorities, as an important component of Chinese culture, is the common spiritual asset of the Chinese nation; all ethnic groups of China have created diverse and splendid cultures in the course of their historical development; the interaction and blending of the cultures of all ethnic groups enhance the vitality and creativity of Chinese culture by constantly enriching and developing the connotation of Chinese culture, which, in turn, improves the cultural identity and centripetal force of the Chinese nation." Therefore, the protection and development of ethnic minority culture are tantamount to the inheritance and prosperity of the Chinese culture. In this sense, respect for the culture of ethnic minorities is the synonym for an ardent love for Chinese culture. It is the only way of building a common spiritual home for people of all ethnic groups.

6.7 The Identity of Chinese Culture: Unity in Diversity

Defined as the agglomeration of all the cultures of the 56 ethnic groups of China, Chinese culture does not equate to the culture of the Han people. The Chinese nation's pluralistic integration determines the diversity of its culture. To guarantee the equality of the 56 constituents of the Chinese nation, people of all ethnic groups shall have equal access to the achievements of China's economic and social development; to consolidate the solidarity of the Chinese nation, the 56 ethnic groups must jointly build the identity of Chinese culture, which becomes a keyword for the exaltation

---

[32]*Retain the Ethnic DNA: Protection of the Traditional Residences of the Ethnic Minorities*. China Construction News. April 24, 2014.

of the collective identity of people of all ethnic groups. As the "root of ethnic unity and soul of ethnic harmony," Chinese cultural identity has a bearing on the underpinning and psychological consensus of the Chinese nation. While addressing the delegates attending the 7th National Conference of Friendship of Overseas Chinese Associations, Xi Jinping stated: "No matter where a Chinese is, he always bears the distinctive brand of the Chinese culture, which is the common heritage of all the sons and daughters of China."[33]

Currently, China is committed to solving the problem of economic and social modernization of the 1.3 billion citizens of the country. All Chinese nationals are making heroic efforts to realize the first centenary goal of the country, that is, the completion of building a moderately well-off society in all respects by 2021 when the Communist Party of China commemorates the 100th anniversary. At the same time, the great tasks of maintaining state unity, consolidating ethnic solidarity, and realizing the rejuvenation of the Chinese nation render it necessary to build a common spiritual home for the people of all ethnic groups. Most of the materialization achievements created by economic growth are characteristics of standardization, socialization, or even worldwide convergence. However, people's acceptance of material well-being convergence in economic life cannot substitute or change their demands for diverse cultural expressions. It is just like the relationship between "hardware" and "software" in a computer: If a computer is not backed by versatile and advanced software, no matter how sophisticated the hardware configuration is, it possesses no powerful functions. As to a country, this is a problem of economic "hard power" and cultural "soft power."

The process of economic and social development in China has reached an extremely urgent stage for the needs of "soft power" to support the country, the nation, and the people. In meeting with outstanding young representatives from all walks of life, Xi Jinping declared: "It is difficult for a nation without inner strength to be self-reliant, and a cause that lacks a cultural buttress cannot be sustained for long."[34] Therefore, the cultural construction under the guidance of the socialist core values, including prosperity, democracy, civility, harmony, freedom, equality, justice, rule of law, patriotism, dedication, integrity, friendship, has become a fundamental issue for the cohesion of Chinese culture identity. Chinese culture is the cultural symbol of state unity and spiritual engine of the Chinese nation's rejuvenation. Its motive force comes from the cultures of all ethnic groups, which are deeply rooted in Chinese soil. In this sense, the protection, inheritance, and development of the culture of all ethnic groups, in particular the cultures of ethnic minorities, are the only ways to the integration, promotion, and identification of Chinese culture. However, we have to bear in mind that its realization is much more complicated and enduring than the economic development. The "unity in diversity" of the Chinese nation can be understood from the following two aspects: Firstly, none of the 56 ethnic groups shall be left behind in the process of economic and social modernization; secondly,

---

[33] Xi Jinping. *The Governance of China*, p. 64.
[34] Xi Jinping. *The Governance of China*, p. 53.

people of all ethnic groups shall "appreciate the culture and values of others as he does his own" in the construction of a common spiritual or cultural home.

Both the concept of "unity" in "China as a unitary multi-ethnic state" and the idea of "oneness" in "the Chinese nation's unity in diversity" are defined as integration of "multi-ethnicity" and "pluralism." From the aspect of ethnic factors, "unity" does not equate to "sameness"; from the point of cultural factor, "oneness" is not tantamount to "uniformity." Both "unity" and "oneness" are pluralistic integration, which means the components of "unity" and "oneness" complement each other in a shared and mutually beneficial order, instead of negating the diversity. "Integration" means to "establish more intimate and symbiotic ties" among the various ethnic groups and cultural types.[35] The system of regional ethnic autonomy and the ethno-national policies of China serve as the "coordination mechanism in a shared and mutually beneficial order for people of all ethnic groups." The construction process of Chinese culture identity is a protracted and arduous task.

Identity, as a psychological phenomenon, consciously or unconsciously makes a stable, regular, mobile, or random expression in each individual's social life experience. Therefore, the identity that people are concerned about is actually a complicated matter. In *Sources of the Self: The Making of the Modern Identity*, an attempt to articulate and write a history of modern identity, the Canadian Philosopher Charles Taylor concluded that "the topic of identity is actually more profound and multifaceted than any possible expression of it."[36] While discussing the problem of "identity" in the category of sovereign state, we tend to focus mainly on national identity. Outwardly a rather simple topic, it has been known worldwide as "identity anxiety" with "globalization symptoms" due to its complicatedness.

As the birthplace of the modern nation-state, referring to the type of state that joins the political entity of a state to the cultural entity of a nation, Western Europe is the forerunner for the construction of an alliance of nation-states, the European Union. In addition, it seems that this type of "supranational union," a type of multi-national political union where negotiated power is delegated to an authority by governments of member states, demonstrates the tendency of surpassing or even replacing the nation-state. The development of the EU created an ideal of building a "European nation"; however, it is accompanied by the conservative mentality of "shrinking back into the individual caves."[37] Moreover, some EU member states are facing the real domestic challenge of separatist movements, which often appeals to economic interests. Therefore, the construction and identity of the nation-state are still widespread problems in the existing state pattern of the world.

In China, the "one nation" for the construction of state nation is the Chinese nation, a collective term for the 56 ethnic groups of China. As the national characteristics of the identity of the Chinese nation, Chinese culture functions as the spiritual tie connecting people of all ethnic groups. The history of China, in particular, the century of national humiliation between 1840 and 1949, has given spiritual power for the forma-

---

[35]Lazlowo (1997): 135–136.

[36]Taylor (2001): 39.

[37]Isaacs (2004): 4.

tion and development of the Chinese nation, "patriotism being the spiritual strength of the Chinese nation's solidarity." China's reality, especially the rapid economic and social growth since the 1980s, has granted motive force for the development and prosperity of the Chinese nation, "reform, opening up and innovation being the driving forces that spur us to keep pace with the times."[38] Therefore, the Chinese nation is neither a nihilist coinage nor an original fait accompli. It is a continuously integrated state nation during its rejuvenation process. For a unitary multi-ethnic state like China, the identity of Chinese culture and the self-identity of the 56 ethnic groups with their respective cultures are inseparably interconnected. They go hand in hand and complement each other. Neither of these two cultural identities excludes the other; otherwise, it would be a distortion of the inclusive nature of the Chinese culture.

Symbols of cultural identity include equality, tolerance, unity, mutual assistance, and harmony. However, non-identification with Chinese culture will inevitably lead to oppression, discrimination, exclusion, alienation, and division. Following a simplified approach to dealing with the long-standing and complicated ethno-national issues, some people argued that the policy practices of recognizing the identity of ethnic minorities and protecting their rights and interests would result in a "weakened identification with the Chinese nation" among the ethnic minorities. Therefore, they strongly suggested that the system of regional ethnic autonomy be abolished. Deng Xiaoping ascribed the most important cause of this kind of radical mentality to "revolutionary impetuosity," namely eagerness for success regardless of objective reality. In the history of the Chinese Communist Party, such rashness was shadowed with big-nation chauvinism and local national chauvinism, collectively known as "two kinds of national chauvinism."

In general, big-nation chauvinism has a sense of superiority and a spillover effect, while local national chauvinism is characteristic of conservativeness and resistance. There exists a causal relationship between the two, the trumpeting of the former tending to trigger the response of the latter. While confirming the positive role of nationalism in fighting against imperialism and colonial liberation movements, Marxism resolutely opposes national chauvinism in domestic ethnic relations, describing it as a toxin, which will exert detrimental effects on domestic ethnic relationships. Therefore, the Communist Party of China has always opposed "two kinds of nationalism." *The Constitution of China* adopted by the First National People's Congress in 1954 provides that: "in the struggle to safeguard ethnic unity, it is necessary to combat big-nation chauvinism, mainly Han chauvinism, and to combat local national chauvinism. The state will do its utmost to promote the common prosperity of all ethnic groups."

In spite of that, serious problems in the field of ethnic affairs management were not uncommon in the early days of the People's Republic of China. Some officials of the Han ethnicity even arbitrarily concluded that all things related to the ethnic minorities were of inferior quality.[39] In regard to this, Mao Zedong pointed out:

---

[38] Xi Jinping. *The Governance of China*, p. 40.
[39] *The Selected Documents on the Governance of Xinjiang: 1949–2010.*

"Such a situation is intolerable for the Chinese Communists because this simplified and radical mentality is characteristic of the Han chauvinism, which can be defined as an irrational belief in the superiority of the Han people while the ethnic minorities are considered weak or inferior."[40]

While combating Han chauvinism, the Chinese Communists are also clearly aware of the harms of local national chauvinism, which would "jeopardize ethnic unity and ultimately inflict unfavorable effects on the rights and interests of the ethnic minorities."[41] The local national chauvinism, under the historical conditions at that time, was mainly manifested as a negative and conservative attitude toward the socialist reform in the compact communities of the ethnic minorities. Moreover, the national separatism consciousness which existed in the ethnic minority elites was utilized by the imperialist powers to provoke inter-ethnic estrangement or resentment.

The solution to "two kinds of national chauvinism" remains a hard nut in today's ethnic affairs management. If this problem is not effectively addressed, both the integration of the Chinese nation and the construction of a common spiritual home for the various ethnic groups will be castles in the air. As to the ways of eliminating the effects of "two kinds of national chauvinism" on the various ethnic groups of China, Deng Xiaoping once made a dialectical argument. He stated: "Upon the Han people's renunciation of Han chauvinism, the ethnic minorities' abandonment of local national chauvinism will be achieved without extra effort. Ethnic unity will come as soon as Han chauvinism and local national chauvinism are abolished."[42] Although the manifestations of the "two kinds of national chauvinism" in contemporary China are largely different from those of the past, Deng Xiaoping's argument is still applicable. In the national conference on ethnic affairs held in 2014, Xi Jinping pointed out: "both Han chauvinism and local national chauvinism are formidable enemies of ethnic unity for the former leads to ethnic discrimination while the latter is likely to breed a separatist tendency." The Chinese government's policies of respecting cultural diversity and protecting ethnic minority cultures incarnate the idea of "appreciating the culture or values of others as one's own".

Every nation's culture has its own unique qualities and expressions. In this regard, we should never judge the merits or demerits of other nation's culture by using our own yardsticks. As the unique logo which distinguishes a nation from the others, culture is esteemed and inherited by all the people of an ethnic group, which is a matter of course and beyond any reproach. Though the Han people constitute approximately 92% of the total Chinese population, it does not mean that Han culture is equal to Chinese culture. In the common spiritual home of the Chinese nation, the diversity of ethnic minority cultures adds luster and splendor to Chinese culture. Therefore, the mutual respect and understanding in the cross-cultural exchanges between the Han people and the ethnic minorities are the foundation for the peaceful coexistence, mutual cooperation, and harmonious development among people of all ethnic groups. Experiences at home and abroad have testified that "if you don't know how to respect

---

[40]Mao (1990): 128.

[41]*The CPC's Documents on the Governance of Xinjiang: 1949–2010*, p. 120.

[42]Deng Xiaoping. *The Selected works of Deng Xiaoping. Volume I*, p. 165.

other people and their culture, the cross-cultural communication will be a failure."[43] The rule applies to domestic ethnic relation and international relations.

Driven by the rapid economic and social development since China introduced the reform and opening-up policy, the multi-directional population movement has led to an increasingly extensive ethnic engagement and contact, forming a wider range of social interaction. In this interaction, the widespread problem of "cross-cultural sensitivity" came into being. In inter-ethnic communication, people's entrenched prejudices against the "grotesque" or "bizarre" folkways or customs will, unavoidably, bring about misunderstandings or even disrespectful behaviors. The novelty-seeking descriptions, mocking appraisals, or exclusionary attitudes in literary works, films, newspaper, or Web site articles, including unintentional violation of the customs or taboos of ethnic minorities, will cause adverse reactions in ethnic relations, or even complaints and protests. For example, a news report covered in the Web site of China News Service, *the Lisu people: chain smokers living in the mountainous villages in Yunnan*, highlighted the blackened fingers of the Lisu villagers, which, the journalist groundlessly claimed, was due to long-term pipe smoking. As a matter of fact, the "blackened fingers" of the local people were in fact dyed as a result of shelling green walnuts during harvest season.[44] In addition to violating the ethical standards of news reporting, the reporter's fake story unintentionally hurts the self-esteem of the Lisu people.

In any countries of the world, it is common to observe disparity between the theoretical concept of state policies and the actual degree of realization. It is impractical to expect "immediate effect" upon the establishment of any system, law, or policy. The superiority of the system design and prestige of state laws must be constantly realized in practice. Of course, having a law does not mean that every aspect of it can be fully realized. Chinese affairs need to be observed with a dynamic vision. As a developing country, China's social system and regional ethnic autonomy system (including human rights) are in a constant process of development and improvement. There is no one advanced concept or institutional model in the world that, as soon as it is established, is capable of fully reflecting its superiority. Admittedly, the existence and emergence of problems in ethnic relations are normality; it is also justified to solve existing problems and prevent new problems from occurring. The Chinese government has long been attaching great importance to the interests, aspirations, and demands of ethnic minorities for the purpose of enhancing the harmonious coexistence of all ethnic groups. With the ever-increasing ethnic engagements and exchanges, the policy principles of dealing with ethno-national issues, including equality, unity, mutual assistance, and harmony, need to be promoted throughout China with greater efforts. Only through the coexistence and common prosperity of the cultures of all ethnic groups can the development of Chinese culture be endowed with modern significance.

---

[43]Cultural Patterns and their Dissemination Modes: Proceedings on Cross-cultural Communication (2003): 453.

[44]*False News Hurt the Feelings of the Lisu People: an Apology from China News Service.* September 26, 2015.

In the construction of a socialist society with Chinese characteristics, the CPC put forward the ideas of respecting differences and tolerating diversity. China's policy practices of protecting and developing the culture of ethnic minorities are not for the purpose of strengthening cultural differences among various ethnic groups; rather, they are for the construction of a common spiritual home for people of all ethnic groups. In this sense, unity in diversity, that is, maintaining state unity while respecting the differences of various ethnic groups, is the Chinese wisdom for the realization of Chinese culture identity.

China proposes building a socialist harmonious society in the Western development process. This society is characterized by democracy and rule of law, fairness and justice, sincerity and honesty, vitality, stability and order, and people existing harmoniously with nature. For a multi-ethnic country, the harmonious relationship between different ethnic groups is one of the most important factors for maintaining social harmony. We should fully respect and understand different traditions, languages, culture, customs, and psychological identities formed in the historical development of all ethnic groups; we should not ignore their existence, and we cannot use force to handle transformation. We should actively create conditions to reduce and eliminate the development gap of all ethnic groups. This sums up the concept of "respect for differences, tolerance of diversity" in ethnic affairs. Recognition of diversity gives full respect and understanding to characteristics of ethnic traditional cultures; reducing and eliminating the ethnic gap in economic development and living standards are common requirements in the effort to achieve fairness and justice. Diversity is the basis of mutual exchange, cooperation, absorption, learning, and innovation; unity is the organized and coordinated integration of the diversified interactive relationship.

References

Baima, L. (2005). The Central Government's Authority in Implementing the Reincarnation of Living Buddha in Tibetan Buddhism. *Journal of Tibetan Studies,* (1), 24–27.

Bianba, C. (2015, March 18). *The formation of the bilingual education system in Tibet.* Xinhuanet.

Cultural Patterns and their Dissemination Modes: Proceedings on Cross-cultural Communication. Beijing: Press of Communication University of China (2003).

Deng, J. (2000). *The tea road.* Hohhot: Inner Mongolia People's Press.

Diamond, J. (2000). *Guns, germs, and steel: The fates of human societies.* Shanghai: Shanghai Translation Publishing House.

Feng, K. (1994). *Racial concept in modern China.* Nanjing: Jiangsu People's Press.

Gu, C. (2004). *The western missionaries and modern China.* Shanghai: Shanghai People's Press.

Isaacs, H. (2004). *Idols of the tribe: Group identity and political change.* Taipei: Li Sui Culture Co., Ltd.

Islam and Terrorism. Taipei: Xiquan Press (2006).

Grang, M. (2005). *Cultural geography.* Nanjing: Nanjing University Press.

Lazlowo, E. (1997). *Destiny choice.* Beijing: The SDX Joint Publishing Company.

Mao, Z. (1990). *The selected works of Mao Zedong* (Vol. IV). Central Literature Publishing House.

Morin, E., & Kern, A. (1997). *Earth motherland.* Beijing: SDX Joint Publishing Company.

On the Ethno-national Issues of China by the CCP Leadership. Beijing: The Nationalities Publishing House. 1994.

Pinker, S. (2015). *The better angels of our nature*. Beijing: Citic Press Group.
Rubruck, W. (1985). *The journey of William Rubruk to the eastern parts*. Beijing: Zhonghua Book Company.
Sun, H., & Hu, Z. (2007). *The languages of China*. Beijing: The Commercial Press.
The Collected Documents on the Ethnic Affairs of China. Beijing: The Central Document Publishing House (1990).
Taylor, C. (2001). *Sources of the self: The making of the modern identity*. Nanjing: Yilin Press.

Conclusion: A Long Way to Go to Solving the Ethno-national Issues of China

As early as the time when the CPC was based in Yan'an (1935–1948), it began to seek a solution to the ethno-national issues of China. This process has been a six-decade undertaking, since the PRC's founding in 1949. In the early days of reform and opening-up, the CPC made a clarion call to build socialism with Chinese characteristics. The solution to the ethno-national issues of China, as an integral part of such socialism, has witnessed many twists and turns. It was after suffering many setbacks in nation-building that the reform and opening-up of China made ideological and practical breakthroughs. The CPC was deeply aware that, to achieve the goal of solving the country's ethno-national issues, it was imperative to follow the tide of the times, respond to the wishes of the people; and this awareness created a powerful force for advancing the cause of the Party and the people. The Chinese Communists united the people and led them in launching the great new revolution of reform and opening-up, in removing all ideological and institutional barriers to China's development, and in embarking on the path of socialism with Chinese characteristics. Thus was China able to stride ahead to catch up with the times. Of course, there is still a long way to go to solving the ethno-national issues of the country.

I

Prevalent in all countries of the world, ethno-national issues have their peculiarities in that other social problems, due to their graduation characteristics, can be addressed by adopting corresponding measures, while ethno-national issues in the broad sense, including issues of race, ethnicity, language, religion, cultural diversity, and immigration, continue to create new problems with the changing times. In this regard, the resolution of ethnic issues is a challenge confronted by countries throughout the world. For example, the influx of several million Muslim immigrants into Europe has caused numerous social problems in France and Germany. As the oldest nation-state, Britain did not foresee that Scotland would seek independent statehood by referendum. The USA, as a country of immigrants, could not have anticipated that

© China Social Sciences Press 2020
S. Hao, *China's Solution to Its Ethno-national Issues*, China Insights,
https://doi.org/10.1007/978-981-32-9519-3

Spanish would be widely spoken in the state of California. As a result of increased documented and undocumented migration of Mexican and other Hispanic people into California and the transformation of many aspects of the culture of California, the state is now known as "Mexifornia" due to its rapid feature of "Hispanicization".[1] All these show that although capitalist countries have experienced a history of several hundred years, they have not come up with a successful way to address their ethno-national problems. As for China, the process of solving its ethno-national issues is generally effective and successful, for the Chinese government neither blindly proclaims that the historical legacy of ethno-national problems of the country has been solved "once and for all" nor improperly belittles its concepts and policies to address ethno-national issues.

Generally, ethno-national issues refer to the relationship between different ethnic groups; relationships between ethnic groups, within the multi-ethnic country. China's ethno-national affairs, through regional ethnic autonomy, and the political, economic, cultural, and social aspects of various ethnic policies, has to coordinate the relationship between the 56 ethnic groups, particularly the relationship between the Han and minority ethnicities; and to enable ethnic equality, solidarity, mutual assistance, and harmony between ethnic minorities. The fundamental task of achieving this goal is to speed up the economic and social development of the compact communities of ethnic minorities and to gradually reduce and eliminate the regional development gap. For a populous developing country like China, the development gap between different regions, between urban and rural areas, between different social classes in living conditions, education, employment, and income also constitute real inequalities. However, due to peculiarities in history, natural geography, language and culture, life customs, and value systems, ethnic minorities have encountered more prominent and complex problems and more diversified and significant real inequalities in adapting to a Han culture dominated society that was in rapid transition from tradition to modernity. The nation is required to give more attention and support, especially from eastern areas, to ethnic minorities and their inhabited areas to make greater efforts at self-reliance.

The system of regional ethnic autonomy and the various ethno-national policies of China are effective and successful for they are based on the national conditions of the country, which can be understood from the following two aspects: historically, China has been a unified multi-ethnic state; in reality, the country is still in the preliminary stage of socialism and will be so for a long period of time. The most fundamental experience for the "China mode", which merits extensive world attention and has no shortage of appreciation in the international community, is that this development path is deeply rooted in the national conditions of the country. It offers Chinese wisdom and a Chinese approach to solving the problems facing mankind. If the historical process of interaction, peaceful co-existence, and "grand unity" among the people of all ethnic groups is ignored, the century of foreign powers' infiltration and aggression of China between 1840 and 1949 would inevitably lead to national disintegration. Thus, throughout the one-hundred odd years of modern China, the

---

[1]Huntington S. *Who Are We: the Challenges to America's National Identity*, p. 204.

thread of nationalistic-racial protest against foreign elements in Chinese life formed a distinct theme of history, now coming to the surface and now going underground.

The system of regional ethnic autonomy, due to its enshrined principles of respect for cultural diversity and narrowing the regional development disparity, guarantees ethnic equality and unity. Ethnic equality is a core principle followed by the CPC and the Chinese government when handling ethnic relations. Irrespective of their size, history, or levels of development, all ethnic groups in China are equal in every aspect of life. No discrimination or oppression against any group can be tolerated. They have the right to equal participation in national and local affairs, regardless of whether their populations are concentrated or dispersed. Ethnic unity is the bedrock of China's ethno-national policies. It is reflected in harmonious, friendly interactions between different ethnic groups, whose members learn from and help each other in a spirit of mutual respect, trust, and understanding. It is built upon the notion that all ethnic groups in China, including the Han and minority groups, are interdependent: they breathe the same air, share the same future, aspire to the same goals, and work together for common prosperity. Likewise, only by upholding and improving regional autonomy can people of all ethnic groups be united for the rejuvenation of the Chinese nation.

The reform and opening-up of China, which is termed as "socialism with Chinese characteristics", embodies the requirements of the socialist system's development and improvement for the purpose of giving full play to its superiority. China has no intention of exporting its development mode to any other country. However, China hopes that the international community can understand and respect its brand of socialism, just as China respects the social systems and development paths of other countries. A quotation from *the Analects* of Confucius vividly expresses this point: "The gentleman seeks harmony, not uniformity." In spite of its great achievements in the past four decades, China is still a developing country with inadequate composite national strength and global influence. Therefore, it cannot rest on its laurels and must press ahead with major policy changes. In terms of economic development, system construction, rule of law and social management, China has been drawing on the achievements of other civilizations to do full justice to the strengths of China's socialist system. Xi Jinping pointed out: "We need to learn from the achievements of foreign political civilization, but we must not give up the fundamentals of China's political system."[2]

In the Chinese top leadership's public speeches, we can find frequent usages of "a land area of 9.6 million square kilometers", "a population of 1.3 billion" and "56 ethnic groups", which are terse summaries of the development reality and national conditions of China. In the CPC's 18th National Congress held in 2012, Xi Jinping put forward the two centenary goals.[3] As far as the population size of China is concerned,

---

[2]Xi (2014).

[3]To build a moderately prosperous society in all respects by the time, the Communist Party of China celebrates its centenary in 2021, and to turn China into a modern socialist country that is prosperous, strong, democratic, culturally advanced, and harmonious by the time the People's Republic of China celebrates its centenary in 2049.

it can be said that no country or any ruling party in the world is shouldering such a grave responsibility. China's reform and opening-up is the institutional guarantee to achieve these goals.

The path, theories, and system of socialism with Chinese characteristics are the accomplishments made by the Chinese people and the CPC in the course of arduous struggle over the past 90-plus years. By integrating theory with practice, it has systematically addressed the fundamental questions of what kind of socialism we should build and how we should build it in China, a vast country with a huge population and a weak economy to start with. Socialism with Chinese characteristics has brought about fast development and rising living standards in China. This fully shows that it is what we must pursue if we are to achieve development and make progress in contemporary China and that only socialism with Chinese characteristics can enable China to develop itself. We must cherish these accomplishments, uphold them all the time, and continue to enrich them.

While meeting with the faculty and students of Peking University, which is consistently ranked as the top academic institution in China, on May 4th, 2014, Xi Jinping declared: "a nation and country must know who they are, where they came from and where they are heading. Keep on going when you have made your choice."[4] The system of regional ethnic autonomy is the correct choice the Chinese people have made. Upholding and improving this system is an integral part of China's reform and opening-up policy. Therefore, the national conference on ethnic affairs in 2014 declared: "regional autonomy for the ethnic minorities is the source of the CPC's ethno-national policies. Any deviation from this origin will inevitably lead to a shaken foundation and subsequent 'domino effect' in the field of ethno-national policies." It is a conclusion arrived at from the collapse of the Soviet Union, the civil war in Yugoslavia and the various kinds of "Color Revolution".

II

Admittedly, there has been divided understanding and assessment regarding China's ethno-national policies. In August 2008, Beijing was due to host its first Olympic Games. The rioters speculated that the violence might affect attendance at the Beijing Olympics. Those who were arrested after the unrest confessed they were employed to undertake the violence, including arson, looting shops, and attacking non-Tibetan civilians.

After the collapse of the Soviet Union, some even speculated that Tibet and Xinjiang would break away from China. In fact, such alarmist talks were merely the sensational hype of the separatists, who have long coveted to split China and the Chinese nation. In addition, some took an almost gleeful delight in seeing the rare occurrences of sensational incidents, for example, the self-immolation protests by

---

[4]Xi Jinping. *The Governance of China*, p. 171.

Tibetans after the 2008 Tibetan unrest and the terrorist attacks in Xinjiang after the July 2009 riots in Ürümqi.

As a matter of fact, such hype can be in large part ascribed to the "Cold War mentality", for some people have always wished the so-called effect of "nationalism over Communism" can be repeated in China. Though the state of geopolitical tension between powers in the Eastern Bloc (the Soviet Union and its satellite states) and powers in the Western Bloc (the USA, its NATO allies and others) was terminated with the Soviet dissolution, the Cold War continued to influence world affairs as many of the economic and social tensions that were exploited to fuel Cold War competition remain acute.

Motivated by the hangover of the "Cold War mentality", some Western countries attempted to launch the "fourth wave of democratization" throughout the world by taking advantage of the various forms of "color revolution". China became one of their most important targets. Thus, "narrating the tragic story" of the Tibetans and Uyghurs under the rule of China became the life-saving straw for the exiled separatist forces represented by the Dalai Lama and Rebiya Kadeer. They are crystal clear that the endorsement of the Western politicians, organizations, and public opinion, including the moral sympathy for the "weak", can only be won by catering to the mainstream Western ideology.

After 1994, the Dalai clique started to alter its tactics, shifting its attempts from achieving open independence to disguised secession by cloaking them with what is called the "Middle Way Approach". In 1988, the Dalai Lama addressed the European Parliament and offered what was later called *the Strasbourg Proposal*, which elaborated on the Middle Way Approach and a vision of reconciliation, resembling what some historians say was a suzerainty relationship between China and Tibet. The proposal basically calls for the establishment of a democratic Tibet with complete sovereignty over its domestic affairs and non-political foreign affairs, with China retaining its responsibility for Tibet's foreign policy and maintaining its military presence temporarily. Claiming China's regional autonomy for ethnic minorities was only a "political vase" for decorative purposes, the Dalai Lama demanded "a high degree of autonomy", which denies the leadership of the central government and Tibet's present social and political systems, and proposes to establish an "autonomous government" under which "Tibetans" (in truth the Dalai clique) take full charge of all affairs other than diplomacy and national defense.

Rebiya Kadeer, an ironclad separatist colluding with terrorists and Islamic extremists, traveled to the USA after being released early on medical grounds. In November 2006, she became the president of the separatist World Uyghur Congress. On June 5, 2007, at a conference on democracy and security held in Prague, Kadeer met with the then US President George W. Bush, who praised people like her for being "far more valuable than the weapons of the US army or oil under the ground." In May 2012, while in Tokyo for a conference engagement, Kadeer visited the Yasukuni Shrine, which is controversial because some of the dead honored there are Japanese war criminals. She called on the Japanese government to support the exiled Uyghur groups financially and politically. Every now and then, some Western politicians would grant audiences with these "political refugees", which seriously violates the core interests of China and hurts the feelings of the Chinese public. It is beyond Chinese people's understanding why Western societies support the Dalai Lama and Rebiya Kadeer.

The political games in Western democracy, including catching votes by fair means or foul, canvassing for electorates with luxurious promises and dishonoring these vows when elected, are known to all. As a matter of fact, the Western society insists that they showcase the superiority of the Western polity, in particular, the universal value of freedom of speech. Nevertheless, if such "freedom" violates the interests of others, or intervenes the rights of others, including the long-cherished values, cultural traditions, or choice of development mode of other countries, it can by no means be defined as "freedom" in the sense of "democracy". In fact, whether in the human rights traditions of Western countries or in *the Universal Declaration of Human Rights*, such freedom is subjected to restriction of legal regulations. "The sole purpose of establishing such restriction is to ensure due respect for the rights and freedoms of others, and to meet the legitimate needs of morality, public order, and universal welfare in a democratic society."[5] Therefore, if such "due recognition and respect" for racial, ethnic, or religious differences are denied, the tragedy of the *Charlie Hebdo* shootings will surely be repeated. The French satirical weekly magazine has been the target of two terrorist attacks, in 2011 and 2015, respectively. Both were presumed to be in response to a number of controversial Muhammad cartoons it published. In the second of these attacks, 12 people were slaughtered, including publishing director Stephane Charbonnier and several other prominent cartoonists. As a response, up to 3.7 million people, including leaders of Europe, took to the streets in cities across France to honor the victims of the shootings and also to voice support for freedom of speech. It is, however, far from adequate to prevent the reoccurrence of such atrocities. Of course, it is justified for the Western society to uphold the freedom of speech and condemn the terrorist attacks. However, freedom of speech must by no means be utilized as an excuse to offend the religious belief of others.

It should be noted that the Western countries' policy toward the ethnic minority affairs of China has changed over time. On August 31, 1907, the convention between the UK and Russia concluded the *Anglo-Russian Entente* in St. Petersburg, declaring China had merely suzerainty, rather than sovereignty, over Tibet. 101 years later, the British government, the creator of the so-called Tibet issue, made a written statement in the name of its Foreign and Commonwealth Office, recognizing Tibet as a part of China and acknowledging China's sovereignty over it. In the final analysis, London confessed it had been wrong regarding its position in Tibet. However, such penitence came much too late.

In his memoirs, Gyalo Thondup, the second-eldest brother of the 14th Dalai Lama, who several times acted as the Dalai Lama's emissary, admitted the Dalai clique had received generous armed support from the Central Intelligence Agency (CIA) of the USA in the 1959 Tibet Uprising. He added that his collaboration with the CIA was his most regret act in his lifetime. The USA archives disclosed also showed that the

---

[5]The Selected International Documents on Human Rights (2002): 6.

CIA not only sent agents to help the Dalai Lama to flee but also purposefully trained militants to support his forces and airdropped a large quantity of weaponry during the armed rebellion. In his autobiography, the Dalai Lama criticized the CIA for supporting the Tibetan independence movement "not because they [the CIA] cared about Tibetan independence but as part of their worldwide efforts to destabilize all Communist regimes".

While meeting with Gyalo Thondup in 1982, Zhongxun Xi, who was then serving as deputy chair of China's national legislature, stated: "In the Dalai Lama's hypothesis, 'Greater Tibet' covers Tibet, Qinghai, parts of Sichuan, Gansu, Yunnan, and Xinjiang. In total, this represents an area larger than one quarter of Chinese territory. It is sheer fantasy and does not conform to China's history and national conditions. In addition to the Tibet Autonomous Region, China has established several autonomous prefectures or counties in the Tibetan-inhabited regions of Sichuan, Yunnan, Gansu, and Qinghai. Such administrative division takes into account the distribution of different ethnic groups with a view to their future development. It is conducive to the common prosperity and development of people of all ethnic groups."[6] Today, the Chinese government's response to the Dalai Lama's demand for "a high degree of autonomy", or the so-called Middle Way Approach, whose essence is to set up an independent Tibetan state free of any control from the central government, remains unchanged, for the system of regional ethnic autonomy conforms to the national conditions of China.

In September 2009, a delegation of British parliamentarians visited Tibet at the invitation of the National People's Congress of China. While talking with their Chinese counterparts during their visit, these British MPs expressed their endorsement of the Dalai Lama's peace initiatives, including "not seeking the independence of Tibet" and "Tibet's high degree of autonomy", suggesting that China follow the pattern of Scottish Parliament, "a decentralization model based on state unity and a high degree of autonomy for Scotland", to address the "issue of Tibet". Actually, were these British political elites really confident of their seemingly successful model of Scottish Parliament while selling it to China?

In November 2013, the Scottish Parliament passed *the Independence Referendum Bill*, setting out the arrangements for the independence of Scotland. A referendum on Scottish independence from the UK took place the next year. The referendum question, which voters answered with "Yes" or "No", was "should Scotland be an independent country?" The "No" side won, with 55.3% voting against independence. Alex Salmond, the leader of the Scottish National Party (SNP) for over twenty years, resigned as Scottish First Minister, saying that "for Scotland, the campaign continues and the dream shall never die." After the vote of Brexit, the prospective withdrawal of the UK from the European Union, Nicola Sturgeon, the new First Minister of Scotland, confirmed in June 2016 that the Scottish government has formally agreed to draft legislation to allow a second independence referendum to take place. On 29 March 2017, Theresa May, Prime Minister of the UK, triggered Article 50 of *the Treaty on European Union*, formally allowing the process of the withdrawal from

---

[6]Xi (2013): 249.

the European Union. Prior to that day, the Scottish Parliament voted 69–59 in favor of another independence referendum.

Facts speak louder than words. The Chinese people will never lap up whatever Western society throws at them. Some political and intellectual elites of the Western countries, with a firm conviction of their infallibility and moral superiority, applauded the Dalai Lama's demand for "Tibet's high degree of autonomy". Strongly believing the supremacy of western democracies, they are used to lecturing China about what should be done. As Gideon Rachman, the chief foreign affairs commentator of *the Financial Times*, put it, "the independence referendum of Scotland provides a successful model for the world to deal with national separatism."[7] In his grand blueprint, the anticipated recipients for this "model" include Tibet, Xinjiang, or even the Taiwan region of China.

Perhaps the British politicians will be sensible enough to take some remedial action, for example, to draft an anti-secession law, for the purpose of deterring Scotland's declaration of independence. It was exactly thanks to the constitutional principle of the indivisibility of the various regions of Spain that the Spanish Constitutional Court successfully blocked the independence referendum of Catalonia in 2014. Similarly, Article 4 of *the Constitution of China* clearly provides: "all autonomous areas for ethnic minorities are inseparable parts of the People's Republic of China". This principle bases itself on the national condition of China as a unified multi-ethnic state.

After the collapse of the Soviet Union, there was much debate on the ethno-national policies of China in domestic academia. Some suggested that "the ethnic identity for the minority nationalities and regional ethnic autonomy should be renounced" under the context of the "de-politicization of the ethno-national issues". Others believed that China should follow the US-style "melting pot" policy, a fusion of nationalities, cultures, and ethnicities. However, such "successful experiences" fail to conform to the reality of China.[8] Since the 1970s, there had been a craze for the concept of "ethnic group", a category of people who identify with each other based on similarities such as common ancestry, language, society, culture, or nation, in the Western society. Against this backdrop, some Chinese scholars believed that the substitution of "56 nations" with "56 ethnic groups" would effectively discourage and contain secession activities in China for the notion of "ethnic group" removes the inherent political features of ethnic identity in the Chinese discourse. These people, divorcing themselves from the reality, were convinced that they had found a short cut to addressing the complex ethno-national issues.

However, such reasoning would mislead the public. According to this simple logic, the menacing risks of the independent referendums in Quebec, Catalonia, and Scotland would cease to exist overnight with the nominal gesture of replacing "nation" with "ethnic group". As a matter of fact, those countries in which the idea of "ethnic group" has been prevalent did not take this magic cure-all. Instead, the Canadian Congress passed a motion on November 27, 2006, declaring: "Quebec forms

---

[7]Rachman (2014).
[8]Sha (2014).

a nation within Canada". Similarly, the Spanish Congress and British Parliament also afforded the residents of Catalan and Scotland the identity of "nationality" or "national minority".

The Resident Identity Card Law of China promulgated in 2003 regulates that all Chinese citizens over the age of 16 apply for identification cards, the official unified form of personal identification in the country. The identity card contains basic information regarding the individual, including name, gender, date of birth, identification number, and ethnicity. In accordance with *the Law of China on Regional Autonomy forEthnic Minorities*, "all the nationalities shall have the freedom to use and develop their own spoken and written languages." Within the ethnic minority regions, identity cards possess a corresponding text in the respective minority languages. In other words, resident identity cards within designated ethnic minority regions are allowed to have bilingual texts. Therefore, cards may contain accompanying text in Zhuang, Uyghur, Yi, Tibetan, Mongolian, or Korean depending on the region. The identity cards of the Han people can only have Chinese characters displayed, while the ethnic minorities within their representative autonomous regions can have their personal name displayed in both their native language and Chinese characters.

In the USA, an optional national identity system is the Social Security Number (SSN), a nine-digit number issued to US citizens, permanent residents, and temporary residents. Its purpose was to identify individuals for the purposes of social security, but it is now also used to track individuals for taxation purposes. The SSN has therefore become a de facto national identification number, despite the fact that originally it was expressly not for this purpose. Different from the identity cards of China, the SSN does not show gender, date of birth, race, or ethnicity of cardholders for fear of infringing on the privacies of citizens. Ironically, some Chinese scholars maintain that it thanks to the non-existence of a unified identity system and regional autonomy for ethnic minorities in the USA that the country is exempt from the nightmares of national secession. Indeed, such naive reasoning induces people to make unrealistic fantasies about the complicated ethno-national problems.

Xi Jinping pointed out: "some suggested that China should renounce the system of regional ethnic autonomy for it is a model of the former Soviet Union. However, this does not tally with the facts in any way. I would like to emphasize again that the Chinese government will uphold and improve this system."[9] This is China's confidence in its own system design and practical results in solving its problems. Xi added: "We will not take the old path of a rigid closed-door policy, nor an erroneous path by changing our flag. China should draw on the achievements of all other cultures but never forget our own origin. We must not blindly copy the development models of other countries nor accept their dictation." [10]

---

[9]Hao (2015).

[10]Xi Jinping. *The Governance of China*, p. 30.

III

Upholding and improving the system of regional ethnic autonomy is a basic principle that China has consistently been emphasizing, for "practice has proved that the system, due to its conformity to the national conditions of China, has played an important role in safeguarding state unity and territorial integrity, strengthening ethnic equality, promoting the development of ethnic minority regions and enhancing the cohesion of the Chinese nation." As one of the basic political systems of China, regional ethnic autonomy is still undergoing an improvement process for the social development stage and the composite national strength of China is not sufficient to prop the superiorities of advanced system design.

We must be realistic enough to know that we are not going to find answers to complex issues in one go. As a developing country, China's social system and regional ethnic autonomy system are in a constant process of development and improvement. There is no one advanced concept or institutional model in the world that, as soon as it is established, is capable of fully reflecting its superiority. China's regional ethnic autonomy system is in line with the basic national conditions. The achievements made in practice still need to be constantly developed and improved. In this regard, the system itself must be based on the economic and social base of the ethnic autonomous regions. Any advanced system design and its advantages can only be gradually displayed through the accumulation of practice and experience. As a consequence, no matter how progressively a system is designed, it needs to be amended to adapt to changing circumstances. Therefore, every effort must be made to improve a system during its implementation, which is exactly what China has been doing in enhancing the governance capacity of the country. Ethnic relationships are a long-standing and complex field in the social relations of China. In this regard, China neither evades nor covers up historical, current or future problems.

China's identification of ethnic minority status and implementation of regional ethnic autonomy has solved the issues of equal status and autonomous rights in socio-political fields. However, equality is not the equality of political rights but covers the economic, cultural, and social aspects of life. True equality in political rights can only be achieved after equality in economic, cultural, and social life, and other aspects have been achieved. However, due to historical economic and cultural differences, ethnic minorities enjoy legally endowed equal rights but cannot fully enjoy socially endowed rights and interests under the law, which is a kind of phenomenon of "real injustice". Therefore, only by continuously reducing and ultimately eliminating gaps between various ethnic groups can we achieve true equality.

In general, all multi-ethnic states possess cultural diversity and various types of economic life. China has many ethnicities in its vast land, with significant cultural differences, such as language, clothing, dwellings, rituals, religious beliefs, values, and behaviors. There are also significant economic and social development gaps, as many minorities in the mid-twentieth century were still engaged in 'slash and burn' mountain agriculture, hunting and gathering and other primary production activities. Cultural differences, particularly between those minorities that came into close contact with each other, inevitably produced a puzzle to mutual adaptability; and economic and social development differences, in helping supply each other's needs, caused a contradictory inequality. These are common issues for the country and ethnic autonomous governments. Therefore, China has devoted itself to resolving two important issues related to the ethnic minorities: respecting, protecting, and inheriting ethnic minority cultures; and improving, developing, and enhancing ethnic minorities' economic productivity.

China's regional ethnic autonomy system uses fairness and justice as its basic principles. Its institutional design and legal norms in political equality, economic development, cultural prosperity, and social security are advanced in the world. China's ethnic autonomous regions are, however, mostly socio-economically underdeveloped areas. Advanced institutional arrangements and a backward economic base constitute the first contradiction that must be solved if China is to uphold and improve the regional ethnic autonomy system. Deng Xiaoping, architect of China's reform and opening-up, said, "Regional ethnic autonomy is just empty talk if the economy has not been developed". The fundamental task of China's ethnic affairs is to speed up economic and social development of minorities and their inhabited areas, and gradually reduce and eliminate interethnic economic, cultural, and social life developmental differences so that people of all ethnicities in ethnic autonomous regions and across China can enjoy commonwealth and prosperity.

The national conference on ethnic affairs held in 2014 specifically listed some typical misconceptions in dealing with ethnic minority affairs, for example, taking the phenomenon of multi-ethnicity as a "burden", ethno-national issues as "sources of trouble", and ethnic minorities as "outsiders". These misunderstandings bring about indiscriminate policies in dealing with ethnic minority affairs in a simplified or radical manner, which will, in turn, provide fodder for another attack by the "three evils", including forces of terrorism, separatism, and religious extremism, on China's ethno-national policies.

The hostile forces in Western countries tried every means to interfere in the internal affairs of China by cashing in on ethnic and religious issues. The rampant recessionary activities of the Tibetan government-in-exile based in Dharamsala of India and the Turkistan Islamic Party founded by Uyghur jihadists pose serious threats to the security and stability of China. In the practice of addressing its ethno-national problems, China must rise to these challenges. In addition, the influences of the "three evils" have been significantly enhanced by the diversified means of propaganda. However, emphasizing one-sidedly the external factors, or even exaggerating their negative impact, will inevitably conceal domestic problems. Therefore, "running our own affairs well" has long been established as the top priority by the Chinese government.

In terms of ethnic affairs, we should unswervingly concentrate on the theme of "unity and common prosperity for the people of all ethnic groups", which fully embodies the fundamental contradiction in Chinese society in the field of ethno-national issues, namely the discrepancy between the urgent development desire of the ethnic minorities and their insufficient self-development capacity. Therefore,

China has been making every effort to speed up the economic development and social progress of ethnic minority regions.

In the completion of building a moderately well-off society in all respects by 2021, we are quite confident that the economic, social, and other undertakings in the ethnic minority regions will experience a fundamental improvement. In this process, these regions are confronting the demanding tasks of poverty reduction, environment protection, and improvement of people's livelihood. Moreover, these problems have become more complicated and varied with the nationwide mobility of the ethnic minority population.

Attracted by more employment opportunities and better living conditions, a huge number of rural laborers have migrated into urban areas to seek employment and make a living. According to the fifth national population census, 88.4 million people had migrated from rural to urban areas by the end of 2000. Similarly, large numbers of ethnic minorities have left their native places and migrated to the economically developed coastal provinces since China's economic reform in the late 1970s. Among the total 277.5 million migrant workers in 2015, people of minority ethnic groups accounted for 10%. The urbanization rate of the ethnic minority population increased from 23.36% in 2000 to 32.84% in 2010. In addition, it is in full swing with no signs of slowing down.

With the influx of ethnic minority populaces into cities, urban administrators are facing a variety of challenges, such as creating an inclusive social atmosphere which tolerates ethnic and religious differences, meeting the ethnic minorities' special needs in their religious beliefs, folkways, or customs and resolving ethnic conflicts. Above all, effective measures must be taken to prevent widespread problems during the urbanization process, including ethnic minorities' social exclusion and marginaliza- tion, as well as racial or ethnic segregation. The floating ethnic minority populaces, who differ from the mainstream urban society in the fields of language, culture, religious belief, folkways and customs, naturally encounter immense difficulties in adapting to the alien urban environment. Therefore, accommodating and embrac- ing the minority nationalities has become a demanding task for the ethnic affairs administration of China.

Due to the ever-increasing economic, cultural, and social engagements and contacts among people of all ethnic groups, the ethno-national policies of China have become all-inclusive in scope and content. As a basic political system of China, regional ethnic autonomy incarnates the combination of state unity and self- government for ethnic minorities. It is the sacred duty of the whole country to uphold and improve the system. Therefore, Xi Jinping emphasized that ethnic minority affairs involve all aspects of society, which gave fresh impetus to the ethnic affairs management of China. The implementation of ethno-national policies is an important part of the modernization of state governance system and capacity.

IV

China's solution to its ethno-national issues is undoubtedly an important aspect of the image of the country for equal rights, and interests of ethnic minorities are established as one of the universal and important human rights perspectives in the international community. As we know, China is a large country with 1.3 billion people, in which the population of the 55 ethnic minorities is more than 100 million. While reporting news related to ethnic minorities of China, some Western media, however, are used to turning a blind eye to the great achievements of the ethnic minority regions; rather, they are concerned only about the so-called incidents, such as, the self-immolation protests of Tibetans, the Uyghur unrest in Xinjiang, or the Dalai Lama's audience with Western politicians. Of course, the people involved in these incidents accounted for an extremely small percentage of the total ethnic minority population.

Such phenomena can only be explained by the Western society's stereotypical idea about China. It has already become a habit for some in the West to speak ill of China's political system. Although they should be naturally endowed with reason and inclined to use it, whenever it comes to China they choose to look at it through tainted glasses. These naysayers casually disregard the fact that China's political system has developed and is evolving in accordance with the country's unique national conditions. Instead, they revel in their ignorance of China's reality and hold fast to their mean, even malicious predisposition toward China's political system out of their irrational, subjective and unprofessional ideological biases. Yet, their deep-rooted ideological prejudice has led them to make one failed prediction after another about China. Their erroneous judgments are only a litany of short-sighted calumnies against the Party and the nation.

Those Western politicians and media speaking ill of China are again showing how much they have staked in the inertia of their outdated thinking and how reluctant they are to put an end to their sport. Their desire is to impose upon China the political standards with which they are familiar and which favor their interests. Believing that the truth entails a loss to themselves, they have no compunction about making false claims and consider it excusable to speak so dishonorably. They can only look at China's politics through a prism of ideology rather than in an objective manner, and thus they cannot make sensible judgments in this regard. We hope these critics without true knowledge of China can visit the country someday to learn more about it. The trend of reform and opening-up over the past four decades has justified the path the Chinese people have chosen and the wishful thinking of the naysayers goes against the Chinese people's aspirations for continued development and better lives. Despite the flood of information that poured into China after reform and opening-up, Chinese society has managed to deal with it and accumulated collective wisdom. In this process, the leadership of the Party Central Committee has been instrumental. This is what Chinese people truly expect. Nonetheless, some Westerners who fail to figure out Chinese people's opinion want to be backseat drivers. They should have been more objective and modest in the face of China's long history and great practice.

As mentioned earlier, China's process of solving its ethno-national issues cannot be divorced from the current social development stage of the country, namely the preliminary stage of socialism with Chinese characteristics. Under the influence of production factor endowments and national policies, the imbalance of economic development among different regions will exist in the long term. Neither the prosperity of economically developed metropolises, such as Beijing, Shanghai, Guangzhou, or Shenzhen, nor the dire destitution of the 14 contiguous poverty-stricken areas can be utilized to represent the real development status of China. Similarly, the abovementioned "incidents" occurring in the compact communities of Tibetans or Uyghurs fail to paint the whole picture of the ties among the various ethnic groups of China.

During the process of eliminating poverty and chalking up larger social spaces, the ethnic minorities gained more development confidence and cultural self-esteem, thus bringing about an accelerated development of cultural industry, eco-tourism, featured products, and catering industry. For example, "Lamian" (literally "hand-pulled noodles"), whose preparation involves taking a lump of dough and repeatedly stretching it to produce a single long noodle, was first created by the Muslim Hui People in northwestern China. Eateries serving Lanzhou-style or Qinghai-style "Lamian" are very popular throughout China where they have formed a staple diet for centuries. They are increasingly found in the Chinatowns of Singapore, Malaysia, the USA, and Australia.

As a matter of fact, the promotion of "Lamian" throughout China and beyond reflects the factor of cultural identity in the process of China's multi-ethnic integration. Instead of taking a clear-cut stance, cultural identity is the self-consciousness formed in daily life by concerted cooperation and harmonious integration among people of all ethnicities. Only through such conscious accumulation in the civil society can the identity of Chinese culture be sublimated after experiencing identities of ethnicity culture and locality culture. In this sense, "none of the 55 ethnic minorities shall be left behind" in the building of a shared spiritual home for the Chinese nation. It can be accounted for from the following two aspects: firstly, the ethnic minority cultures enrich the variety of Chinese civilization; secondly, the spiritual value of ethnic minority cultures is an integral part of the fine quality of Chinese civilization.

The ethnic minority affairs of China, as part of the internal affairs of the country, shall be subjected to no foreign interference. At the same time, introducing China's ethno-national policies and achievements to the outside world is an indispensable part of the international community's comprehensive and accurate understanding of China. Since 1991, the State Council Information Office of China has publicized a large number of White Papers on the topics of religious and ethnic minority affairs of the country, as well as human rights, culture, and ecological environment. Correspondingly, the channels for cultural diplomacy have been expanded, including introducing the cultural classics or academic works of China to the outside world. These efforts, however, were often dismissed by the Western media as a political "propaganda" campaign of the Chinese government. Actually, it is no exaggeration to say that every country's foreign policy has elements of "propaganda". As the only superpower of the world, the US boasts the most powerful machine of "ballyhoo". Spread by both government and media entities, the media of the US disseminates

American cultural information, official positions on world affairs, and daily summaries of international news for the purpose of advertising American values and creating negative images of countries with different social systems. The external publicity of China is aimed at facilitating the international community's knowledge and understanding about the country. In his speech at the UNESCO Headquarters on March 27, 2014, Xi Jinping pointed out: "On the planet, there are more than 200 countries and regions inhabited by over 2500 ethnic groups with a multitude of religions. Can we imagine a world with only one lifestyle, one language, one kind of music and one style of costume?"[11] Xi's judgment of the world comes from his deep understanding of China's national conditions of diverse ethnicities, religions, languages, and cultures.

One of the important features of China's reform and opening-up is to integrate the country into the world and contribute to the peaceful development, mutual benefit and cooperation of the "global village". In this regard, some of China's policy ideas and achievements in resolving its internal affairs will also be extended to its foreign relations, as "diplomacy is the extension of domestic affairs". The basic principles advocated and guaranteed by the ethno-national policies of China, including equality, unity, mutual assistance and harmonious co-existence, share similar connotations with many foreign relation proposals put forward by the Chinese government, for example, "openness and inclusiveness", "mutual benefit and win-win cooperation", "seeking common ground while reserving differences", and "a community of shared future for mankind".

The facts speak for themselves about China's international cooperation. In developing its relations with other countries, China acts on the principles of sincerity, practical results, affinity and good faith, and values friendship, justice, and shared interests. The enduring and vigorous friendship between China and other developing countries is rooted in equality, sincerity, win-win cooperation, and common development. History is a mirror that one must look into in order to take off the spectacles tinted with political bias and get the facts straight. One should respect the history of China's development and appreciate the ethnic harmony and social stability in China.

In the practice of addressing its ethnic and religious affairs, China resolutely opposes any discrimination against a specific ethnic group or religion; in its foreign relations, "China will never falter in its support for the Arab states in safeguarding their national cultural traditions and will oppose all discrimination and prejudice against any ethnic groups or religions. We should work together to advocate tolerance toward different civilizations and prevent extremist forces and ideas from creating division between us."[12] Therefore, recognizing the conceptual unity of China's internal affairs and foreign relations is conducive to understanding the internal affairs of China and helpful in comprehending its foreign relations. While addressing the faculty and students of Peking University, Xi Jinping pointed out: "There are no two

---

[11]Xi Jinping. *The Governance of China*, p. 262.

[12]Xi Jinping. *The Governance of China*, p. 315.

leaves exactly alike on earth."[13] The road of socialism with Chinese characteristics is still being forged ahead, and the process of solving the ethno-national problems of China is also being continuously advanced.

China emphasizes that its development pattern, "socialism with Chinese characteristics", which bases itself on the unique historical and cultural backgrounds of the country, is not for the sake of plowing its own furrow; rather, it intends to convey to the world the quintessence of "unity in diversity" and "harmony without uniformity". On the face of it, China's answer to its ethno-national problems and related ethno-national policies are directed to the ethnic minorities and their compact communities; however, their goal is to build a community of shared future and realize the great rejuvenation of the Chinese nation. To preserve unity in diversity and to achieve harmony in differences will be an arduous journey in itself. It will take more than drum beating and gong clanging to get there. China will forge ahead along this road in defiance of considerable hardship.

V

Just after becoming General Secretary of the Communist Party of China in late 2012, Xi Jinping announced what would become the hallmark of his administration. "The Chinese Dream," he said, is "the great rejuvenation of the Chinese nation." Xi's "Chinese Dream" is described as achieving the Two Centenaries: the material goal of China becoming a "moderately well-off society" by 2021, the 100th anniversary of the Chinese Communist Party, and the modernization goal of China becoming a fully developed nation by 2049, the 100th anniversary of the founding of the People's Republic of China. In May 2013, Xi called upon the Chinese people "to dare to dream, work assiduously to fulfill their dreams and contribute to the revitalization of the nation".

Therefore, the overall layout of the development strategy for the next five years becomes the central task for China's 13th Five-Year-Plan (2016–2020). The proposal sets a target of "maintaining medium-high growth," highlighting the ideas of innovation, coordination, green development, opening-up, and sharing to fulfill its goals. China's development has been gradually integrated and interwoven with the rest of the world, while the world's development also goes with the Chinese people's dream for a better future. The series of social and economic development initiatives are the further improvement in the scientific development concept on the basis of coordinating the situations at home and abroad. The development of the ethnic minority areas will definitely see a fundamental progress in the second phase of the transformative economic reform in China.

The traditional economies of ethnic minority regions, including mountain agriculture, arid agriculture and grassland animal husbandry, demand to be transformed and upgraded with technology, policy and market innovation support. In addition, the

---

[13]Ibid., p. 171.

tourism and cultural industries of these regions need to be innovated to gain access to a wider development space. At the same time, imbalanced economic and social development has long existed between the compact communities of ethnic minorities and the remaining parts of China. Therefore, the regional, urban–rural and interethnic development gaps have presented demanding tasks for coordinated development. It is, however, the only solution to the unbalanced east–west population distribution demarcated by the aforementioned "Hu Line".

As the source of the major river systems of China, including the Yangtze, Huanghe, and Lancang Rivers, the bio-diverse Western regions function as the ecological barrier of the country. The construction of ecological security while speeding up economic growth has become the focus of green development. With the full implementation of the "Belt and Road Initiative", the ethnic minority regions, in particular the frontier regions, are gaining development momentum due to their strategic geographical advantages. The concepts of "cooperation, inclusiveness, and mutual benefit" in international diplomacy and the practices of people-to-people bond, which provides public support for implementing the "Belt and Road Initiative", render it necessary to enhance the self-development capacity of the frontier regions.

These development concepts are targeted to realize the goal of a "sharing development", which means "common prosperity for people of all ethnic groups". In other words, none of the 56 constituents of the Chinese nation shall be left behind in terms of sharing the well-being of building a moderately well-off society and the rejuvenation of the Chinese nation. Currently, the most demanding task of building a well-off society in an all-round way is to eradicate poverty. Though China's poverty reduction strategy has achieved remarkable success, the Chinese government is fully aware that the fight remains tough as the country still has a large population living in profound poverty, and the solutions to their problems are becoming increasingly costly and complex. Faced with these major problems, China has entered the crucial stage of poverty reduction.

It is an essential requirement of socialism as well as a key mission of the CPC as the ruling party to eradicate poverty, improve people's living standards, and achieve common prosperity among the people. Since the 18th CPC National Congress held in 2012, aimed at eliminating poverty and better protecting the people's rights to live and to develop in impoverished areas, the CPC Central Committee led by General Secretary Xi Jinping has committed China to pursuing innovative, balanced and eco-friendly development featuring openness and sharing, to making best use of its political and institutional strengths, and to implementing the basic strategy of taking targeted measures for poverty alleviation. The central authorities are determined to mobilize all members of the CPC and of society to achieve poverty eradication by ensuring that progress in development-oriented poverty alleviation is coordinated with overall economic and social development by attaching equal importance to poverty alleviation and ecological protection, and by integrating poverty alleviation with social security.

Based on statistics collected at the end of 2014 for the population living in poverty, the government has worked out specific schemes to actualize the overall goals: first, helping 30 million people who have the ability to work and possess productive skills to escape from poverty by supporting them in developing their industries; second, helping 10 million people escape from poverty by transferring them to locations where they can find employment; third, helping 10 million people whose land does not provide subsistence to escape from poverty by relocating them to other places; fourth, bringing all the impoverished population under the coverage of the rural subsistence allowance system and eradicating poverty through the guarantee of social security.

At the end of 2015, the CPC Central Committee and the State Council jointly issued *the Decision on Winning the Fight against Poverty*, defining the overall goals of poverty eradication for the 13th Five-Year Plan period. By 2020, the state is committed to ensuring that the impoverished rural population has stable access to adequate food and clothing, compulsory education, and basic medical services and housing; to realizing a growth rate of per-capita disposable income in poor rural areas higher than the national average; to achieving indices of major basic public services close to the national average levels; to ensuring that the rural population living below the current poverty threshold and all impoverished counties are all lifted out of poverty; and to solving the problems of regional poverty.

Based on the *National Plan for Poverty Alleviation in the 13th Five-Year Plan Period* and the *Annual Poverty Reduction Plan*, central government departments have drawn up specific schemes and guidance for poverty alleviation. Local governments of the provinces and equivalent units have comprehensively implemented the central government plan, worked out local plans for poverty alleviation in the *13th Five-Year Plan* period and published their "1 + N" targeted poverty alleviation policies (one overall policy plus a number of supporting policies). All sectors have included poverty alleviation into their specialized industrial plans in the *13th Five-Year Plan* period and made poverty reduction a priority in implementation.

At the same time, poverty eradication for ethnic minorities has been accelerated. The government has developed a series of special support policies to accelerate poverty eradication for ethnic minority groups and regions inhabited by ethnic minorities. *The Outline for Development-oriented Poverty Reduction for China's Rural Areas* (2011–2020) maps out 14 contiguous impoverished areas, 11 of which are in ethnic autonomous areas, and 592 key counties for national development-oriented poverty alleviation work, 263 of which are in ethnic autonomous areas. All these show that the Western regions, in particular, the compact communities of the ethnic minorities, are the major targets for China's development-oriented poverty alleviation. During the implementation of *the Thirteenth Five-Year-Plan*, China's solution to its ethno-national problems will be advanced on the basis of the concepts of innovation, coordination, green development, opening-up, and sharing. In the process of fulfilling the central task of economic development, the Chinese people of all ethnic groups are working hard to build China into a great modern socialist country that is prosperous, strong, democratic, culturally advanced, harmonious, and beautiful.

Chinese culture values the harmonious co-existence between different ethnic groups and cultures. The Chinese nation itself is proudly born out of thousands of years of integrating diverse ethnic groups and does not provide a breeding ground for racial discrimination or parochial nationalism. Throughout China's history, it has never colonized, plundered, or enslaved any vulnerable nation. In line with this peaceful tradition, China is committed to working with global partners to build a community with a shared future for mankind.

References

Hao, S. (2015). Adhering to and improving the system of regional ethnic autonomy: The guideline of the working conference on the Ethnic Affairs of China. *Journal of Minzu University of China, 2.*

Rachman, G. (2014, February 25). Let Scotland referendum become a model. *The Financial Times.*

Sha, B. (2014). Are the ethno-national policy models of America or India be applicable in China? *Journal of Minzu University of China, 4.*

The Selected International Documents on Human Rights. (2002). Beijing: Peking University Press.

Xi, J. (2014, September 5). A speech on the 60th anniversary of the founding of the National People's Congress. *People's Daily.*

Xi, Z. (2013). *On the united front.* Beijing: Central Party Literature Press.

Bibliography

Andersons, B. (2003). *Imagined communities: Reflections on the origin and spread of nationalism.* Shanghai: Shanghai People's Press.

Bai, G. (1999). *National self-determination in the international law.* Beijing: The Chinese Overseas Publishing House.

Baima, L. (2005). The central government's authority in implementing the reincarnation of Living Buddha in Tibetan Buddhism. *Journal of Tibetan Studies, 19*(4), 26–28.

Brzezinski, Z. (1988). *Competitive plan: A geopolitical strategy for US-Soviet competition.* Beijing: China Translation Corporation.

Candler, E. (1989). *The unveiling of Lhasa.* Lhasa: Tibet People's Press.

Chen, J. (1998). *History of Taiwan independence movement.* Taipei: Qianwei Press.

Chinese Tibetology Research Center. (2009). *The democratic reform in Tibet and the Dalai Lama's exile.* Beijing: People's Press.

Dalai Lama. (1990). *Autobiography of the 14th Dalai Lama.* Taipei: Linking Publishing Services.

Delager. (1998). *The history of Tibetan Buddhism in Inner Mongolia.* Hohhot: Inner Mongolia People's Press.

Deng, J. (2000). *The tea road.* Hohhot: Inner Mongolia People's Press.

Deng, X. (1994). *The collected works of Deng Xiaoping.* Beijing: People's Press.

Diamond, J. (2000). *Guns, germs, and steel: The fates of human societies.* Shanghai: Shanghai Translation Publishing House.

Duara, P. (2003). *Rescuing history from the nation: Questioning narratives of modern China.* Beijing: Social Science Academic Press.

Ekwa, R. B. (2005). *Self-image of the Tibetans.* Beijing: China Tibetology Research Center.

Engdahl, W. (2009). *Behind the hegemony: The all-dominant strategy of the United States.* Beijing: Intellectual Publishing House.

Fairbank, J. K. (2000). *The great Chinese revolution, 1800–1985.* Beijing: World Affairs Press.

Fairbank, J. K., & Liu, G. J. (1985). *The Cambridge history of China: Late Qing 1800–1911.* Beijing: China Social Sciences Press.

Feng, K. (1994). *Racial concept in modern China.* Nanjing: Jiangsu People's Press.

Feng, K. (1999). *The concept of race in modern China.* Nanjing: Jiangsu People's Press.

Feng, T. (2001). *Japanese Samurai's observations of China in 1862.* Beijing: The Commercial Press.

de Carla, J. (2003). *The history of Spain.* Beijing: The Commercial Press.

de Coulanges, Fustel. (2006). *The ancient city: A study on the religion, laws and institutions of Greece and Rome.* Guiling: Guangxi Normal University Press.

Ge, J. (1997). *The history of internal migration in China.* Fuzhou: Fujian People's Press.

Greenfield, L. (2010). *Nationalism: Five roads to modernity.* Shanghai: The SDX Joint Publishing Company.

© China Social Sciences Press 2020

S. Hao, *China's Solution to Its Ethno-national Issues*, China Insights,

https://doi.org/10.1007/978-981-32-9519-3

Gu, C. (2004). *The Western missionaries and modern China*. Shanghai: Shanghai People's Press.

Hao, S. (2015a). Adhering to and improving the system of regional ethnic autonomy: The guideline of the working conference on the ethnic affairs of China. *Journal of Minzu University of China, 91*(2), 216–219.

Hao, S. (2015b). Regional autonomy for ethnic minorities: New formulations on the national conference on ethnic minority affairs. *Journal of the Minzu University of China, 99*(6), 312–316.

Hao, S., & Chen, J. (2012). *The ethno-national issues of Taiwan: From "Barbarians" to "Taiwanese Aborigines"*. Beijing: Social Science Academic Press.

Hao, S., & Du, S. (2007). *The history of Outer Mongolia*. Beijing: Social Science Academic Press.

Hobsbawm, E. (1999a). *The age of empire: 1875–1914*. Nanjing: Jiangsu People's Press.

Hobsbawm, E. (1999b). *The age of revolution: Europe 1789–1848*. Nanjing: Jiangsu People's Press.

Hsu, I. C. Y. (2008). *The rise of modern China: 1600–2000*. Beijing: World Book Incorporation.

Hu, S. (1981). *From the Opium War to the May Fourth Movement*. Beijing: People's Press.

Huang, Y. (1995). *The history of the relationship between Tibet and the Chinese Central Government*. Lhasa: Tibet People's Press.

Huang, G., & Shi, L. (2005). *Ethnicity classification of China: The origin of 56 ethnic groups*. Beijing: The Ethnic Publishing House.

Huc, E. R. (1991). *Travels in Tartary, Tibet, and China during the years 1844-5-6*. Beijing: China Tibetology Press.

Ippolito Desideri. (2004). *An account of Tibet: The travels of Ippolito Desideri of Pistoia*. Lhasa: Tibet People's Press.

Isaacs, H. (2004). *Idols of the tribe: Group identity and political change*. Taipei: Li Sui Culture Co., Ltd.

Jampel Gyatso. (2011). *Zhou Enlai and the peaceful liberation of Tibet*. Beijing: China Social Sciences Academic Press.

Jin, C. (2009). *The history of China in the 20th century*. Beijing: Social Sciences Academic Press.

Jin, H., & Sai, H. (2011). *The comprehensive history of Inner Mongolia*. Beijing: People's Press.

Jin, K. (2012). *Sun Yat-sen and the founding of the Tongmenghui*. Changchun: Jilin literary and history Publishing House.

Kennedy, P. (1992). *The rise and fall of great powers*. Beijing: World Affairs Press.

Khan, R. (2014). *Afghanistan and Pakistan: Conflict, extremism and resistance to modernity*. Beijing: Current Affairs Press.

Krone, M. (2005). *Cultural geography*. Nanjing: Nanjing University Press.

Kymlicka, W. (2004a). *Politics in the vernacular: Nationalism, multiculturalism, citizenship*. Taipei: Left Bank Culture Press.

Kymlicka, W. (2004b). *Rights of minorities: Nationalism, multiculturalism and citizenship*. Taipei: Left Bank Culture Press.

Landers, D. S. (2001). *The wealth and poverty of nations: Why some are so rich and some so poor?*. Beijing: Xinhua Press.

Lattimore, O. (2005). *Inner Asian frontiers of China*. Nanjing: Jiangsu People's Press.

Lazlowo, E. (1997). *Destiny choice*. Beijing: The SDX Joint Publishing Company.

Lenin, V. (2009). *Collected works of Lenin*. Beijing: People's Press.

Li, A. (1986). *Research on Kai-shek Chiang*. Taipei: Taiwan Tianyuan Book Company.

Li, J. (2010). *1959: The 14th Dalai Lama's fleeing to India*. Taipei: Lianjing Publishing House.

Li, S. (2003). *Xinjiang: History and current situation*. Urumqi: Xinjiang People's Press.

Liang, J. (2012). *The British Empire and Tibet: 1774–1904*. Lanzhou: Lanzhou University Press.

Liang, Q. (1989). *The selected works of Qichao Liang*. Beijing: Zhonghua Book Company.

Liu, X. (2001). *The issues of Outer Mongolia*. Taipei: Nantian Book Company.

Liu, Y. (2011). *Sea and land: A study of east-west communication in medieval times*. Beijing: Peking University Press.

Mackerras, C. P. (2013). *Western image of China since 1949*. Hong Kong: Open Page Publishing Co., Ltd.

Mann, M. (2015). *The dark side of democracy: Explaining ethnic cleansing*. Beijing: Central Compilation &Translation Press.

Mao, Z. (1991). *The selected works of Mao Zedong*. Beijing: People's Press.

Marx, K., & Friedrich, E. (1997). *The complete works of Marx and Engels*. Beijing: People's Press.

Masaaki, M. (2013). *The challenges of Kublai Khan*. Beijing: Social Sciences Academic Press.

Menzies, G. (2005). *1421: The year China discovered the world*. Beijing: Jinghua Press.

Morin, E., & Kern, A. (1997). *Earth motherland*. Beijing: SDX Joint Publishing Company.

Patterson, T. (2007). *The political culture of the US*. Beijing: Orient Publishing House.

Pinker, S. (2015). *The better angels of our nature*. Beijing: Citic Press Group.

Pole, J. (2007). *The pursuit of equality in American history*. Beijing: The Commercial Press.

Polo, M. (2000). *The travels of Marco Polo*. Shanghai: Shanghai Bookstore Publishing House.

Rizhkov, N. (2008). *The tragedy of the great power: The disintegration of the Soviet Union*. Beijing: Xinhua Publishing House.

Rubruck, W. (1985). *The journey of William Rubruk to the eastern parts*. Beijing: Zhonghua Book Company.

Seitz, K. (2007). *China: The revival of a world power*. Beijing: International Cultural Publishing Company.

Sha, B. (2014). Are the ethno-national policy models of America and India applicable in China? *Journal of Minzu University of China, 82*(4), 124–129.

Shakya, T. (2011). *The dragon in the land of snows: A history of modern Tibet since 1947*. Taibei: Left Bank Culture Press.

Shen Z. *A brief history of the Sino-Soviet relations*. Beijing: Xinhua Press.

Shen, Z., & Liu, S. (2014). *Tibet and Tibetans*. Beijing: China Tibetology Press.

Snow, E. (1984). *Red star over China*. Beijing: Xinhua Press.

Stalin, J. (1979). *The selected works of Stalin*. Beijing: People's Press.

Stavrianos, L. (1988). *A global history: The world before 1500*. Shanghai: Press of Shanghai Social Sciences Academy.

Stavrianos, L. (1992). *Lifelines from our past: A new world history*. Beijing: China Social Sciences Press.

Stein, R. (1999). *Civilizations of Tibet*. Beijing: China Tibetology Press.

Sun, H., & Hu, Z. (2007). *The languages of China*. Beijing: The Commercial Press.

Sun, Y. (1982). *The completed works of Sun Yat-sen*. Beijing: Zhonghua Book Company.

Sun, Y. (2000). *Three principles of the people*. Changsha: Yuelu Book Company.

Sun, Y. (2007). *Theories and ideologies for "Taiwan Independence"*. Beijing: Jiuzhou Press.

Sun, Z. (2003). *Map scaling and territory formation during the reigns of Kangxi, Yongzheng and Qianlong*. Beijing: Press of Renmin University of China.

Taylor, C. (2001). *Sources of the self: The making of the modern identity*. Nanjing: Yilin Press.

Taylor, M. (1995). *Discovering Tibet*. Beijing: China Tibetology Press.

The Soviet Union Academy of Sciences. (1997). *The nation-state building history of the Soviet Union*. Beijing: The Commercial Press.

Toynbee, A. (1966). *Historical research*. Shanghai: Shanghai People's Press.

Turner, S. (2004). *Tashilhunpo monastery of Tibet*. Lhasa: Tibet People's Press.

Ulanhu. (1999). *The selected works of Ulanhu*. Beijing: The Central Document Publishing House.

Voltaire. (1995). *On folkways and customs*. Beijing: The Commercial Press.

Vyigotski, L. (1979). *Diplomatic history*. Beijing: SDX Joint Publishing Company.

Wallerstein, I. (2013). *The modern world-system*. Beijing: Social Sciences Academic Press.

Wang, G. (1998). *China transformed: Historical change and the limits of European experience*. Nanjing: Jiangsu People's Press.

Wang, M. (2008). *Choice of nomads: The nomadic tribes in Northern Asia vs. the Han Empire*. Guilin: Guangxi Normal University Press.

Wang, X. (2000). *Modern history of Sino-Japanese cultural exchange*. Beijing: Zhonghua Book Company.

Wang, X. (2009). *The governance of Tibet by the People's Republic of China: 1949–2009*. Beijing: People's Press.

Weatherford, J. (2006). *Genghis Khan and the making of the modern world*. Chongqing: Chongqing Press.

Wood, F. (1997). *Has Marco Polo been to China?* Beijing: Xinhua Press.

Wright, M. C. (2002). *The last stand of Chinese conservatism: The Tongzhi Restoration 1862–1874*. Beijing: China Social Sciences Press.

Wu, Y., & Zhou, X. (2000). *Modern Islamic thoughts and movement*. Beijing: Social Science Academic Press.

Xi, J. (2014). *The governance of China*. Beijing: Foreign Languages Press.

Xi, Z. (2013). *Zhongxun Xi: On the united front*. Beijing: Central Party Literature Press.

Xiao, Q. (2007). *The history of Mongol-dominated Yuan Empire*. Beijing: Zhonghua Book Company.

Xiao, Z. (1979). The several "Xinjiangs" during the reign of the Qing dynasty. *Chinese Journal of History., 82*(8), 67–69.

Xiao, Z., & Yang, W. (1986). *A Chronicle of Sino-Western relations before the Opium War*. Hubei People's Press.

Ya, H. (1984). *The biography of the 13th Dalai Lama*. Beijing: The People's Press.

Ya, H. (1987). *The biography of the 10th Panchen Lama*. Lhasa: Tibet People's Press.

Yang, T. (2014). The abdication of the last Qing Emperor and the "Republic of Five Races". *Journal of Modern Chinese History, 96*(2), 120–125.

Yao, D. (2007). *Ten papers on the history of the northern nomads of China*. Guiling: Press of Guangxi Normal University Press.

Yoda, Y. (2004). *The foundations of Japan's modernization: A comparison with China's path towards modernization*. Shanghai: Shanghai Far East Publishing House.

Yōichi, K. (2003). *Criticism of modern Japanese*. Changchun: Jilin People's Press.

Zeng, J., & Liang, Z. (2005). *Personal accounts of Ching-kuo Chiang*. Taipei: The Unity Press.

Zhang, X. L. (1977). *Historical documents on east-west communication*. Beijing: Zhonghua Book Company.

Zhang, Z. (2007). An analysis of the Congressional Human Rights Caucus related to China. *The Chinese Journal of American Studies, 93*(2), 126–129.

Zhang, Z. (2009). *The US-China relations and Tibet: Historical evolution and decision analysis*. Beijing: Chinese Literature and Art Publishing House.

Zhou, H. (2001). *Xinjiang Society during the Republic of China*. Urumqi: Xinjiang University Press.

Zhou, W., & Zhou, Y. (2015). *The comprehensive history of Tibet*. Beijing: China Tibetology Press.

Index

© China Social Sciences Press 2020
S. Hao, *China's Solution to Its Ethno-national Issues*, China Insights,
https://doi.org/10.1007/978-981-32-9519-3

Printed by Printforce, the Netherlands